157 cosmographic ① as junction of audience

AMERICAN AUTOBIOGRAPHY

WISCONSIN STUDIES IN
AMERICAN AUTOBIOGRAPHY

William L. Andrews, General Editor

American Autobiography

Retrospect and Prospect

Edited by

PAUL JOHN EAKIN

The University of Wisconsin Press

The University of Wisconsin Press
114 North Murray Street
Madison, Wisconsin 53715

3 Henrietta Street
London WC2E 8LU, England

5 4 3 2 1

Printed in the United States of America

Library of Congress Cataloging-in-Publication Data
American autobiography: retrospect and prospect/
    edited by Paul John Eakin
    298 pp.   cm.—(Wisconsin studies in American autobiography)
    Includes bibliographical references and index.
    1. American prose literature—History and criticism.
2. Autobiography. I. Eakin, Paul John. II. Series.
PS366.A88A44   1991
810.9′492—dc20   90-12971
ISBN 0-299-12780-X
ISBN 0-299-12784-2 (pbk.)   CIP

Contents

AMERICAN AUTOBIOGRAPHY

Introduction

PAUL JOHN EAKIN

When I set out in the fall of 1986 to draw up a brief report on contemporary criticism of nineteenth-century American autobiography, I was quite surprised by the meagerness of my findings. Resources were scattered and difficult to locate, and it turned out that even the most frequently studied autobiographies of the period had rarely been studied *as autobiographies*.[1] How can so extensive a literature—I am thinking of the hundreds of entries in the listing of Louis Kaplan—have left so faint a trail in our scholarship? On consideration, however, this state of affairs is hardly surprising, for despite the lively interest in autobiography both in and out of academe at the present time, study of the genre has not yet been institutionalized in our curricula, where autobiography—and indeed nonfiction prose in general—continues as a kind of poor relation.

It is not self-evident what texts would be included in a course on nineteenth-century American autobiography. Reaching forward into the early twentieth century, we might expect to find works by Henry Adams, Henry James, and Mark Twain. Reaching back into the eighteenth century, Benjamin Franklin's autobiography and Jonathan Edwards's "Personal Narrative"—that familiar pair—would be likely to appear. But what about the century that stretches in between? Even the best-known candidates—*Walden* (1854) and "Song of Myself" (1855)—are not always recognized as autobiographies.[2] Slave narratives, such as those by Frederick Douglass, Harriet Jacobs, and others that have been featured in major recent studies by William L. Andrews, Houston A. Baker, Elizabeth Fox-Genovese, and Henry Louis Gates, would surely make the list, but what else would round it out? Would traditional classics such as Francis Parkman's *The California and Oregon Trail* (1849) and Richard Henry Dana's *Two Years Before the Mast* (1840) be counted in? And what other texts would be tapped—the *Personal Memoirs of*

U. S. Grant (1885), Elizabeth Cady Stanton's *Eighty Years and More: Reminiscences, 1815–1897* (1898), the *Life of P. T. Barnum* (1855), Lucy Larcom's *A New England Girlhood* (1889)? When it comes to nineteenth-century American autobiography, there is nothing comparable to the consensus about the canon of nineteenth-century British autobiography that is emerging in the work of Avrom Fleishman, Susanna Egan, Linda H. Peterson, and others. The fluid state of the field reflects not only a lack of knowledge of the surviving primary literature but continuing uncertainty about generic definition as well.

If the study of autobiography—American or other—is only now finding a place in our departments of language and literature, that may be just as well, for our thinking about this late arrival stands a chance of escaping some of the shortcomings of our traditional conception of American literature as a whole. Some years ago, in an essay entitled "What Is American Literature?" William C. Spengemann exposed the narrowness of our working definition of the field: "*Those few works of fiction, poetry, and the drama which have been written in any place that is now part of the United States or by anyone who has ever lived in one of these places and which now rank among the acknowledged masterpieces of Western writing*" (123). Spengemann identified the kinds of criteria informing this institutional practice as "linguistic, political, belletristic, and aesthetic" (125), buttressed by a "provincial (not to say racist) notion that the progress of Anglo-Saxon culture forms the armature of New-World history" (128). As long as they subscribe to so impoverished a definition of their field, Americanists seem doomed to increasingly stale exercises as they endlessly conjugate the features of a tiny, closed canon of masterworks. The way out of this exclusivist cultural cul-de-sac, Spengemann suggests, is not for the faint of heart, for he proposes a new construction of "American literature" in which "the word 'American' signifies everything having to do with civilization in the New World since the European discovery, and 'literature' includes every written document that will respond to literary analysis" (135). The magnitude of the subject so conceived is indeed staggering, and Spengemann contends that historical and critical analysis of so heterogeneous a literature would require as a first step an elaborate labor of bibliographic and taxonomic organization.

Following Spengemann, definition of the literature to be studied and constitution of a corpus of texts go hand in hand. Together they provide the foundation for the subsequent work of history and criticism: you need to have a working definition of the genre to serve as a principle of selection in establishing a census of the relevant texts; once you have such a census, you can use it to test and refine the criteria posited in your initial definition.[3] If we were to adopt this inclusive approach in the case of autobiography, we would begin with Louis Kaplan's *A Bibliography of American Autobiographies*, which lists more than 6000 examples before 1945, and Mary Louise Briscoe's supplement, *American Autobiography, 1945–1980*, which adds another 5000 titles. The Kaplan and Briscoe volumes, however, are essentially descriptive in nature, indispensable bibliographic tools to facilitate the research of others. In themselves, they are interpretive only insofar as (1) they are based on an implied definition of autobiography that excludes some items from the list (in the case of Kaplan, for example, "most episodic accounts," manuscript autobiographies, and so forth), and (2) they include a "subject index" whose rubrics (autobiographers' occupations, where they lived, ethnic affiliation, period of publication, and so forth) suggest some of the potential uses to which the data compiled might be put.

To my knowledge, however, the resources of Kaplan and Briscoe have been little examined by scholars so far. Thomas Cooley and Lawrence Buell are notable exceptions. Through a brief review of Kaplan's listings up to 1865, Cooley sketches out a typology of the principal varieties of popular narrative in the nineteenth century—conversions, criminal confessions, captivities, and so forth. Again, Buell, in his essay on "Autobiography in the American Renaissance" for the present volume, uses Kaplan's inventory as a basis for generalizations about the nature of autobiographical practice in the period.[4]

The comparative neglect of Kaplan and Briscoe is a sign of the long-standing perplexity of both historians and literary critics about a kind of imaginative literature that claims a basis in referential fact. Except in the case of literary biographies of writers, however, attention to the referential dimension of autobiography is not a familiar exercise for critics and literary historians who, when they deal with autobiography at all, have been intent on demonstrating the literariness of such texts, validating their status as imaginative art. Hence it is inevitable that study of the autobiographies of writers should dominate the field.[5]

Meanwhile, historians remain largely skeptical of Wilhelm Dilthey's claim for autobiography as "the germinal cell of history" (quoted in Stone 11). Facts *in* texts are one thing; texts *as* facts are quite another, and Hayden White's insistence on the *textuality* of history has been largely ignored by practicing historians, who prefer to assign White's disquieting observations about the necessarily mediated condition of all historical knowledge to some other discipline—literary theory or historiography—where they can be safely ignored. As historians turn increasingly to the practice of oral history, however, this state of suspicion may fade, for they are likely to trust themselves to gather such data with an appropriate objectivity (never mind the dangers of the literary, the fictive, which will inevitably be present). No one better expresses the fundamental issue posed by autobiography's problematic dual status as literature and history than Albert E. Stone:

I remain uneasy over the tendency to treat autobiography chiefly as a branch of imaginative literature and thus to stress artistic creation over the equally complex processes of historical recreation, ideological argument, and psychological expression. *Life* is the more inclusive sign—not *Literature*—which deserves to be placed above the gateway to the house of autobiography. (19)

As long as we subscribe to *literature* as the sign of autobiography, assuming a traditional aesthetic construction of this governing term, most of the works recorded in Kaplan-Briscoe are likely to go unread. Lawrence Buell estimates, for example, that in the period from 1800 to 1870 only a fraction of the autobiographers recorded in Kaplan ("not more than one in ten or fifteen") "were creative writers either by trade or avocation" (see p. 48 in this work). In recent years, however, a number of scholars investigating special varieties of American autobiography—by women, by blacks, by Native Americans, by immigrants—have embraced the broadly inclusive perspective that the Kaplan-Briscoe corpus represents, and their work may serve to suggest its possibilities.

The Kaplan-Briscoe census poses a lesson in point of view: if you think you already have in hand a comfortably compact list of masterworks—the autobiographies of Franklin, Adams, and James, say[6]—you may be put off by the scale of such an inventory, where texts swarm in a classless state, unsorted by traditional notions of aesthetic privilege; if you are engaged in constructing a canon of previously unrecognized works, however, quantity may become a desideratum, and literary quality may be left to fend for itself. Literary quality is always a matter of relative judgment anyhow, whether we like it or not, and inevitably complicit in mainstream values that underwrite canonic exclusion in the first place. It is worth noting, in this connection, that the current emphasis on autobiography as an imaginative art has led to the neglect of the autobiography of even so archetypically American a figure as Thomas Jefferson.[7] It all depends on whether your field of inquiry is that of the dominant culture or that of one of the various subcultures existing at its margins. The classlessness of the apparently all-inclusive Kaplan-Briscoe census, moreover, is itself deceptive, for access to the media of communication is controlled by the literate class that governs the circulation of texts.[8] Indeed, no small part of the significance of the contemporary interest in oral history, the gathering in the field of the lives of ordinary and often unlettered people, as in the work of Jane

Hallowell Coles and Robert Coles, for example, in their *Women of Crisis* volumes (1978, 1980), resides in its potential to represent the otherwise textually excluded.[9]

In dealing with the literature of the oppressed, for obvious reasons the magnitude of the bibliographic task may seem small in total number of texts, when measured against the mass of the Kaplan-Briscoe corpus. The work of recovery may be proportionally great, however, because, given the marginal status of such authors, the survival of their texts is more likely to have been left to chance than in the case of texts preserved in what Raymond Williams terms the "selective tradition" of the dominant culture (39). This enterprise of reconstruction has proceeded most thoroughly in the areas of black American and Native American autobiography. One of the striking things to emerge from this research is evidence of the extent to which the primary texts owe their very existence to the sponsorship of members of the dominant culture, white Northern abolitionists in the case of the ex-slaves, white anthropologists in the case of the Indians. Writing about the period preceding the appearance of the first Native American autobiography (defined as the product of collaboration between an Indian informant and a white writer or editor), Arnold Krupat brings home the stark reality of the power of the literate class over the life of texts. There *were* no Native American autobiographies until the 1830s for the breathtakingly simple reason that the Indian was not recognized as a person with a *culture* in the received white construction of that term. Perceived by the whites as "wholly other" (5), "the antithesis of culture, its zero degree" (36), the Indian therefore possessed "nothing worthy of textualization" (5).

The most obvious benefit of research devoted to the marginalized literatures of autobiography, besides its implicit affirmation of the intrinsic worth of the material studied, is that it sheds new light on the perennial problem of generic definition. Elizabeth Bruss and Philippe Lejeune have exposed the limitations of the prescriptive approach to genre that has colored so much of the work on autobiography; formalist or essentialist definitions, they argue, offer an inadequate measure of constantly changing modes of autobiographical practice.[10] It is precisely this picture of autobiographical practice that scholars who pursue the recovery of texts inclusively and inductively are in a position to formulate. Setting aside narrow, traditional categories of aesthetic merit in favor of a broad definition of literature as the history of discourse, they are determined to read everything and report back on what was written. The value of any definition of the genre must be tested against an authoritative account of actual autobiographical practice.

Lest anyone be tempted to discount this work at the margins as marginal, without bearing on the practice of mainstream autobiography, I want to emphasize that our understanding of either member of this heuristically relational pair, *mainstream* and *margin*, is enhanced by study of the other. One of the most important contributions of this research so far has been its delineation of the values and assumptions of the dominant culture, especially its received models of self and life story. The mark of the dominant culture on the ostensibly self-authorizing performance of the autobiographical act is most tangibly preserved in collaborative autobiographies, a form that occupies a large place in the literature of the oppressed. In these products of cross-cultural exchange, the balance of power is distinctly lopsided: the informant—dispossessed Indian, enslaved black—is empowered to speak only by submitting to the terms set forth by the white member of the pair.

Slave narratives offer a textbook illustration of this play of cultural politics, as William L. Andrews has shown, for white editors and amanuenses explicitly state within these texts the rules that govern the discursive situation. For example, the white editor of the story of ex-slave Charles Ball (1836) assures the white reader that Ball's "bitterness of heart" "has been carefully excluded from the following pages" (quoted in Andrews 82). The employment of *expressives*, John Searle's term for speech acts designed to express the psychological state of the speaker, was taboo, and Andrews brings home to us again and again the irony of this *antiautobiographical* premise that governed the early slave narrative. Not until the slave narrative reached its culmination at mid-century did the black subject's memory of the truth of his experience take priority over what the white reader was prepared to accept as fact. Only gradually did blacks emancipate themselves from this discursive bondage, achieving more distinctly autonomous forms of identity and self-expression.[11]

Arnold Krupat's investigation of Native American autobiography tells a similar story. In such texts the presence of the Indian is displaced by white models of the Indian, and his history of this special variety of American autobiography becomes in effect a history of the *theories* that constitute part of the evolving ideology of the person in the United States: the nineteenth-century Indian as Romantic hero, Carlylian actor on the stage of world history, is supplanted by the twentieth-century Indian as the anthropologist's representative type of a vanishing culture. In texts, as in all else, Native Americans were dispossessed by the whites. Despite the pervasive presence of the dominant culture in the Native American autobiography and the slave narrative, however, it would be hasty to conclude that the voice of the other has been totally suppressed in these cross-cultural collaborations. In an extremely suggestive phrase, Andrews speaks of reading the early slave narratives as "an exercise in creative hearing" (36), a sensitive work of recuperation dedicated to registering the "silences" of such texts. The hope, of course, would be to recover something of the nature of the identities of the oppressed, their own views of self and life story. [12]

In immigrant autobiography, no less than in the slave narrative and Native American autobiography, the impress of the dominant culture's models of self and life story is central and profound, for the freedom from the authorizing discipline imposed by the collaborative relation proves to be only partial. [13] Allegiance to authorized models has been so thoroughly internalized by these autobiographers that their representation in immigrant lives is ensured even without the mediation of a white sponsor, whether editor or scholar. William Boelhower's essay for this collection, a semiotic analysis of "The Making of Ethnic Autobiography in the United States," argues that the concept of a normative American self was "rigidly codified" by the end of the nineteenth century. *The Americanization of Edward Bok* (1920) by Edward Bok, *The Making of an American* (1924) by Jacob Riis, *An American in the Making* (1917) by Marcus E. Ravage—these and other texts document the existence of what Boelhower identifies as "the received behavioral script of the rhetorically well-defined American self" (see p. 125 in this work). The titles reflect, moreover, a conscious sense of the cultural construction of the person.

Of special interest in Boelhower's inquiry, however, is his demonstration of the reciprocity of influence in the relation between mainstream and ethnic cultures, a salutary corrective to any simplistic, one-way construing of cultural influence that "mainstream-marginal" and similar formulations might seem to promote. [14] Although the idea of an American self was sufficiently coherent to be perceived by aspiring immigrants as specifiable and hence available for imitation, it was nonetheless scarcely a stable concept. According to such nativist observers of the American scene as Henry Adams and Henry James, the American self was undergoing a crisis of redefinition at the turn of the century, precipitated in no small part by the very presence of the aliens who tried to embrace it. As they sought through assimilation to make themselves over as Americans, immigrants and immigrant autobiographers transformed the principle of identification itself, of Americanness, for good. Boelhower interprets ethnic autobiography accordingly as "an act of higher criticism and an instrument of cultural construction" that led to the creation of "new American types and new narrative perspectives" (see p. 138 in this work). Thus mainstream and margin were equally subject to the fires of the melting pot. To recognize the interdependency between the national culture and any of its various subcultures, moreover, is to accept the appropriateness of a broad, inclusive conception of the canon of American autobiography. One model for the history of the genre in the United States might well be the ongoing interplay between dominant and marginal texts.

One of the risks of my emphasis on the influence of the dominant culture—its models of self and life story—on various subgenres of American autobiography is that it might seem to imply that these satellite literatures are essentially fringe phenomena, derivative in nature, lacking the kind of genuine originality, for example, that Boelhower discerns in immigrant texts. The dangers of such a cultural myopia are addressed by Carol Holly's essay in this collection on nineteenth-century women's autobiographies. Holly criticizes Estelle Jelinek's too-exclusive preoccupation with dominant male models—models of self as public figure and of life story as career—which leads Jelinek to characterize women's autobiographies in wholly negative terms, defining them by what they lack. Conceding that nineteenth-century women were indeed often victims of a patriarchal ideology of subordination that cast them as domestic helpmates and little else, Holly draws on the work of Carroll Smith-Rosenberg and others to argue nevertheless that "the ideology of separate spheres also created the social space for women to exert some control in defining themselves and shaping their lives" (see p. 218 in this work). What emerges from this enabling perspective is a fresh view of women's lives as structured by an alternative model of identity, one in which affiliation rather than accomplishment, relationship rather than career, are the defining characteristics.

In sizing up autobiographies of those who are culturally marginalized by reason of class, gender, or race, we need to be careful not to repeat unwittingly in our critical practice the original injustice of domination and exclusion. To begin with, autobiography in the West is itself hardly value-neutral as a literary kind. Krupat has emphasized the mismatch, for example, between the genre's characteristic markers—"egocentric individualism, historicism, and writing" (29)—and Native American concepts of selfhood, time, and literary expression. In order to assess the Indian contribution to the literature of autobiography in the United States, he proposes accordingly, in his essay for the present volume, an alternative to the traditionally individualist cast of Western autobiography, a "synecdochic" model of selfhood to conceptualize the characteristic form of collective identity in a tribal culture. In a parallel essay in this volume, Sau-ling Cynthia Wong's critique of Boelhower's model of immigrant autobiography singles out the limitations of its

Eurocentric bias. For Wong, Boelhower's exclusive concern with works by European immigrants steeped in the Judeo-Christian tradition and his commitment to an ahistorical brand of structuralist theorizing combine to produce a conception of American immigrant autobiography that fails to provide an adequate measure of the experience and texts of Chinese and other non-European ethnic groups.

To observe scholars at work on the manifold varieties of American autobiography—black, immigrant, women's, Native American—is to be reminded that the study of the genre, by its own definition a referential art, necessarily involves the study of culture. The play of models of self and life story is pervasive—in the experience of the subject, in the conventional assumptions of the genre, and (not least) in the mind of the critic—and shapes both the autobiographies Americans have written in the past, and those that Americans are writing now and in the time to come.

Although we have identified an extremely rich and comprehensive corpus of American autobiographies, thanks to the efforts of Kaplan, Briscoe, Lillard, Brumble, Jelinek, Brignano, and many others, the history of this literature in the United States remains largely unwritten. The earliest contribution is Robert F. Sayre's pioneering study, *The Examined Self: Benjamin Franklin, Henry Adams, Henry James* (1964).[15] Sayre argues that Augustine and Franklin represent the two major traditions, religious and secular, of the American practice of self-examination in autobiography. As its title suggests, however, Sayre's perspective reflects precisely the culturally restrictive definition of literary canon that Spengemann attacks; to define a "tradition" by moving chronologically from title to title on the received short list of masterworks and to perform the work of literary history become conveniently synonymous. That Sayre should have proceeded to emplot the history of American autobiography in this way is hardly surprising, however, given the ahistorical formalism of the New Criticism that colored so much of the scholarship of that period.[16] The assumption that the challenge of writing a history of the genre in the United States could be met by finding a way to arrange a small number of masterpieces in a coherent sequence of some kind persisted, and various all-purpose skeleton keys to American autobiography were proposed in the years following Sayre's initial foray. These included a cultural monomyth of success (Spengemann and L. R. Lundquist, 1965); a recurring prose form, "the interpreted design" (David Minter, 1969); political unrest (James M. Cox, "Autobiography and America," 1971); and a "prophetic mode" of discourse (G. Thomas Couser, 1979).[17]

The most comprehensive treatment of the history of American autobiography to date is Albert E. Stone's book, *Autobiographical Occasions
and Original Acts: Versions of American Identity from Henry Adams to Nate
Shaw* (1982). The subtitle, which stresses a diachronic movement *from*
Adams *to* Shaw, emphasizes the historical ambition of this major project. In his preface Stone credits Wilhelm Dilthey with inaugurating concern for the relation between autobiography and history, and he remains
faithful to the spirit of Dilthey in his willingness to place autobiography
above other modes of cultural expression as the most subtle and wide-
ranging reflection of both "the diversities of American experience" and
"the richness of American memories and imaginations" (1). The challenge posed by Stone is "to understand autobiography as both representative cultural history and stubbornly singular story" (18), to pursue
the representative without compromising the integrity of the individual
instance.

In practice, however, the broad historical purpose of Stone's project,
the construction of cultural narrative from the instances of individual
story, gives way to a literary criticism rather different in its aims. What
the book offers is a discrete series of comparatist forays or probes into
typical aspects of American autobiographical writing—women's autobiography, black autobiography, fiction in autobiography, violence in
autobiography, and so forth. The two or three texts featured in each
chapter are presented as representative works, exemplifying the characteristic features of the particular variety of American autobiographical
writing under study. What we learn from these texts has less to do with
history than with literature, less to do with American culture than with
the performance of autobiography. The yoking of Stone's title and subtitle, juxtaposing performance and history, may represent an attempt
to bridge this gap between his wishful historical program and his substantial achievement as a literary critic.

In suggesting the limitations of Stone's attempt to negotiate a distinctly *historical* passage between the individual and the representative
significance of an autobiography, I think it is necessary to add that the
notion that there is some cultural totality of American experience,
whose origins could be traced and plotted, may prove in the end to be
one of the most enduring of Americanists' illusions. The true history
of American autobiography and the culture in which it is produced and
consumed may turn out to be the history of identifiable groups within
the culture and of the network of relations among them. In this sense,
the cultural pluralism of Stone's book, with its multiple perspectives
addressing now the texts of one group in the culture and now those
of another, is especially suggestive, and may point the way for other

historians of American autobiography in the time to come. Interestingly, Sayre's thinking seems to have evolved toward something like this position: shifting away from his earlier concern with unifying a narrow canon of masterworks, he asserts in 1977 that any "adequate history of American autobiography" must be "plural in genre" and "pluralistic in subject matter" ("The Proper Study," 248–49).

If overviews of the history of American autobiography remain sketchy and highly speculative so far, work on the sources, assumptions, and practice of the genre in particular periods is a different story. Daniel B. Shea writing on colonial autobiography, Lawrence Buell on Transcendentalist autobiography, or Thomas Cooley on late nineteenth-century autobiography all represent important attempts to conceptualize distinct periods of autobiographical activity. Cooley, for example, dates the rise of modern autobiography in America from the practice of late nineteenth-century autobiographers such as Adams, Twain, Howells, and James, who abandoned the traditional, unitary concept of the self as innate and changeless in favor of a situational model of identity as "the shifting deposit of a continuing process of adaptation" (19). This difference, he believes, reflects the emergence of modern, developmental psychology, as opposed to the traditional faculty psychology that Thoreau and the Transcendentalists shared with Franklin and the Puritans.

Speaking of the New England Transcendentalists, Buell observes that "the most egoistic movement in American literary history produced no first-rate autobiography, unless one counts *Walden* as such." "Although they attached great theoretical importance to the self," he adds, "most of what they themselves wrote seems quite impersonal, including their own private journals" ("Transcendentalist," 268). Given the problematic status of the Transcendentalist literature of the first person, it is rather curious that the origins or "traditions" of this writing should have been studied repeatedly and in considerable detail. Shea's study of colonial autobiography left him convinced that Quaker and Puritan modes of self-presentation are reflected in the writings of Thoreau and Whitman, Dickinson and Adams. Similarly, Sacvan Bercovitch has made an elaborate case for the contribution of the Puritan model of selfhood to nineteenth-century American culture (*Puritan Origins*).

Whether or not the Transcendentalists' preoccupation with the life of self-culture yielded works that can be properly identified as autobiographies, however, is another matter. If Transcendentalist autobiographies do not seem very much like autobiographies to the modern reader, that may be because they derive, as Bercovitch suggests, from a "Protestant-libertarian model of the self" ("Ritual," 146) which is "self-effacing, exemplary, and self-transcending" (142) as opposed to the "Rousseauesque self" (146), the *I* "affirmed as a discrete presence, essentially private and unique" (142).[18] In Buell's essay for the present volume, "Autobiography in the American Renaissance," which addresses the paradoxes of the Transcendentalist conception of self, he concludes, in fact, that "although the autobiographical mode strongly marks American writing from the start, especially in Puritan New England but in other regions as well, autobiography in the strictest current sense does not fully flower as a literary genre in America much before the time of Henry Adams" (47–48).

Although *Walden* inevitably remains the test case for any account of American autobiographical writing in the mid-nineteenth century, Buell is careful to contextualize it in terms of the generic practice of the period. Thus he compares Thoreau's narrative to autobiographies by Frederick Douglass, P. T. Barnum, Lydia Sigourney, John Neal, and Walt Whitman, as well as to the general features of the surviving texts recorded in Kaplan. The resulting picture of actual autobiographical practice in the period is a relatively new development, and highly significant. Whereas before the literary historical space of autobiography was a largely unvisited terrain, demarcated on one side by a highly selective (and therefore questionably representative) literary canon and on the other by the largely unread volumes in Kaplan, now a working sense of the life of texts and a concomitant sense of the tastes and expectations of the reading public in particular periods is beginning to emerge.

A large share of this work of description has been performed by scholars researching one of the various subgenres of American autobiography. For example, texts of cross-cultural provenance—the life of the ex-slave, the life of the Christianized Native American—offer a peculiarly sensitive register of the popular autobiographical conventions of the 1830s, 1840s, and 1850s. Thus Krupat is able to locate J. B. Patterson's *Life of Ma-Ka-tai-me-she-kia-kiak or Black Hawk* (1833) in the period context of Indian biography and western American autobiography; thus A. LaVonne Brown Ruoff can specify the distinctive features of George Copway's *The Life, History, and Travels of Kah-ge-ga-gah-bowh* (1847) by referring to contemporary parallel developments in Indian captivity, slave, and missionary narratives. These are signs of the increasing fund of literary historical knowledge on which any authoritative, large-scale reconstruction of the history of American autobiography must be based.

The aims of this collection of essays, implicit in the preceding discussion, are soon told. In order to facilitate the study of American autobiography, I want to draw together in a single volume a wealth of literary, cultural, and bibliographical information that is not readily available elsewhere at the present time. Taken together, the commissioned essays offer a comprehensive picture of the state of the field today. From a variety of critical perspectives, they assess the work that has already been done; they also map out new lines of inquiry, and sometimes they proceed to demonstrate them by way of example. Because autobiography is by definition a referential art, because the self that is its principal referent is in fundamental ways a construct of culture, the issues raised and the texts studied in these essays tend to reflect broadly cultural rather than exclusively literary concerns. Shifting and conflicting models of self prove to be a focal topic. The pool of representative American autobiographies is considerably enlarged and certainly differently construed from its characteristic appearance in many earlier studies. Thus, in addition to commentary on Thoreau, Adams, and James, there are readings of Lucy Larcom, William Apes, and Emma Goldman. It is especially significant, moreover, that in several essays well-known, lesser known, and virtually unknown autobiographers figure *in relation to each other* for the first time in criticism, as they once did in the day of their original publication.

The essays are divided into two major sections. In the first, Daniel B. Shea, Lawrence Buell, Susanna Egan, and Albert E. Stone characterize the practice of American autobiography in particular periods. My own division into four periods was necessarily rough and heuristic, and I abandoned any notion of coverage at the outset. Instead, I encouraged each contributor to this section to devise an approach and to demarcate temporal boundaries that seemed to make the best sense of the material available for study.

The make-up of the second section reflects my own view that the pluralist nature of American culture has been decisive in the development of American autobiography. In an effort to work toward a more inclusive picture of the variety of autobiographical writing in the United States, I invited essays on women's autobiography (by Carol Holly and Blanche H. Gelfant), Native American autobiography (by Arnold Krupat), Afro-American autobiography (by William L. Andrews), immigrant autobiography (by William Boelhower and Sau-ling Cynthia Wong), and oral autobiography (by Jane Hallowell Coles and Robert Coles). I have placed the Coles' essay last because it represents an important contrast in form, style, and perspective to the rest of the essays in the volume. Here critical and historical commentary yield to a personal testimony of an altogether different sort, in which two leading practitioners of the art of gathering life histories in the field trace the evolution of their work over a period of more than twenty years.

Appropriately, they choose the interview as their format here, for it is the medium in which they conduct their work. They argue that their success in making contact with people from radically different economic, social, and cultural circumstances has been directly a function of their willingness to abandon the constraints of narrowly defined academic and professional postures.

The various subgenres represented in the second section, however, give only a partial portrait of the hugely various practice of American autobiographical writing today. Most readers will easily identify significant categories that are not treated here: Chicano autobiography, working-class autobiography, gay autobiography, "as-told-to" autobiographies by celebrities, autobiographies by veterans, by convicts, and so forth. I should add that I did not seek to impose on the contributors any single, unifying definition of "American autobiography" of my own design. The potential futility of such a move, moreover, is suggested in several of the essays, notably those by William Boelhower, Sau-ling Cynthia Wong, and Arnold Krupat, which explore the vexed issue of generic definition. What the contributors have done, collectively, is to describe the practice of autobiographical writing of various kinds by various kinds of Americans. It remains for others, in the time to come, to situate American autobiographical writing in the larger context of the history of the genre as a whole. To undertake this task will be to avoid the risk of positing a narrowly national teleology to the development of American autobiography.[19]

Any reader of this volume will recognize the size of the subject and how much remains to be done with it. For my own part, I want to thank all of the contributors, who have both individually and collectively enlarged my sense of the richness of the field. Martha Banta and Susan Gubar made important suggestions about the book in its early stages, Rebecca Hogan gave wise and timely advice later on, and William L. Andrews advised and encouraged throughout. Lawrence Buell, Carol Holly, Arnold Krupart, and Albert E. Stone read the introduction with care, and I hope I have put their criticism to good use. Barbara Hanrahan and Raphael Kadushin of the University of Wisconsin Press have been invaluable in guiding these pages into print. Needless to say, any shortcomings in the governing conception and program for this project are my own.

NOTES

1 See Eakin, "L'autobiographie." Commentary on nineteenth-century American autobiography has been greatly enriched by the appearance in 1989 of three new books: G. Thomas Couser, *Altered Egos*; James M. Cox, *Recovering Literature's Lost Ground*; and Joseph Fichtelberg, *The Complex Image*.

2 See Granger, for example, who applies Philippe Lejeune's well-known definition of the genre to *Walden*, and concludes that it is not an autobiography.

3 Philippe Lejeune's current project to compile an exhaustive inventory of all of the autobiographies written in France in the nineteenth century illustrates both the problems and the promise of adopting Spengemann's inclusive stance. For Lejeune's account of this project, see "Cote Ln 27"; for additional commentary, see Eakin, "Foreword." For an illustration of Lejeune's procedure and his findings to date, see "Autobiography and Social History in the Nineteenth Century." Lejeune adopts membership in a social group as the only possible organizing principle for the otherwise baffling heterogeneity of his corpus of nineteenth-century French autobiography. Lillard, Kaplan, and Briscoe also feature an individual's occupation as a principle of classification.

4 For a more manageable sample than the hundreds of entries in Kaplan, see Carlock's list of more than a hundred titles published between 1840 and 1870.

5 Daniel B. Shea's work on colonial autobiography is an exception here, to be explained in part by the fact that the scholarly territory was opened up for settlement by Perry Miller, who placed a premium on the broad social and cultural context of the literature to be studied.

6 See, for example, Sayre, *The Examined Self*.

7 See Cox, "Recovering Literature's Lost Ground." Renza joins Cox in noting the tendency of contemporary criticism to stress the fictive, literary dimension of autobiography, attenuating "autobiography's explicit, formal claim to be a legitimate personal-historical document" (273).

8 See Lejeune, "The Autobiography of Those Who Do Not Write," 198.

9 Lejeune ("The Autobiography of Those Who Do Not Write"), Patai, and others emphasize the shaping hand of the dominant culture at work in the gathering of oral history.

10 See Bruss, and Lejeune, "Autobiography and Literary History." For examples of the formalist approach, see Fleishman, Lejeune (in his early books and essays), May, and Spengemann.

11 No other variety of American autobiography has been studied in greater depth and with more sophistication than the slave narrative. For a comprehensive account of the scholarship, see William L. Andrews's essay in this collection.

12 In "Base and Superstructure in Marxist Cultural Theory," Raymond Williams reminds us that the hegemony of the dominant culture, by which he understands "a central system of practices, meanings and values" (38),

is neither total nor static. In particular, he directs attention to the existence of "alternative" and "oppositional" cultures, "those practices, experiences, meanings, values which are not part of the effective dominant culture" (40). Arnold Krupat directed my attention to this essay, which articulates a theoretical model that could be applied to the relation between "dominant" and "other-than-dominant" texts.

13   See also working-class autobiography for a parallel instance of cultural influence. Regenia Gagnier's study of nineteenth-century British working-class autobiography reminds us that the individualist bias of the models of self and life story in traditional bourgeois autobiography was ill-equipped to express the typically collective nature of working-class experience. For some of Gagnier's subjects, the very act of presuming to write an autobiography in the first place felt like a betrayal of class solidarity. Scholars such as Gagnier, David Vincent, Nan Hackett, and Simon Dentith have demonstrated the richness of the field of British working-class autobiography. American working-class autobiography, on the other hand, remains largely unexplored, and it was one of my chief disappointments in preparing this collection that I could not locate anyone—literary critic or labor historian—to tackle this subject.

14   Boelhower's emphasis here parallels that of Werner Sollors, who stresses "the cultural interplays and contacts among writers of different backgrounds, the cultural mergers and secessions that took place in America" (*Beyond Ethnicity*, 14–15). See also his critique of the concept of cultural pluralism, which, he argues, tends to interfere with proper recognition of the fact that "American culture . . . abounds in ethnogenesis on the basis of trans-ethnic contacts" ("Critique," 276).

15   William L. Andrews has called my attention to the existence of an earlier volume than Sayre's, *Witnesses for Freedom: Negro Americans in Autobiography* (1948), by Rebecca Chalmers Barton. See his essay in this collection.

16   Sayre makes a similar assessment of *The Examined Self* in the revised edition published in 1988.

17   It is hardly surprising that literary critics are not necessarily suited by taste and training to undertake the work of history, and studies of autobiography are no exception. Lejeune has noted that most attempts to write the history of the genre have yielded a series of disconnected chapters or monographs on individual masterworks (*L'Autobiographie*, 48), and even the best of these, *The Value of the Individual: Self and Circumstance in Autobiography* (1978) by Karl Joachim Weintraub, does not escape this belletristic tendency to accept the classic, canonized mastertext as conveniently representative, a comprehensive synthesis of the dominant features of its cultural context. The easy metonymies of privilege and power that rationalize the part (the class, the gender, the race) as equivalent to the whole (the country, the culture) are fast losing their once unquestioned authority to persuade. Lejeune's discussion in *L'Autobiographie en France* of the problems of writing the history of autobiography remains the best introduction to the subject. Avrom Fleishman's succinct but illuminating summary of the history of the genre

from Augustine to the nineteenth century is exemplary in its wary avoidance of untested commonplaces.

18 Quentin Anderson shares Bercovitch's stress on the difference between the comparatively abstract and absolute individualism embraced by Emerson, Thoreau, and Whitman and the more politically engaged, historically contingent variety espoused by Rousseau and the English Romantics. For Anderson, however, Transcendentalist autobiography represents not a conservative tradition dedicated to "transforming the energies of radical individualism into a force against social change" as Bercovitch would have it ("Ritual," 149), but rather a bold, doomed project of single, separate persons "to make it alone because they were faced by a society they could find no other way of dealing with" (Anderson, 30).

19 In raising this last point, I am echoing the words of Lawrence Buell, who underscored the limitations of an exclusively Americanist perspective in a letter he wrote in response to an earlier draft of this introduction.

WORKS CITED

Anderson, Quentin. "Making It Alone." *Review* 5 (1983): 17–30.

Andrews, William L. *To Tell a Free Story: The First Century of Afro-American Autobiography, 1760–1865.* Champaign-Urbana: University of Illinois Press, 1986.

Baker, Houston A. *Blues, Ideology, and Afro-American Literature.* Chicago: University of Chicago Press, 1984.

Bercovitch, Sacvan. *The Puritan Origins of the American Self.* New Haven: Yale University Press, 1975.

Bercovitch, Sacvan. "The Ritual of American Autobiography: Edwards, Franklin, Thoreau." *Revue française d'études américaines* 14 (1982): 139–50.

Brignano, Russell C. *Black Americans in Autobiography: An Annotated Bibliography of Autobiographies and Autobiographical Books Written Since the Civil War.* [1974]. Rev. ed. Durham: Duke University Press, 1984.

Briscoe, Mary Louise, et al., eds. *American Autobiography, 1945–1980: A Bibliography.* Madison: University of Wisconsin Press, 1982.

Brumble, H. David, III. *An Annotated Bibliography of American Indian and Eskimo Autobiographies.* Lincoln: University of Nebraska Press, 1981.

Bruss, Elizabeth W. "Introduction: Literary Acts." In *Autobiographical Acts: The Changing Situation of a Literary Genre.* Baltimore: Johns Hopkins University Press, 1976, 1–18.

Buell, Lawrence. "Transcendentalist Self-Examination and Autobiographical Tradition." In *Literary Transcendentalism: Style and Vision in the American Renaissance.* Ithaca: Cornell University Press, 1973, 265–83.

Carlock, Mary Sue. "American Autobiographies, 1840–1870: A Bibliography." *Bulletin of Bibliography and Magazine Notes* 23 (1961): 118–20.

Coles, Robert, and Jane Hallowell Coles. *Women of Crisis: Lives of Struggle and Hope*. New York: Delacorte, 1978.

Coles, Robert, and Jane Hallowell Coles. *Women of Crisis II: Lives of Work and Dreams*. New York: Delacorte, 1980.

Cooley, Thomas. *Educated Lives: The Rise of Modern Autobiography in America*. Columbus: Ohio State University Press, 1976.

Couser, G. Thomas. *American Autobiography: The Prophetic Mode*. Amherst: University of Massachusetts Press, 1979.

Couser, G. Thomas. *Altered Egos: Authority in American Autobiography*. New York: Oxford University Press, 1989.

Cox, James M. "Autobiography and America." [1971]. In *Recovering Literature's Lost Ground*, 11–32.

Cox, James M. "Recovering Literature's Lost Ground through Autobiography." [1978]. In *Recovering Literature's Lost Ground*, 33–54.

Cox, James M. *Recovering Literature's Lost Ground: Essays in American Autobiography*. Baton Rouge: Louisiana State University Press, 1989.

Dentith, Simon. "Contemporary Working-class Autobiography: Politics of Form, Politics of Content." In *Modern Selves: Essays on Modern British and American Autobiography*. Ed. Philip Dodd. London: Frank Cass, 1986, 60–80.

Eakin, Paul John. "L'autobiographie américaine au XIXe siècle: tendances récentes de la recherche." *Romantisme* 56 (1987): 118–23.

Eakin, Paul John. "Foreword." In Philippe Lejeune, *On Autobiography*. Ed. Paul John Eakin. Minneapolis: University of Minnesota Press, 1989, vii–xxviii.

Egan, Susanna. *Patterns of Experience in Autobiography*. Chapel Hill: University of North Carolina Press, 1984.

Fichtelberg, Joseph. *The Complex Image: Faith and Method in American Autobiography*. Philadelphia: University of Pennsylvania Press, 1989.

Fleishman, Avrom. *Figures of Autobiography: The Language of Self-Writing in Victorian and Modern England*. Berkeley and Los Angeles: University of California Press, 1983.

Fox-Genovese, Elizabeth. *Within the Plantation Household: Black and White Women of the Old South*. Chapel Hill: University of North Carolina Press, 1989.

Gagnier, Regenia. "Social Atoms: Working-Class Autobiography, Subjectivity, and Gender." *Victorian Studies* 30 (1987): 335–63.

Gates, Henry Louis. *The Signifying Monkey: A Theory of Afro-American Literary Criticism*. New York: Oxford University Press, 1988.

Granger, Michel. "*Walden*, ou l'autographie de Henry D. Thoreau." *Revue française d'études américaines* 14 (1982): 199–210.

Hackett, Nancy Ann. *The Evolution of Nineteenth Century Working-Class Autobiography*. Ph.D. diss. University of Iowa, 1983. Ann Arbor: UMI, 1987.

Jelinek, Estelle C. *The Tradition of Women's Autobiography: From Antiquity to the Present*. Boston: Twayne, 1986.

Kaplan, Louis, et al. *A Bibliography of American Autobiographies*. Madison: University of Wisconsin Press, 1961.

Krupat, Arnold. *For Those Who Come After: A Study of Native American Auto-biography.* Berkeley and Los Angeles: University of California Press, 1985.

Lejeune, Philippe. *L'Autobiographie en France.* Paris: Colin, 1971.

Lejeune, Philippe. "Autobiography and Literary History." [1975]. In Lejeune, *On Autobiography,* 141–62.

Lejeune, Philippe. "The Autobiography of Those Who Do Not Write." [1980]. In Lejeune, *On Autobiography,* 185–215.

Lejeune, Philippe. "Autobiography and Social History in the Nineteenth Century." [1982]. In Lejeune, *On Autobiography,* 163–84.

Lejeune, Philippe. "La Cote Ln 27: Pour un répertoire des autobiographies écrites en France au XIXe siècle." [1984]. In *Moi aussi.* Paris: Seuil, 1986, 249–72.

Lejeune, Philippe. *On Autobiography.* Ed. Paul John Eakin. Minneapolis: University of Minnesota Press, 1989.

Lillard, Richard G. *American Life in Autobiography: A Descriptive Guide.* Stanford: Stanford University Press, 1956.

May, Georges. *L'Autobiographie.* Paris: Presses Universitaires de France, 1979.

Minter, David L. *The Interpreted Design as a Structural Principle in American Prose.* New Haven: Yale University Press, 1969.

Patai, Daphne. "Introduction: Constructing a Self." In *Brazilian Women Speak: Contemporary Life Stories.* New Brunswick: Rutgers University Press, 1988, 1–35.

Peterson, Linda H. *Victorian Autobiography: The Tradition of Self-Interpretation.* New Haven: Yale University Press, 1986.

Renza, Louis A. "The Veto of the Imagination: A Theory of Autobiography." In *Autobiography: Essays Theoretical and Critical.* Ed. James Olney. Princeton: Princeton University Press, 1980, 268–95.

Ruoff, A. LaVonne Brown. "George Copway: Nineteenth-Century American Indian Autobiographer." *a/b Auto/Biography Studies* 3 (1987): 6–17.

Sayre, Robert F. *The Examined Self: Benjamin Franklin, Henry Adams, Henry James.* [1964]. Rev. ed. Madison: University of Wisconsin Press, 1988.

Sayre, Robert F. "The Proper Study—Autobiographies in American Studies." *American Quarterly* 29 (1977): 241–62.

Shea, Daniel B. *Spiritual Autobiography in Early America.* [1968]. Rev. ed. Madison: University of Wisconsin Press, 1988.

Sollors, Werner. *Beyond Ethnicity: Consent and Descent in American Culture.* New York: Oxford University Press, 1986.

Sollors, Werner. "A Critique of Pure Pluralism." In *Reconstructing American Literary History.* Ed. Sacvan Bercovitch. Cambridge: Harvard University Press, 1986, 250–79.

Spengemann, William C. "What Is American Literature?" *The Centennial Review* 22 (1978): 119–38.

Spengemann, William C. *The Forms of Autobiography: Episodes in the History of a Literary Genre.* New Haven: Yale University Press, 1980.

Spengemann, William C., and L. R. Lundquist. "Autobiography and the American Myth." *American Quarterly* 17 (1965): 501–19.

Stone, Albert E. *Autobiographical Occasions and Original Acts: Versions of American Identity from Henry Adams to Nate Shaw*. Philadelphia: University of Pennsylvania Press, 1982.

Vincent, David. *Bread, Knowledge, and Freedom: A Study of Nineteenth-Century Working Class Autobiography*. London: Europa, 1981.

Weintraub, Karl Joachim. *The Value of the Individual: Self and Circumstance in Autobiography*. Chicago: University of Chicago Press, 1978.

White, Hayden. "The Context in the Text: Method and Ideology in Intellectual History." In *The Content of the Form: Narrative Discourse and Historical Representation*. Baltimore: Johns Hopkins University Press, 1987.

Williams, Raymond. "Base and Superstructure in Marxist Cultural Theory." In *Problems in Materialism and Culture: Selected Essays*. London: Verso, 1980, 31–49.

PART I

Four Centuries of
American Autobiography

CHAPTER 1

The Prehistory of
American Autobiography

DANIEL B. SHEA

> Men can do nothing without the make-believe of a beginning. Even Science, the
> strict measurer, is obliged to start with a make-believe unit, and must fix on a point
> in the stars' unceasing journey when his sidereal clock shall pretend that time
> is at Nought . . . . No retrospect will take us to the true beginning; and whether
> our prologue be in heaven or on earth, it is but a fraction of the all-presupposing
> fact with which our story sets out.
>
> George Eliot, *Daniel Deronda*

In the beginning (as it were), autobiography had no America. If autobiography is memory's form, and if "America" in the Renaissance was
an icon of the future that focused errant Anglo-European imaginings
about the New World, then early American autobiography is a hope-
less solecism. Autobiography, itself in the process of being invented,
would have to wait until 1809 to take its proper name, and America,
while claiming a national identity in 1776, would take generations more
to earn and define one. In this earliest period one does as well to think
of Shakespeare's Miranda as the very figure of an American autobiography conceived but not yet born. "Oh brave new world that has such
creatures in't," she says in *The Tempest*, confronting the representatives
of a fallen Old World. Innocent of the kind of history known to her
father, she can understand the past only as a version of the future. " 'Tis
new to thee," Prospero responds indulgently (V.i.182–84). Her brief
autobiography is a wonder indeed, the effort of a purely prospective
imagination to give shape to wisps of dimly remembered experience.
" 'Tis far off," she pleads, "And rather like a dream than an assurance

that my remembrance warrants" (I.ii.44–46). The writing of American autobiography, properly speaking, would be left to the New World descendants of Miranda and Ferdinand.

And yet America, as the explorers came upon it, was not vacant of memory and imagination and did not lack for peoples whose calling forth of their past was a life source for them in the present. To stipulate a beginning for a form of Anglo-European writing on the American continent is to invent in George Eliot's words an "all presupposing fact" that ignores the pre-existent oral literature of a multitude of Indian tribes. Our access to that continuity of song and story comes primarily from its later emergence into print, a process begun in the nineteenth century that eventually resulted in such a recognizable artifact as the Indian autobiography.[1] To inquire about Indian autobiography in the sixteenth, seventeenth, and eighteenth centuries, as we count them, is to court a further solecism. What we seek did not exist in the form in which we have learned to seek it. What was there we can know about only through a kind of archaeological inference. As Arnold Krupat has pointed out, it is a difficulty of knowing not only what was said but of "how they said it" (3). In an oral, tribal culture the autobiographical act (to speak anachronistically) would have been literally performative, beyond the ken of (because prior to) our intricate theories about metaphorically performative texts. From our familiar (because familial) idea of autobiography, we should have to subtract notions of the individual and of the self's motivation and teleology and dispense with much of our accustomed formal sense of narrative causation and closure; and even then, having made appropriate subtractions, we should still not have begun the positive work of archaeological recovery.

Such attempts, as they have begun to appear in contemporary studies of Indian autobiography, admittedly have the quality of rough sketches, a static representation of those preliterate voices that had risen and fallen through a chromatic range whose colors and limits we cannot know unmediated. The attempt, nevertheless, is an act of imaginative sympathy that has begun to yield rewards. Looking through the medium of later, published narratives, H. David Brumble has given some estimate of the shape of original tellings. Granting the full complexity of tribal variations, he distinguishes six kinds of preliterate autobiographical narratives: the "coup" tales, by which warriors elaborated their triumphs in striking the enemy; less formal and usually more detailed tales of warfare and hunting; self-examinations; self-vindications; educational narratives; and tales of the acquisition of shamanic powers (22–23).

It is possible, of course, to shape these categories into shadowy primitive reflections of Anglo-European ideal forms. The coup tales then become a version of the classical vaunt or Anglo-Saxon hero's *beot* (boast); self-examinations and self-vindications take their place in the literature of confession; the educational narratives of Indian tribes appear continuous with all autobiography that has posterity as its most important audience; and narratives recounting the acquisition of mysterious, enabling powers may seem to have something of the pattern, less individually self-conscious, of the saint's coming into grace or the growth of a poet's soul. Critical imperialism, however, is self-defeating; assimilating strangeness by familiarizing it leaves the would-be knower sunk in his or her original ignorance. And given the ultimate equality of cultures as cultures, the notions of original and reflection are meaningless because they are always reversible. One could as easily maintain that Indian stories of origins are the type of all autobiography; to speak of the earth's manifold becomings and narratively, communally, to trace them to their root becomes in an alternative view the great human act distortedly mirrored in that addiction of modern Western civilization, its endless rewritings of Genesis in the first person.

In developmental terms, the New World offered a kind of evolutionary "niche" favoring the growth of the parent culture's autobiographical tendencies. Both Renaissance and Reformation were fertile in forms of what evolutionary biologists call *preadaptation*, which, in concert with a hospitable environment, would result in an eventual flourishing of American autobiography. The evolutionary metaphor means most when it is most strictly limited. It has, in particular, no teleological implications, as if somehow certain strains of Anglo-European literature aspired internally to the condition of American autobiography. But two strains, notable for their adaptive survival in the New World, deserve notice against the implicit selectivity of the host environment.

The first is the flourishing of the Renaissance idea of the self as microcosm in a period when the discovery and exploration of the macrocosm seemed to offer transformative possibilities directly to the person of the explorer. The conjunction of outward and inward exploration, a union of vehicle and tenor familiar from the "Conclusion" to *Walden*, has a long prehistory, one characterized by dialectical attempts to accommodate the impact of literal exploration to assumptions about human nature, and to adjust figural representations of the self to physical discovery.[2] The hypothesis to be tested, William Spengemann has pointed out, was "the Renaissance traveler's generally unspoken but nevertheless strongly felt sense that a voyage to the New World made a new man" (30).

It is no accident that one of the names most closely associated with New World exploration, that of Samuel Purchas, appears prominently as well in the literature of seventeenth-century microcosmography. His 1619 *Microcosmus, or the Historie of Man*, is a moody meditation on ambition written in the spirit of Ecclesiastes, its subtitle promising to relate the "Wonders of [Man's] Generation, Vanities in his Degeneration, [and the] Necessity of his Regeneration." Purchas's famous multivolume collection of Renaissance travel writing, *Hakluytus Posthumus, or Purchas His Pilgrimes* (1625), an editor's pilgrimage through new dimensions of the enlarged macrocosm, would seem to declare him a spokesman for an age of optimism and discovery. For Purchas, though, physical possession of the world without spiritual self-possession makes of the discoverer only a latter-day Alexander, "as if the World had not beene Morsell bigge enough for that vaine ambitious appetite, which then would have beene as sicke for new Worlds, as hee had beene eager of this" (*Microcosmus*, 773). Like Thoreau, Purchas arrived at the moral of his journeying while traveling locally, arguing (as all autobiographers must) the ascendancy of text over experience. "Least Travellers may be greatest Writers," he claims. "Even I which have written so much of travellers and travells, never travelled 200. miles from Thaxted in Essex, where I was borne . . ." *Hakluytus* 1:201).

For many of the travelers of whom Purchas spoke, on the other hand, New World autobiography would be a tale of literal transformations. The *Relation* of Alvar Nuñez Cabeza de Vaca, which had appeared in its Spanish original in 1542, could seem at times to promise an outdistancing of original sin, a kind of salvation through locomotion: "I have already stated that throughout all this country we went naked, and as we were unaccustomed to being so, twice a year we cast our skins like serpents" (Quinn 2:41). At a minimum, the discovery of tobacco promised relief from the direst effects of the Fall: kidney stones, wind, menstrual cramps, evil breath, worms, joint problems, swellings, toothache, chilblaines, venomous bites, wounds, and carbuncles in the catalogue of John Frampton's *Joyfull Newes Out of the Newe Founde Worlde*, a 1577 translation from the Spanish of the Sevillian physician, Nicholas Monardes. The possibility beckoned of an even greater transport: not the self rehabilitated, but the self beside itself, a state enjoyed by the Indians when, chewing tobacco and coca together, they "goe as thei were out of their wittes, like as if they were dronke which is a thyng that dooeth give them great contentment to bee in that sorte" (Quinn 2:32). Between Purchas and Frampton, the nadir and zenith of an as yet unwritten New World autobiography had been marked out. The American "I" might eventually discover that there was truly nothing new under the sun, but for some time to come, the environment would encourage it to write a narrative of deliverance, even into witless content, from its accustomed ordinary self.

THE TRAVELER'S SHADOW

Woven into the writings of the Renaissance discoverers and explorers, as John Seelye and Wayne Franklin have made us aware, there is a discernible thread of autobiography. These were not writers who made a point of setting their lives intact before the reader. Still, it is difficult to escape the feeling, as they categorize strange flora and fauna and, in their descriptions of the natives, puzzle over all that is and is not part of their own identity's birthright, that they are writing about a life's definitive event. We see the traveler's shadow cast before him on the terrain he writes about.

Though only recently read as he might be, Captain John Smith has always had preeminence among this group. The investment of self in deed and the ambition of textual heroism have seemed the chief characteristics, since their first publication, of such works as *A True Relation of Such Occurences and Accidents of Noate as Hath Hapned in Virginia* (1608), *A Description of New England* (1616) and *The Generall Historie of Virginia, New England, and the Summer Isles* (1624). In a volume published in the year before his death, *The True Travels, Adventures, and Observations of Captaine John Smith* (1630), Smith returned to the early ground of a lifetime of becoming. Within several sentences of the mention of his birth, he describes himself orphaned at thirteen and ready to sell his scholar's "Satchell, bookes, and all he had," intending to go to sea, "his minde being even then set upon brave adventures" (3:153–54). In the kind of originary scene by which memory and imagination create a self, Smith isolates his hero in a version, which appears consciously mythical, of the squire's preparation for his knighthood:

Here by a faire brooke he built a Pavillion of boughes, where only in his cloaths he lay. His studie was Machiavills Art of warre, and Marcus Aurelius; his exercise a good horse, with his lance and Ring; his food was thought to be more of venison than any thing else; what he wanted his man brought him. The countrey wondering at such an Hermite . . . (3:156).

By reputation, if not chronology, John Smith stands first in the line of American self-writers who found that they could not write themselves into the New World text without writing the native identity to some extent as their own. His famous narrative of his rescue by Pocohontas begins with an image of Smith defining himself as the bringer of a civilized and scientific cosmos to the Indians, introducing them to the compass and demonstrating by that

Globe-like Jewell, the roundnesse of the earth, and skies, the spheare of the Sunne, Moone, and Starres, and how the Sunne did chase the night round about the world continually; the greatnesse of the Land and Sea, the diversitie of Nations, varietie of complexions, and how we were to them Antipodes, and . . . they all stood as amazed with admiration (2:147).

Smith's audience in this passage is as much onlooker at his cosmos as he is at theirs. What his English audience then experiences in the Pocahontas episode is an initiation through the autobiographical hero into that culture to which *it* is antipode. Whether Smith literally escaped death by the intervention of Powhatan's daughter is irrelevant to the narrative reality of initiation, the hero's death as Englishman and his rebirth as Powhatan's son, a transformation effected by the prepubescent (Pocahontas was eleven) spirit of the New World, an Ariel in skins (Kupperman 65n). Thomas Morton's *New English Canaan* (1647), though its narrator emerges more cautiously and obliquely than the narrator in Smith's writing, similarly projects an English identity ("Mine Host") against the language and behavior of the native culture, and then through ritual—the evocation of masque, the dancing of Englishmen and "lasses in beaver coats" about the May Pole—textually deploys antipodes of race and identity toward the end of their coming together. It is that act, autobiographical in the largest sense, over which Mine Host ultimately presides.

Morton's narrative in the third book of *The New English Canaan* celebrates the secular faith of the Renaissance in a metamorphic self, but its unhappily chosen ground in Puritan New England constitutes a thoroughly hostile environment. For while *renaissance* and *reformation* seem to express a kinship through the idea of rebirth, the characteristic patterns of their autobiographical testimonies reveal that they differ in essential ways. Morton's models for the self are Ovidean, his transformative sense of the New World environment is Virgilean, and his satiric approach to the Puritans' piety is both socially and politically temporal (Shea, *"Old Adversary"*). His Puritan judges, who three times cast Morton out of their narrative of salvation history, authorized only one sort of autobiography: the narrative of rebirth through divine grace. Migrating from Old to New England, that strain of the autobiographical mode enjoyed a successful adaptive survival in rocky soil that encouraged the rigors of spiritual introspection and discouraged Humanist fantasies of an autonomously willed self that charms and is charmed by the natural environment. (Properly to understand the efflorescence of the autobiographical mode among the New England Transcendentalists, one must appreciate the way in which these two strains later intermingle, potentiating by profoundly disturbing one another.)

NEW ENGLAND SOUL-WRITING

As monolithic descriptions of New England Puritanism have yielded to descriptions that are more nuanced and more aware of heterodoxy, the frame around spiritual autobiography in the colonial period has also had to be enlarged. The center of the picture has traditionally been the narrative of conversion, a staple of New England's literary and religious history ever since such narratives, written or oral, were required of petitioners for membership in the churches of the Massachusetts Bay area. The attraction of a decentered picture is that it allows for a greater variety of autobiographical texts by freeing the definition of autobiography in this period from its attachment to narrative in the first person. Criticism benefits, of course, from such a move, but not at the expense of historical understanding. The critic's sense of a continuity of discourse, from Puritan histories to autobiography, from diaries to poetry, is buttressed by a historical awareness that the Puritan urnarrative of God's saving activity in time and on the glorious cynosure of the New England stage diffused itself through a variety of interrelated forms.

In such histories, for instance, as William Bradford's *Of Plymouth Plantation* (1650) and Edward Johnson's *Wonder-Working Providence of Sion's Saviour in New-England* (1654),[3] the person of the narrator is largely effaced except in his role as inditer of the deeds, sufferings, and backslidings of a chosen people. Yet these historians are biographers of a community, and the experience on which they draw is ultimately autobiographical; it is the soul's story, adumbrated in Exodus or Canticles, of its movement from bondage to sin, of escape from the seductions of Babylon to the love feast of divine grace. In that narrative, as Edward Gallagher has suggested in speaking of Johnson's history, the wilderness of the elect soul is transformed into "a fruitful land . . . a well ordered Commonwealth . . . a Temple of the Lord" (vii). So Mary Griswald saw her experience in the brief spiritual narrative recorded along with those of fifty other petitioners for church membership by Thomas Shepard at Cambridge: "But after, I thought I must be filthy still and afterward I heard the deliverer shall come from Sion and shall turn iniquity from Jacob. I wished I had a part in it and I heard of [a] fruitful desert as a fruitful field" (*Confessions*, 188). So too the otherwise unnamed Brother Crackbone's wife who, although she finds her heart eventually set "at liberty," must first endure a wilderness experience: "And so came to New England. I forgot the Lord as the Israelites did and when I had a new house yet I thought I had no new heart" (*Confessions*, 140; Caldwell, 183–86).

The ubiquity of the Puritan autobiographical mode becomes even more obvious when we hear Thomas Shepard, as stenographer of his congregation's confessions, intruding his own first person into their testimonies and occasionally rendering that testimony in the third person (*Confessions*, 47). In such a case, the pastor's authority over the extended autobiographical text of his congregation becomes explicit, but it must also be remembered that Shepard had been more than a collaborator from the beginning, shaping his congregation's experience from the pulpit in Cambridge. And at only a slight remove in this echoic voicing of souls, there is in fact *The Autobiography of Thomas Shepard* (1646),[4] his own autobiography as redundancy would rightly distinguish it, and its companion *Journal* (1640–44), the former rendering the speaker's original conversion, the latter tracing the ongoing process by which the life of grace regularly came within a hair of pronouncing its death sentence while moving ineluctably toward ultimate sanctification (*God's Plot*, 25). The network of autobiographical discourse in New England Puritanism repeats itself and returns upon itself. The continuity of pastor's and parishioners' self-inquisitions appears also in *The Diary of Michael Wigglesworth, 1653–1657*, and it is not surprising that the ostensibly non-autobiographical poetry of Wigglesworth's *Day of Doom* (1662) should seem less cosmic than personal for the diarist who writes self-damningly: "I sometimes find such a monster of iniquity in myself that I can see nor tast no excellency in communion with god, how seldom is it that I have a living sight of him? this Lord I groan under as my greatest plague" (64).

The great monument of Puritan autobiographical writing—so designed, one feels, by its author—is the *Diary of Cotton Mather* (1681–1724). And yet for a writer whose every gesture was autobiographical, the forms of his shaping a textual self can seem interchangeable variations on a theme. Properly, Mather's autobiography is *Paterna* (1688–1727), which he began writing as an instructional version of his life intended for his son Increase. Paradoxically, the autobiography never names its author; and after an initial genetic narrative, many of its passages have been copied from the diaries. It might even be argued that Mather's shapelessly epical history of the Puritan New England experiment, the *Magnalia Christi Americana* (1702), is his largest autobiographical gesture. Self and history are interdependent. Without divine favor, the autobiographical self cannot exist. As Mather says in a birthday entry in his diary, "What! And is the *fifty-third* Year of my Life this Day finished? A Life so forfeited; a Life so threatened; such a dying Life; yea, and such a barren One!" (2:334). Without the urgent and identifying voice of the self-as-historian, through, there will be no textual life for the great deeds of Christ in America. Discursively to enact the lives of the Puritan fathers, the founding and becoming of Harvard College, and the wonders and mysteries of divine providence was to write large and public versions of those "G.D.'s" of his diary, the daily entries of "goods devised" that took on for Mather the status of life events.

The equivalence of history and autobiography in his writing may well have been an inherited characteristic, not only of the tribe but of the family. The *Autobiography* (1685–1715) of Cotton's father Increase wrought in fact a more exquisite variation on the relation between divine activity in time and the writing about it. At one point, having prayed for deliverance from disease, Increase argues that the very fact of writing out his experience should dispose Providence to favor the answering of his prayers, lest "if hee should not answer me graciously, others after my decease, that should see the papers which I had written and kept as remembrances of my walking before God, would be discouraged" (294). While the end is edification, text here takes priority over experience; it is as if the referent, experience, needed somehow to keep in mind that it must eventually subsume itself in autobiography.

It is unfortunate that for every reader who studies Puritan spiritual autobiography, there will be ten who browse the poetry of Anne Bradstreet and Edward Taylor with little sense of how arbitrary is the line they have implicitly drawn between genres. Although both Bradstreet and Taylor wrote out brief autobiographical statements in prose (Shea, *Spiritual Autobiography* 92–100, 113–18), their poetry too needs to be seen in its continuity with the extensive web of Puritan writing about the soul, collected in nodes of "I," alternatively prose or poetry. Characteristically, Anne Bradstreet's domestic poetry counts the poet's losses, past or prospective, of children and grandchildren, father and house and husband, even of her own life; and then, seeming to isolate her from the communal faith, it questions the ways in which Providence has arranged her life. Readers who make much of what they take to be her lapses from an hypothesized Puritan creed need to launch themselves on the fullness of the Puritan autobiographical text and to hear the voice of Anne Bradstreet in company with the soul-keenings in Shepard's collection of testimonies or the diaries of Wigglesworth and Cotton Mather.

Similarly, Edward Taylor's two series of "Preparatory Meditations" (1682–1725), read collectively, can appear to be artificially repetitive exercises in the repletion and emptying of the waters of grace. Yet the same process is observable in Shepard's *Journal* and Mather's *Diary*. It is the nature of grace to reinvent itself autobiographically again and again. The experience of conversion is psychologically unstable because its custodian is the doubting fallen self, and open-ended because it is understood to be perfectible only at the vanishing point of eternity. These are the conditions of soul-writing, and it is the Puritan pastor's awareness of those conditions that informs Taylor's long poem, *God's Determinations Touching His Elect* (c. 1685), a work whose matter is that of spiritual autobiography, cast into a drama of already chosen saints not yet visible to themselves. The dialectic between Satan's counsels of despair and Christ's reassurances, objectified in the poem's dramatic exchanges, is spiritual autobiography turned inside out and pastorally directed toward the goal of church membership.

GENDER: THE MOVABLE CENTER

If reconsiderations of genre in the early period profit the study of autobiography, so too do new understandings of the relation between gender and self-writing. Feminist criticism may find limitations and obstacles in the materials of autobiography in a period dominated first by a male ministerial vocabulary for the soul and then by a pantheon of founding fathers. But the prospect remains that continuing literary archaeology will bring to light previously unread autobiographical writing by women, particularly in the textual private space of diaries, a form at once companionate and exploratory, submissive in its externals to chronology and domestic regimen but providing in fact a terrain of wide freedom within the self.[5] And for the women's autobiographical writing that we have presumed was already well understood, readings authorized under a new dispensation will have the critical impact of discovering new texts.

The voice that ought to be heard first among colonial women is Anne Hutchinson's, but hers was a fragment of autobiography, its few lines scattered through the transcript of her heresy trial and invented, with whatever intrepidity, only in response to external interrogation. Governor John Winthrop's charge to her, "We do not call you to teach the court but to lay open yourself," constituted something less than an unencumbered invitation to autobiography (Hall, 315). What Anne Hutchinson finally revealed to the Massachusetts Bay authorities was that the source of her doctrinal errors was also the source and essence of autobiography. Granting her need to discriminate among the voices that spoke to her, those of Moses and John the Baptist, of Christ and potentially even of the antichrist, Anne Hutchinson said that she knew what she knew "by an immediate revelation . . . by the voice of his own spirit to my soul" (Hall, 337). An antinominan voice would be an autonomous, self-authorizing voice, heretical only in that it is the daring hypothesis, while never quite the actuality, of any autobiography. That voice was banished from Massachusetts Bay less for what it had said than for what it might be imagined to say. The interdicted "I" of Anne Hutchinson was therefore prophetic of women whose autobiographical writing, having been driven or exiled to some margin or frontier, effects a rediscovery of the center of all autobiography.

The Indian captivity narrative of Mary Rowlandson (1678), for instance, has often and accurately been described as a version of the soul's deliverance from bondage to Satan, a pattern it shares with the comparable narrative of John Williams (1707). But in its succession of "removes" from the narrator's seat of domesticity and from the persona developed during her pretextual lifetime, Rowlandson's narrative also entertains the possibility of a "life," hideous but imaginable nevertheless, that would annihilate the one we understand her to have lived so far. The narrator is indeed delivered from that possibility as event. Mary Rowlandson does not, like Mary Jemison and other captives, "go Indian." The narrator's principal activity, however, surrounded by a literal wilderness, is to write at a figurative frontier where the previously given persona would have to be surrendered to its extinguishing other. Images of herself eating raw liver, conversing with King Philip and engaging herself in economic freedom as tribal seamstress, eventually nudge into existence the image of herself as other in the form of one of her master's three squaws, a "severe and proud dame" (61) named Weetamoo. Having once been told by her captors that she is dead to her husband, Mary Rowlandson must write, even retrospectively, out of that imagined possibility. The result is occasional brief glimpses through the other end of the telescope, a reversal of Puritan autobiographical perspective; she wonders at the mystery of Providence in preserving Indians from certain defeat or starvation; the once-grieved mother of earlier removes observes that the death of a papoose leaves more room in the wigwam and confesses, when the noises of mourning relatives reach her, that "I could not much condole with them" (56).

For Sarah Kemble Knight as well, autobiographical life does not begin until, in the *Journal* of her travels from Boston to New Haven in 1704, she finds herself at a frontier of role and identity. Stopping at an inn one night, she encounters the question of gender that implicitly calls forth the sharp articulations of her entire work: "I never see a woman on the Rode so dreadfull late . . . ," says a more conventional sister.

"Who are You? Where are You going?" In the floating world of travel, the diarist is free to enter into textual negotiation between the luxuriant inner space of imagination, where she is "agreably entertained without a thou't of anything but thoughts themselves" (9), and the rude comic texture of the society she spies on. A closet poet about to set her head to the pillow, she overhears in the closet next to her a set of male voices loudly debating their world and wishes them "tongue tyed." The situation is incipiently symbolic, and Madame Knight reaches beyond her own experience to link it with the recollection of another female traveler, a friend similarly provoked by the loud absurdities of men "contriving how to bring a triangle into a square" (10). Her immediate revenge is her poetry, an invocation to Rum to finish its work on the enemies of her sleep, but in a larger sense it is the entire journal that establishes the ascendancy of her voice, in satiric portraits of clownish topers "tyed by the Lipps to a pewter engine" and in the general formidableness with which she approaches the dangers of her physical and autobiographical journey—"Sometimes seeing my self drowning, otherwhiles drowned, and at best like a holy Sister Just come out of a Spiritual Bath in dripping Garments" (6). No spiritual autobiographer, Madame Knight seeks all the same the language of rebirth to express her arrival in her text at a truer self than Boston had ever permitted.

More directly related to the antinomian pattern of Anne Hutchinson were Quaker autobiographers like Elizabeth Ashbridge (1774), whose narrative of the early part of her life develops further the close connection between a theology of the spirit within and the emergence of woman's autobiographical voice. Quaker spiritual egalitarianism, since the time of George Fox, had argued a scriptural rationale for women as preachers, the role denied to Anne Hutchinson. In the autobiography of Elizabeth Ashbridge, and to a lesser extent in that of Jane Hoskens (1771), the typical journeying toward Truth of the nascent Quaker is also a narrative of the process by which the female speaker comes to an awareness of a voice within. Elizabeth Ashbridge dramatizes better than anyone of her time and place the fearsome power of opposition to that discovery, in introjected scorn for a prophetic self, in voices that encourage self-destruction, and centrally in the autobiographical plot, in the figure of an abusive, alcoholic husband, whom the narrative finally blesses and redeems.

For contrast's sake, one need only turn to the diaries of men whose power and responsibility made their autobiographical records into extensions of the managed worldly estate. The *Diary* (1674–1729) of Samuel Sewall of Massachusetts assimilates the point of view of eternity more habitually and tellingly than those of William Byrd (1709–12; 1739–41) and Landon Carter (1752–76) of Virginia. But a regional emphasis alone can tend to coax cliché out of these texts: Sewall, the Puritan judge, spelling a life from the divine alphabet of nature and experience; Byrd, the Virginia gentleman and New World Pepys, simultaneously in touch with London, the classics, and the variable moods of his wife and slaves; Carter, the stringently tempered master of Sabine Hall, a Faulknerian figure who curses and feels cursed by his slaves and who watches the degradation of his son with a mixture of moral contempt and physical fear. What ties these diarists together is the ambition, reflected in their dutiful entries, of an ordered external world, an ambition that cannot entirely concede its illusoriness without undermining the foundation of their sense of autobiography. The "I" in their writing is confident that it speaks from the center of the real world, whereas in the autobiographical succession from Anne Hutchinson, the "I," finding itself set out at an apparent margin, disputes the given real and invents a text that acknowledges a journeying rather than a fixed center.

EDWARDS, WOOLMAN, FRANKLIN

It says much about the resistance of early American autobiography to adopting a prematurely final form, one binding on its heirs, that its canonical triad of classics, the *Personal Narrative* of Jonathan Edwards, the *Journal* of John Woolman, and the *Autobiography* of Benjamin Franklin should so thoroughly eschew anything like classical finish and closure. These works, so often written about together and apart, could not help but seem fragments, minor and peripheral, in the fully literary culture of eighteenth-century England. In America, they begin to suggest the way in which the autobiographical self's heedlessness about form and its penchant for improvisation become in a textual democracy the moral equivalent of form. Edwards's spiritual autobiography (c. 1739), for instance, while a compacted treatise on the theology and psychology of conversion, also has the quality of afterthought, as though the narrator had come to the end of an entire community's awakenings only to discover that he had not inquired into his own. Its structure, clear enough in the general movement from empty, willed strivings after grace, through the early ardor of a "new sense" of divine things, to the more settled balance of citizenship among the saints, nevertheless seems fluid and directionless at times. The autobiographical persona, at moments of compelling verbal intensity, appears ready to surrender itself to its recreations of sweetness or to an abyss in the self opened up by the language of bottomless depravity. Closure looms as a remembered duty, not a formal ambition.

John Woolman's *Journal* (1774) ends abruptly in a dream, one felt to be so slight an addition to his life that the Quaker editorial committee preparing his manuscript for publication felt free to overlook or ignore it. Like Elizabeth Ashbridge, who also died on a missionary trip to the British Isles and whose autobiography Woolman may have read in a manuscript copy, Woolman followed the Inner Light wherever it led him. His narrative, too, derives itself from the originary experience of distinguishing "the language of the pure Spirit which inwardly moves upon the heart" (31), and at times that language came to Woolman in dreams. The last recorded of them allegorizes slavery, the moral issue at the center of the *Journal*, in the form of "an old Negro man" hanged to feed a fox-cat, a hybrid beast of cunning and idleness, while a woman at tea observes only that "at the sight of the old man a dying, she could not go on with tea drinking" (161). The great summary power of Woolman's final image comes not from any artificial sense of rhetorical arrangement but from its connectedness with the deep source of the autobiographer's moral vision, which, figured as Light, is both the origin and the essential subject of his *Journal*.

Edwards and Woolman confuse, as they should, rigid categories of gender and genre. At its most androgynous, Edwards's narrative divides its energies between the solar figure of a judging and empowering authority and the responsive radiance of the self as a little white flower "opening its bosom" and "diffusing around a sweet fragrancy" (30). In Woolman, inner and outer space depend upon one another as enabling vision and moral arena, and in the spiritual democracy of Quaker autobiography there is no place even for Edwards's hierarchy of sun and flower. The movement to Franklin's *Autobiography* (1771–90) in this triad seems discontinuous, not because it is a movement from ministerial to secular life, but because Franklin's narrative energy is monistic, confidently and competitively single-gendered in its orientation toward the related goals of wealth—understood as no more than a sufficiency for well-being—and public service. By an autobiographical standard of male teleology, John Barnard (1767) of Marblehead, a latter-day Puritan, and the Anglican Samuel Johnson (1768–70), founder of King's College (Columbia) and American sponsor of George Berkeley, despite their ministerial status, have more in common with Franklin than with Edwards and Woolman.

Although it is the most written-about of early American autobiographies, Franklin's four-part narrative has always disarmed readers by its consciously provincial deshabille, then rearmed them by the steady cunning of its didactic design. As if in deference to Franklin's pose of casual self-invention, the scholarly work of a definitive text and a biography of his autobiographical book have only recently appeared (Lemay and Zall; Seavey). It may be that the usefulness of the figure of the young apprentice printer as a touchstone for estimates of the national character has not diminished. The use is likely to change, however, as the national autobiography undergoes successive rewritings. The absence from Franklin's text of any interiority and the controlled projection of the negative self into items of technologically revisable "errata" continue to suggest that the durability of the autobiography of the American Way is also its vulnerability. In Edwards the negative self is expressed in magnitudes of nihility; in Woolman, by the selfish desire to express self alone. In both cases, autobiographical drama arises from a conflict that threatens the text's ideal self. But in Franklin the negative self is unacknowledged by the persona except as the quite rational failure to achieve moral perfection and in the objectified and distanced form of an assortment of poets, sots, and enthusiasts. Readers since D. H. Lawrence who have expressed dissatisfaction with the autobiography's complacent formula for success may instead be reacting to the absence of energetically positive and negative versions of the self, registering their sense of an empty center where one expects to find dimensions of the self functioning as opposed actors.

The real drama in Franklin, therefore, is a rhetorical one. The narrator dismisses moral perfection as unattainable or, if attainable, a form of foppishness. What he cannot afford to dismiss is the possibility of rhetorical perfection, the success at any rate of the *Autobiography*'s argument for the mechanically improvable life. So confident of his rhetoric is the narrator that he tempts the reader by revealing his secret, the only truly dangerous secret confided by the text; he will argue, not dogmatically but deferentially, not sermonically but by an ingratiating series of anecdotes inculcating method; he has come before us not dressed for a public ball but in his morning coat. It is as if the criminal had left clues daring his pursuer to catch him. The reader is permitted to attack "the dummy American," as D. H Lawrence called Franklin's persona, because to do so is to fall into a trap, to be exposed as the reader who fails to see that the rhetoric knowingly and with indulgent irony comprehends the dummy of patterned behavior and is willing to sacrifice the ideal of perfection in exchange for the more realistic aim of improvement. The great risk Franklin runs is that in exposing irony as the secret of his diplomacy, his mission to the reader will fail entirely. If the reader refuses to recognize the autobiographical country from which he comes—its utilitarian language, its allegiance to method, its charts and maps for the self—it is because the text, winking, has dared us to tug hard on the string of its rhetorical undoing. Under the morning

coat, confirming the suspicions of many of his readers, the Enlightenment autobiographer would then stand naked as Adam.

THE CENTRIFUGAL REPUBLIC

As autobiographer, Benjamin Franklin does not carry us into the period
of the New Republic. Properly to accomplish that movement would require a personal narrative embodying the crisis of familial and generational identity described in Jay Fliegelman's treatment of the literature
surrounding the American Revolution. No single text answers adequately to that description, and the autobiographical writings of
veterans of the War for Independence, such as Joseph Plumb Martin's
*Narrative of the Adventures, Dangers, and Sufferings of a Revolutionary
Soldier* (1830), are the military memoirs of the common soldier rather
than perspectives on the transformation from a colonial to a national
identity. The autobiography of that metamorphosis would be, in a
sense, the autobiography of Rip Van Winkle's missing years. Among
the founding fathers, the ablest candidates are John Adams and Thomas
Jefferson, although their mutual friend, Benjamin Rush, who rein-
troduced the two ex-presidents after the rupture in their friendship, also
deserves mention. The importance of Jefferson's *Autobiography* (1821)
has been convincingly stated by James Cox as an extension, beyond the
ground of personality, of both the idea of American autobiography and
American literature, but its relative impersonality must still be reckoned
with as a felt absence. Adams, the New Englander, needed no encouragement to improve his time and justify his days by the writing of both
a diary and an autobiographical narrative. The diary, the more introspective and revelatory of the two works, was begun in college. The
autobiography was begun in 1802 after he had left the presidency; like
Franklin's, it is composed in stages and runs increasingly into the shape
of the memoirs of a public man.

By an extended definition, Adams and Jefferson are responsible for
the most important autobiography of the early republic, a collaborative
one that can be seen as a shape within the shape of the correspondence
between them that ended with their deaths on July 4, the only other act
of collaboration that challenges their literary one for interest. In their
letters to each other, Adams and Jefferson function virtually as an autobiographical divided self, energized by difference but each dependent
on the other as a unique kind of audience. One side, Federalist and dark
realist, situates itself in a mental habit called Massachusetts and writes
out of irascible compulsion; the other, meditative and Republican, draws
its philosophic calm from a sanguine state of mind called Virginia.

Together they compose without nullifying their differences, and the starting point for their shared autobiographical act is articulated when Adams says, "You and I ought not to die, before We have explained ourselves to each other" (Cappon, 358). Situated near the end of their lives but in the youth of the nation, Adams tends to be the voice of memory, Jefferson that of prophecy. It is Adams who asks the autobiographical question that also occurred to his great-grandson Henry: "Would you go back to your Cradle and live over again Your 70 Years?" (Cappon, 464). Jefferson, while he answers yes, indulges in retrospect only under provocation and declares, more typically, "I steer my Bark with Hope in the head, leaving Fear astern" (Cappon, 467). The unity of this autobiography is accomplished in the heart rather than the head. As Jefferson says, "I am sure that I really know many, many things, and none more surely than that I love you with all my heart . . . " (Cappon, 569). And his profession is completed when Adams, become a widower and speaking in the year before their deaths, refers to John Quincy Adams as "our John . . . almost as much your boy as mine" (Cappon, 606–7). In the fiction of this autobiography, the safety of the Republic will be guaranteed by a president descended on both sides from presidents.

Even in the earliest period, the biography of American autobiography fails to tell a tidy story. Soon all pretensions to coherence give way before a pluralism of forms and voices. African-American autobiography begins in the colonial period under a culturally recognizable rubric as the narrative of a Christianized pagan in such "as told to" autobiographies as those of James Gronniosaw (1770) and John Marrant (1785) and the more textually autonomous life of Olaudah Equiano (1789), an African and an English citizen exposed to New World horrors. In its narrative, the Equiano text touches the North American continent infrequently, but its essential shape adumbrates much African-American self-writing. The New World is a descent into hell, and slavery is the condition of the Fall. The self is in fact a fallen prince, tracing its nobility back to the "charming fruitful vale" of a faraway kingdom; and although the kingdom will not literally come again, freedom is its essential condition, and the text prophesies and then celebrates a return to that royal status. In the more familiar forms of the next century, the African-American autobiographer would begin to spell his or her own name narratively, becoming increasingly a fugitive from the slave owner and an escapee as well from the custody of the amanuensis. At the turn of the century, the status of outsider takes on a new attraction in the rogues' autobiographies of Stephen Burroughs (1798) and Henry Tufts (1807) and in John Filson's fictionalized autobiography (1784) of the archetypal American borderer, Daniel Boone. Such would be the centrifugal nature of a democracy, as Tocqueville would explain, in which language and action instinctively reject conceptions of the ideal. Though he isolated the naive formula of a democratic literature ("I have only to look at myself" [183]) in all its apparent simplicity, Tocqueville could not have predicted its endless fissions in autobiography. Any outsider would eventually have his or her inside narrative to tell, and none could claim the center with any authority. Even in the beginning it was so.

NOTES

1 Debating several forms of reference—*Native American, Indian, Amerindian*— H. David Brumble III chose *Indian* for the reason that "this is how most of the Indians I have met refer to themselves" (ix). I have followed Brumble's practice, since in the case of a people who thought of themselves as simply *the people*, any term based on Anglo-European assumptions represents an introjected fiction; hence there are no stronger reasons than usage and preference for choosing among them.

2 Analogously, Robert Lawson-Peebles has written recently of two opposed models, the Columbian *Otro Mundo* and the Vespuccian *terra nuoua*, which apply as well to the microcosm of autobiography as to the macrocosm of landscape description. The concept of an Other World is traditional and "contains ordering strategies, including the rhetoric of inexpressibility, which stretch back like a lifeline to the Old World." The triumphant Vespuccian model asserts novelty and a distinct vocabulary of the New World, "but it can also be dangerous because it involves an approach towards literal inexpressibility" (10). Columbus felt himself sufficiently inarticulate before what he saw to write, almost despairingly, "I told the men with me that, in order to make a report to the Sovereigns of the things they saw, a thousand tongues would not be sufficient to tell it, for it looks like an enchanted land" (119).

3 For a suggestive treatment of this history as a form of role-playing in which the historian acts as "representative autobiographer for New England" (292) see Perry.

4 The use of the term *autobiography* for such writings as Shepard's spiritual narrative or Franklin's memoirs is of course the practice of later editors. Throughout, I use the titles of modern editions, but I give the date, when known, of original composition.

5 The journals of Esther Edwards Burr (1754–57) and Sarah Wister (1777–97) are particularly interesting. Both enlist the relational audience of a correspondent for the fullness of their self-articulation, in contrast to the isolated male selves in the diaries of Wigglesworth, Shepard, Edwards, and Mather. (But see those later, august lovers, Adams and Jefferson, in their correspondence.)

The Derounian edition of Sarah Wister includes both the lighthearted emergence of a younger persona into experience both concretely and romantically observed and, in the "Devotional Journal," the more sober and virtually posthumous meditations of the mature Quaker Wister became.

WORKS CITED

Adams, John. *Diary and Autobiography of John Adams*. Ed. L. H. Butterfield. Cambridge: Harvard University Press, 1961.

Adams, John. *The Earliest Diary of John Adams*. Ed. L. H. Butterfield. Cambridge: Harvard University Press, 1966.

Andrews, William L. *To Tell a Free Story: The First Century of Afro-American Autobiography, 1760–1865*. Champaign-Urbana: University of Illinois Press, 1986.

Ashbridge, Elizabeth. *Some Account of the Fore-Part of the Life of Elizabeth Ashbridge . . . Wrote By Herself*, ed. Daniel B. Shea. In *Journeys in New Worlds: Early American Women's Narratives*, ed. William Andrews. Madison: University of Wisconsin Press, 1990. This volume also contains the autobiographical writings of Mary Rowlandson, Sarah Kemble Knight, and Elizabeth House Trist.

Barnard, John. "Autobiography of the Rev. John Barnard." In Collections of the Massachusetts Historical Society, 3rd ser., vol. 5. Boston: 1836.

Bradford, William. *History of Plymouth Plantation*. Ed. Samuel Eliot Morison. New York: Knopf, 1952. Reprint. New York: Modern Library, 1967.

Brumble, H. David. *American Indian Autobiography*. Berkeley and Los Angeles: University of California Press, 1988.

Burr, Esther Edwards. *The Journal of Esther Edwards Burr, 1754–1757*. Ed. Carol F. Karlsen and Laurie Crumpacker. New Haven: Yale University Press, 1984.

Burroughs, Stephen. *Memoirs of Stephen Burroughs*. Ed. Philip F. Gura. Boston: Northeastern University Press, 1988.

Byrd, William. *The Secret Diary of William Byrd of Westover, 1709–1712*. Ed. Louis B. Wright and Marion Tinling. Richmond, VA: Dietz, 1941.

Byrd, William. *Another Secret Diary of William Byrd of Westover, 1739–1741*. Ed. Maude H. Woodfin and Marion Tinling. Richmond, VA: Dietz, 1942.

Caldwell, Patricia. *The Puritan Conversion Narrative: The Beginnings of American Expression*. Cambridge: Cambridge University Press, 1983.

Cappon, Lester J., ed. *The Adams-Jefferson Letters*. 2 vols. Chapel Hill: University of North Carolina Press, 1959.

Carter, Landon. *The Diary of Colonel Landon Carter of Sabine Hall, 1752–1776*. 2 vols. Ed. Jack P. Greene. Charlottesville: University Press of Virginia, 1965.

Columbus, Christopher. *The Log of Christopher Columbus*. Trans. Robert H. Fuson. Camden, ME: International Marine Publishing, 1987.

Cox, James. "Jefferson's *Autobiography*: Recovering Literature's Lost Ground," *The Southern Review* 14 (1978): 633–52.

Edwards, Jonathan. "An Account of His Conversion, Experiences, and Religious Exercises, Given by Himself" [*Personal Narrative*]. In *Jonathan Edwards: A Profile*. Ed. David Levin. New York: Hill and Wang, 1969.

Eliot, George. *Daniel Deronda*. Ed. Graham Handley. New York: Oxford University Press, 1984.

Equiano, Olaudah. *The Interesting Narrative of the Life of Olaudah Equiano, or Gustavus Vassa, The African. Written by himself.* 2 vols. London: the Author, 1789. First American Edition: New York, 1791.

Filson, John. *Filson's Kentucke* ["The Discovery, Purchase and Settlement of Kentucke" and "The Adventures of Col. Daniel Boone"]. A facsimile reproduction of the original Wilmington Edition of 1784. Louisville, KY: John P. Morton, 1930.

Fliegelman, Jay. *Prodigals and Pilgrims: The American Revolution Against Patriarchal Authority, 1750–1800.* Cambridge: Cambridge University Press, 1982.

Frampton, John. *Joyfull Newes Out of the Newe Founde Worlde. Written in Spanish by Nicholas Monardes, Physician of Seville and Englished by John Frampton, Merchant Anno 1577.* 2 vols. Ed. Stephen Gaselee. London: Constable, 1925.

Franklin, Benjamin. *The Autobiography of Benjamin Franklin. A Genetic Text.* Ed. J. A. Leo Lemay and P. M. Zall. Knoxville: The University of Tennessee Press, 1981.

Franklin, Wayne. *Discoverers, Explorers, Settlers: The Diligent Writers of Early America.* Chicago: University of Chicago Press, 1979.

Gronniosaw, James. *A Narrative of the Most Remarkable Particulars in the Life of James Albert Ukawsaw Gronniosaw, an African.* [1770]. Ed. W. Shirley. Bath: S. Hazzard. First American edition: Newport: n.p., 1774.

Hall, David, ed. *The Antinomian Controversy, 1636–1638. A Documentary History.* Middletown, CT: Wesleyan University Press, 1968.

Hoskens, Jane. *The Life and Spiritual Sufferings of that Faithful Servant of Christ, Jane Hoskens, A Public Preacher Among the People Called Quakers.* Philadelphia: William Evitt, 1771.

Jemison, Mary. *A Narrative of the Life of Mrs. Mary Jemison.* Canandaigua, NY: D. Beamis, 1824.

Johnson, Edward. *Wonder-Working Providence of Sion's Saviour in New England.* Intro. by Edward Gallagher. Delmar, NY: Scholars' Facsimiles & Reprints, 1974.

Jefferson, Thomas. "Autobiography of Thomas Jefferson." In *The Life and Writings of Thomas Jefferson*. Ed. Adrienne Koch and William Peden. New York: Random House, 1944.

Johnson, Samuel. *Samuel Johnson: His Career and Writings*, vol. 1. *Autobiography and Letters*. Ed. Herbert and Carol Schneider. New York: Columbia University Press, 1929.

Knight, Sarah Kemble. *The Journal of Madam Knight.* Ed. Malcolm Freiberg. Boston: David R. Godine, 1972.

Krupat, Arnold. *For Those Who Came After: A Study of Native American Autobiography.* Berkeley and Los Angeles: University of California Press, 1985.

Kupperman, Karen, ed. *Captain John Smith: A Select Edition of His Writings.* Chapel Hill: University of North Carolina Press, 1988.

Lawson-Peebles, Robert. *Landscape and Written Expression in Revolutionary America.* Cambridge University Press, 1988.

Lemay and Zall. *See* Franklin, Benjamin.

Marrant, John. *A Narrative of the Lord's Wonderful Dealings with John Marrant, a Black . . . .* Ed. Rev. W. Aldridge. London: Gilbert and Plummer, 1785.

Martin, Joseph Plumb. *Private Yankee Doodle; Being a Narrative of Some of the Adventures, Dangers, and Sufferings of a Revolutionary Soldier.* Ed. George F. Scheer. Boston: Little, Brown, 1962.

Mather, Cotton. *Diary of Cotton Mather.* 2 vols. New York: Frederick Ungar, 1957.

Mather, Cotton. *Magnalia Christi Americana. Or, the Ecclesiastical History of New England.* Research Library of Colonial Americana Reprint. New York: Arno, 1972.

Mather, Cotton. *Paterna: The Autobiography of Cotton Mather.* Ed. Ronald A. Bosco. Delmar, NY: Scholars' Facsimiles & Reprints, 1976.

Mather, Increase, *The Autobiography of Increase Mather.* Worcester: American Antiquarian Society, 1962.

Morton, Thomas. *The New English Canaan of Thomas Morton.* Ed. Charles Francis Adams, Jr. Boston: The Prince Society, 1883.

Perry, Dennis R. "Autobiographical Role-Playing in Johnson's *Wonder Working Providence.*" *Early American Literature* 22 (1987):291–305.

Purchas, Samuel. *Hakluytus Posthumus, or Purchas His Pilgrimes.* 20 vols. [1625]. Glasgow: J. MacLehose & Sons, 1905–07.

Purchas, Samuel. *Microcosmus, or The Historie of Man.* [1619]. Facsimile Edition. Amsterdam: DaCapo Press, 1969.

Quinn, David B. *New American World: A Documentary History of North America to 1612.* 5 vols. New York: Ayer, 1979.

Rowlandson, Mary. *The Soveraignty & Goodness of God, . . . Being a Narrative of the Captivity and Restauration of Mrs. Mary Rowlandson.* In *Puritans Among the Indians: Accounts of Captivity and Redemption.* Ed. Alden T. Vaughan and Edward W. Clark. Cambridge: Harvard University Press, 1981.

Seavey, Ormond. *Becoming Benjamin Franklin: The Autobiography and the Life.* University Park: Pennsylvania State University Press, 1988.

Seeley, John. *Prophetic Waters: The River in Early American Life and Literature.* New York: Oxford University Press, 1977.

Sewall, Samuel. *The Diary of Samuel Sewall, 1674–1729.* 2 vols. Ed. M. Halsey Thomas. New York, Farrar, Strauss, and Giroux, 1973.

Shea, Daniel B. *Spiritual Autobiography in Early America.* Republished with a new Preface and Bibliographical Supplement. Madison: University of Wisconsin Press, 1988.

Shea, Daniel B. "Our Professed Old Adversary": Thomas Morton and the Naming of New England. *Early American Literature* 23 (1988): 52–69.

Shepard, Thomas. *God's Plot: The Paradoxes of Puritan Piety, Being the Autobiography & Journal of Thomas Shepard.* Ed. Michael McGiffert. Amherst: University of Massachusetts Press, 1972.

Shepard, Thomas. *Thomas Shepard's "Confessions."* Ed. George Selement and Bruce C. Wooley. Collections of the Colonial Society of Massachusetts. Boston: 1981.

Smith, John. *The Complete Works of Captain John Smith.* Ed. Philip L. Barbour. 3 vols. Published for the Institute of Early American History and Culture. Chapel Hill: University of North Carolina Press, 1986.

Spengemann, William. *The Adventurous Muse: The Poetics of American Fiction, 1789–1900.* New Haven: Yale University Press, 1977.

Taylor, Edward. *The Poems of Edward Taylor.* Ed. Donald Stanford. New Haven: Yale University Press, 1960.

Taylor, Edward. "Spiritual Relation." In *Edward Taylor's "Church Records" and Related Sermons.* Ed. Thomas and Virginia Davis. Vol. 1. *The Unpublished Writings of Edward Taylor.* Boston: Twayne, 1981.

Tocqueville, Alexis de. *Democracy in America.* Ed. Richard D. Heffner. Mentor Edition. New York: New American Library, 1956.

Tufts, Henry. *The Autobiography of a Criminal.* Ed. Edmund Pearson. New York: Duffield, 1930.

Wigglesworth, Michael. *The Diary of Michael Wigglesworth, 1653–1657.* Ed. Edmund S. Morgan. Gloucester: Peter Smith, 1970.

Williams, John. *The Redeemed Captive Returning to Zion.* In *Puritans Among the Indians: Accounts of Captivity and Restoration, 1676–1724.* Ed. Alden T. Vaughan and Edward W. Clark. Cambridge: Harvard University Press, 1981.

Wister, Sarah. *The Journal and Occasional Writings of Sarah Wister.* Ed. Kathryn Zabelle Derounian. Cranbury, NJ: Associated University Presses, 1987.

Woolman, John. *The Journal and Major Essays of John Woolman.* Ed. Phillips P. Moulton. New York: Oxford University Press, 1971.

CHAPTER 2

Autobiography in the American Renaissance

LAWRENCE BUELL

The first two-thirds of the nineteenth century were pivotal for the history of American autobiography. During these years, the term *autobiography* passed into common usage; many of the great early American autobiographies (like Franklin's and Thomas Shepard's) were first published in full, and it became obvious that the autobiographical mode would continue to be an ingredient of American literary distinctiveness no less important than it had been before 1800 and also far more multiform. A number of the works today taken as central reference points for the study of the American Renaissance have a strong autobiographical dimension: Emerson's major essays, Thoreau's *Walden*, Whitman's *Leaves of Grass*, many of Emily Dickinson's lyrics, Hawthorne's *The Scarlet Letter* (certainly "The Custom House" and, some would argue, even the romance proper), Frederick Douglass's *Narrative*, and all of Melville's novels through *Pierre*.

Yet the period was not particularly rich in the kind of developed autobiography that one most immediately associates with the term since Rousseau: the detailed, complex secular narrative of the author's unfolding mind and fortunes during a substantial portion if not the entirety of his or her life span. Although this type of work had been pioneered during the colonial period by the founding fathers, and Franklin's *Autobiography* in particular was already reckoned an American classic, no succeeding work in the same vein that is widely read today was produced until the *Life and Times of Frederick Douglass* (1881, rev. 1892). In short, although the autobiographical mode strongly marks American writing from the start, especially in Puritan New England but in other regions as well, autobiography in the strictest current sense does not fully flower as a literary genre in America much before the

47

time of Henry Adams.[1] The present essay has developed as a reflection on that paradox.

First, some confirming statistics that will give us a better sense of what the period's autobiographical output was like. Of the 6377 entries in Kaplan's standard *Bibliography of American Autobiographies* (1962), roughly one-eighth were written between 1800 and 1870. Of these, two-thirds to three-quarters fall into two rough categories: spiritual narratives, mostly produced by clergymen, and diverse types of topical narratives of extreme suffering (e.g. Indian captivities, slave narratives, and prisoner-of-war experiences) or adventures with romantic or sensational interest (criminal's confessions, maritime and/or military exploits, frontier and forty-niner narratives, etc.) Roughly speaking, though by no means invariably, this distinction implies also a distinction in class: religious narrative being more a gentry-class product, the topical narrative of adventure or suffering being generally plebeian. Frequently, however, generic lines crossed; almost as symptomatic of the period was a composite like Alfred M. Lorrain's *The Helm, the Sword, and the Cross* (1862), the memoirs of a man who was, successively, a mariner, a soldier, and a preacher.

Altogether, then, the narratives of Jonathan Edwards and Olaudah Equiano were closer to the antebellum norm than Franklin's *Autobiography*. Among antebellum autobiographical works read today for their literary interest, by far the most typical was Frederick Douglass's *Narrative* (1845), and Richard Henry Dana's *Two Years Before the Mast* (1840) and Francis Parkman's *The Oregon Trail* (1849) were a great deal more typical than *Walden* in structure if not in authorship, both being relatively straightforward descriptive narratives. The narratives of Douglass, Dana, and Parkman all presented variants on three oft-repeated—indeed by their time almost prefabricated—American autobiographical subgenres that had roots going back to the previous century: the experiences of the slave, the sailor, and the frontier adventurer, though Dana and Parkman made it clear from the first page that they were actually well-educated gentlemen.

Like their predecessors, even the most obscure of the early nineteenth-century autobiographers, whatever their protestations to the contrary, presumably had literary aspirations: to arouse readerly interest, to inspire or at least to inform, and in most cases also to sell. Yet very few, probably not more than one in ten or fifteen, were creative writers either by trade or avocation, if one judges the creative impulse by whether they published another work of narrative, poetry, drama, or literary prose other than sermons. Whereas for an antebellum writer to produce an amount of poetry equal in verbiage to the average autobiographical narrative was an almost sure sign of a strong commitment to letters, to publish an autobiography usually signified nothing more than that one had had a remarkable inner or outer adventure that one wanted oneself and/or the world to profit by. Possibly this helps explain why women with literary aspirations seem to have produced a disproportinately small number of autobiographies. (The ratio of male to female authors in Carlock's bibliography for 1840–70 is almost 5 to 1, and in Kaplan's 10 to 1 for the same period, as against a 3 to 1 male-to-female ratio for creative writers generally, according to my own recent study of antebellum New England.) For although nineteenth-century women writers, like women in any professional field, labored under a certain stigma, women who did write were more apt to define themselves as writers and to pursue a thoroughgoing literary professionalism than did their male counterparts.[2]

In short, although it would be obtuse if not self-contradictory to deny literary standing to antebellum American autobiography, it does seem clear that autobiography was not yet being practiced in America as a form of artistic endeavor on the same footing as that of poetry and prose fiction or even more kindred nonfictional genres like the literary essay, the narrative history, or the sermon. Peculiar though it may seem to say this of the most bourgeois of all nineteenth-century civilizations and the most self-preoccupied of all Western literatures, Americans of the mid-nineteenth century clearly had very severe reservations about the appropriateness of celebrating the lifeline of the private, secular self in public narrative discourse. In the most ambitious attempt to date to read the popular mood of antebellum America through its written utterances, Lewis O. Saum finds a strongly pietistic restraint: "the self stood as no accommodating channel to enhancement or perfection; it stood rather as an endlessly frustrating, dark-hued impediment" (108). Although Saum sees this mood as antithetical to the tenor of the period's literary high culture, there too one finds versions of the same skepticism: America's high canonical writers tended either to link celebration of the self to its possibilities of transcendence (the Emersonian strain) or to critique the naïveté of that Transcendentalist hope (Steele). Given this similarity in cultural climate at both the elite and popular levels, it is no wonder that America's only canonical work of fully-developed autobiography before the late nineteenth century was Franklin's personalized version of the famous-figure memoir, and that we produced no equivalent in nonfictional prose, poetry, or prose fiction to Rousseau's *Confessions*, Wordsworth's *Prelude*, or Carlyle's *Sartor Resartus*.

At the same time, the antebellum period was also a time when pressures were being brought to bear on traditional literary forms that would ensure that they became more autobiographical and that auto-biography would become practiced in America as a more self-conscious art. One source of pressure that was changing literary fashion was slowly infiltrating America from abroad: the lyricization of poetry owing to the Romantic movement, and the development of the protagonist-centered novel (frequently told in the first person), from the eighteenth-century picaresque memoir to the nineteenth-century bildungsroman, in which an essentialist model of character at least theoretically gives way to a model of character as a developing process. Romanticism encouraged the writer to exploit the "I" as the principal literary subject, thereby encouraging stylized confessional modes like the Transcendentalist essay and Whitman's and Dickinson's lyric per-sonae. The protagonist-dominated novel as it developed from *Robinson Crusoe* and *Pamela* through *Great Expectations* and *Jane Eyre* contributed toward an erosion of the boundary in both directions between factual and fictitious autobiography, as in Melville's *Typee*, a compound of fic-tion in the Crusoe vein with "nonfictional" maritime narrative. On the one hand, writers were encouraged to push autobiography over into the domain of fiction, as Melville essentially did; on the other hand, they were encouraged to autobiographicalize traditional fictive forms, as Dickinson did when she turned hymns into monodramas.

These crossings between autobiography and the fictive were regulated by the strong entrenchment, in some cases for more than a century, of a number of autobiographical subgenres by the time American letters began to become markedly belletristic toward the end of the colonial era. The exploration narrative, the narrative of conversion, the spiritual journal, and the criminal's confession were all by then established and popular types. Their persistence in mutated form as a force in American literature beyond the colonial period was ensured by at least two other factors apart from mere cultural inertia and the change in literary ethos described above. One was the markedly utilitarian cast of an emerg-ing American civilization, owing to the material and social exigencies of nation-building and to the traditional religiocentrism of many of its subcultures. These led readers at least publicly to value literature that strongly emphasized didactic and/or informational content, as the tradi-tional types of autobiographical narrative tended to do well into the nineteenth century, notwithstanding the evident increase in melodra-matization (in captivity narrative, for instance) after the late eighteenth-century introduction of the novel to the American literary marketplace (Van Der Beets xx–xxiv). Second was the unprecedented and increasing value American civil religion set on the individual as a social unit. The Declaration of Independence claimed as an inalienable right the individual (white male's) life, liberty, and pursuit of happiness; a half-century later, Emerson, as Myra Jehlen puts it, "completed the development of the modern concept of individualism . . . by projecting an individual who possesses the world in his own image" (77). This historical movement, which achieved its most ambitious culmination in Emersonian Transcendentalism, led directly to the I-centered master-pieces of Thoreau and Whitman.

American literary history thus presents the appearance of having sustained a vigorous autobiographical impetus from its beginnings to 1865. Indeed, as we attempt to reduce the heterogeneous and refractory materials of those two-and-a-half centuries to some sort of conceptual unity, one of the first patterns that suggests itself is the "autobiographical motif," tempting us even to picture autobiography with some justice as "the preeminent kind of American expression" (Sayre *Autobiography*, 147). It looms up as distinctive and constitutive both in the "Puritan legacy" interpretation of American literary history and in the older, Turner-inspired, frontier-genesis interpretation. From either standpoint, Thoreau's *Walden*, for instance, can be retrospectively read as an emanation from American origins: as latter-day spiritual autobiography or wilderness exploration narrative. At the same time, however, as the case of *Walden* also demonstrates, the impression of autobiography as a unifying motif in American literary history is misleading, because the various forces promoting the persistence of the autobiographical mode in America were in some ways at odds with it, and with each other as well.

To begin with, traditional religious narrative and the various types of traditional topical narratives obviously differed in their concentration on interior vs. exterior experiences. Second, both traditional modes differed from romanticist autobiography in their comparatively conventionalized patterning of experience. The "I" in Mary Rowlandson's captivity narrative (1682) is by no means completely lacking in individuality; indeed, this work inaugurated a new subgenre; but the narrator's impulse is to minimize that individuality rather than to flaunt it, in contrast to Thoreau's insistence that living a mere mile from town has put him in a different land from his countrymen and that, in principle, looking through the eyes of another is the greatest miracle of which we can conceive. Rowlandson's anxiety is all on the other side: to bring the uncanniness of her traumatic experience under control by imposing upon it a paradigm of ordeal by wilderness redeemed through grace and thereby to effect some degree of reintegration into a community in which, confessedly, she fears she will never again feel truly at home.

In other words, American autobiography of the colonial period tends to normalize its self-presentations so that the "unique" histories of extra-ordinary spirituality, physical endurance, and so forth that afford the pretext for publishing this or that particular life are rendered exemplary and typical, and uniqueness is seen to consist more in circumstance than in self. This normalizing impulse has at least three sources. One is the desire to turn the story of one's inner life into a ritual of theological and social consensus that Sacvan Bercovitch *The Puritan Origins* identifies with Puritan writing and its progeny. Another is the pragmatic subordination of self to circumstance that is proper to exploration and discovery narratives. A third and perhaps most pervasive source is the tendency of the genre itself over the course of time to conventionalize both persona and the repertoire of reported experiences. When Jonathan Edwards sat down to write his "Personal Narrative," it would probably not even have occurred to him to create anything more original than relatively simple variations on a preestablished plot or a protagonist that dwelt more than fleetingly on the secular business that undoubtedly consumed the great majority of a typical Edwards day.

Operating under such internalized self-constraints, an autobiographer will tend to do any or all of the following: to shift the focus of concentration from self to context, to feature typical aspects of self, and to register embarrassment or self-consciousness about those irrepressible dimensions of one's life or personality that seem idiosyncratic. All three impulses persist in the writing of the American Renaissance and thereby limit the scope of its autobiographical achievement. In *The Oregon Trail*, for instance, Francis Parkman declares that the chief reason he went on his adventures was a fascination with Indian culture; but although the book is technically a first-person narrative that follows Parkman's wanderings day by day, it is much more an anecdotal narrative anthropology than an account of what the Indians meant to him. Only sparingly does Parkman make himself the protagonist of a memorable episode. The book's subjective dimension must usually be inferred from Parkman's adjectives rather than from self-dramatization. And Parkman broaches no more than obliquely what we now understand to be a more personal motive for undertaking the journey and writing the book: the desire to conquer ill health by proving himself a man (Townsend). The descriptive genre of the frontier narrative, approaching a subject of national interest in a chronicle-of-events format already familiar to the reading public, serves as the acceptable recourse for making public a private struggle that he did not want to share too openly. So he shares it indirectly, not for the most part focusing upon his desire to know (and thereby, frontiersman-like, symbolically to subdue) Indians or upon his desire to prove himself, but filling the book primarily with Indian anecdote and stories of adventure he has witnessed.

A more notorious case of withholding is Thoreau's *Walden* (1854), which is remarkable for the extent of its refusal to do what it seems to promise to do. Thoreau declares that he shall retain the first person because he has no other option and because in any case he expects "of every writer, first or last, a simple and sincere account of his own life" (3). In fact, as every reader quickly finds, the book is organized more in terms of issues or topics than in terms of the protagonist's life and adventures. When he describes particular actions, his practice is to turn them into exempla; and some key information we might reasonably expect from "a simple and sincere account" is deliberately kept mysterious by resort to parable, such as his particular reasons for the timing and location of the Walden experiment and his reasons for leaving the pond. The conclusion seems inescapable that Thoreau was bumping up against the limits of Emerson's dictum—not original with him but long since part of the fiber of American autobiographical thinking: "That which is individual & remains individual in my experience is of no value. What is fit to engage me & so engage others permanently, is what has put off its weeds of time & personal relation" (7:65).

Thoreau's masterpiece appears to register strong dissent from this normalizing imperative, yet proceeds to accommodate it anyhow. The persona in *Walden* seems at first glance too alienated to fit Emerson's confident equation between interiority and universality; at the outset, he seems to stand on the principle that his experiment has led him into a completely different mental realm from others. This alienated stance is developed throughout the book thematically, in the form of irreverent challenges to public opinion, and rhetorically, through metaphorical and tonal convolutions that underscore the distance between him and us. Thus far Thoreau seems to have set the stage for a fuller presentation of the saga of a self than any previous American autobiographer. And indeed *Walden*'s successive revisions do make the final product stylistically an even more individuated, idiosyncratic work than the original. But the finished version is in other ways less personal and autobiographic: more packed with environmental detail, more elaborated with mythic overlay, and more committed point-by-point to the strategy of representing this or that "personal" experience as exemplary. Even the persona's withdrawal is itself universalized into a shareable remedy recommended as good for everybody: "the tonic of wildness"—a phrase, indeed, already included in the first draft (317).

Thus the result of Thoreau's rhetorical individuations and his particularization of environmental detail is, paradoxically, to accentuate the tendency, present from the start, of the persona to dissolve into the text of his exempla. *Walden* can thereby be said both to build upon American autobiographical practice and to veer away from it. Bercovitch shrewdly formulates the first of these movements as follows:

the self projected by Edwards, Franklin, and Thoreau is neither discrete nor antagonistic, but . . . self-effacing, exemplary, and self-transcending. There is an invitation lurking in each of them: how would you like to disappear?—to disappear into the American army of Christ (Edwards), to disappear into American institutions (Franklin), to disappear into American nature (Thoreau) (Bercovitch "The Ritual", 142).

Yet Thoreau's escape is by far the most complete, being an escape not only from solipsism but from the teleology that shapes the plots of his two great predecessors. Whether this rules *Walden* out as a true autobiography is a perennial question, one's answer to which ultimately depends on the literal-mindedness of one's conception of genre; but it is quite clear that, relative to Edwards and Franklin, Thoreau elaborates autobiographical consciousness to the near eclipse of the autobiographical lifeline that provides the other two their primary organizing principle.[3]

Looking at the whole of Thoreau's literary career, we see a broader pattern of vacillation, ending in a greater degree of repression, over how much to indulge or play down the dramatization of a persona that never ceases to want to think of itself as distinct and oppositional. The basic rhythm of the entries in Thoreau's later *Journal* follows a relatively predictable log-of-excursions pattern that is less introspective than the *Journal* before 1850. On the public level, Thoreau accommodates himself more to the literary marketplace, one conspicuous sign of which is the tendency of his later excursions (to Maine, Cape Cod, and Canada) to resemble popular magazine accounts more closely than do his first two books; the latter three projects are much less subject-oriented, more linear in narration, and more literal in mode of description. Thoreau's later excursions move back to a more conventional kind of travel narrative than he had previously practiced, as if to acknowledge the strength of the conservative literary mainstream represented by Parkman and Richard Henry Dana, Jr.[4]

These cross-currents in Thoreau's work reflect a widely-shared edginess about self-disclosure in autobiographical writing that sets a limit on the period's achievement in that vein yet also constitutes one of the period's distinctive achievements. If there is a single motif that fundamentally distinguishes this period of American autobiographical writing, it is the presence of a creative instability, taking place within the traditional impulse to objectify or universalize the self, as to how far to think and write about the "I" as a figure distinct from an established public or narrative role. The Transcendentalist movement that constituted Thoreau's chief intellectual matrix is the best known and most studied case of this. More conspicuously than any other contemporaneous literary school, Transcendentalism "stood for" the valorization of the "I", yet on condition that the "I" be grounded in the universal rather than in the particular. Thus the most seasoned presentation of Emerson's philosophy of individualism is *Representative Men* (1850), a series of case studies that purports to evaluate the achievements of great men as models of human potential; and in *Woman in the Nineteenth Century*, Fuller celebrates but subsumes individual achievement to a theory of the sexes that rests on mythic prototypes.

The three autobiographies of Frederick Douglass provide an especially illuminating example here. The first version (*Narrative*) is a slave narrative in which the psychological complexity of self-characterization is perforce limited in the interest of stressing the representativeness of his condition as a slave; in fact one motive for writing it was to counter public skepticism as to whether so accomplished a speaker could really have been a slave (Blassingame, lii). The second and especially the third versions, reflecting Douglass's later rise to prominence and fame, tell an increasingly individuated life story that even in its earlier phases is not so circumscribed in its self-representation as the *Narrative*. In the *Narrative*, for example, the climax of chapter 1 presents as the child's rite of passage from innocence to experience the whipping of his Aunt Hester, "the blood-stained gate, the entrance to the hell of slavery, through which I was about to pass" (25). In subsequent versions, this event comes much later, and a new incident is substituted as "my first introduction to the realities of slavery" (*Bondage*, 50): the traumatic desertion of the young Frederick by his grandmother, who takes him from the shelter of her cabin to the old master's plantation and leaves him there. This shift goes along with a much fuller presentation of the growth of the author's mind and of impressions of family and environment that have nothing directly to do with slavery as such ("The squirrels, as they skipped the fences, climbed the trees, or gathered their nuts, were an unceasing delight to me" [*Life and Times*, 30]).

The significance of Douglass's shift from relatively "typical" to relatively "personal" experience is easily exaggerated. It is arguably more a shift from one conventional persona to another than a philosophical change in Douglass's view of the propriety of featuring private experiences as opposed to common ones. The first autobiography was a slave narrative, the second and especially the third were the memoirs of an eminent public figure, for which a greater emphasis on the uniquely personal, even to the point of biographical and genealogical trivia, was not only appropriate but expected. What is more striking about the later additions, and harder to explain simply on grounds of genre, is their tendency to complicate episodes that in the first version were more straightforwardly narrated. The *Narrative*, for example, ends with a definitevely succinct account of Douglass's maiden speech at an antislavery meeting: "I felt myself a slave, and the idea of speaking to white people weighed me down. I spoke but a few moments, when I felt a degree of freedom, and said what I desired with considerable ease" (119). In later versions, by contrast, Douglass stresses his awkward inarticulateness throughout the whole performance: indeed, "I am not sure that my embarrassment was not the most effective part of my speech, if speech it could be so called" (*Bondage*, 358). In the *Narrative*, the passage serves as the coda that summarizes and leads back into the whole book's confident, eloquent denunciation of slavery. The revision, more exploratory and nuanced, self-consciously corrects the original (in case anyone should be listening) and substitutes scrupulous psychologizing for rhetorical force. The result is that both persona and protagonist project more of a sense of an inner life interacting with public role.

Now, this development in a sense simply follows logically from the *Narrative* and from slave narrative generally, a principal theme of which is that bondage artificially and cruelly limits the slave by imposing on a complex human being a role that denies the slave's humanity. That very likely has something to do with why Douglass makes the switch of examples to dramatize the child's awakening to slavery. He wants to show that "SLAVE-children *are* children, and prove no exceptions to the general rule" (*Bondage*, 39). He might well have supposed that the sensation of being suddenly deprived of a mother-figure's support would strike a more universal chord than the comparatively externalized and exotic experience of being present at a whipping. The latter proves that slaves are treated unjustly; the former proves that slaves are not, in fact, stereotypical slaves. For slave narrative to press the slave's subjective personhood beyond a point is to transform the genre by shifting it from documentary to real-life bildungsroman, and this is precisely what happened in Douglass's two later autobiographies; but that transformation also represented an extension of one of the earlier genre's motifs.

Douglass's literary pilgrimage as autobiographer up from slave narrative, without altogether leaving it behind (a transformed version of the *Narrative* occupies four-fifths of *Bondage* and one-third of *Life and Times*), is another kind of epitome (to set alongside the Transcendentalist essay) of the shift in American autobiographical practice that occurs in the nineteenth century. The parallel is more than merely fortuitous between Emerson's restiveness with a neoclassical discourse committed to a doctrine of generalized identity or a sectarian discourse committed to a common morphology of development, and Douglass's revision of his autobiography so as to make it more individuated than it was in its initial version. Douglass reveals the common basis in two vignettes at the end of *My Bondage and My Freedom*: two incidents when hostility toward Douglass by Yankee passengers in railroad cars evaporated when prominent whites who happened to be present recognized him and made a point of showing respect to him (402–405). Douglass apparently cites these cases as proof that racism is not, after all, invincible. The wary reader, however, will find in them proof merely that Douglass received a special exemption. At the conscious level, Douglass remained committed to an ethic of solidarity with other blacks still in bondage; but he became increasingly seen by the American public as a kind of Emersonian "representative man," a remarkable case of individual achievement, and the structure of his second and third autobiographies reflects that public image. At the same time, Douglass would probably not have internalized the success-story model of autobiography, nor would Emerson have become fascinated with the prospect of individual greatness in himself and others, were it not for the continuing dominant American tendency to justify individual achievement on the grounds of social representativeness.[5]

The foregoing juxtaposition of Thoreau and Douglass can serve as a kind of allegorical diptych of mid-century American autobiographical attitudes: Thoreau would illustrate the actual self-limitedness of the persona who ostensibly sets out to be the thoroughgoing advocate of individuation, and Douglass the thrust toward individuation exerted from within an initial commitment to inventing a socially representative self. Within these cross-currents, other period autobiographies can be placed.

To broaden the discussion and give a more nuanced account of variations in autobiographical practice let us turn now to four other less often discussed autobiographies by mid-nineteenth-century figures in which the creative instability surrounding the "I" function appears in different lights: P. T. Barnum's *Life of P. T. Barnum* (1855), Lydia Sigourney's *Let-*

ters of Life (1866), John Neal's *Wandering Recollections of a Somewhat Busy Life* (1869), and Walt Whitman's *Specimen Days* (1882). In addition to being historically symptomatic, all are fascinating documents in their own right, worthy of more scrutiny than they have received.

These works share the following features: the authors' careers have been highly distinctive, even unique; they know this and wish to exploit the fact, yet it also causes them a degree of embarrassment that leads them into strategies of self-consciousness and self-effacement that limit the unfolding and individuation of the "I" figure.

Barnum's *Life* is conspicuous in this group, and indeed in period autobiography generally, for its unabashed awareness of the growing market for the genre, on which it desires to capitalize. At the threshold of our period, Franklin, Adams, and Jefferson produced their memoirs at least nominally as family affairs, on roughly the same footing as their wills and testaments, not as saleable commodities. Barnum, on the other hand, tells us that he writes at the encouragement not merely of friends but of publishers, who have assured him "that such a work would have an extensive circulation" (iii). The preface reminds us that we have reached the decade when the American book market has become conspicuously larger than the British.

Given Barnum's candid hankering for commercial success, we should not be surprised to find his autobiography in many ways the most traditional of the four. More than any of the others, it reflects a previous model, Franklin, as in the last chapter, where Barnum gives his equivalent of Franklin's scheme of virtue: ten "rules for success in business," stressing predictable values like organization, thrift, honesty, and energy ("Let your pledged word ever be sacred"; "Avoid extravagance"; "Let hope predominate, but be not too visionary," etc.) (394–98). The book is also even more reminiscent than Franklin's of picaresque fiction and the criminal's confession and of previous narratives that intermix these, such as the highly popular *Memoirs of Stephen Burroghs* (1798), a New England con man of the late eighteenth century.

Barnum bends the Franklin model in several ways, however. Their autobiographical protagonists and personae are in some ways quite similar: they depict themselves as advancing by dint or wit, energy, and the power of benign manipulation of their fellow citizens; they ingratiate themselves by drolly parading their errata (as Franklin calls his mistakes) while at the same time making clear that they have a high opinion of themselves as self-made men and important public figures. For Barnum, however, amusement becomes at least theoretically a much more important point of doctrine than for Franklin. Barnum solemnly diagnoses as "the great defect of our American civilization . . . a severe and drudging practicalness" that "loses sight of the true aims of life, and concentrates itself upon dry and technical ideas of duty, and upon a sordid love of acquisition" (399). This is, of course, the showman's self-defense. Ironically, however, it comes two pages after his earnest-seeming rules of business success. Similar ironies recur throughout the book, but that does not make them any less confusing. How serious is Barnum, anyhow? The rest of the book shows not only that we cannot know, but that Barnum himself probably does not know, either. For example, he makes a point of stressing at odd times his commitment to temperance and Bible-reading. Naturally he hopes to induce his audience to think well of him, to see him as a cut above the average mountebank; but it is not unreasonable to assume that the confusion of evangelist and barker exists in the person as well as the persona.

Consciously or unconsciously, Barnum thus opens up the solemn-frivolous contradiction that Franklin holds in suspension by betraying his drollery (both mimetically and rhetorically) without advocating it as a principle. A similar effect results from Barnum's comparative decentering of focus, so that much of the book, particularly the first third, consists not of self-presentation but of an anthology of jokes that people Barnum knew played on each other. Barnum is partly humble, partly defensive about this centrifugalism. "Perhaps I should apologize for devoting so much space . . . to practical jokes and other incidents not immediately relating to myself," but "I feel myself entitled to record the sayings and doings of the wags and eccentricities of Bethel [Connecticut, his home town], because they partly explain the causes which have made me what I am" (105). This can't be taken completely at face value (for Barnum knows that amusing anecdotes will help to sell the book), but to the extent that it can, it makes an arrestingly Whitman-esque claim: "such as it is to be of these more of less I am" ("Song of Myself," line 328, 1892 ed.) Whereas Franklin finally made himself into a patriarch, Barnum will remain comparatively a man of the people, which proves that showmanship ought to be considered socially representative and sanctioned, not freakish or deviant. This in turn explains and justifies the scattering of the book into hundreds of vignettes of drollery, many not directly involving Barnum. He remains the central barker and ticket collector; but just as in life that act is not one of direct self-display but the display of a collection of exhibits the public will see as striking, so the literary autobiography cannot be the solo narrative of the showman's life but an account of the figure of the showman gradually and partially emerging from a clutter of surrounding events to which he must accommodate himself, and by which he is sometimes even victimized, in order to succeed.

The comic haphazardness of development that Franklin imputes to his projected self thus becomes at times positively entropic in Barnum. Barnum's hide-and-go-seek, shape-changing experimentalism, in turn, masks both a more aggressive belief in the social worth of the ordinary individual than Franklin's, and a greater degree of uncertainty as to how the individual ought to present the plot of his life. These two ostensibly incompatible motifs really go together: when the self is to be socially defined and in effect constituted by social approval, it must prepare to be self-effacing; yet if the social story is the story of the lives of its individuals, the individual must somehow remain the central figure in the process. This unstable compound is the formal equivalent of the ambiguity Tocqueville diagnosed when he found Jacksonian democracy at once individualistic and conformist; and it is fitting that Barnum presents himself in his *Life* as a good Jacksonian democrat.

In our other three autobiographies, the anxiety of the persona-public relation is developed not just as a topic but also as a distinct rhetorical device. Sigourney's *Letters of Life* is formally the most conservative of the three, although in substance the most innovative. Sigourney's flat-character reputation, dating from the prefeminist era of scholarship, as a purveyor of meretriciously sentimental gift-book verses, has anesthetized most literary historians to the significance of a number of landmark features in her career, not the least of which was that hers was the first full-dress autobiography written by an American author of either sex whose primary vocation was creative writing. That may partly explain the seeming diffidence of casting it nominally in the form of a series of epistles to the dedicatee, a "dear friend" whose request for "a particular account of my own life" "ought to be sacred to my much indebted heart" (5). This gesture of intimacy smoothly assimilates a standard framing device of manuscript autobiography to a standard framing convention of a publicly-accepted fictional genre that also happened to be strongly female-identified: the epistolary novel. Once having set this tone, however, the persona makes only sparing allusion to the interlocutor; what started as self-conscious gesture becomes in fact a stabilizing element.

More complex and suggestive is the obliquity with which Sigourney pursues the story of her emerging sense of literary vocation. Note that it begins with her first childhood transgression: the secret perusal of *The Mysteries of Udolpho*: "the first surreptitious satisfaction, and not partaken without remorse" (28). Here and elsewhere, the stilted, passive style—so easy to hold against Sigourney—cannot be discounted as ineptitude. It is part of an important presentational strategy to minimize the role of the "I" as active agent, perhaps even in her own eyes. The protagonist will yield to literary temptation, of course ("the fascinations of that fearful fiction-book seemed to me too strong to be resisted" [29]); but the persona cannot, despite the evidence of great and continuous productivity from a very early age, dramatize that commitment as the main plot of her life. Rather, the two halves into which her account roughly divides, childhood (chapters 1–8) and adulthood (chapters 9–14), are topically oriented in such a way as to put home life (with parents, then with husband) before literary life. The mere two chapters primarily devoted to literary reminiscences, furthermore, are curiously depersonalized. The first consists mainly of samples of her juvenilia strung together by slender commentary; the second, the book's climactic chapter and by far the longest, consists of a chronologically-arranged annotated bibliography of the various books Sigourney has published.[6]

The record is altogether a striking mixture of literary modesty and self-advertisement, dramatizing the offsetting point that personal literary aspirations mustn't come first but also asserting that they have given her life its ultimate direction. Or to put the matter another way, Sigourney accepts society's proposition that literary professionalism is tolerable only when it does not "interfere with the discharge of womanly duty" (324); she structures her recollected life accordingly, so that the literary achievement comes after and (she argues) as an outgrowth of a domesticity that she refuses to see as other than fully satisfying; and so she can finally approach her auditor with a minimum of self-consciousness, secure that the compartments into which she has divided her existence make both an authentic and a publicly shareable unity.

Sigourney's circumspect presentation of her literary commitments should not, incidentally, be seen as an exclusively feminine reflex by any means, although her particular form of caution reflects her acceptance of a gender-specific role. An analogous and indeed sometimes far greater circumspection runs strong among male writers as well. Thoreau nowhere parades his literary identity in *Walden*, for instance, even though we know that writing was his main form of purposive endeavor during his sojourn there. To present himself as squatter with pen in hand would have destroyed the masculinist illusion. Male and female writers of the period both labored in the face of public skepticism about the legitimacy of their vocation, though the grounds of skepticism differed.

John Neal and Walt Whitman are less secure than Sigourney and Barnum in their self-presentations. Both chafe at the limits imposed on the autobiographer and proclaim their despair at being able to produce

anything like a conventional narrative. Neal starts each major section
with a journal entry, running from 1866 to 1868—the period when he
was presumably biting his pen—beginning with what he claims as
his fourth desperate stab at the project, (whose inception he name-
droppingly ascribes to "the suggestion of my friend Longfellow" [1]).
He bemoans his indecision as to whether to proceed chronologically
or topically (10), ultimately resolving to try both at once, as when he
coordinates profiles of his parents with an essay on the Friends' reputation for superstition. All this makes for a much more self-consciously
turbid and unstable text than the autobiographies of Sigourney and
even Barnum, which is very much in keeping with Neal's vaunting and
paranoid sense of himself as a Renaissance man of multiple but irre-
gular accomplishments, impossible to sum up tidily and undervalued
by his neighbors and the public. Like Barnum, Neal prefers to think on
the level of the anecdotal snippet and build his chapters around strings
of these: for example, all the fists fights he remembers having from age
nine to age seventy (chapter 6). But Neal presents these not as distilled
vignettes but as feats of mental improvisation: the author in the act of
recreating his past through precarious extemporizing, much the same
approach that Neal claims he uses in his public lectures.

Whitman's *Specimen Days* looks even more improvisational. "I obey
my happy hour's command," declares Whitman, expecting that "I shall
send out the most wayward, spontaneous, fragmentary book ever
printed" (1). The style is improvisational not just in following out the
mood of the present moment of writing, but in relying for much of its
reminiscences on quoted diary material that itself took the form of
squibs. Whitman does not even attempt to organize by chapter units,
but follows instead a journalistic format of captions followed by short
paragraphs, usually no more than a paragraph or two. The convention
of linear autobiography is vestigially preserved, however, by sketches
of chapters in the author's lifeline, prefaced by genealogical information about both his family lines. Indeed, this narrative is the only major
thread that Whitman sustains from beginning to end. Otherwise, Whitman is quite right in suggesting that "the book is probably without any
definite purpose that can be told in a statement" (3). *Specimen Days* can
thus be fairly viewed as the period's most conspicuous case of the autobiographer's ambivalence toward his or her genre. Whitman nominally
adopts the genre but treats it so cavalierly that his subject becomes not
so much the shape of his life as the impossibility of meaningfully
shaping it in the terms normally available to the autobiographer. The
ambivalence toward genre that Barnum, Sigourney, and Neal contain
virtually explodes in Whitman.

It is very much to Whitman's purpose that the two major topical centers in *Specimen Days* are not coordinated with each other, and neither is seen to have produced a conclusive result. These are his Civil War reminiscences and his nature notes of the 1870s, during the period when he partially recovered his health after a paralytic stroke in 1872. The first of these sections concludes with the assertion that the inner history of the war will never be written, although "the preceding notes may furnish a few stray glimpses into . . . those lurid interiors, never to be fully convey'd to the future" (117). Concerning the second, Whitman confesses, just before ending, that originally he intended his materials as "hints and data of a Nature-poem that should carry one's experience a few hours, commencing at noon-flush, and so through the after-part of the day"; but he later decided that nature is not to be smoothed out or meddled with (293). These valedictions to his two major subjects of commentary are in keeping with Whitman's use of autobiographical structure: to supply a nominal principle of coherence that at the same time justifies a strategy of inconclusion.

Looking at *Specimen Days* in terms of Whitman's literary development from his first mature book, the 1855 edition of *Leaves of Grass*, it seems in some ways an even more logical result for him than the body of old-age poems he was concurrently writing and annexing to the parent volume. A little like Douglass in this respect, Whitman began by experimenting with a relatively representative persona but then moved toward a more individuated self-dramatization. In Whitman's poetry of the late 1850s and 1860s, as has often been noted, the "I" becomes more intimate and particularized, less cosmic, than in the first two editions of *Leaves of Grass*, as the speaker more openly and lyrically admits his fallability, his mortality, his need of comrades. *Specimen Days* is, so to speak, the next step in that process of particularization: the life-record of a vulnerable and finite being presented in more detail, the "I" still closer to the everyday Whitman. Not that *Specimen Days* is a wholly intimate work—far from it. The persona is objectified by the voice(s) of the Victorian sage-like essayist, and the book looks outward more often than inward, preoccupied as it is with scenes of the war; snapshots of the New Jersey countryside, the prairies, the Rockies; lists of flora and fauna; summary assessments of eminent persons; and so forth. The persona and his field of vision are each developed and claimed to be complementary, but are tentatively coordinated at best. Altogether, Whitman can be read not so much as stating flat doctrine but as musing about his career-long tackings and shiftings as an auto-biographical writer when he asserts that "the most profound theme than can occupy the mind of man . . . is doubtless involved in the query:

What is the fusing explanation and tie—what the relation between the (radical, democratic) Me, the human identity of understanding, emotions, spirit, &c., on the one side, of and with the (conservative) Not Me, the whole of the material objective universe and laws, with what is behind them in time and space, on the other side?" (258).

Whitman's dictum gropingly sums up not only his own practice but the two related lines of development we have been tracing through American autobiography during the period of its emergence as a form of consciously literary discourse. One is a commitment, in keeping with traditional autobiographical practice, of objectifying the self either through its effacement in favor of a narrative of events (usually itself somewhat stereotyped, as in slave or frontier narrative), or through the subordination of the "I"'s uniqueness to shared, communal models of the self: the convert, the slave, the famous self-made man, the successful domestic/professional woman, the frontiersman. The other—opposite yet symbiotic, indeed called into being by the pressure of the first as it exerts itself within an "I"-centered transatlantic culture accentuated by America's exceptionally "I"-centered civil religion—is the development of the more individuated "I" at the level of either protagonist or persona but especially the latter, an "I" that explicitly or implicitly proclaims its boundlessness in relation to social and literary norms, its impatience with preexisting narrative frames, its inability to be typed and formulated even by itself. This bipolarity leads to an epistemological/literary oscillation that constitutes one of the fundamental distinguishing features of mid-nineteenth-century American autobiography as distinct from that of previous eras.

This bipolarity is most intricately inscribed in *Walden*. Never was there an autobiographical text so tortuous with regard to the issue of the "I"'s exemplary status. On the one had, it embroiders extensively on the literal and symbolic quest-into-nature-and-return story that forms the heart of traditional exploration and discovery narratives. Into this, furthermore, is infused a strong element of post-Puritan didacticism, which takes much of its force from a vision of the Walden sojourn as exemplifying two of the period's most widely shared and admired models of selfhood, especially for males: the workingman/pioneer's ethic of economic self-sufficiency and the gentlemanly ethic of pastoral retreat. But as if in recoil against the very deftness with which it draws on these models, the text also, on the other hand, is at pains to represent the "I"'s experience as anomalous, to warn its reader against imitation, to mystify its explanations so as to make that experience unfathomable, and to establish that even this comparatively liberated "I" is an insufficient token of the author's total self, which declares itself to have many more avatars than are recorded there.

The wonderful intricacy and fussiness into which Thoreauvian rhetoric is thereby led is not typical of the period in the sense of having precise duplicates elsewhere. Yet it does have an array of counterparts in Neal's testy impetuousness, Whitman's studied vagaries, the rhetorical convolutions of Sigourney's "passivity," Douglass's career-long narrative self-presentation, and Barnum's uneasy reinvention of Franklin by jerry-building his autobiography as a compound of earnestness and hoaxing, personal glimpses and local folklore. These analogues are hardly surprising, coming as they did when mobility and expansion were America's two most conspicuous social motifs, and the nation had hardly yet finished deciding whether it was to be one, two, or many.

The autobiographical scene just summarized can be evaluated either as a state of burgeoning possibility or as a state of cultural erosion. Indeed, it was both. The self-presentations of mid-nineteenth-century autobiographers make it clear that American self-conceptions had, for better or for worse, begun to proceed toward the contemporary climate recently characterized by Robert Bellah and his associates in *Habits of the Heart*, in which individuals aspiring to self-actualization seem caught between a "culture of separation" and a "culture of coherence" (277–83). After Barnum's carnivalization of Franklin and Thoreau's near-total inversion of him in "Economy," after Sigourney's and Douglass's struggle between individual and communalistic modes of life-narrative, after Thoreau's and Neal's and Whitman's restiveness with narrative teleologies, it became inevitable that future American authors of literary pretension would find themselves working among a plurality of autobiographical models, with less trust in the viability of any one, unless they were able to internalize a model as the mark of a coherent subculture with which they could imaginatively identify. Surely it is significant in this regard that the only widely used American autobiographical plot of the early nineteenth century to yield a distinguished literary tradition in the twentieth century is slave narrative. Otherwise, as a national literary culture, we remain, as compared with our colonial and early national predecessors, an "I"-centered culture deeply unsure about the viability of our available myths of self-realization.

NOTES

The research and writing of this essay were facilitated by generous support from the Guggenheim Foundation and Oberlin College.

1 Previous commentators have noted this, for example, Stone (16) and especially Cooley (3–25), whose first chapter contains the fullest discussion to date of the paucity of developed American autobiography before 1865. For a helpful, up-to-date overview of existing scholarship on nineteenth-century American autobiography, see Eakin.

2 See Buell (*New England*, 377–78) for statistics and professionalism by gender for New England writers between the Revolution and the Civil War. In explaining the comparative gender imbalance in the bibliographies of Kaplan and Carlock, I am inclined to discount the two most tempting explanations: the underrepresentation of women's writing in the sources usually consulted by precontemporary researchers, and the reluctance of precontemporary women writers to say "I"—although in view of Jelinek, the most thorough study of American women's autobiographies, both must be accorded some weight. As the present article notes, antebellum male writers themselves had considerable trouble writing developed autobiography, and among literary professionals, women writers were pioneers in this respect. Where differential socialization seems to have constrained, or rather channeled, women's autobiographical expression most conspicuously was in directing them on the whole more toward the domestic sphere than toward narratives of adventure or public event, although Jelinek (69–78) cites a number of instances of the latter from our period.

3 "Transcendentalist Self-Examination and Autobiographical Tradition" (Buell, *Literary Transcendentalism*, 265–83), presses the distinction between Transcendentalist first-person discourse, including *Walden*, and true autobiography. In response, Sayre "The Proper Study," 252) very reasonably states the other side of the case. Two important arguments for regarding *Walden* as an autobiography on the strength of its status as an act of speech or consiousness are made by Blasing (1–23) and Gunn (29–54). Some critics have been discerned in *Walden* a strong, if largely implicit, narrative line; for example, Schwaber contends that Thoreau's "moral development is central to the book's aesthetic excellence" (68). This may be true with regard to Thoreau's life history, but with regard to Thoreau's artistry, Blasing is surely more correct in asserting that "neither the *Journal* nor *Walden* was conceived as a chronological transcription of a process of growth; instead, each seems to deny a linear process of change" (18). The best defense of *Walden* as legitimate autobiography is finally to deny that narrative is a crucial ingredient (Gunn, 43); conversely, the case for grouping Thoreau with colonial and revolutionary autobiographers is most convincingly made on the macro-level of Thoreau's exemplary (Bercovitch, *The Puritan Origins*; "The Ritual") or prophetic (Couser) modes.

4 Thoreau's accommodation to marketplace factors is briefly discussed by Gilmore (35–51), and much more extensively by Fink. Concerning *Walden*, both Gilmore and Fink argue persuasively that the first version was more

popularly oriented than the version actually published. Fink also shows, however, with extensive reference to popular travel writing of the period among other genres, that Thoreau made systematic albeit ambivalent attempts to normalize his style during the 1840s and 1850s, reaching an effectual compromise in his later lecture-essays. This is not to say that marketplace considerations were the only reason for the diminution of the self-conscious "I" in *The Maine Woods, Cape Cod,* and *A Yankee in Canada,* or that the diminution of the "I" was Thoreau's only or even primary project to the extent that he sought to alter his style in the interest of popular consumption. Probably at least as important a reason for Thoreau's less reflexive, less interiorized later style was his increasing interest in the environment as subject relative to himself. Once Thoreau found his vocation as literary/literal surveyor, the need to survey himself probably became less pressing.

Incidentally, Thoreauvians will recognize that I have slightly oversimplified chronology in referring to the "later" Thoreau of the three posthumous travel books, since "Ktaadn," the first chapter of *The Maine Woods,* was written before *A Week* was published and while *Walden* was still in process.

5 For an illuminating previous discussion of Douglass's self-fashioning through revision, see Gates (115–24) and especially Andrews (218–39), who also discusses the choice of the incident used by Douglass's in *Bondage* to dramatize his indoctrination into slavery (219). For Douglass's desire to represent himself in terms of a version of the ideal of the American self-made man, see Martin (253–78). For a concise account of the generic constraints on self-representation in slave narrative, see Olney (150–53). For the argument that Douglass's *Narrative* itself "offers a profound endorsement of the fundamental American plot, the myth of the self-made man," see Smith (27–8) and especially Andrews (97–166), who persuasively argues concerning slave narratives of the 1840s in general thay they focus on the figure of the persona to a greater degree than their predecessors. For the argument that slave narrative *qua* autobiographical genre is coopted by a white ideology of individual achievement, see Niemtzow.

6 Jelinek shows that this approach of telling the story of one's literary career through bibliography and excerpt was not uncommon among nineteenth-century American women autobiographers, nor was the tendency to structure one's life so as to circumscribe or even omit mention of one's literary commitments. In the latter respect, although Jelinek sees Sigourney's diffidence as typical, she appears to me rather to have been quite bold, not only for her time, but for the next generation as well.

WORKS CITED

Andrews, William L. *To Tell a Free Story: The First Century of Afro-American Autobiography, 1760–1965.* Urbana and Chicago: University of Illinois Press, 1986.

Barnum, Phineas Taylor. *Life of P.T. Barnum.* New York: Redfield, 1855.

Bellah, Robert N. et al. *Habits of the Heart: Individualism and Commitment in American Life.* New York: Harper & Row, 1986.

Bercovitch, Sacvan. *The Puritan Origins of the American Self.* New Haven and London: Yale University Press, 1975.

Bercovitch, Sacvan. "The Ritual of American Autobiography: Edwards, Franklin, Thoreau." *Revue Française d'etudes Americaines* 7 (1982): 139–49.

Blasing, Mutlu Konuk. *The Art of Life: Studies in American Autobiographical Literature.* Austin and London: University of Texas Press, 1977.

Blassingame, John W., ed. *The Frederick Douglass Papers.* Vol. 1. New Haven and London: Yale University Press, 1979.

Buell, Lawrence. *Literary Transcendentalism: Style and Vision in the American Renaissance.* Ithaca and London: Cornell University Press, 1973.

Buell, Lawrence. *New England Literary Culture: From Revolution through Renaissance* Cambridge: Cambridge University Press, 1986.

Carlock, Mary Sue. "American Autobiographies, 1840–1870: A Bibliography." *Bulletin of Bibliography* 23 (1961): 118–20.

Cooley, Thomas. *Educated Lives: The Rise of Modern Autobiography in America.* Columbus: Ohio State University Press, 1976.

Couser, G. Thomas. *American Autobiography: The Prophetic Mode.* Amherst: University of Massachusetts Press, 1979.

Douglass, Frederick. *My Bondage and My Freedom.* [1855]. Reprint. New York: Dover, 1969.

Douglass, Frederick. *Narrative of the Life of Frederick Douglass, an American Slave.* [1845]. Reprint. New York: Signet, 1968.

Douglass, Frederick. *Life and Times of Frederick Douglass.* [1892]. Reprint. New York: Collier, 1962.

Eakin, Paul John. "L'autobiographie américaine au XIXe siècle: tendances récentes de la recherche." *Romantisme* no. 56 (1987), 118–23.

Emerson, Ralph Waldo. *The Journals and Miscellaneous Notebooks of Ralph Waldo Emerson.* 16 vols. Ed. William H. Gilman et al. Cambridge: Harvard University Press, 1960–82.

Fink, Stephen. *Prophet in the Marketplace: Thoreau's Early Development as a Professional Writer.* Princeton: Princeton University Press. Forthcoming.

Franklin, Benjamin. *The Autobiography of Benjamin Franklin.* [1790, 1791, 1793, 1818]. Ed. J. A. Leo Lemay and P. M. Zall. Knoxville: University of Tennessee Press, 1981.

Gates, Henry Louis, Jr. *Figures in Black: Words, Signs, and the 'Racial' Self.* New York and Oxford: Oxford University Press, 1987.

Gilmore, Michael T. *American Romanticism and the Marketplace.* Chicago and London: University of Chicago Press, 1985.

Gunn, Janet Varner. *Autobiography: Toward a Poetics of Experience.* Philadelphia: University of Pennsylvania Press, 1982.

Jehlen, Myra. *American Incarnation: The Individual, the Nation, and the Continent.* Cambridge and London: Harvard University Press, 1986.

Jelinek, Estelle C. *The Tradition of Women's Autobiography: From Antiquity to the Present.* Boston: Hall, 1986.

Kaplan, Louis. *A Bibliography of American Autobiographies*. Madison: University of Wisconsin Press, 1962.

Martin, Waldo E., Jr. *The Mind of Frederick Douglass*. Chapel Hill and London: University of North Carolina Press, 1984.

Neal, John. *Wandering Recollections of a Somewhat Busy Life*. Boston: Roberts, 1869.

Niemtzow, Annette. "The Problematic of Self in Autobiography: The Example of the Slave Narrative." In *The Art of Slave Narrative: Original Essays in Criticism and Theory*. Ed. John Sekora and Darwin T. Turner. Macomb: Western Illinois University, 1982, 96–109.

Olney, James. " 'I Was Born': Slave Narratives, Their Status as Autobiography and as Literature." In *The Slave's Narrative*. Ed. Charles T. Davis and Henry Louis Gates, Jr. New York and Oxford: Oxford University Press, 1985, 148–75.

Parkman, Francis. *The California and Oregon Trail*. New York: G. P. Putnam, 1849.

Rowlandson, Mary. *A Narrative of the Captivity and Restoration of Mrs. Mary Rowlandson*. [1682]. Vol. 14 of *Original Narratives of Early American History, Narratives of Indian Wars, 1675–1699*. Ed. C. H. Lincoln. New York: Barnes & Noble, 1952.

Saum, Lewis O. *The Popular Mood of Pre-Civil War America*. Westport and London: Greenwood, 1980.

Sayre, Robert. "The Proper Study—Autobiographies in American Studies." *American Quarterly* 29 (1977): 241–62.

Sayre, Robert. "Autobiography and the Making of America." *Autobiography: Essays Theoretical and Critical*. Ed. James Olney. Princeton: Princeton University Press, 1980, 146–68.

Schwaber, Paul. "Thoreau's Development in 'Walden.' " *Criticism* 5 (1963): 64–77.

Shanley, J. London. *The Making of "Walden", with the Text of the First Edition*. Chicago: University of Chicago Press, 1957.

Sigourney, Lydia H. *Letters of Life*. New York: Appleton-Century-Crofts, 1866.

Smith, Valerie. *Self-Discovery and Authority in Afro-American Narrative*. Cambridge and London: Harvard University Press, 1987.

Steele, Jeffrey. *The Representation of the Self in the American Renaissance*. Chapel Hill and London: University of North Carolina Press, 1987.

Stone, Albert E. *Autobiographical Occasions and Original Acts*. Philadelphia: University of Pennsylvania Press, 1982.

Thoreau, Henry. *Walden*. Ed. J. Lyndon Shanley. Princeton: Princeton University Press, 1971.

Townsend, Kim. "Francis Parkman and the Male Tradition." *American Quarterly* 38 (1986): 97–113.

Van Der Beets, Richard, ed. *Held Captive by Indians: Selected Narratives 1642–1836*. Knoxville: University of Tennessee Press, 1973.

Whitman, Walt. *Specimen Days*. Vol. 1 of *Prose Works 1982*. Ed. Floyd Stovall. New York: New York University Press, 1963.

CHAPTER 3

"Self"-Conscious History: American Autobiography after the Civil War

SUSANNA EGAN

INTRODUCTION

Writing of Hawthorne, Henry James refers to the Civil War as "that great convulsion" that took a complacent generation by surprise: "their illusions were rudely dispelled, and they saw the best of all possible republics given over to fratricidal carnage" (*Hawthorne*, 144). For him, the war marks an era in the history of the American mind; the world became more complicated than it had seemed, the future more treacherous, success more difficult. For Americans, of course, one nation under God was involved in the painful process of Reconstruction in the south, of expansive and questionably imperialistic movement west, of industrialization and reshuffling of the sources of power in the east and north, of reevaluation of autonomy vis-à-vis Europe as the ex-colonies felt their way to becoming an international power. In the political republic and in what William Dean Howells calls "the republic of letters" ("Autobiography," 798), democracy was distinctive of the American scene. But Americans also shared the moral and intellectual dilemmas that beset their European relatives. Indeed, as James complained, it was unfair that no European writer had to deal with America, but the American must somehow deal with Europe (Matthiessen, 296). Quite apart from the sociological and technological transformations engendered throughout the Western world by the Industrial Revolution, new ideas in science, psychology, economics, and the treatment of history were revolutionizing the ways in which autobiographers thought about themselves.[1]

Every autobiography, Thomas Cooley suggests, implies a theory of human nature; it is from this premise that he distinguishes this period of postwar turbulence for American autobiography. As traditional sources of stability are undermined, autobiographers make repeated efforts to recollect their past and discover whatever continuity may establish their identity in a pluralistic universe. These are the autobiographers born in the 1840s, writing out of the period that Emerson describes as "the Fall of Man," from perspectives that Cooley describes as "recognizably 'modern.'" From the failed education of Henry Adams to Sherwood Anderson's apparent success, Cooley describes a period of re-search and redefinition in American autobiography. Periods in history, however we slice them, tend to be creations of our own myth-making. Cooley's particular slice is plausible, however, because it grows out of contemporary perceptions of the significance of the Civil War, not just to the male world of the battlefield, government, or boardroom, but also to the heterogeneous identities—female, black, Indian, immigrant—that constitute and create postwar America. (For the Chicano, of course, the American occupation of Northern Mexico a few years earlier in 1846 is the turning point.)

As part, it may be, of American democracy, participation in the making of history is a crucial and distinctive feature of American autobiography in this period. Again and again we find that the self is important essentially in the context of change or place or ethnic group, as an active participant in the definition of any of these or as an active intelligence through which current events are perceived and understood. In one way or another, it is common for autobiographers of this period to identify their purpose as political; they not only review a past in order to make sense of it, but they also reach forward to predict or possibly shape a future. Each, in a distinctive way, creates autobiography not as memoir (suggestive of an established context that defines a public self) but as history in the making, with the self, in varying degrees of objectivity, as participant. The defining of self and of time and place is reciprocal, creating what Albert E. Stone has described as the web of text and context. Furthermore, if we recognize these autobiographers as the immediate heirs or contemporaries of Rousseau, Goethe, De Quincey, Gorky, or Proust, the giants of European autobiography, we can appreciate the significance of their role in creating an American literature; for these characters written into specific times and places identify themselves repeatedly as American.

This is not, of course, a new point. Despite Mark Twain's truism that "there is not a single human characteristic which can be surely labeled as 'American'" (Wecter, 917), critics today look back on American literature in this period and recognize a distinct tendency toward the identification of what is American. Robert F. Sayre, for example, describes autobiographical examination as accounting for more lives than the writer's own: "they comment profoundly on the American experience" (*Examined Self*, vii). Or, again: "America and autobiography have been peculiarly linked . . . . An American seems to have needed to be an American first and then an autobiographer" ("Making of America," 147). James M. Cox describes autobiography as growing out of the political necessities and discoveries of the American and French revolutions ("Autobiography," 253) so that it becomes "an act of life, a making of experience" (263). G. Thomas Couser describes "an ongoing and almost obsessive inquiry into what it means to be an American" (9).

What matters for our present purpose is that just as the Civil War drew attention to an independent America struggling, in Faulkner's terms, like Jacob and Esau for inheritance of the future, so also it drew attention to the nature of America in relation to Europe, in relation to Europeans immigrating to the Promised Land, in relation to the places that constitute America—New England, the South, the West—and, most important, in relation to notions of what America could or should be. By 1917 and entry into World War I, numerous autobiographers were concerned about roads not taken, but it is also true to say that Stein, Fitzgerald, or Hemingway in Paris, were writing distinctly American literature, a plant that could flourish without identity crisis only after the self-creation of this postwar half century.

AMERICAN PERSPECTIVES

"He studied the universe from himself," Howells writes of Oliver Wendell Holmes. "I do not know how one is to study it otherwise; the impersonal has really no existence" (*Literary Friends*, [1902]132). Howells's assumption that the personal perspective is the crucial lens for perception of the universal is common to autobiographers of this period. They assume the role of historians who put themselves in the picture; Henry Adams returns to the steps of Santa Maria di Ara Coeli both in the footsteps of Gibbon and in order to establish his perspective. They become biographers who create their own places and times in terms of other people; James, Adams, Howells, Twain, and Washington are just a few of the major autobiographers of this period who also wrote biographies of other people who were significant to their own sense of themselves. Or they write in the third person, about themselves as if they were others, as if they were in a literal but nontechnical sense defaced, of interest only as figures of their times. (Conversely, of course, what happens is significant precisely because it is important to the self.[2]) The autobiographer assumes he is useful rather than egocentric; his purpose repeatedly is to record and thereby to create American history.

Howells writing on Holmes, as on all his other literary friends and acquaintances, is writing part of his autobiography in terms of a context that is of interest and importance beyond his own part in it. (He recognizes Twain's genius, for example, and suspects that he himself will be remembered only as Twain's correspondent.) He is also creating that context for American literature and history and for his own part in both. Henry Adams feels the need for this sense of context (less humbly, in the end, one feels, than Howells); indeed, Robert E. Spiller describes him as "thwarted, as all American writers have been until very recently, by the absence of a matured and autogenous literary culture" (1096). Henry James refers bitterly to "this naked vacuous America" (Matthiessen, 290) and flees to Europe in order to recreate Americans (as he loved to hold Minnie Temple) "translated from this changing realm of fact to the steady realm of thought" (Matthiessen, 261).

James called it a "complex fate" to be American (Matthiessen, 290), and Howells energetically described him as in fact "American to his heart's core to the day of his death" (M. Howells, 2:395). With more constant ambivalence than any of his contemporaries, James sought the tight fit of European culture, and then recognized the tight fit of that available in New England (Son and Brother, [1914]178); he lived in England for most of his adult life, but returned with fully engaged imagination to the New York of his boyhood after the deaths of his father and his brother; he wished to be neutral in his national perspective but was deeply disturbed by the Civil War and distressed by Hawthorne's death to the extent of writing a brief life of Hawthorne in 1887.

He was not alone in this difficulty of identifying his cultural affinities. Adams, after feeling foreign and uncouth in London as a young man, learned to be completely at home throughout Europe; yet his filial responsibilities throughout his writing life attached him more clearly and firmly than James to the new American world. Howells writes to his son in 1894 to warn him against the poison of Europe getting into his soul (M. Howells, 2:52). Yet he also dreams (Impressions, [1896] 96–97) of taking towels and bathgowns to the Duke of Wellington and refusing the proffered tip with a gentlemanly bow on the grounds that he is an American.[3]

Like James or Twain or Adams, Howells returns to the world of his boyhood with intense poignancy, recreating the deeply felt personal flavors of memory. But these writers create also the more objective context of the time, the place, of Boston and Quincy or New York, or the river and logcabin life of the midwest. Their later struggles with Europe grow out of their sense, very early established, of being themselves Americans. This original context controls the perspective on each of these lives and is important to each writer precisely for the clarity that it provides.

AUTOBIOGRAPHER AS HISTORIAN

Just as nationality helps to define the autobiographer's role in the world, so the egocentric imperatives of autobiography repeatedly yield to the larger design of reporting on one's world, commenting in a prophetic vein, or reliving one's life as historian for times that are rapidly changing. Carlyle, Ruskin, and Arnold were similarly engaged in England, Burckhardt in Europe. For autobiography, however, it seems a new and distinctive undertaking that the writer's life should unfold, develop, or signify so explicitly in relation to his times.

Ernest Samuels describes Adams's *Education* (1918) as the drama of a potential participant which becomes the drama of the detached observer (*Major Phase*, 374). Kicking his heels on the sidelines of the Civil War and of every American government that came after it, Adams describes his nonparticipation as the ironic failure of a manikin inadequately prepared to control, predict, or even understand the political or economic life of his times. The objective nature of this perception of what is, after all, himself, is clarified by his breadth of context. *Sub specie aeternitatis*, Adams seeks his ancestry in the first vertebrate, the ganoid fish called Pteraspis, which comes to represent random change in place of coherent evolution and so becomes a symbol, grinning horribly, of everything, both personal and political, that is inexplicable. He begins, for example, by accepting Darwinism as a common-law deity, but finds that it fails both in this arch-example of nonevolution and also in its moral, social, and political analogies: "That two thousand years after Alexander the Great and Julius Caesar, a man like Grant should be called—and should actually and truly be—the highest product of the most advanced evolution, made evolution ludicrous . . . . The progress of evolution from President Washington to President Grant, was alone evidence enough to upset Darwin" (266). Adams's pessimism becomes so intense, his search for unity so persistently baffled at every turn by multiplicity, as to require the witty, taciturn style of detachment that is his hallmark. Ironically, U. S. Grant (1885) shares his feeling, part of much topical thinking in historiography, that great men are merely chance products of their time, that Napoleon swinging the tassels in his chariot does not control the tides of the times, though Adams might go further and call his autobiographical manikin the victim of his circumstances. America, the republic led by exceptional men (including the Adamses), becomes a mechanistic jungle with a dynamo for its symbol and with cosmic catastrophe just around the corner.

Adams has no time for Carlylean heroes, despite the fact that one could indeed alter the course of history by killing off a few-score men; his ironic narrator is concerned (like his *bête noir*, General Grant, indeed,) with setting the record straight, ensuring that the past makes sense or is of value to the future. His historical and prophetic purposes are closely connected to a positive anchoring of American identity within the vast scope of global history. He finds it important, for instance, to recognize Teutonic laws and customs as antecedents to American democracy; "we the people" do not rebel but, rather, reaffirm the oldest political traditions of the Teutonic race (Samuels, *The Young Henry Adams*, 256). His concern as historian and as autobiographer is the danger of disconnection from the past in American thought; the American mind, he writes, "stood alone in history for its ignorance of the past" (Adams, *The Education*, 328).

American democracy allows him no privileges of aristocratic descent. For the man and the historian both, the future turns upon flexible and intelligent reading of the past. His manikin persona, then, becomes a figure in a board game moved from point to point for his constantly shifting analysis of relation. Despite his repeated attempts to control the figure imaginatively, his constructions, like his cathedrals, like the St. Gaudens statue for his wife's grave, remain reflections of his intellectual distress and represent his keen sense that the time is out of joint. The personal, the subjective, are generalized, universalized by phrase-making and by symbols. Like any suggestion of developmental cause and effect, they are subsumed into this representative figure of the time; the potential Empedocles or Tiresias or, in a different vein and more modestly, Macaulay or Disraeli, becomes in autobiography an objective ironic exemplar.

BIOGRAPHY AS AUTOBIOGRAPHY

Reading Trollope's autobiography, Adams comments on "how coolly and neatly a man like Trollope can destroy the last vestige of heroism in his own life." Adams's irony is antiheroic. "I object," he writes, "to allowing mine to be murdered by any one except myself" (Samuels, *Middle Years*, 192). But it is not just heroism that is leaked like sawdust out of the ironic manikin; he abjures, as we have also noted, the intimate, the personal, and the private to which the autobiographer can make such exclusive claim. Adams's hiatus of a twenty-year period and the absence of any reference to his wife are startling and have received much and varied explanation. Such blanks, however, are in fact part of a common trend at a time when the private autobiographer is so frequently representative or serviceably public. We might compare such an omission with James's "obscure hurt," which he could well be describing only to assure us that his autobiography does not explicate the secret and the obscure.[4] Or we should consider Howells, who refers in correspondence to his emotional difficulties in including his wife in his autobiography. He is reduced to the cryptic summary: "Forty-seven years we were together here, and then she died" (*Years of My Youth*, [1916] 194). James is able to be more expansive about the emotional quality of a relationship that is not his own. He writes in sympathy about the "long, long years of exquisite, of heroic devotion, the most perfect thing of its kind one has ever known" (M. Howells, 2:284). Although Howells cannot write about his own wife, he can, in the year of her death, become expansive on the subject of Twain's marriage and the character of Twain's wife, calling his friend "My Mark Twain" in his imaginative reach behind what he calls the mask of the fictive name.

Howells prefers the mask of fiction.[5] "No man, unless he puts on the mask of fiction, can show his real face or the will behind it" (*Years of My Youth*, 110). He creates his boy's town for himself and for all boys. He resurrects his parents in his novel, *New Leaf Mills* (1913), carefully checking on the details of the original experience and reconstructing what must have been, in his now adult understanding, his parents' relationship with each other. In *Years of My Youth*, he deals more directly and intimately with the neuroses of his childhood but explains: "I came to deal with my own state of mind as another would deal with it, and to combat my fears as if they were alien" (81). Adams, too, resorts to fiction; his *Democracy* and *Esther* work through many of the themes that trouble *Mont-Saint-Michel and Chartres* and *The Education*. Twain and James more emphatically than Howells raise the question of what counts as autobiography, in that the significantly private is certainly absorbed into the voluminous fiction.

But it is also in the framework not of overt fiction but of the explicitly other-referential art of biography that these autobiographers hide themselves, only to be identified by those with whom they share a common history. So Charles Adams reacts to the recreation of Quincy and Boston in *The Education* and writes to his brother: "You brought it all back out of the remote past! . . . Oh dear! Oh dear! I'm a boy again" (Samuels, *Major Phase*, 334–35). James finds himself overwhelmed by "its suggestion and recall and terrible thick evocation," so that he feels himself "as it were, sticking fast in it, even as an indiscreet fly in amber" (Samuels, *Major Phase*, 336). Similarly, Adams identifies himself in James's *William Wetmore Story and His Friends*, which spells out for him the ignorance and inadequacy of the "*type Bourgeois-bostonien*," their knowledge of their own ignorance leading to self-distrust, their nervous self-consciousness, their irritable dislike of America, their antipathy to Boston: "So you have written not Story's life, but your own and mine— pure autobiography" (Samuels, *Major Phase*, 318). Just as Adams's recreation of Quincy and Boston takes his brother back to childhood, so James's recreation of Story's world is both James's own and Adams's too. Biography, autobiography, and history overlap in such a way that author, subject, and contemporary reader become representative and impersonal.

The manikin is homunculus scriptor for his time and place, suppressing or disguising what is most personal, choosing forms that conceal or minimize the self. (St. Gaudens, delighted by *Chartres*, addressed Adams as "you old poeticus under a Bushelibus" [Samuels, *Major Phase*, 308].) Even James, that most sensitive self-consciousness, dawdling and gaping over his "poor dear inward life" (*Small Boy*, [1913] 191) as he had dawdled and gaped in boyhood at the world around him, receiving "an impression or an accession," feeling "a relation or a vibration" (*Small Boy*, 27), describes himself as always eager to exchange his lot for that of another, presumed happier, but not in envy, rather because of his rich sense of other *as* other and therefore unattainable. His small boy becomes other to the aging autobiographer in the clarity of recall and in the tenderness with which the old man filters his boy's perceptions. P. T. Barnum's circus, in retrospect, was surely "of the last meanness," but he had "plucked somehow the flower of the ideal" (*Small Boy*, 173). (Howells, too, knows that all was not, could not have been, as idyllic as he now portrays it.) Such tension between the writer in the present and the "other" past self, which is so revealing of the individual self and of the problems of self-creation, suggests also that constant reach for context and objectivity attempted when writing about people other than the self.

James's small boy and young man, furthermore, like Adams's manikin in relation to the politics of his time, are defined in terms of their relation to significant others, particularly in relation to Henry James Sr. and to William. So James creates the context for his consciousness.

Letters are important, from William, from his father, and from his
brother Wilkie in the war; they serve to locate the young James in the
same way as the attention he gives to the Albany cousins, so interesting
for their numberless bereavements. So the more public figure of Ten-
nyson becomes part of this context; he is disappointingly unTennyso-
nian, but he likes James's story and recognizes James as the author of
the story he has liked. The prominent poet, in other words, vouches
for the coherent existence of the aspiring novelist in stark contrast to
Mr. Lewes, who returns to the young man his own work, which his
friend, Mrs. Greville, had importunately loaned to George Eliot, thus
forcing the ironical but painful recognition both that James's work is
not liked and that he is not identified as its author; in this case, the
disconnection in Lewes's mind between James as writer and James as
man dissolves the possible public context (Samuels, *Middle Years*, 90,
81–82). Such validation, failed or achieved, of the central consciousness
enables what would otherwise be an intensely private and subjective
self to merge, like homunculus scriptor, with the time and the place,
to become "other" and thus representative.

So James's "obscure hurt," the mysterious "physical mishap" (*Son and
Brother*, 276), becomes part of what he calls a huge comprehensive ache,
from one's own poor organism or from the enclosing social body rent
with a thousand wounds. So contagious was the tension of the time
"that almost any tension would do, would serve for one's share" (*Son
and Brother*, 278). Even that, in other words, which is emphatically subjective if only because it remains so deliberately mysterious, becomes
part of the whole context in which the self is an object of history. Paul
John Eakin stresses the connection that James himself made at the time
between the war and his own injury: "What the autobiographer actually
reconstructs for us with no little precision is the curious way in which
the young noncombatant became in his own eyes a veteran" (*Fictions*,
104). Even at his most personal, in other words, the autobiographer sees
fit to make himself most universal.

James's "personal history" assumes "a shape almost too familiar at
first for recognition . . . . I had in a word," says James, "to draw him forth
from within rather than meet him in the world before me . . . and to
make him objective, in short, had to turn nothing less than myself inside out" (*Son and Brother*, 344–45). (We may note in passing the inter-
change or interrelation between first and third-person pronouns in this
sentence.) This common use of the self as other, as part of a historical
context in which biography of the other helps to define the self, is also
apparent and explicit in the titles of many of these autobiographies: *The
Education of Henry Adams, Notes of a Son and Brother, A Boy's Town*. We

may look beyond these intellectual and self-conscious autobiographies to their contemporaries with titles like *Life on the Mississippi* (1883), *An Indian Boyhood* (1902), *Twenty Years at Hull House* (1911), *The Making of an American* (1901), *Up from Slavery* (1901), *A New England Girlhood* (1889), and *The Souls of Black Folk* (1903). Such titles enforce connection between the one life and all others that it may represent. They enforce attention also to place as the context that serves in part to justify autobiography.

PLACE AS CONTEXT

Howells describes the importance of a particular environment in the memories that help to constitute autobiography. The autobiographer is part of a context, a place, "and his hope of a recognizable self-portrait must lie in his frank acceptance of the condition that he can make himself truly seen chiefly in what he remembers to have seen of his environment" (*Years of Youth*, 57). Indeed, he wrote to Harper & Bros. in May 1914 that "without the carefully painted background of time and place, it will be a lifeless portrait of me" (*Years of Youth*, xviii). With ink, he feels, rather than blood running in his veins, he may look east and to England for his literary opinions. ("From West to East," he writes in *My Literary Friends and Acquaintances*, "the difference was as great as I afterwards found it from America to Europe" [46].) It is important for him, however, to identify Mark Twain as a fellow westerner: "We were natives of the same vast Mississippi Valley . . . we were akin in our first knowledges of woods and fields, as we were in our early parlance" (*Literary Friends*, 264). Howells positively relishes Twain's use of regional language for its "long-remembered savor" on his "mental palate"; significantly, he describes Twain's use of English "as if it were native to his own air, as if it had come up out of American, out of Missourian ground" (*Literary Friends*, 266).

Twain's regionalism is important, of course, for American literature at large; for autobiography it may be important to link his repeated and never satisfactory attempts at autobiography with the oral traditions of western narrative.[6] Howells describes him pacing in the nightgown, which he preferred to pyjamas, telling "the story of his life, the inexhaustible, the fairy, the Arabian Nights story, which I could never tire of even when it began to be told over again" (*Literary Friends*, 260). Howells's admiration for Twain's autobiography is unbounded: "If you have gone this gait all through," he writes to Twain in 1906 after reading a portion, "you have already gone farther than any autobiographer ever went before. You are nakeder than Adam and Eve put together, and truer than sin" (M. Howells 218–19). But Twain himself, in his night-gown mode, declares, "I have thought of fifteen hundred or two thousand incidents in my life which I am ashamed of but I have not gotten one of them to consent to go on paper yet" (*The Autobiography*, [1917] 224). His childhood, like Howells's own, finds most fluent expression in fiction. In his repeated attempts at complete autobiography, he resorted to dictation in order to become a voice from the grave. But it is precisely this unshaped, undetermined narrative, this episodic entertainment so dependent on audience response, that resurrects the particular time and place which Twain recognized as the source of his genius. The midwest made him and he, in turn, made the midwest.

Grant describes the move west as a direct result of the Civil War, the opening up of a frontier by men whom the war had made restless. Even while Howells looks east, traveling as a passionate pilgrim, approaching the Holy Land of Boston by way of the Grand Trunk Railway from Quebec to Portland (*Literary Friends*, 18), he comes to recognize that California, which had seemed exile, is different now that people are being born there every day. And Bret Harte, coming east on a princely progress from the Pacific, is reduced to recreating California again and again (*Literary Friends*, 251).

This world that is new even to the New Englander is part, of course, of the whole issue of sharing the North American continent with the British Loyalists and French to the north, the Spaniards to the south and the Indians to the West. Howells, Grant, and Adams all express concern at the Mexican war and the annexation of Texas. The values of a free republic come into conflict with the taste for power and the pull of imperialism, and autobiographers identify themselves not only by a particular region but also by what it is they understand America to be about. James writes in 1887 from an essentially dislocated generation (that grew up in "troglodytic Boston") when he describes Emerson's life in Concord with nostalgia: "fifty years of residence in the home of one's forefathers, pervaded by reading, by walking in the woods and the daily addition of sentence to sentence" (Matthiessen, 439). The serenity of pale, quiet Concord, the homogeneity of ancestry and place, represent that unity of explanation so favorable to autobiography. It is a unity for these autobiographers only as it serves memory and feeds the roots of language. For some, like Twain or Adams, it may inflect their voice and color their personality, to the end. But it is common, too, for the autobiographer to move from such identification of the self with a particular place to a larger and essentially moral purpose for writing autobiography.

MAKING AMERICA

Lucy Larcom's autobiography recreates a New England that has long since gone. Like Howells, she has had to learn to appreciate her local flora and fauna as distinct from those in English poetry and authentic in their own right; they become a resource for her American writing as the Mississippi is a resource for Twain. New England is Larcom's essential habitat, but she leaves it behind to become a missionary teacher in the west, exchanging the gray ledges of the Massachusetts coast for an endless sea of green. Like the immigrants from the old world, Americans, uprooted by whatever circumstances, move forward not so much into a post-Edenic wilderness (though nostalgia for childhood is common) as with purpose and enthusiasm for a cause that is almost invariably connected to the importance of being American.

For Henry Adams, the responsibility to understand what has happened is outweighed by the appalling responsibility to predict what will happen. Adams, however, finding his education run riot at the Chicago World Fair, receiving the dynamo as a "symbol of infinity" (380), must have crossed paths with Jane Addams, who was concerned with the unemployment and the smallpox epidemic that followed the World Fair. (He shared none of her concerns, but did know that the new woman set free since 1840 would show the world new meaning by 1940.) For Jane Addams, as for numerous autobiographers of this period, the significance of autobiography, as of life work, is political at a far more practical level than for Henry Adams. If the Civil War introduced to American literature that realism that Howells so admired in English literature, and if Howells's distinction is his ability to sit as James describes him, with his window opening close onto the American city street, these autobiographers of social causes also define their work in terms of the American scene and the making of American history.

Jane Addams, for example, travels in England, Europe, and Russia to learn her life work, but it is in the streets of Chicago that she identifies the needs of the immigrant population, of the working woman, of first-generation American children; it is her response to this religious and cultural variety that makes her work necessarily so distinctive. Unsuccessful attempts at Hull House to pool spiritual resources in some sort of communal worship contrast with the high church evening service that she has experienced as part of the routine at Oxford House in England. Their work and not their faith, she concludes, provides the appropriate community bond in a new and polyglot society.[7]

The industrial and economic conditions that troubled the social conscience in England were, of course, vastly magnified by the size of the

United States and by the speed of its growth. Where Howells took his conscience and his concern that no one in a republic should depend on the charity of another (or get something for nothing), Jacob Riis took his camera, thus providing the kind of evidence that prompted action. But his own sufferings as a boy in New York and his imagination and energies for the reform of what he had suffered and seen work also to transform him from a Dane into an American.

Riis's autobiography is a circular work in which he leaves for the land of promise only to find a lifetime of strenuous effort, but he returns to the homeland of happy memories as an elderly man only to recognize that he has made himself, indeed, American. The triumph of this achievement is presented in terms of all the good fortune for which he has worked very hard (and which he therefore deserves); the poor boy disdained by the rich girl earns the right to be her husband, the penniless immigrant becomes the respected friend of Teddy Roosevelt. It is Franklin's story in a new key and, like Franklin's, it is both personal and exemplary; its purpose is the identification by personal review and example of the good American. Whereas Grant establishes his solid worth by the (extraordinary) statement that his "family is American, and has been for generations, in all its branches, direct and collateral" (3), immigrant autobiographers need to adjust the meaning and value of their backgrounds to the new meanings and opportunities of their adopted country. They need, in short, to become assimilated.[8]

Riis is a reporter, not an historian or novelist. Curiously, though, his relatively simplistic myth of the making of an American bears comparison with Howells's more complex, more self-conscious attention to the identification and definition of a good man, and comparison, again, with Alexander Berkman's intense investigation of the nature of an anarchist (1912). Where Riis suggests that his alternatives in the face of the suffering he saw around him were to tell or turn anarchist, Berkman moves backward from his *Attentat*, his failed attempt on the life of Frick, to fierce compassion and concern for his fellow inmates in prison. America has failed for Berkman to be "a glorious free country, where men walked erect in the full stature of manhood" (20). Having been, like Riis, out of work on the streets, warming himself with newspapers, he moves to a sympathy with his fellow prisoners that surprises him—it is so untheoretical—and that alters him quite profoundly. After caring for a cause on behalf of humanity in general, he learns the value, repeatedly, of the individual. He is, necessarily, a disappointment to his anarchist associates, but he explores his motives at every stage in a manner that is both intense and reflective. His attempted statement, the killing of Frick, fails. It is fragmented, like the clarity of his anarchist purpose as translated at his trial by a blind interpreter who renders what he has to say word for word and not in coherent sentences. His failure to reach his audience, either the public by his deeds or the court by his words, turns him in upon himself and his particular context of fellow prisoners, the homeless, voiceless, and deprived. It is to these that he devotes the rest of his life and, despite the breakdown at the end, Berkman's autobiography, with its final questionable gesture of "work to do," takes from its special context a meaning that is different from that originally intended, a meaning that extends beyond him as subject or as instrument in a cause to him as part of an American community in need of a hearing.

THE MELTING POT

As the most prominent white autobiographers defined America by means of their own lives, so they created the standard or norm (just as they held, of course, the political power) that persuaded immigrant, black, Chicano, or Indian autobiographers to underplay their difference from these white exemplars and to stress their capacity for assimilation. Like Adams from the Brahmin caste, Twain or Howells from the midwest, like James in his use of New York or Addams in her use of Chicago, these minority writers begin by carrying baggage, their own history, their culture and language, or the stain of slavery; but in each case, what could be their full and authentic voice is muted or adjusted to suit a white audience and often to suggest conformity with the white culture.

Lacking the usual external confirmations of parentage and date or place of birth, the ex-slave was compelled to use an essentially forward focus for autobiography. Henry Louis Gates, for example, has described Frederick Douglass's attempts (1892) not long before his death to establish his birthdate and his distress at his identity being limited by his personal memory.[9] Frequently unable to identify themselves in any more certain form, ex-slaves write less on behalf of themselves than on behalf of their whole race in order to prove to the white reader that they are a coherent and equivalent people. Far more pronouncedly than the white, the black autobiographer is Representative Man. In this capacity, of course, Booker T. Washington plays an important part in minimizing the threat these recently discovered Americans pose to the peace or stability of the white race. He incorporates his Atlanta speech into the text of his autobiography, for example, with all the acclaim that it received, both as authentication of his public role and as significant evidence of his conformity with white expectations.

Up from Slavery achieved speedy recognition as a classic almost certainly because it minimizes black suffering and sturdily reiterates white, Christian values. (Christianity as adopted by the Afro-American or the Indian represents white civilization, seems to offer equality with whites, and too often becomes part of the ironic gap between apparent values and those that are realized in white treatment of Americans of color.) Not only does Washington pose no threat, he even implicitly suggests that the black race is primitive and in need of much help before it can be seen as truly equivalent to the white. Whereas Washington's own self-help and selfless industry may be endorsed for the white reading public by men like Carnegie and President McKinley, his delight at the Duchess of Sutherland's photograph arriving to bless Tuskegee at Christmas suggests just how profoundly his sense of worth is contaminated by notions of a white hierarchy above him (an attitude so distinctly in contrast to Howells's dream about the duke's towels as to open the whole issue of the franchise and the failed ideal of democracy). Indeed, given what he is able to tell us of his own history, Washington's personal achievements and international acclaim necessarily both cooperate and conflict within his personality.

What is more remarkable, however, than the celebrated achievement of one black autobiographer is the fact, as William L. Andrews has pointed out, that ninety black autobiographers told their stories during the same period. Andrews mentions the quantity of black autobiography and goes on to define its particular characteristics at this time: "After the Civil War," he writes, "black autobiography becomes much more concerned with the consolidation of power, the institutionalization of power, and the manipulation of power" ("Forgotten Voices," 21). He refers to the Algeresque titles of many black autobiographies and, paradoxically, the common effacement of self in the institution or cause that is useful. He identifies the end of this particular stage of black autobiography with William Pickens's revision of *The Heir of Slaves* (1911) which appeared in 1923 as *Bursting Bonds.* The significant move that Pickens makes is to reject conformity with white expectations, indeed to reject white control, in order to assert an independent and autonomous black perspective.

Such autonomy is acquired only gradually within the format of autobiography itself. Robert B. Stepto examines the stages whereby the black autobiographer moves from dependence on the white writer (in the form of prefaces and afterwords that frame and authenticate the black narrative) to an independent production whose authority is internal. Douglass is remarkable for his explicit control over his own written life despite his use of such white support, and particularly interesting for the revisions to which he submits his autobiography. He demonstrates through these revisions the importance of the black voice as a political voice serving a purpose beyond the personal. Again and again we see examples of amazing endurance and courage in slave writings and in the early days of freedom. Zilpha Elaw, for example, preaches in the slave states regardless of her personal risk (Andrews, *Sisters of the Spirit*, 49–160). Black autobiography develops significantly in this period, however, in that it determines not just the objective, historical identity or political purpose of the autobiographer but also, increasingly, the manner in which that autobiographer is seen to exist. "It is a peculiar sensation," writes Du Bois, "this double-consciousness, this sense of always looking at oneself through the eyes of others" (*Souls of Black Folk*, 3). Writing about the relationship in literature of black women with white, Minrose C. Gwin refers to the black woman's clear need expressed in autobiography "for human recognition and the white woman's inability or unwillingness to acknowledge either the need or the person behind it" (*Black and White Women*, 52).

It is not surprising, given the limited and mixed attention that the black American received in the north and in the south during Reconstruction, that these autobiographers should define their human worth in white terms or that this self-evaluation from outside, as it were, should compete within the text with the autobiographer's determination to be free from such restraints. For black women such restraints could be multiplied from within their own community; it is Andrews, again, who points to the dry humor with which Julia Foote, prevented by black ministers from preaching, writes in 1879 that "even ministers of Christ did not feel that women had any rights which they were bound to respect" (*Sisters of the Spirit*, 207), thus paraphrasing Chief Justice Roger B. Taney's conclusion to the Dred Scott decision in 1857 that black Americans "'had no rights which the white man was bound to respect'" (*Sisters of the Spirit*, 20). Julia Foote chops up the whip that is used on her in childhood. (Lucy Delaney snatches shovel, tongs, and broomstick in turn from the mistress who wants to whip her.)

Convinced of her calling, Foote is able to assert her independence within a very particular context. For many of these autobiographers, Christianity is both a spiritual equalizer and a moral force in terms of which the unvalued black was able to set and assert a personal valuation. As assumed by Christian ministers or by pioneers for the race, this personal valuation, in terms respected by the dominant white culture, is explicitly reasonable. These black autobiographers demonstrate indeed a finely tuned tension and ambivalence between expression of black individualism and commitment to white cultural values.

The self-expression is discreet and controlled. Commitment to the acceptable social values of industry, usefulness, and cooperation is pragmatic, leading through this period to the acquisition of such skills and power as would enable blacks to operate collectively for the advancement of the race. What we see in autobiography, in other words, is the appreciation of the individual personality, comprehension of the particular history that has created it, and a forward-looking motivation for life-writing as for life that may do much to explain the understatement of the past.[10]

If black autobiographers walked a tightrope on the way to self-definition and full participation in their own perspective on and contribution to American history, Chicanos and Indians were also under pressure to record their past and thus become part of the increasingly complex American story. Genaro M. Padilla makes the point that "Chicano autobiography as a distinct cultural utterance begins with that historical moment when the United States violently appropriated northern Mexico in the mid-nineteenth century" ("The Recovery," 288). In ways that relate to the black experience, "Mexicans inscribed themselves upon history as a warrant against oblivion" ("The Recovery," 289). Describing the complex sense in which the individual and racial history interlock, Padilla demonstrates an astonishing variety of Chicano selves, from religious to political to military, from the revolutionary to the Texas ranger, all responding to the destabilization of a culture and effectively establishing "identity as a destabilized condition" ("The Recovery," 292). If this is a painfully modern predicament, we may also recognize the role of the great white imperialist of letters, Hubert Howe Bancroft, who spent the 1870s collecting oral and written histories from Hispano-Mexicans. These new Americans responded ambivalently both to the Americanization they had experienced and to the culture whose erasure they were witnessing, but they produced hundreds of transcriptions of their lives into letters even as the originals were changing beyond recognition.[11]

As Bancroft tracked down the Chicano story, so numerous anthropologists were gleaning vast amounts of information (much of it also still untapped) in their pursuit of the Indian story. Our period was one of intense acculturation for American Indians, who were under pressure to assimilate, to become good Americans.[12] Arnold Krupat has discussed the distinctions between the written traditions of the east and the oral traditions that were essentially western, and we are paying more attention these days to the nature and value both of oral narrative and of what he calls "bicultural composite authorship." It is indicative of the seriousness of Indian assimilation, however, that the notion of an

extended story in which personal experience accounts for character formation or is central to a whole history is foreign to North American
Indian expression; the Indian identified himself essentially in terms
of his tribe, not at all as a unique individual. As Krupat puts it, "the
individual who spoke only for himself spoke, therefore, for no one else"
(*For Those Who Come After*, 11). What happens in autobiography, then,
is the shaping of the Indian narrative by the white interviewer for a
white audience. The interviewer, by all accounts, was frequently very
close to the narrator and sensitive in questioning and in attention.
Beyond the problems of interpretation and editing, however, we face
the initial problem of the motivation for autobiography, and we must
consider whether Indian autobiography was in fact a significant tool
in the process of Indian assimilation into white culture.

Like the representative black, the Indian speaks to the white reader
on behalf of all Indians, very commonly concentrating on the beliefs
and customs of a dying culture, either to reject them (Sam Blowsnake
has converted to the Peyote Cult and sees his former ways as errone-
ous), or to express indignation at white treatment of Indian people, or
to voice the nostalgia that must have been nurtured by Indian enthusiasts and anthropologists. A. LaVonne Ruoff has written about George
Copway as an original Indian autobiographer establishing a form "that
is reflected in the life histories of later Indian writers" (13). Ruoff also
makes the point that the strong tribal and cultural identity of the Indian makes his autobiography more akin to eighteenth-century slave
narratives, in which the African heritage finds a place, than to the
nineteenth-century black autobiography, which works entirely within
the context of the white culture of North America. David H. Brumble
has also commented on the fact that whereas ex-slaves lacked an
authenticating history and therefore imagined themselves into the
dominant white culture, the activity of autobiography turned the Indian
away from the white context because it was specifically the Indian context that was to be recreated. For the Indian, as for the black, however,
"the English written word became a powerful, new weapon in the . . .
battle for cultural survival" (Ruoff, 13). Assimilation, after all, is a matter both of absorption and of continuity.

The Indian autobiographer had models within his culture for personal
narrative, but they are, compared with Western traditions of autobiography, episodic and oriented to specific purposes. Brumble explores
Sam Blowsnake's *Confessions* as a reinvention of autobiography based
on an assortment of narrative possibilities, Native and European, that
were available to him. Another possibility for autobiography is that of
Charles Eastman, the assimilated Indian, who writes of his Indian boy-

hood as an episodic adventure sequence to delight the white reader. "What boy," he asks, "would not be an Indian for a while . . . ?" (*Indian Boyhood*, 1). His name is Hakada, the "pitiful last one." He survives the Sioux massacre as a child and spends much of his youth fleeing the Washechu, or white man. Yet he describes his life in the wild as that of the authentic Indian, the life that any boy would choose if he could; today, on the reservations, people live differently. The return of his father, long presumed dead, in Western clothes, concludes the Indian boyhood; his father introduces him to Christianity and sends him to school. We may remember Washington's complicity in "civilizing" Indians—they resist parting with blankets and pipes—and recognize that for Hakada to become Charles Eastman is a complete translation to the white man's world, a translation in which personal memory and tribal feeling are logged in the white man's museum.

SOME CONCLUSIONS

When the United States entered the war in 1917 because "the world must be made safe for democracy," it did so as an independent and coherent world power with significant experience of the aspirations of the democracy it sought to defend and of their modification under the stress of a fast-growing and polyglot *demos*. The white man's museum, representing what is formative and what, accordingly, matters in a nation's history, may describe the dominance of the white invader and ex-slave owner, but it also includes distinctive contributions to American expression and self-definition in the form of autobiographies by American Indians, Afro-Americans, and Chicanos, by immigrants, and by those able and determined women to whom Adams gives credit for the creation of the future.

Under glass, then, preserved as the making of America in this period of prolific autobiography, we may note a couple of curiosities. Firstly, we may comment on the remarkable number of autobiographies that were revised, updated, reattempted, or succeeded by later volumes. "People begin to say," Howells notes, "and not without reason, in a world so hurried and wearied as this, 'Ah, here he is again with his re-collections'" (*Literary Friends*, 242). But he was by no means alone in his repeated attempts to identify and recreate his context, his family and friends, and his past. We can, in his work as in that of most of his contemporaries, see odd contradictions between self-assertion and self-effacement, between a Wordsworthian refreshment of age at the fountain of youth, and a spider-web sensibility whose first purpose is to catch, as James puts it "every air-borne particle in its tissue" (Matthiessen, 359). I have described this complex, repeatedly other-referential autobiography as historiography, with the spider, or *bricoleur,* at the centre.[13] Indeed, Mutlu Konuk Blasing describes Adams's enterprise as solipsistic, a making of history even out of his personal theories of history: "Adams presents his progress from certainty to confusion as a journey through two centuries, which also happen to encompass all American history" (100). For a period remarkable for the disintegration of the historical sense, I have called this kind of achievement the making of America by means of the self-definition of Americans.

Secondly, this autobiography, which is so largely and frequently conscious of its extra-personal dimensions, runs into problems of critical definition. Autobiography as a genre is still subject to refinements and sophistication of definition, but the works we have been considering here seem more subject than most to generic confusion. For example, Sayre describes Adams's *Education* as an epic, Blasing describes it as comic, J. C. Levenson says it is not autobiography, and Alfred Kazin describes it as a book about the nineteenth century and finds that the letters are the true autobiography. Or again, Blasing suggests that James's genuine autobiography is neither the three volumes so identified nor the elements of self buried in the fiction but, rather, the Prefaces to the novels which tell the story of the story or provide a reconstruction of the artist's inner life. And while it is true that Adams and James may provide in their intellectual complexity some very particular problems, and that Howells may have turned autobiography into a form almost as anecdotal and prolific as Twain's talk, these literary giants were not out of step (bestriding the narrow world) with their contemporary autobiographers. Autobiography in this period was as various in form and in reassessment, revision, and sequel as it was responsive to and creative of its time and place.

Finally, it may be possible to generalize and suggest that just as the "I" is the centre of the bildungsroman, so this prolific, reiterated, revised, and inclusive production of autobiography represents, by virtue of its preoccupations and its elusive nature, the center of the democracy that consciously created itself in letters as in life during this period, as history in process.

NOTES

1 Darwin's work was available in America after the Civil War. Comte, Mill, and Tocqueville were among those most influential in political thought, Burkhardt and Dilthey in historiography, Bergson and, at home, G. Stanley Hall and William James were important in the new science of psychology.

To list is to omit, but these names may indicate the originality or reorganization of thought in areas affecting autobiography.

2 "The value of outer events which affect [the] self lies in the fact that they do so" (Wilhelm Dilthey, quoted in Stone, 11).

3 See Twain's bias most fully spelled out in *The Innocents Abroad* and *A Connecticut Yankee in King Arthur's Court*.

4 But see Eakin, *Fictions*, especially pp. 99–109, and Eakin, "Henry James's 'Obscure Hurt,' " for full and sophisticated analysis of this "hurt."

5 See Jacobson.

6 For discussion of western autobiography and the oral tradition, see Krupat, "American Autobiography." See also Krupat, *For Those Who Come After*: "when the eastern autobiographer looked to Europe for a model of the self, he also found a formal model for his book. But, if the western autobiographer, looking to the Indian, found a valuable experiential model, he found no textual model whatever" (43).

7 See also Louise De Koven Bowen (1926). And for energy and inspired contribution to society of which autobiography forms a part, see Elizabeth Cady Stanton (1898) and Julia Ward Howe (1899). For extended discussion of women's autobiographical writing, see Jelinek, *The Tradition of Women's Autobiography*, especially chapter 8.

8 See also Antin (1912), Bok (1921), Stern (1917), and Eaton (1915). Tuerk has written on Jewish American autobiography and some of the problems of immigration and assimilation in this period. See also Ling for discussion of the Eaton sisters and the disguises assumed by Asian autobiographers.

9 For black autobiography in general see Brignano. Andrews ("Forgotten Voices") includes a useful bibliography of black autobiographies written between 1865 and 1930.

10 I am indebted to William L. Andrews for clarification of the pragmatic approach to assimilation expressed in black autobiography of this period.

11 Sau-ling Cynthia Wong very kindly directed me to this material, which clearly opens a new and important area for textual and for theoretical study.

12 Krupat, (*For Those Who Come After*) quotes Francis Paul Prucha's summation of the goals of the "Friends of the Indian" to this effect (58). For an annotated bibliography of American autobiography, see Brumble (1981). For an important study of the lives of Indian women, see Bataille and Sands (1984), which includes an annotated bibliography. For analysis of the methodology of Indian autobiography and its place in American literature, see Krupat's work *passim*.

13 See Rowe (especially 120–31) on Adams's *bricolage*, taking things apart and putting them together in different relations.

WORKS CONSULTED

Adams, Henry. *Esther.* New York: Henry Holt, 1884.
Adams, Henry. *Mont-Saint-Michel and Chartres.* Boston: Houghton Mifflin, 1905.
Adams, Henry. *Democracy: An American Novel.* New York: Henry Holt, 1908.
Adams, Henry. *The Education of Henry Adams: An Autobiography.* Boston: Houghton Mifflin, 1918.
Addams, Jane. *Twenty Years at Hull-House.* New York: Macmillan, 1911.
Andrews, William L. "Forgotten Voices of Afro-American Autobiography, 1865–1930." *a/b: Auto/Biography Studies* 2 (Fall 1986): 21–27.
Andrews, William L. ed., *Sisters of the Spirit: Three Black Women's Autobiographies of the Nineteenth Century.* Bloomington: Indiana University Press, 1986.
Antin, Mary. *The Promised Land.* Boston: Houghton Mifflin, 1912.
Bancroft, Hubert Howe. *History of California.* Vols. 1–7. San Francisco: The History Company, 1884–1889.
Bancroft, Hubert Howe. *Pastoral California.* San Francisco: The History Company, 1888.
Bancroft, Hubert Howe. *Literary Industries.* San Francisco: The History Company, 1890.
Bataille, Gretchen M., and Kathleen Mullen Sands. *American Indian Women: Telling Their Lives.* Lincoln: University of Nebraska Press, 1984.
Berkman, Alexander. *Prison Memoirs of an Anarchist.* New York: Mother Earth, 1912.
Blasing, Mutlu Konuk. *The Art of Life: Studies in American Autobiographical Literature.* Austin: University of Texas Press, 1977.
Bok, Edward. *The Americanization of Edward Bok: The Autobiography of a Dutch Boy Fifty Years After.* New York: Charles Scribner's Sons, 1921.
Bowen, Louise De Koven. *Growing Up With a City.* New York: Macmillan, 1926.
Brignano, Russell C. *Black Americans in Autobiography: An Annotated Bibliography of Autobiographies and Autobiographical Books Written Since the Civil War.* Durham, NC: Duke University Press, 1974.
Brumble, David H., III. *An Annotated Bibliography of American Indian and Eskimo Autobiographies.* Lincoln: University of Nebraska Press, 1981.
Brumble, David H., III. "Sam Blowsnake's Confessions: *Crashing Thunder* and the History of American Autobiography." In *Recovering the Word: Essays in Native American Literature.* Ed. Brian Swann and Arnold Krupat. Berkeley and Los Angeles: University of California Press, 1987, 537–51.
Butterfield, Stephen. *Black Autobiography in America.* Amherst: University of Massachusets Press, 1974.
Chona, Maria. *Papago Woman.* Ed. Ruth M. Underhill. New York: Holt, Rinehart & Winston, 1979.
Cooley, Thomas. *Educated Lives: The Rise of Modern Autobiography in America.* Columbus: Ohio State University Press, 1976.
Copway, George. *Life, History, and Travels of Kah-ge-ga-gah-bowh.* Albany, NY: Weed and Parsons, 1847.

Couser, G. Thomas. *American Autobiography: The Prophetic Mode*. Amherst: University of Massachusetts Press, 1979.

Cox, James M. *Mark Twain: The Fate of Humor*. Princeton: Princeton University Press, 1966.

Cox, James M. "Autobiography and America." *Virginia Quarterly Review* 47 (1971): 252–77.

Douglass, Frederick. *Life and Times of Frederick Douglass: Written by Himself.* [1892]. London: Collier Books, 1962.

Du Bois, W. E. Burghardt. *The Souls of Black Folk: Essays and Sketches*. A. C. McClurg, 1903.

Eakin, Paul John. *Fictions in Autobiography: Studies in the Art of Self-Invention*. Princeton: Princeton University Press, 1985.

Eakin, Paul John. "L'autobiographie américaine au XIXe siècle: tendances récentes de la recherche." *Romantisme* 56 (1987): 118–32.

Eakin, Paul John. "Henry James's 'Obscure Hurt': Can Autobiography Serve Biography?" *New Literary History* 29 (1987–88): 675–92.

Eastman, Charles Alexander. *Indian Boyhood*. [1902]. Boston: Little, Brown, 1922.

Eaton, Winnifred. *Me, a Book of Remembrance*. New York: Centuary Company, 1915.

Gates, Henry Louis, Jr. *Figures in Black: Words, Signs, and the "Racial" Self*. New York: Oxford University Press, 1987.

Grant, U.S. *Personal Memoirs of U.S. Grant*. [1885]. New York: The World Publishing Co., 1952.

Gwin, Minrose C. *Black and White Women of the Old South: The Peculiar Sisterhood in American Literature*. Knoxville: University of Tennessee Press, 1985.

Howe, Julia Ward. *Reminiscences 1819–1899*. New York: Houghton Mifflin, 1899.

Howells, Mildred, ed. *Life in Letters of William Dean Howells*. 2 vols. New York: Doubleday Doran, 1928.

Howells, W. D. *A Boy's Town*. New York: Harper & Bros. 1890.

Howells, W. D. *Impressions and Experiences*. [1896]. Freeport, NY: Books for Libraries Press, 1972.

Howells, W. D. *Literary Friends and Acquaintances: A Personal Retrospect of American Authorship*. [1902]. Bloomington: Indiana University Press, 1968.

Howells, W. D. "Autobiography, A New Form of Literature." *Harper's Monthly* 119 (1909): 795–98.

Howells, W. D. *New Leaf Mills: A Chronicle*. Harper & Bros., 1913.

Howells, W. D. *Years of My Youth*. [1916]. Bloomington: Indiana University Press, 1975.

Jacobson, Marcia. "The Mask of Fiction: William Dean Howells's Experiments in Autobiography." *biography* 10 (1987): 55–67.

James, Henry. *Hawthorne*. London: Macmillan, 1887.

James, Henry. *A Small Boy and Others*. London: Macmillan, 1913.

James, Henry. *Notes of a Son and Brother*. London: Macmillan, 1914.

James, Henry. *The Middle Years*. London: Collins & Son, 1917.

Jelinek, Estelle C. "The Paradox and Success of Elizabeth Cady Stanton." In *Women's Autobiography: Essays in Criticism*. Ed. E. Jelinek. Bloomington: Indiana University Press, 1980, 71–92.

Jelinek, Estelle C. *The Tradition of Woman's Autobiography: From Antiquity to the Present*. New York: Twayne, 1986.

Kaplan, Louis, with James Tyler Cook, Clinton E. Colby Jr., and Daniel C. Haskell. *A Bibliography of American Autobiographies*. Madison: University of Wisconsin Press, 1961.

Kazin, Alfred. *An American Procession*. New York: Alfred A. Knopf, 1984.

Krupat, Arnold. "American Autobiography: The Western Tradition." *Georgia Review* 35 (1981): 307–17.

Krupat, Arnold. *For Those Who Come After: A Study of Native American Autobiography*. Berkeley and Los Angeles: University of California Press, 1985.

Larcom, Lucy. *A New England Girlhood: Outlined from Memory*. [1889]. New York: Corinth Books, 1961.

Levenson, J.C. *The Mind and Art of Henry Adams*. Boston: Houghton Mifflin, 1957.

Lillard, Richard G. *American Life in Autobiography: A Descriptive Guide*. Stanford, CA: Stanford University Press, 1956.

Ling, Amy. "Revelation and Mask: Autobiographies of the Eaton Sisters." *a/b: Auto/Biography Studies* 3 (Summer 1987): 46–52.

Lurie, Nancy Oestreich. *Mountain Wolf Woman, Sister of Crashing Thunder: The Autobiography of a Winnebago Indian*. Ann Arbor: University of Michigan Press, 1961.

Matthiessen, F. O. *The James Family*. New York: Knopf, 1947.

Padilla, Genaro M. "The Recovery of Chicano Nineteenth-Century Autobiography." *American Quarterly* 40 (September 1988): 286–306.

Padilla, Genaro M., ed. *Chicano Autobiographies: An Anthology*. Albuquerque: University of New Mexico Press, 1989.

Pickens, William. *The Heir of Slaves*. Boston: Pilgrim Press, 1911.

Pickens, William. *Bursting Bonds*. Boston: Jordan & More, 1923.

Radin, Paul. *Crashing Thunder: The Autobiography of a Winnebago Indian*. [1926]. Lincoln: University of Nebraska Press, 1983.

Riis, Jacob A. *The Making of an American*. [1901]. London: Macmillan, 1970.

Rowe, John Carlos. *Henry Adams and Henry James: The Emergence of Modern Consciousness*. Ithaca: Cornell University Press, 1976.

Ruoff, A. LaVonne Brown. "George Copway: Nineteenth-Century American-Indian Autobiographer." *a/b: Auto/Biography Studies* 3 (Summer 1987): 6–17.

Samuels, Ernest. *The Young Henry Adams*. [1948]. Cambridge: Harvard University Press, 1965.

Samuels, Ernest. *Henry Adams: The Middle Years*. Cambridge: Harvard University Press, 1958.

Samuels, Ernest. *Henry Adams: The Major Phase*. Harvard University Press, 1964.

Sayre, Robert F. *The Examined Self: Benjamin Franklin, Henry Adams, Henry James*. Princeton: Princeton University Press, 1964.

Sayre, Robert F. "Autobiography and the Making of America." *Autobiography: Essays Theoretical and Critical.* Ed. James Olney. Princeton: Princeton University Press, 1980, 146–68.

Spengemann, W. C., and L. R. Lundquist. "Autobiography and the American Myth." *American Quarterly* 17 (1965): 501–19.

Spiller, Robert E. "Henry Adams." In *Literary History*, 1080–1103.

Spiller, Robert E. et al., eds. *Literary History of the United States.* [1946]. 3rd ed., rev. New York: Macmillan, 1963.

Stanton, Elizabeth Cady. *Eighty Years and More: Reminiscences, 1815–1897.* [1898]. New York: Schocken Books, 1971.

Stepto, Robert B. *From Behind the Veil: A Study of Afro-American Narrative.* Champaign-Urbana: University of Illinois Press, 1979.

Stern, E. G. *My Mother and I.* New York: Macmillan, 1917.

Stone, Albert E. *Autobiographical Occasions and Original Acts: Versions of American Identity from Henry Adams to Nate Shaw.* Philadelphia: University of Pennsylvania Press, 1982.

Tuerk, Richard. "Assimilation in Jewish-American Autobiography: Mary Antin and Ludwig Lewisohn." *a/b: Auto/Biography Studies* 3 (Summer 1987): 26–33.

Twain, Mark. *The Innocents Abroad, Or The New Pilgrim's Progress.* Hartford, CT: American Publishing, 1869.

Twain, Mark. *Roughing It.* Hartford, CT: American Publishing, 1872.

Twain, Mark. *Life on the Mississippi.* Boston: James R. Osgood, 1883.

Twain, Mark. *A Connecticut Yankee in King Arthur's Court.* New York: Charles L. Webster, 1889.

Twain, Mark. *The Autobiography of Mark Twain: Including Chapters Now Published for the First Time.* [1917]. Ed. Charles Neider. New York: Harper & Bros., 1959.

Washington, Booker T. *Up From Slavery: An Autobiography.* [1901]. New York: Dodd, Mead, 1965.

Wecter, Dixon. "Mark Twain." In Spiller et al., eds., *Literal History*, 917–39.

CHAPTER 4

Modern American Autobiography: Texts and Transactions

ALBERT E. STONE

The last fifty or sixty years do not necessarily make a distinct and self-evident period in American cultural life; or if years fall into a unity for some, that coherence is not recognized by others. What rationale, then, for opening this survey of representative texts and transactions with the 1930s, or indeed any succeeding boundary decade? One might assert that, realistically speaking, the Depression and the coming of World War II mark the farther reaches of most adult American memories and historical imaginations. The world of the thirties is the first world remembered by this generation's parents or grandparents, and there are autobiographies by both men and women to document that horizon. A broader explanation holds that during that decade fundamental changes in cultural consciousness occurred which suggested, at least at the time, a real break with the past. Whether fact or fancy, these changes affect the writing and reading of autobiography as individual versions of history. But autobiographies are imaginative creations, too, and part of literary history. In characterizing the literary thirties, a trend away from the modernist experiments (often ahistorical) of the twenties can be perceived. This movement is typified by the succession of spokesmen: in poetry, from Eliot and Pound to Sandburg and MacLeish; in drama, from O'Neill to Odets; in fiction, from Fitzgerald to Steinbeck, from Toomer to Wright. Is autobiography as nonfictional prose susceptible to similar shifts and paradigms which bespeak the pressures of public as well as artistic events?

As simultaneously expressive experiment and historical record, autobiography confirms but also complicates such contrasts between one era's elite art and another's demotic realism. Furthermore, autobiographies and eras don't correlate as easily, at least in this century, as James M. Cox argued in his trailblazing essay "Autobiography and America." More generally, nevertheless, life history provides a valuable resource for speculating concretely about cultural change and the larger problem of periodizing history. As Fredric Jameson points out in "Periodizing the Sixties", there is the existential fact that "veterans of a decade who have seen so many things change dramatically from year to year, think more historically than their predecessors." (178) If true of the sixties, perhaps it is also true of earlier decades and generations in this century of rapid, often violent transformations. Jameson therefore defends periodizing while warning against facile generalizations about "massive kinship and homogeneity or identity within a given period." He argued instead that any era is characterized by the interplay of what is dominant—culturally, economically, politically—and what is deviant and original. In fact, "it is surely only against a certain conception of what is historically dominant or hegemonic that the full value of the exceptional—what Raymond Williams calls the 'residual' or 'emergent'—can be assessed. Here, in any case, the 'period' in question is understood not as some omnipresent and uniform shared style or way of thinking and acting, but rather as the sharing of a common objective situation, to which a whole range of varied responses and creative innovations is then possible, but always within that situation's structural limits." (178)

Given the limits of this collection's agenda, it is impossible to describe in detail the "common objective situations" within and against which American autobiographers have written over the past half-dozen decades. It will prove easier to argue the value of the exceptional, the residual, the emergent. For in a true sense, each autobiography is a *sui generis* artifact reflecting a particular vision of past, present, and future. Nevertheless, as a critical desideratum, the grounding of an individual text in its manifold cultural conditions is an essential part of any evaluation. At its inception, personal history represents a historically conditioned transaction between a surviving witness or participant and available records of the past. These embrace memories above all, but also correspondence, interviews, diaries, photographs, newspapers, and other library resources. What results is an account designedly individual and partial. Hence the reservations some social scientists like Herbert Blumer voice about the reliability of autobiographical data as historical or sociological evidence. Nonetheless, autobiographies are useful in throwing light on the time-bound perceptions of past events and on the effects of, and responses of individuals to, the structural features (e.g. institutions and social process) of given historical moments. Autobiographies are even more valuable in demonstrating how, and under what interplay of remembered and applicable circumstances, people put into words the stories of their development as selves in their world. Given the notorious weakness of memory, the autobiographical act as history is more trustworthy as a record of the author's reactivations than of the actor's original behavior and perceptions.

Resources for investigating and ordering these problematic relations between texts and contexts are rich and rapidly growing, thanks to the scholarship of many critics and cultural historians cultivating this fertile field of American studies. An essential tool is the bibliography. Over the past few decades, five basic collections have appeared: Richard G. Lillard, *American Life in Autobiography, A Descriptive Guide*; Louis Kaplan et al., *A Bibliography of American Autobiographies*; Russell C. Brignano, *Black Americans in Autobiography: An Annotated Bibliography of Autobiographies and Autobiographical Books Written since the Civil War*; Patricia K. Addis, *Through a Woman's I: An Annotated Bibliography of American Women's Autobiographical Writings, 1946–1976*; Mary Louise Briscoe, Lynn Z. Bloom, and Barbara Tobias, *American Autobiography, 1945–1980*. Especially where annotated, these volumes help identify literally hundreds of personal narratives published annually. Although all sorts and conditions of Americans, from the most famous to the previously quite unknown, have become autobiographers, it is true that the past half-century has seen a remarkable efflorescence of personal histories by a wide spectrum of amateur and professional writers. Kaplan's subject index indicates the range in 1962 of social groups, occupations, ideologies, and geographical origins which were well or poorly represented. The index also identifies significant historical events in which autobiographers played a part. In addition, Kaplan and the others draw attention to the growing numbers of autobiographical subjects not fitting obvious categories. Among these are "accounts of spiritual development, physical infirmity, and mental illness" (Kaplan, 326), and the life-stories of immigrants, exiles, prisoners, and expatriates.

From bibliographies and other channels (ranging from *Publisher's Weekly* and Sunday book reviews to women's reading clubs and word-of-mouth advice from college-age children fresh from courses on American autobiography), present-day readers have in large numbers been attracted to autobiographies. Increased self- and group-consciousness among women and blacks, the paperback revolution since World War II, book clubs, and other new sales outlets have encouraged the spread of this consumer group, whose common denominator is an interest in others' lives and storytelling styles. These accounts appear now in a variety of conventional forms and new narrative modes: memoirs and confessions, testaments and apologies, diaries and journals, collaborations and collections of letters. A communication network has developed in which authors and audiences are brought together, "superintended" (as the British narralogist Tony Bennett puts it) by editors, ghostwriters, publishers, saleswomen and admen, reviewers and critics, schoolteachers, peer groups, and sometimes even politicians, psychiatrists, and priests. Thereby a simple entry in Brignano or Addis is transformed from isolated text into social occasion and cultural transaction. By means of text-acts like those of Lincoln Steffens, Black Elk, Gertrude Stein, Eleanor Roosevelt, and W. E. B. Du Bois—to cite five familiar Depression-era autobiographies—complex messages are exchanged, often in a peculiarly affective way. Historical facts, social attitudes and values, political and ideological commentary, and a range of personal experiences and emotional states are preserved, transmitted, and discussed.

Indeed, every autobiographical publication is a critical and collective activity as well as idiosyncratic creative expression. In Jean Starobinski's familiar formulation, autobiography is "discourse" and "history." By turning a lifetime into a pattern of words, the autobiographer's imagination makes a narrative shape, or *fictio*, resemble chronicle, novel, myth, melodrama, dream. But that same activity always reactivates a past shared with others, one now available to be tested by still others as having actually occurred more or less as stated. Retrospective examination and reflection, together with the often shared and always superintended process of composition, exert controls over the notoriously fickle, self-serving, present-oriented operations of memory and desire. Autobiographers need and court readers, especially sympathetic ones who will generously confirm the identity of the self who writes and the self who lived. But most autobiographers also expect skeptical readers. Indeed, their own historical consciousness activated by writing, and their propensity to confess as well as commit deceptions and errors, draw attention to the different kinds of truth aimed at and/or achieved.

To read and exploit autobiographies as history, then, not only requires critical attention to the text, to what is said and not said, but involves going beyond the text in order to grasp a sometimes elusive set of aims and putatively "truthful" assertions. For these purposes a variety of aids is now available: biographies, historical and literary critiques of a period, an author's single other work or entire career, as well as other autobiographies for contrast and comparison. How these might work together may be illustrated for readers of Richard Wright's *Black Boy*.

Alerted by the well-nigh unrelieved bitterness of the actor's early family life and by the author's attitudes toward blacks' emotional ties in general, readers can turn for help to Michel Fabre's masterful biography, *The Unfinished Quest of Richard Wright* in order to get a clearer fix on the emotional distance between the two Richard Wrights and their worlds. Additional clarification is available by contrasting Wright's childhood and youth with a sample of parallel accounts by Du Bois, Zora Neale Hurston, James Baldwin, Malcolm X, Claude Brown, Maya Angelou, or Anne Moody. Finally, various critical perspectives on Wright as literary ancestor to many of these other autobiographers are found in the growing number of discussions of black autobiography by George E. Kent, Sidonie Smith, Stephen Butterfield, Robert Stepto, Regina Blackburn, and Houston A. Baker. While literary-minded readers might use such resources to define Wright's status within stylistic tradition, historians can use the same text and its contextualizing materials (including Wright's sequel, *American Hunger*) to assess what is deviant and original and what was shared in the common situation blacks faced before, during, and after the Depression. Oppression and poverty may have been well-nigh universal features of the common historical situation, but that is not to say that Wright's memories of food (its scarcity at the orphanage, its abundance on Uncle Hoskins's table) mean the same thing as , say, Maya Angelou's recollection of eating powdered eggs in the Store in Stamps. This linkage of biscuits and powdered eggs suggests that many autobiographers often make history in ways close to current models of women's history—with their emphasis on private and domestic experience—as well as recording the more public, less intimate concerns of (male) textbook histories.

The necessity of assistance from scholars, biographers, and other writers for clarifying an autobiographer's struggle with literal and symbolic truth is differently illustrated in the case of Gertrude Stein. Even sympathetic readers of *The Autobiography of Alice B. Toklas* question the tricky ways in which Stein aggrandizes her role as creative genius yet simultaneously hints at her own deceptions in constructing a touchingly oblique love story. *Everybody's Autobiography*, its sequel, cannot expose or explain all of these eloquent deceptions, whose true function is to articulate the personal myth of Gertrude Stein. Counter-claims and corrections by others—e.g., by Ernest Hemingway in *A Moveable Feast*—are usually just as difficult to decode. On critical issues having to do with biography or literary criticism, it is necessary again to seek help from critics like Richard Bridgman and Wendy Steiner and biographers like John Malcolm Brinnin or Janet Hobhouse. Yet biography must never be blindly accepted as the measuring rod of other compari-

sons and interpretations. In fact, a common feature of current understandings of autobiography as a distinct kind of narrative is its distance
from biography. Among other challenging innovations likely to be
underestimated by biographers, the first edition of *Alice B. Toklas* is illustrated by a remarkable series of photographs by Man Ray and Carl
Van Vechten. The multiple function of these photographs as historical,
psychological, and artistic messages over and around the text has been
analyzed by Paul Alkon, and the general principles suggested about
"visual rhetoric" can be applied to other illustrated autobiographies like
Margaret Mead's *Blackberry Winter* and the recent anthology of brief
autobiographies each built around a family snapshot, *A World Unsuspected*, edited by Alex Harris.

Two perennial problems in interpreting any autobiographical act are
here highlighted. One is the overdetermined nature of all assertions in
autobiographical texts and the problem of their "truth" value to others
as compared to the author. Closely allied is the matter of the nature of
the communication, which originates in the autobiographer's context
but is reactivated in each reader's. In ways subtly different from other
literary or historical narratives, autobiography conventionally presupposes a "pact" or "contract" by which creator and consumer tacitly
agree on each others' co-creating roles, duties, and liberties. For many
readers in the past, this understanding was explicitly historical: the
autobiographer was expected to subordinate imagination to the attempt
to communicate trustworthy, verifiable, subjective messages. Proposed
terms of individual arrangements are often announced in a preface or
introduction, whose presence once assured readers that they were not
beginning a novel but a "true story." However, this convention has
recently broken down. A number of contemporary autobiographers
(not all of them practicing novelists) use prefaces to manipulate and
question the concept of any trustworthy pact. "If the reader prefers, this
book may be regarded as fiction," Hemingway states in the preface to
A Moveable Feast. "But there is always the chance that such a book of
fiction may throw some light on what has been written as fact." Critics
who treat most fully this question of the changing nature of such
reciprocal understandings (and mystifications) are Philippe Lejeune,
Le Pacte autobiographique, and Elizabeth Bruss, *Autobiographical Acts: The
Changing Situation of a Literary Genre.*

Whether intended or taken as imaginative creation or historical reconstruction, an autobiography is part and parcel of cultural history.
At publication, it is embedded in one situation; then each reader reem-
beds the story in her or his own private and social context. Whether as
bestseller or unnoticed work, the autobiography then begins its unique

history. Culturally important American life-stories have often become reembedded in later moments and different sets of circumstances, with new or renewed meanings. A signal instance of rebirth is *Black Elk Speaks: Being the Life Story of a Holy Man of the Oglala Sioux*. John G. Neihardt's collaboration with Black Elk, a more than usually collective transaction in 1930 and 1931, produced a unique history of cultural conflict from 1863 to 1890. The text went largely unnoticed in 1932, but when reissued in paperback in 1961, it soon fired the imaginations of a large, and since faithful, readership. *Black Elk Speaks* contributed to and drew new significance from the spiritual quests of sixties Americans. This social impact may or may not include members of the Sioux nation, however, whose responses are seldom preserved in Wasichu libraries.

If *Black Elk Speaks* typifies the historical phenomenon of delayed influence, a later collaboration represents an immediate and steady success. As a powerful political and spiritual message, *The Autobiography of Malcolm X* rapidly assumed the status of a sixties and seventies monument. It is possible that the most important act of the Black Muslim preacher's life was telling his story to Alex Haley. Its fame and force derive from a concatenation of circumstances. These included Malcolm X's tragic assassination, paperback publication at a key juncture in racial politics, early critical reception by white critics who, like Warner Berthoff, hailed it a "contemporary classic," and, most pertinent factor of all, the raw energy and honesty of Malcolm X's oral performance as stimulated and recorded by Alex Haley. Though it is difficult to assess precisely the cultural influence of any literary/historical work, *The Autobiography of Malcolm X* has reached perhaps millions of readers of both races, many of whom acknowledge that their feelings about race, violence, religion, and global politics have been permanently affected by it. This hypothesis, though based on twenty years' experience in predominantly white classrooms, does not mean that black readers respond like white readers or that women of whatever race can ignore Malcolm X's misogyny and his belated efforts to overcome it.

If autobiographies, despite and because of their over-determined nature as narratives, are unique sources of historical information and, occasionally at least, of power and influence, they are by the same token literary documents within a distinct tradition and network. Though definitions vary, the fact than an autobiography is a nonfiction story of a self's public and private experiences is the basis of most contracts or working assumptions. As a special kind of imaginative experience, autobiography has grown steadily in popularity with readers and critics. This surge of interest originated in the 1960s. The cultural history of that decisive decade could scarcely be conceived without recognizing the impact on American minds of new modes of personal writing: the New Journalism; oral history à la Studs Terkel; faction, metafiction, and surfiction; the revised diary; and the testamentary essay. Public life was represented and criticized in highly idiosyncratic prose experiments like *The Autobiography of Malcolm X*, Norman Mailer's *The Armies of the Night*, Hunter Thompson's *Hell's Angels*, George Jackson's *Soledad Brother*, and Michael Herr's *Dispatches*. At the same time, the inner reaches of American consciousness were explored in other texts and types of personal prose. Within a dozen or fifteen years (extending into the seventies), the national literature of nonfictional prose was enriched as perhaps in no previous period of history.

In autobiography, this flowering was anticipated by two texts of the fifties whose authors revised successive editions in such extended exercises of retrospective imagination as to turn each virtually into a sixties phenomenon. Vladimir Nabokov's *Speak, Memory* and Mary McCarthy's *Memories of a Catholic Girlhood* were followed by other artfully mysterious narratives in which clear-cut boundaries between autobiography and fiction seemed all but obliterated. Frank Conroy's *Stop-time*, Frederick Exley's *A Fan's Notes*, Lillian Hellman's *An Unfinished Woman* and *Pentimento: A Book of Portraits*, and Maxine Hong Kingston's *The Woman Warrior: Memoirs of a Girlhood Among Ghosts* proved variously, often immensely, popular with readers. But all became cannon fodder for critics who, during the same decade or later, established ongoing critical debates over autobiography and its complex nature as narrative. These discussions have frequently appeared in those scholarly journals receptive to autobiographical studies: *American Quarterly, New Literary History, Critical Inquiry, Journal of Interdisciplinary History, Clio, Biography, Genre, Black American Literary Forum* and *Genders,* among others.

Initial questions have centered on authorship, authority, and narrative techniques and their implications. About their interrelations, Erik Erikson observed in *Life History and the Historical Moment* that "autobiographies are written at certain late stages of life for the purpose of re-creating oneself in the image of one's own method; and they are written to make that image convincing" (125). Though the criteria of literary method and convincing image cover autobiographical acts of any era, the assumption that autobiographies appear at later stages in their creators' life cycles sounds almost quaint to present-day ears, for a noteworthy aspect of autobiography of the past generation has been the numbers of personal histories written by young, previously unpublished writers. Indeed, *The Autobiography of W. E. B. Du Bois: A Soliloquy on Viewing My Life from the Last Decade of Its First Century* stands out in this period, if not as a solitary monument to the traditional old man's memoir, then as something distinct from many of its contemporaries. Du Bois's *Soliloquy* also represents a departure from its own predecessors, *Darkwater: Voices from within the Veil* and *Dusk of Dawn: An Essay Toward an Autobiography of a Race Concept*. More typical than any of these are modern narratives like Maya Angelou's *I Know Why the Caged Bird Sings*, Conroy's *Stoptime*, Kingston's *The Woman Warrior*, Patricia Hampl's *A Romantic Education*, Richard Rodriguez's *Hunger of Memory*, and Susan Allen Toth's *Blooming: A Small Town Girlhood*, all of which announce the arrival of new, young writers, some of whom, like Maya Angelou, have made a career of successive autobiographies.

In fact, the serial or multiple autobiography is today an accepted alternative to the "one life/one autobiography" convention. Creating a running account of even an ordinary life is a plausible response to Malcolm X's question, "How is it possible to write one's autobiography in a world so fast-changing as this?" (408). In reply, successive stories of the self have been written by persons as differently located in American literary culture as Theodore Dreiser, W. E. B. Du Bois, Alfred Kazin, Maya Angelou, Lillian Hellman, and Shirley Maclaine. A special version of this activity is the revised diary or journal, the signal modern instance of which is *The Diary of Anaïs Nin*, now in seven volumes. Nin's artistic and psychological dissatisfaction with memory and the retrospective stance towards experience led the older woman to work with Gunther Stuhlmann so that, in volume 1 for instance, the diurnal ideas and emotions of the young artist and lay psychoanalyst in Paris were reseen as stages in the development of a self in continuous evolution and transformation. A stable, final self frozen in prose is, then, repudiated by autobiographers as polar as Malcolm X, Anaïs Nin and Lillian Hellman, whose variously "convincing" methods of self-recreation are the oral performance, the nightly diary entry, and the book of portraits.

As already mentioned, the collaborative autobiography has become an accepted mode in the modern era for recreating one partner's convincing image. Variations on this collective transaction have proliferated since the early thirties, when Black Elk and John G. Neihardt joined forces to preserve the aged, blind man's boyhood visions and to record the final tragic phase of the white/Native American confrontation on the upper Great Plains. "No good thing can be done by any man alone", Black Elk observes at the outset, (2) and this redefinition of autobiographical convention on the basis of an age-old attitude toward human relationships has reverberated through the years. In addition to Nin and Stuhlmann, other joint enterprises by Stein and Toklas, Malcolm X and Haley, Nate Shaw (Ned Cobb) and Theodore Rosengarten, John

Wideman and his brother Robby, Kesho Scott, Cherry Muhanji, and Egyirba High have appeared—often to popular and critical acclaim. Even more popular, of course, are the ghostwritten autobiographies of politicians and football players which appear and fade in weekly succession. Critical purists may denounce such violations of the code, limiting "true" autobiographies to stories in which author and historical actor are identical. But this merely underscores the protean nature of contemporary texts and the changing practices by which they are produced. Responses to this common practice also reflect sharply divergent views of personal identity and literary genre or form. Thus it may be no coincidence that most collaborations have women, blacks, or Native Americans as subjects. At stake here is the hoary myth of the self-sufficient American male, whose central role since Franklin was reaffirmed in 1965 by William C. Spengemann and L. R. Lundquist. "This notion of individual identity, in fact, may well be the central belief of our culture," they declared. "With all its ramifications—personal responsibility, individual destiny, dissent, vocation, and so forth—it forms the core of our being and the fabric of our history" (516). A similar conflict between myth and ideology characterizes another early example of autobiographical criticism, Carol Ohmann's relocation of *The Autobiography of Malcolm X* in the Franklinian lineage of American success stories. Such interpretations, insightful as they are regarding particular texts and textual features, betray an insensitivity to social and ideological divisions in our society, including collective (rather than atomistic) assumptions about personal identity honored in subgroups and by oppressed genders.

Involved in these formal developments and cultural splits are the same literary techniques deployed in virtually all autobiographical texts. The artistic resources for creating convincing images are, as James Olney and Francis Russell Hart early enumerated, narration with its characteristics of pace and momentum; metaphors of self through which verbal patterns and bridges are constructed from narrative details; description, reflection, argument, and meditation; and other common literary features including characterization, dialogue, dramatic scenes, and synecdoche. If chronological narrative is the verbal construct representing a character's movement through time and history, then metaphor is the medium by which other levels of being and consciousness are communicated. Various vivid and highly metaphoric patterns distinguish many contemporary autobiographies. Readers of all degrees of sophistication recognize the linked references to clothing and name-changes in *The Autobiography of Malcolm X*, which stand for the multiple transformations and continuities in Malcolm Little's life. Intertextuality, too, is established through common patterns of metaphor with different personal meanings—Nabokov's butterflies, for instance, and Mary McCarthy's tin butterfly. The balance between narrative movement and changes on the one hand and metaphoric clues to pattern and continuity on the other is frequently struck in an autobiography's opening and closing sections. Thus the Prologue and Epilogue of *Stop-time* announce and then repeat a pattern in Conroy's youthful experience, tying together automobiles, games, fears of death and insanity, and stoic endurance into an explanatory image, episode, or other synecdoche. Thereby metaphor sometimes implies a psychological stability at variance with the actor's historical experience and states of being. When that occurs, autobiography demonstrates its power to compress into one image or scene the author's dual sense of unruly reality and ideal order.

Some metaphors of self are embedded in dreams and visions which fuse transcendent and temporal existence. This is memorably exemplified in the Great Vision in *Black Elk Speaks*. First, the nine-year-old boy in airy transport looks down on himself and his people represented by the image of the hoop of peoples, at the center of which blooms the holy tree, where the red road and the black road intersect. The ideal state of being in both nature and nation is represented by the red road, while the black road pictures bitter history in the forms of highways, railroads, rifle barrels, and other prophetic symbols of the Wasichu's fateful thrust into the round world of Black Elk and his people. Such compressions of pace and pattern are not limited to modern spiritual narratives like Black Elk's, Thomas Merton's, or Annie Dillard's. They are found everywhere in this mode of writing from Jonathan Edwards to John Woolman to Henry David Thoreau. All spiritual autobiographers wrestle with the problem Merton expresses via metaphor in recording his ecstatic moment of divine illumination in Havana's Church of St. Francis. "The strange thing about this light was that although it seemed so 'ordinary' in the sense I have mentioned, and so accessible, there was no way of recapturing it. In fact I did not even know how to start trying to reconstruct the experience or bring it back if I wanted to, except to make acts of faith and love" (279). A useful overview of American religious autobiographies has been prepared by Robert F. Sayre. A more extended and theoretical approach to such texts and transactions is found in Janet Varner Gunn's *Autobiography: Toward a Poetics of Experience*.

Characterization and dialogue are equally common devices for treating actual persons as literary figures. If metaphor and synecdoche indicate autobiography's connections with poetry and prayer, the representation of characters in action, with strings of words in their often long-dead mouths, typifies the fictional and dramatic resources of the autobiographal act. Fiction is the privileged narrative model for most present-day readers, so the question routinely arises, is not autobiography a form of failed fiction—"in effect a novel written in the present with one's past life as its subject," as Burton Pike has phrased it (337)? Some authors and readers admit that statements about all actual or historical figures—Du Bois's Booker T. Washington, say, or Exley's Frank Gifford—can only be literary constructs, never statements of fact. "Obviously, autobiography does not appeal to us as readers because it is more true to the facts than is fiction, " Alfred Kazin has written, "it is just another way of telling a story, it tells another kind of story, and it uses facts as a strategy" ("Autobiography as Narrative," 213). The author of *A Walker in the City* and other autobiographies concluded in 1964 that a writer simply cannot employ fictional devices without actually creating fictional texts.

Vigorously dissenting from this opinion is another practicing autobiographer. In the 1957 version of *Memories of a Catholic Girlhood*, Mary McCarthy finally achieves an autobiographical text which expresses both her imaginative and historical aims. There, *Memories* combines previously published stories from *The New Yorker* and *Harper's Bazaar* and newly written interchapters printed in italics. The function of these added sections is to comment on the stories with their often conflicting claims and characterizations. Since she is a well-known novelist, she wonders, "Can it be that the public takes for granted that anything written by a professional writer is *eo ipso* untrue?" (9). In this case, doubts are further complicated by the autobiographical fact that the young girl Mary, as the result of family and religious conflicts, became an inveterate liar. Consequently, in the initial "To The Reader," McCarthy spells out the terms of her pact or autobiographical contract.

Many a time, in the course of doing these memoirs I have wished that I were writing fiction. The temptation to invent has been very strong, particularly where recollection is hazy and I remember the substance of an event but not the details—the color of a dress, the pattern of a carpet, the placing of a picture. Sometimes I have yielded, as in the case of the conversations. My memory is good, but obviously I cannot recall whole passages of dialogue that took place years ago. Only a few single sentences stand out: "They'd make you toe the chalk line," "Perseverence wins the crown," "My child, you must have faith." The conversations, as given, are mostly fictional. Quotation marks indicate that a conversation to this general effect took place, but I do not vouch for the exact words or the exact order of the speeches (9–10).

Several critics subsequently caught up in this dispute about truth in autobiography come down on the side of Mary McCarthy. One is Barrett

J. Mandel, for whom the fact that this statement occurs in "To The Reader" is crucial. Though certain critics deny all claims by autobiographers that their narratives are nonfiction, Mandel believes readers seldom have trouble telling one from the other. By experience, they know how writers in one genre borrow from other genres or modes. "Of course it is true that autobiographers use techniques of fiction, but such usage does not turn an autobiography into a fiction any more than Dvořak's use of folk motifs turns the *New World Symphony* into a folk song. At every moment of any true autobiography (I do not speak here of auto-biographical novels) the author's intention is to convey the sense that 'this happened to me,' and it is this intention that is always carried through in a way which, I believe, makes the result different from fic-tion" (53).

John Eakin carries Mandel's argument further, using the extreme cases of Mary McCarthy and Lillian Hellman to do so. The fact that these two highly imaginative autobiographers once publicly accused each other of lying and that a suit for libel was pending against Hellman at the time of her death, indicates that the question of truth in autobiog-raphy is no tea-table debate. As Lejeune and Bruss point out in their discussion of pacts, modern societies like that of the United States accord legal status to the truth value of autobiographies. "Autobiog-raphers convicted of 'insincerity' risk fines for libel, imprisonment for fraud" Eakin points out ("*Reference*," 30). *Memories of a Catholic Girlhood* is then analyzed as a text representing an ambiguous but honest re-sponse to the pressures of memory and imagination. Speaking of her dead father's romantic aura—"a certain mythic power that made people want to invent stories about him" (17)—McCarthy discusses family stories which upon closer inspection prove inaccurate or false. Auto-biographical truth frequently includes false statements believed in by the actor self and others which, if not subsequently dispelled, may still be believed by the author. Upon confessing that she has not given the correct names of former teachers and schoolmates while accurately recording family names, McCarthy observes, "*to me, this record lays a claim to being historical—that is, much of it can be checked. If there is more fiction in it than I know, I should like to be set right*" (10). Some readers insist that the previously-published stories contain all the fiction, while the interchapters are in italics precisely to assure us that *they* are the truthful revisions by which "story" is enclosed by "autobiography." Eakin insists, however, that this is oversimplification. The final version about such mysterious details as the tin butterfly is not to be found in the commentary alone. Rather, *both* narrative modes are alternate explanations of McCarthy's past, so that *Memories of a Catholic Girlhood* is total autobiography, consisting of "a series of earlier recallings" and so is "a series of prototypes for the autobiographical act" ("Reference," 35).

As Eakin's discussion and his earlier book, *Fictions in Autobiography; Studies in the Art of Self-Invention*, attest, "fact" and "fiction," are not stable, separate terms describing the properties of autobiographical texts. Neither authors nor readers can untangle all the centrifugal and centripetal movements of personal narratives except by simultaneously analyzing the content, form, and contexts of any given text. As William C. Spengemann argues in his "Bibliographical Essay" in *The Forms of Autobiography*, whether one defines autobiography as history or fiction or simply emphasizes one feature over the other will depend upon the use to which either choice is to be put. "Those who wish to extract from autobiography information about the writer's life and times will regard the genre as comprising only works that contain this sort of information, while those who feel that our essential being is unconscious usually extend the definition to cover many forms of symbolic expression. Similarly, those who wish to demonstrate the artistry of autobiography have no difficulty including poems and novels in the genre. And, of course, those who maintain that writing refers primarily or solely to itself will find all writing to be autobiographical by definition" (185–86). Being himself committed to one or more of the last three choices, Spengemann opts to devote his book's last chapter to *The Scarlet Letter* as autobiography. His historical account of autobiography as literary form makes this virtually inevitable, since he is convinced that "once the assumption of referentiality is called into question . . . the last distinction evaporates, and the long migration from fact to fiction is complete" (213).

American leaders on this Long March of autobiography and its critics away from facts, history, and the referential function of language include Paul de Man, Burton Pike, Louis Renza, and Michael Sprinker. A common ground on which they meet is succinctly identified in Avrom Fleishman's C position in his essay "The ABC of Historical Criticism." According to this position, literature neither mirrors nor stands in dialectical tension with society. Instead, "literary works have nothing to do with the major institutions of society, since they exist in a tradition with its own line of historical development, or because they are, like all art-works, purely aesthetic objects with their own non-referential mode of existence" (205). Since language and discourse constitute independent systems, intertextuality becomes the only linkage of one discourse to something outside itself. Consequently, the autobiographical "I" as the sign of author/actor ceases to signify. Loose formulations like "autobiography turns a who into a what" must be rephrased to recognize the putative self in autobiography as an "it" existing solely inside the text, distinct from history or realistic fiction; for, as Louis Renza argues, the act of writing autobiography engenders nothing like the cooperative activity of readers assumed by conventional concepts of "pact" or "contract." Being neither a biographical nor fictional communication, the autobiographical situation severs the writer from its readers, who can share neither the writer's past reality nor its imaginative present. Thus autobiography dissolves itself into an endless prelude: "a beginning without middle (the realm of fiction) or without end (the realm of history), a purely fragmentary, incomplete literary project" (295).

The "end of autobiography" and "the disappearance of the self" are accepted realities for some critics, who choose carefully the texts with which to confirm their hypotheses. Others, however, remain unconvinced or unenlightened, not to mention the common reader who blithely persists in purchasing and enjoying autobiographies like *Iacocca* in ignorance of the futility of their belief that this story bears some trustworthy (or untrustworthy) relation to the subject's actual experiences. Thus, there are critics who stress the ideological implications and cultural dangers involved in the premature interment of autobiography. "What this procedure has meant in practice," James M. Cox observes, "is a contraction of the imaginative orbit. Teachers, students, and critics of literature have more and more retreated from the world of fact, leaving it to the historian or the political scientist. If there is too much fact or idea in a piece of writing, it is under threat of abandonment . . . . Thus autobiographies devoted to the emotional consciousness of the writer have been much more subject to investigation that the memoir, particularly the memoir of well-known public figures. More literary attention has been paid Frank Conroy's *Stop-time* than to Grant's *Memoirs*." ("Recovering," 125) Feminist critics, too, have their own reasons for making the same argument. "The death of the subject and of the author," Elizabeth Fox-Genovese writes," may accurately reflect the perceived crisis of Western culture and the bottomless anxieties of its most privileged subjects—the white male authors who had presumed to define it . . . . The virtuosity, born of centuries of privilege, with which these ghosts of authors make their case demands that others, who have something else to say, meet the ghosts' standards of pyrotechnics" (67). For Cox, as for other serious readers, autobiography has never been confined to any literary form, genre, or ideology but is rather a content and a mode of consciousness. Nonetheless, critical debate continues, and modernist and postmodernist interpretations of autobiography must be taken into consideration by the cultural historian. "To be a conscientious historian or historical critic, then," Fleishman concludes, "is to vary one's methods with the object of enquiry, to develop a somewhat different methodology for differing periods of historical and critical investigation. When dealing with modernist works in relation to modern society, it is the autonomist way of thinking that is put to the test. . . . For earlier periods, when the artist's social bond was stronger and the strength of his discomfort with it correspondingly great, dialectical oppositions may come more quickly to hand, although never—let us hope—in ignorance of the specifics of the medium or of the artist's individual development" (218).

Fleishman's plea for a principled pluralism applies, I believe, with special force to autobiography in the field of contemporary culture. So many different kinds of texts are being generated in response to a bewildering range of social conditions and contexts and psychic states (including isolation, anomie, and insanity), that readers and critics are virtually compelled to react in adaptive ways. Indeed, Jameson's and Raymond Williams's models of dominant, residual, and emergent forms of expressive responses to a given social/historical situation can only with difficulty and some injustice be made applicable to all autobiographical transactions. One promising adaptive approach which cuts through dualistic concepts of language and behavior, genre and culture is offered by the narratologist Barbara Herrnstein Smith. In "Narrative Versions, Narrative Theories" she seeks common ground on which all sorts of stories and story-telling situations can be based. In addition to stories' structural features, which if made their exclusive hallmark, separate narrative from time and human agency, stories are also verbal acts resembling other human activity. More precisely, she argues, a narrative might profitably be conceived of as a series of verbal responses to the conditions under which it is created. "Accordingly, we might conceive of narrative discourse most minimally and most generally as verbal acts consisting of *someone telling someone else that something happened.* Among the advantages of such a conception is that it makes explicit the relation of narrative discourse to other forms of discourse and, thereby, to verbal, symbolic, and social behavior generally" (228). More practically, viewing a narrative like autobiography as part of a social transaction discloses aspects which "tend to remain obscure or elusive when we conceive of it primarily as a kind of text or structure or any other form of detached and decontextualized entity. For it suggests not only that every telling is produced and experienced under certain social conditions and constraints and that it always involves two parties, an audience as well as a narrator, but also that, as in any social transaction, each party must be individually motivated to participate in it" (228–29). This relationship of teller to listener, moreover, is always individual and dynamic. It describes historical as well as imaginative occasions, connecting both to ordinary conversation and nonverbal communication. Furthermore, the functions of all narrative transactions will vary not only by occasion but among individual narrators. The critical reader must, therefore, "acknowledge and explore the *multiplicity* of functions that may be performed by narratives generally and by any narrative in particular. We would, accordingly, be less likely to expect to find (or claim to have identified) any single fundamental political purpose or psychological (or transcendental) effect of narratives, whether it be to reflect reality or to supplement it, to reinforce ruling ideologies or to subvert them, to console us for our mortality or to give us intimations of our immortality" (231). Inasmuch as autobiography is a thoroughly overdetermined utterance—potentially historical record, artful story, spiritual confession, and ideological testament all at once—this discourse mode nicely fits Herrnstein Smith's general notions of narrative and its uses. Her theories are culturally inclusive and lend general support to my own adaptive approach to autobiography as individual text and social transaction.

The dynamic ferment in current autobiographical writing, reading, and theorizing can only be sketched in this brief survey. Subgroups of texts, traditions, and social circumstances, all creating new communities of interest, abound. Much more needs to be said about categories already identified but described chiefly in terms of a few, putatively representative texts. Granted the equal status of content with form in defining autobiography, and the wisdom of cultural pluralism as social philosophy, we may note, for example, the continuing vitality of immigrant and prison autobiographies, as well as the larger body of ethnic- and gender-specific stories by women, blacks, Native Americans, Jewish Americans, Asian Americans, and gays and lesbians, among numerous others. In fact, it seems likely that the future history of twentieth-century autobiography will consist of chapters on life stories of members of proliferating subsets of our diverse population, rather than an account of *the* American tradition in autobiography that emphasizes a few mainstream masterpieces, as has been the case with most previous and present-day studies. (One example of a more socially-inclusive critique is my own *Autobiographical Occasions and Original Acts.*) Autobiography thus participates centrally in current controversies over questions of canon. On this point John Eakin has observed that "the notion that there is some cultural totality of American experience, however, may prove in the end to be one of the most enduring of Americanists' illusions; the true history of American autobiography and the culture in which it is produced and consumed may turn out to be the history of identifiable groups within the culture and of the network of relations among them" ("Reference," 28).

If bibliographical updates continue to support this hypothesis, our flourishing literature of the self will reflect in both form and content the varieties of late-twentieth-century lives and imaginations. For many Americans and their subgroups, this means cross-cultural and global consciousness. Contemporary autobiographies often place their subjects and their ways of thinking about the self and others in an international context. Few readers, for example, would deny the Americanness as well as the Europeanness of *Speak, Memory* and *The Diary of Anaïs Nin.* Similarly, biculturalism is both problematic subject and style in works like *The Woman Warrior.* In this transnational historical ethos, not surprisingly, the thought and example of the anthropologist Margaret Mead and the increasing Third World consciousness of writers like Du Bois and Malcolm X have played a part. Hence future criticism and teaching, even more than today, should involve cross-cultural contrasts, so that *Black Boy*, for instance, will no longer be set exclusively within American or black American traditions, but will be compared, say, to Camara Laye's *The Dark Child* as a matter of course. Over all these manifestations of global experience and international consciousness hang memories of the Bomb and the Holocaust, two world events no less profound than the postcolonialist emergence of the Third World. The impact of Hiroshima and Auschwitz is beginning to be registered in autobiography, as Holocaust stories and apocalyptic consciousness already figure prominently in Jewish-American writing generally.

Because world history in this century has proved so overwhelming as to destroy many hopes of coherence and continuity of personality in autobiographers as well as nonwriters, two alternate conceptions of the self and history have been stressed. One choice is frankly to accept the diminution of the separate individual and to write personal history with the author/actor functioning simply as the nexus of social and historical forces. "The world seized and whirled me," W. E. B. Du Bois writes of his peripatetic self (*The Autobiography*, 195), who speaks less in traditionally personal terms than as the voice and consciousness of twentieth-century history from a black perspective. Even more radical an ideologue is George Jackson, whose *Soledad Brother* is a striking instance of an individual story in which personal identity is strenuously repudiated as the ultimate white man's weapon. Francis Russell Hart sees something of the same retreat from private, confessional self-portrayal in other contemporary memoirs. The other extreme is to take refuge in the realm of the psyche and the private imagination, leaving the nightmare of history for others to record. Thus Frank Conroy's childhood and youth are eloquently reenacted with scarcely a single phrase registering the existence of World War II, the Bomb, the Holocaust, or the Third World. Both strategies render problematic the traditional concept (or dream) of historical identity as the aim and end of autobiographical activity. Nonetheless, Hart's 1970 formulation of this rationale still makes sense to some as a way of distinguishing autobiography from other prose narratives: "In understanding personal history one seeks an imaginative comprehension of another's historic identity. 'Meaning' and 'identity' are not the same kind of reality and do not make the same demands. One has no obligation to a fantasy" ("Notes," 488). Today, and for the foreseeable future, the contest continues over the status of this singular self whose responsible autonomy, in many eyes, conveniently serves the needs and values of Euro-American bourgeois late capitalism.

More flexible, though still flawed, is the picture of human personality elaborated over recent decades by Erik Erikson, who applies his psychosocial imagination to the interpretation of autobiography in *Life History and the Historic Moment*. Erikson traces the somatic, psychic, social, and historical dimensions of an individual's gradually cohering (or not coherent) identity. In autobiography, this epigenesis or complex series of stages, crises, and achieved (or failed) integrations can be reenacted in various narrative forms. "There is always some naive self-revelation in any outpouring of autobiographical data," he remarks *à propos* of Gandhi's *Autobiography*, "yet each given medium (diary or conversation, correspondence or autobiography) has its own formal laws and serves tradition and personal style. As to unconscious motivation, we must always remember that the autobiographer has not agreed to a therapeutic contract by which he promises to put into words all that 'comes to his mind' " (123). Central to this psychosocial conception of identity formation is the eight-stage life cycle with its succession of crises and, for the healthy ego, recoveries and integrations. Contemporary social psychologists and psychiatrists—especially American women like Nancy Chodorow and Carol Gilligan—criticize the post-Freudian dynamics and timetable of Erikson's version of American adolescence with its well-known identity crisis and moratorium possibilities. This and other generalizations, they contend, constitute a developmental explanation more applicable to male than to female experience. Similar objections to dominant ideological implications in this and other formulations can be raised on racial and class grounds. Nevertheless, Erikson continues to inspire broad-gauged social scientists like Robert Coles, Heinz Lichtenstein, and the black psychiatrists James Comer and Alvin Poussaint. Especially challenging for autobiography is Lichtenstein's concept of personal myth or core identity posited as an early sameness of response and adaptation to external stimuli, beginning especially with the self's first caregiver. For every social analyst, as for every autobiographer, the perennial dilemma of personal history is how to grasp and communicate continuity as well as change in one's behavior, one's sense of ego identity, and of one's identity in the eyes of others.

Clearly the future agenda of autobiography studies will include searching for ever more adequate and systematic applications of social psychology to autobiographies, not as case histories but as complex records of the dynamic relation between an individual and the environment. But attempts to decode the "naive self-revelation" of some autobiographies must also include similar efforts to interpret the far from naive confessions of other writers like Conrad Aiken, Edward Dahlberg, and Anaïs Nin. Meanwhile, waiting to be collected, published, and interpreted are unnumbered autobiographical texts created daily in the social, commercial, educational, religious, and therapeutic transactions of everyday life. Some of these normally private activities become publicly superintended in meetings of ad hoc groups like Ira Progoff's journal-writing workshops. In other social transactions, bibliotherapy is a recognized medium of psychiatric treatment used by some therapists; it constitutes still another historical occasion and record of demotic discourses about American lives.

Indeed, current production of American autobiographies seems to be more than keeping pace with consumption and criticism. Literary and historiographical critiques, like psychoanalytic readings and ideological commentaries, are engaged in lively conflict on the "Homeric battlefield, on which a host of interpretive options are either openly or implicitly in conflict," as Fredric Jameson describes the current literary/cultural situation ("Political Unconscious," 13). The "death of the self" and "the impossibility of autobiography" are some of the battle slogans flung across this field. Apparently, however, not all contestants hear, and many do not care about, such proclamations, whose ideological implications are not lost on other participants in the cultural debate. Meanwhile, the spontaneous or carefully tended commercial cultivation of life stories continues, as the spate of autobiographies by housewives, penitentiary prisoners, prizefighters, movie stars, retired politicians, and a host of other nonprofessional writers attests. This accumulation of insider reports on ordinary and unusual experiences composes an invaluable historical and cultural resource, which few American libraries are capable of keeping up with. Whether the future historian of, say, black women in late twentieth-century America will find that Nikki Giovanni's *Gemini* or Angela Davis's *With My Mind on Freedom* equal or exceed Ossie Guffy's *Ossie: The Autobiography of a Black Woman* in significance will depend on the ideological questions asked and the theories honored by the historian. For whether written by the self or told to a collaborator, an autobiography is so individual and imaginatively self-contained a social document that it can test, evade, or even submit passively to a given social or psychological theory or political or religious ideology. How an autobiography is to be related to other historical records and issues depends upon the imaginative attention paid to particular gestalts of content, context, form, and tradition.

From the common reader's perspective, autobiography continues to represent a mode of consciousness and self-representation not essentially different from other modes of "configurational thinking", as Louis O. Mink calls the story-telling, contextualizing activities of the human mind. All human beings tell stories about themselves in response to queries from others who likewise presuppose that a narrative, and not a general law or philosophical principle, will be the only adequate response. An autobiography, after all, is but an extended reply to one of the simplest and profoundest of questions: who are you and how did you come to be that way? As Alfred Kazin has wisely observed, this transaction between Americans, whether strangers or lovers, is perennially and vitally important in our mobile, polyglot, pluralistic society. Moreover, it reverberates through all reaches of human communication, and nowhere more clearly than in our society's print and electronic network, "because the experience of being so *much* a 'self'—constantly explaining oneself and telling one's own story—is as traditional in the greatest American writing as it is in a barroom" ("Self as History," 32).

WORKS CITED

Addis, Patricia K. *Through a Woman's I: An Annotated Bibliography of American Women's Autobiographical Writings, 1946–1976.* Metuchen, NJ: Scarecrow, 1983.
Aiken, Conrad. *Ushant: An Essay.* Cleveland: Meridian, 1962.
Alkon, Paul. "Visual Rhetoric in *The Autobiography of Alice B. Toklas.*" *Critical Inquiry* 1 (June 1975): 849–81.
Angelou, Maya. *I Know Why the Caged Bird Sings.* New York: Bantam Books, 1969.

Angelou, Maya. *Gather Together in My Name*. New York: Bantam Books, 1975.
Angelou, Maya. *Singin' and Swingin' and Getting Merry Like Christmas*. New York: Bantam Books, 1977.
Angelou, Maya. *The Heart of a Woman*. New York: Random House, 1981.
Angelou, Maya. *All God's Chillun Got Travelin' Shoes*. New York: Random House, 1986.
Baker, Houston A. *The Journey Back: Issues in Black Literature and Criticism*. Chicago: University of Chicago Press, 1980.
Baldwin, James. *Notes of a Native Son*. Boston: Beacon, 1957.
Baldwin, James. *Nobody Knows My Name*. New York, Dial, 1961.
Baldwin, James. *The Fire Next Time*. New York: Dell, 1970.
Bennett, Tony. "Texts, Readers, Reading Formations." *Bulletin of the Midwest Modern Language Association* 16 (Spring 1983): 3–17.
Berthoff, Warner. "Witness and Testament: Two Contemporary Classics." *Aspects of Narrative*. Ed. J. Hillis Miller. New York: Columbia University Press, 1971, 173–98.
Blackburn, Regina. "In Search of the Black Female Self: African American Women's Autobiographies and Ethnicity." *Women's Autobiography: Essays in Criticism*. Ed. E. Jelinek. Bloomington: Indiana University Press, 1980, 133–48.
Black Elk. *See* Neihardt, John G.
Bloom, Lynn Z. *See* Briscoe, Mary Louise.
Blumer, Herbert. *Critiques of Research in the Social Sciences: I. An Appraisal of Thomas and Znaniecki's 'The Polish Peasant in Europe and America'*. New York: Social Science Research Council, 1939.
Bridgman, Richard. *Gertrude Stein in Pieces*. New York: Oxford University Press, 1970.
Brignano, Russell. *Black Americans in Autobiography: An Annotated Bibliography of Autobiographies and Autobiographical Books Written since the Civil War*. Durham, NC: Duke University Press, 1984.
Brinnin, John Malcolm. *The Third Rose: Gertrude Stein and Her World*. Boston: Little, Brown, 1959.
Briscoe, Mary Louise, Lynn Z. Bloom, and Barbara Tobias. *American Autobiography, 1945–1980: A Bibliography*. Madison: University of Wisconsin Press, 1982.
Brown, Claude. *Manchild in the Promised Land*. New York: New American Library, 1965.
Bruss, Elizabeth. *Autobiographical Acts: The Changing Situation of a Literary Genre*. Baltimore: Johns Hopkins University Press, 1976.
Butterfield, Stephen. *Black Autobiography in America*. Amherst: University of Massachusetts Press, 1974.
Chodorow, Nancy. *The Reproduction of Mothering: Psychoanalysis and the Sociology of Gender*. Berkeley and Los Angeles: University of California Press, 1978.
Conroy, Frank. *Stop-time*. New York: Viking, 1967.
Cox, James M. "Autobiography and America." *Aspects of Narrative*. Ed. J. Hillis Miller. New York: Columbia University Press, 1971, 143–72.

Cox, James M. "Recovering Literature's Lost Ground through Autobiography." *Autobiography: Essays Theoretical and Critical.* Ed. James Olney. Princeton: Princeton University Press, 1980, 123–45.

Davis, Angela. *With My Mind on Freedom, An Autobiography.* New York: Bantam Book, 1974.

Dahlberg, Edward. *Because I Was Flesh, The Autobiography of Edward Dahlberg.* New York: New Directions, 1963.

de Man, Paul. "Autobiography as De-Facement." *Modern Language Notes* 94 (December 1979): 919–30.

Dillard, Annie. *Pilgrim at Tinker Creek.* New York: Harper's Magazine Press, 1974.

Dreiser, Theodore. *A Book About Myself.* New York: Boni & Liveright, 1922.

Dreiser, Theodore. *Dawn.* New York: Fawcett World Library, 1931.

Du Bois, W. E. B. *Dusk of Dawn: An Essay Toward an Autobiography of a Race Concept.* New York: Harcourt, Brace, 1940.

Du Bois, W. E. B. *The Autobiography of W. E. B. Du Bois: A Soliloquy on Viewing My Life from the Last Decade of Its First Century.* New York: International Publishers, 1968.

Du Bois, W. E. B. *Darkwater: Voices from Within the Veil.* New York: Schocken Books, 1969.

Eakin, Paul John. *Fictions in Autobiography: Studies in the Art of Self-Invention.* Princeton: Princeton University Press, 1985.

Eakin, Paul John. "Reference and the Representative in American Autobiography: Mary McCarthy and Lillian Hellman." In *Identità e Scrittura: Studi sull'Autobiografia Nord-Americana.* A. L. Accardo, M. O. Marrotti, I. Tattoni (Rome: Bulzoni Editore, 1988), 21–47.

Erikson, Erik. "Gandhi's Autobiography: The Leader as a Child." *American Scholar* 35 (Autumn 1966): 632–46.

Erikson, Erik. *Life and the Historical Moment.* New York: W. W. Norton, 1975.

Exley, Frederick. *A Fan's Notes: A Fictional Memoir.* New York: Random House, 1968.

Fabre, Michel. *The Unfinished Quest of Richard Wright.* New York: Morrow, 1973.

Fleishman, Avrom. "The ABC of Historical Criticism." In *Research in English and American Literature* vol. 5. Berlin: W. De Gryter, 1987, 205–19.

Fox-Genovese, Elizabeth. "My Statue, My Self: Autobiographical Writings of Afro-American Women." In *The Private Self: Theory and Practice of Women's Autobiographical Writings.* Ed. Shari Benstock. Chapel Hill: University of North Carolina Press, 1988, 63–89.

Gilligan, Carol. *In a Different Voice: Psychological Theory and Women's Development.* Cambridge: Harvard University Press, 1982.

Giovanni, Nikki. *Gemini: An Extended Autobiographical Statement on my First Twenty-one Years of Being a Black Poet.* Indianapolis: Bobbs-Merrill, 1971.

Guffy, Ossie. *Ossie: The Autobiography of a Black Woman.* New York: Bantam Books, 1971. As told to Caryl Ledner.

Gunn, Janet V. *Autobiography: Toward a Poetics of Experience.* Philadelphia: University of Pennsylvania Press, 1982.

Haley, Alex. *The Autobiography of Malcolm X*. New York: Grove, 1965.

Hampl, Patricia. *A Romantic Education*. Boston: Houghton Mifflin, 1981.

Harris, Alex, ed. *A World Unsuspected: Portraits of Southern Childhood*. Chapel Hill: University of North Carolina Press/Duke University Press, 1987.

Hart, Francis Russell. "Notes for an Anatomy of Modern Autobiography." *New Literary History* 1 (Spring 1970): 485–511.

Hart, Francis Russell. "History Talking to Itself: Public Personality in Recent Memoir." *New Literary History* 11 (Autumn 1979): 193–210.

Hellman, Lillian. *An Unfinished Woman: A Memoir*. New York: Bantam Books, 1970.

Hellman, Lillian. *Pentimento: A Book of Portraits*. New York: New American Library, 1973.

Hellman, Lillian. *Scoundrel Time*. Boston: Little, Brown, 1976.

Hellman, Lillian. *Maybe: A Story*. Boston: Little, Brown, 1980.

Hemingway, Ernest. *A Moveable Feast*. New York: Bantam Books, 1965.

Herr, Michael. *Dispatches*. New York: A. A. Knopf, 1977.

Herrnstein Smith, Barbara. "Narrative Versions, Narrative Theories." In *On Narrative*. Ed. W. J. T. Mitchell. Chicago: University of Chicago Press, 1981, 205–19.

Hobhouse, Janet. *Everybody Who Was Anybody: A Biography of Gertrude Stein* New York: G. P. Putnam's Sons, 1975.

Hurston, Zora Neale. *Dust Tracks on a Road*. Philadelphia: J. B. Lippincott, 1943.

Iacocca, Lee (with David Abodaher). *Iacocca*. New York: Macmillan, 1982.

Jackson, George. *Soledad Brother: The Prison Letters of George Jackson*. New York: Bantam Books, 1970.

Jameson, Fredric. *The Political Unconscious: Narrative as a Socially Symbolic Act*. Ithaca: Cornell University Press, 1981.

Jameson, Fredric. "Periodizing the Sixties." In *The Sixties Without Apology*. Ed. S. Sayres, A. Stephanson, S. Aronowitz, F. Jameson, Minneapolis: University of Minnesota Press, 1984, 178–209.

Kaplan, Louis et al. *A Bibliography of American Autobiographies*. Madison: University of Wisconsin Press, 1962.

Kazin, Alfred. *A Walker in the City*. New York: Harcourt, Brace, 1951.

Kazin, Alfred. "Autobiography as Narrative." *Michigan Quarterly Review* 3 (Fall 1964): 210–16.

Kazin, Alfred. *Starting Out in the Thirties*. Boston: Little, Brown, 1965.

Kazin, Alfred. *New York Jew*. New York: A. A. Knopf, 1978.

Kazin, Alfred. "The Self as History: Reflections in Autobiography." In *Telling Lives: The Biographer's Art*. Ed. M. Pachter. Washington: New Republic Press, 1979. Reprinted in *The American Autobiography: A Collection of Critical Essays*. Ed. A. E. Stone. Englewood Cliffs, NJ: Prentice-Hall, 1981, 31–43.

Kent, George E. "Maya Angelou's *I Know Why the Caged Brid Sings* and Black Autobiographical Tradition." *Kansas Quarterly* 7 (Summer 1975): 72–78.

Kingston, Maxine Hong. *The Woman Warrior: Memoirs of a Girlhood Among Ghosts*. New York: A. A. Knopf, 1976.

Laye, Camara. *The Dark Child.* Trans. James Kirkup and Ernest Jones. New York: Noonday, 1954.

Lejeune, Philippe. *Le pacte autobiographique.* Paris: Editions du Seuil, 1975.

Lichtenstein, Heinz. "Identity and Sexuality: A Study of their Interrelationship in Man." *Journal of the American Psychoanalytic Association* 9 (1961): 179–260.

Lichtenstein, Heinz. "The Dilemma of Human Identity." *Journal of the American Psychoanalytic Association* 11 (1963): 173–223.

Lillard, Richard G. *American Life in Autobiography, A Descriptive Guide.* Stanford, CA: Stanford University Press, 1956.

MacLaine, Shirley. *Don't Fall Off the Mountain.* New York, Bantam Books, 1970.

MacLaine, Shirley. *You Can Get There from Here.* New York: W. W. Norton, 1975.

MacLaine, Shirley. *Out on a Limb.* New York: Bantam Books, 1983.

MacLaine, Shirley. *Dancing in the Light.* New York: Bantam Books, 1985.

MacLaine, Shirley. *It's All in the Playing.* New York: Bantam Books, 1987.

Malcolm X. *See* Halley, Alex.

Mailer, Norman. *The Armies of the Night: History as Novel, the Novel as History.* New York: New American Library, 1968.

Mandel, Barrett J. "Full of Life Now." In Olney, *Autobiography: Essays Theoretical and Critical,* 49–72.

McCarthy, Mary. *Memories of a Catholic Girlhood.* New York: Harcourt, Brace, 1957; New York: Berkeley, 1963.

Mead, Margaret. *Blackberry Winter: My Earlier Years.* New York: Morrow, 1972.

Merton, Thomas. *The Seven Storey Mountain.* New York: New American Library, 1948.

Mink, Louis O. "Narrative Form as Cognitive Instrument." In *The Writing of History: Literary Form and Historical Understanding.* Eds., R. H. Canary and H. Kozicki. Madison: University of Wisconsin Press, 1978. 129–49.

Moody, Anne. *Coming of Age in Mississippi, An Autobiography.* New York: Dial, 1968.

Nabokov, Vladimir. *Speak, Momory.* New York: G. P. Putnam's Sons, 1966.

Neihardt, John G. *Black Elk Speaks: Being the Life Story of a Holy Man of the Oglala Sioux,* as told through John G. Neihardt. Lincoln: University of Nebraska Press, 1961.

Nin, Anaïs. *The Diary of Anaïs Nin.* 7 vols. New York: Swallow Press, 1966–1974. [Vol. 1: 1931–34; vol. 2: 1934–39; vol. 3: 1939–44; vol. 4: 1944–47; vol. 5: 1947–55; vol. 6: 1955–66; vol. 7: 1966–74].

Ohmann, Carol. "*The Autobiography of Malcolm X*: A Revolutionary Use of the Franklin Tradition." *American Quarterly* 22 (Summer 1970): 131–49.

Olney, James. *Metaphors of Self: The Meaning of Autobiography.* Princeton: Princeton University Press, 1972.

Olney, James, ed. *Autobiography: Essays Theoretical and Critical.* Princeton: Princeton University Press, 1980.

Pike, Burton. "Time in Autobiography." *Comparative Literature* 28 (Fall 1976): 326–42.

Progoff, Ira. *At a Journal Workshop: The Basic Text and Guide for Using the Intensive Journal.* New York: Dialogue House Library, 1975.

Renza, Louis. "The Veto of the Imagination: A Theory of Auto-biography." In Olney, *Autobiography: Essays Theoretical and Critical*, 268–95.

Rodriguez, Richard. *Hunger of Memory: The Education of Richard Rodriguez.* Boston: D. R. Godine, 1981.

Roosevelt, Eleanor. *This is My Story.* New York: Harper & Bros., 1937.

Rosengarten, Theodore. *All God's Dangers: The Life of Nate Shaw.* New York: A. A. Knopf, 1974.

Sayre, Robert F. "Religious Autobiography." In vol. 2 of *Encyclopedia of the American Religious Experience.* Ed. C. H. Lippy and P. W. Williams. New York: Charles Scribner's Sons, 1988, 1223–36.

Scott, Kesho; Cherry Muhanji; and Egyirba High. *Tight Spaces.* San Francisco: Spinsters/ aunt lute, 1987.

Smith, Sidonie. *Where I'm Bound: Patterns of Slavery and Freedom in Black American Autobiography.* Westport, CT: Greenwood, 1974.

Spengemann, William C. *The Forms of Autobiography: Episodes in the History of a Literary Genre.* New Haven: Yale University Press, 1980.

Spengemann, W. C., and L. R. Lundquist. "Autobiography and the American Myth." *American Quarterly* 17 (Fall 1965): 501–19.

Sprinkler, Michael. "Fictions of the Self: The End of Autobiography." In Olney, *Autobiography: Essays Theoretical and Critical*, 321–42.

Starobinski, Jean. "The Style of Autobiography." Translated in Olney, *Autobiography: Essays Theoretical and Critical*, 73–83.

Steffens, J. Lincoln. *The Autobiography of Lincoln Steffens.* New York: Harcourt, Brace, 1931.

Stein, Gertrude. *The Autobiography of Alice B. Toklas.* New York: Harcourt, Brace, 1933.

Stein, Gertrude. *Everybody's Autobiography.* New York: Cooper Square, 1937.

Steiner, Wendy. *Exact Resemblance to Exact Resemblance: The Literary Portraiture of Gertrude Stein.* New Haven: Yale University Press, 1978.

Stepto, Robert B. *From Behind the Veil: A Study of African American Narrative.* Champaign-Urbana: University of Illinois Press, 1979.

Stone, Albert E. *Autobiographical Occasions and Original Acts: Versions of American Identity from Henry Adams to Nate Shaw.* Philadelphia: University of Pennsylvania Press, 1982.

Terkel, Studs. *Talking to Myself: A Memoir of My Times.* New York: Pantheon Books, 1977.

Thompson, Hunter. *Hell's Angels: A Strange and Terrible Saga.* New York: Ballantine, 1967.

Toth, Susan Allen. *Blooming: A Small-Town Girlhood.* Boston: Little, Brown, 1981.

Wideman, John E. *Brothers and Keepers.* New York: Penguin Books, 1984.

Williams, Raymond. *Marxism and Literature.* New York: Oxford University Press, 1977.

Wright, Richard. *Black Boy: A Record of Childhood and Youth.* New York: Harper & Bros., 1945.

Wright, Richard. *American Hunger.* New York: Harper & Row, 1977.

PART II

Varieties of American Autobiography

CHAPTER 5

The Making of Ethnic Autobiography in the United States

WILLIAM BOELHOWER

There is a popular Italian saying about Naples which in the 1890s would have been particularly applicable to the largest city in the United States, although with a completely different meaning. Allowing for the toponymic substitution, it goes: See New York and die. Nativists, slummers, and European immigrants all had valid reasons for standing agape on the threshold of this urban golden door. In his autobiographical jaunt, *Un italiano in America*, published in 1892, Adolfo Rossi resorted to a frequently used trope to describe his American landing in late 1879, calling New York a tower of Babel (121). Of course, he was referring to the double confusion of tenements and tongues and further noted, "Today, all the down and out, all the helpless of Europe run to America when they are at their wits' end" (58).[1]

Abraham Cahan recounts in his *Bleter Fun Mein Leben* (*Pages From My Life*), the first three volumes of which were published in 1926, what it means to be at wits' end for a Russian Jew. Forced to flee the shtetl because of the pogroms against his people that followed upon the Czar's assassination, he arrived in Philadelphia on 8 June 1882. As Cahan points out, in that year there were fewer than one hundred thousand Jews in the United States, while forty years later there were nearly four million. Such a mass exodus made America "the major center of Jewish population" (197, 196). As for the Italians, the other major contributing population source of the greatest wave of migration ever to inundate the American land, New York was among the four largest Italian cities, rivaling Rome, Naples, and Milan. The wave did not reach its crest until 1910. By then the southern and eastern European flotsam

123

and jetsam it cast upon the shores of the United States in a wasteful display of immigrant *Erleben* was more than enough to provide the raw materials for the birth of a new subgenre of autobiography.[2] By 1911—a sort of *annus mirabilis*—the literary faucet out of which ethnic autobiographies began to flow was turned on for good.

It was in that year too that the Dillingham Commission published its highly influential report identifying the disturbing presence of a *new type* of immigrant, and between 1890 and 1914 some fifteen million newcomers answering to this description came to America primarily from Italy, Russia, Greece, and Austria-Hungary. What is most important, however, is that these new strangers were not melting. On the contrary, just when the old America of Jeffersonian farmers was being brutalized by the aggressive forces of industrialization and urbanization, so-called third-wave immigrants were conspicuously concentrating in the principal cities where they frequently made up a near majority of the population. Indeed, there was literally a *character shift* taking place in these years, or at least the critical issues of the day were perceived in characterological terms. The first restrictive act of federal legislation, passed as early as 1882, excluded a specific racial type from the official American portrait gallery: the Chinese. From this date on, until the final Quota Act of 1924, nativist-inspired legislation tried to resolve the problem of cultural heterogeneity according to Houston Stewart Chamberlain's formula of *Rasse ist Alles*. The question of loyalties, in other words, was often formulated typologically according to an official canon of acceptable identities. In 1890, for example, Jacob Riis applied the method of the vignette to describe "the other half," and his success spawned a whole series of typological studies.

The point is, Anglo-Americans—and New Englanders in particular—were no longer sure what "We the People of the United States" meant. The problem was definitional, and in place of a solution, a clear affirmation of the ritual components of the American Self was called for. In his autobiography *From Alien to Citizen*, published in 1914, Edward A. Steiner could write in all seriousness that experience has led him "to believe that Slavic and Semitic mixtures, and others too, have produced normal children" (326). That the concept of normality was already rigidly codified by the time of Steiner's observation is evident from the ritualistic nod observed in the titles of many immigrant/ethnic autobiographies: *The Americanization of Edward Bok* (1920), by Edward Bok; *The Making of an American* (1924), by Jacob Riis; *An American in the Making* (1917), by Marcus E. Ravage; and the less obvious *The Promised Land* (1911), by Mary Antin.

In fact, the specialty of ethnic autobiographical signification, its unique semiotic *jeu*, largely consists in consciously re-elaborating or simply rewriting the received behavioral script of the rhetorically well-defined American self. Immigrant/ethnic autobiographers quickly learned how to read the blueprint of this official version. Like all initiation rites, the reading process began in the negative and required a stripping away of the "old" self. In Edward Steiner's words, "The American people as a whole clamour with a kind of savage hunger for the assimilation of the immigrant . . . [w]hether or not we threw the immigrant to the dogs did not matter, so long as he was eaten up and his bones gnawed free of anything foreign . . . " (166). The complicity of Steiner's "we" is clearly meant to exonerate him from his own foreign origins and paint his Jewish soul in the official red, white, and blue.

The question of loyalties, which was the natural consequence of Old World bonds not being broken, had a specific geographical origin. "Two decades ago the words 'East Side' called up a vague and alarming picture of something strange and alien: a vast crowded area, a foreign city within our own, for whose conditions we had no concern" (2), Lillian Wald explains in her classic settlement account, *The House on Henry Street* of 1915. The exotic types inhabited well circumscribed urban spaces, and within these boundaries Americans were, in Henry James's words, forced to eat "the fruit of the foreign tree" (117) and adopt "the rich Rutgers Street perspective" (133). The crisis of American identity, therefore, was likewise tied to the nation's coming of age under new urban conditions.

If new values and behavioral codes were to be found, if the sick metropolitan patient were to be etherized and spread out upon a table (a very apt image of the collapse of the Bostonian/Eliotic soul), one would have to analyze *The Spirit of the Ghetto*, as Hutchins Hapgood set out to do in his 1902 book of that name. Modern American reality, with its topology of new forms of democratic chaos and complexity, lay in Mulberry Bend, Jewtown, Chinatown, and Little Italy. Among the many who answered Henry Adams's call to go questing for the new man was Lincoln Steffens, and in a chapter of his autobiography titled "The Ghetto," he nicely sums up the novel social rage of slumming: "I had become infatuated with the Ghetto as eastern boys were with the wild west" (1:244). As Constantine Panunzio described them in his autobiography, *The Soul of an Immigrant*, published in 1928, these territories of the new man were "cities within cities" (183), "impenetrable citadels [where] no amount of Americanization can batter down" their walls (256). But no one better than Jacob Riis confirms how haunted

Americans had become by this new ethnic substitute for the now vanquished Indian as he prowled about in the modern American forest/jungle. Having visited Mulberry Bend and the Five Points area of inner-city New York, Riis says in a chapter of his autobiography significantly titled "I Go to War," "For half a lifetime afterward they were my haunts by day and by night" (42).

When Abraham Cahan submitted his first typological vignettes of life in the Jewish quarter to the *New York Sun* in the late 1880s, the copy editor, a certain Mr. Beach, inquired of the author, "Pardon me. You use a word about which I must ask. What is a Ghetto" (355)? By the time he was writing the first volumes of his autobiography, Cahan could say, "Today, every American city has a Jewish quarter, some of them as large as a city. . . . And every American understands the meaning of the word ghetto" (355). The conceptual scheme Henry Adams used in his *Education* in 1907 unwittingly embodies the Cahanian shift from American unity to ethnic-American multiplicity, thus making his blue-blood autobiography a necessary "study of relation" (xxx). A quintessential American, Adams defined himself at the beginning of the twentieth century as a "weary Titan of Unity" (455). Like other important New Englanders, although not so much a nativist like them, he was an apostle of "Unity, Purpose, Order, Law, Truth, the Universe, God" and tried with feckless might to cope with their opposites: "Multiplicity, Diversity, Complexity, Anarchy, Chaos" (455).

I say "feckless might" because Adams himself suggests that, contrary to the teeming immigrants who easily and even joyfully represented all of his negative categories, his American self was no more than a manikin, a shell, a mere ectoplasm. No longer a substance anchored down by metaphysical values, this self was now a casual set of relations roaming in "a new world which [was not] a unity but a multiple" (457). One could not hope for a better autobiographical homology of the spreading cultural catastrophe of America's multiplying Mulberry Bends, what Henry James in *The American Scene* had already referred to as "the great 'ethnic' question" (120). James too felt a "sense of dispossession" (86), but being less of a metaphysician, for him "the huge looseness of New York" (116) was due to the "ubiquitous alien" (87). In the Yiddish quarter of the East Side, James notes, "multiplication . . . was the dominant note" (130); what upset one was "the claim of the alien . . . to share in one's supreme relation" (85). For both Adams and James, it seems, the old order and the old pattern of identities were dead. As a result, both turned their attention to a study of American relations.

People in the new department of sociology at the University of Chicago—Robert Park, Florian Znaniecki, William Thomas, and later

Louis Wirth—who tried to understand the new American identities turned naturally to an examination of immigrant and ethnic autobiographies. But this academic discipline was quickly infected with popular ideology. Henry Ross, who wrote the first university textbook of sociology, which was largely devoted to social engineering, was a staunch nativist (Staeuble). And certainly it was due to xenophobic pressure and the consequent need to allay spreading nativist fears that most immigrant/ethnic autobiographers sought to pass themselves off as Americans by didactically copying and promoting officially acceptable behavioral codes.

Sacvan Bercovitch discusses the trans-historical foundations of the true-stock American in terms of "The Ritual of American Autobiography." The model self projected in the works of such canonic writers as Franklin and Thoreau, for example, was part of a national script which tended to mythologize the nation's early historical patterns and protagonists, promote a political philosophy of liberalism, and take for its system of values a virulent form of individualism. Needless to say, this self was perennially dressed out in typological rhetoric, in part because its base was stringently monocultural and monolinguistic, in part because it was sheathed in a theory of American exceptionalism. By the turn of the twentieth century, this ritualized ideal self, with its mythic halo, was increasingly hard to match with urban lives in the contemporary scene (Sayre; Spengemann and Lundquist). Simply put, the Puritan, Protestant legacy lacked *hic et nunc* confirmation. Indeed, the alleged and distinctly American self had to be rushed to the intensive care room of ideology, the last refuge for its immediate historical recovery.

It is not at all surprising, given the new demographic texture of the nation, that the self of American autobiography had at its bedside the best foreign practitioners of the genre available. If they ultimately presided over the patient's funeral rather than rebirth, however, they did learn to reconstruct that self by simulation in their own autobiographical projects. Thus, Constantine Panunzio in his autobiography *The Soul of an Immigrant* is more than eager to admit, "I am in a special way happy to have learned the English language and through its medium to have become acquainted with the stalwart thought of the Master minds of the Anglo-Saxon race" (294). Obviously over-aware of his audience, as most of his fellow immigrant/ethnic autobiographers then were, he drums home the anatomy lesson he himself had learned in that big cultural emergency room that urban America had become towards the end of the third wave of immigrant influx: "If my experience has any significance at all, it lies in the fact that it shows what a transformation in the thought-life of the foreign groups could actually take place . . ." (276).

Panunzio, of course, is concerned to present himself as a palimpsest of the model American. Availing himself of a typical ethnic autobiographical strategy, he relies on a troping device to bring home his simulating sleight of hand. His old immigrant self, he declares in playing up to his Americanist audience, has been allowed to die so as to make way for "the unfolding of the American in me" (223). His choice of a trope is more theatrically unveiled when, towards the end of his autobiography and with the volume of ideal rhetoric now turned up as loud as it can go, he says, "I take my hat off to the typical American . . . " (295). Earlier he had even given a typological tag to this simulated resuscitation of a dying autobiographical *figura* by writing, "I am certain that had it not been for my American 'Big Brother' I would not have the deepseated faith in America which is mine today" (223). By means of this enactment Panunzio becomes, by consent, a little American brother, hopefully a perfect simulacrum of Big Brother: "There is one man in all America who has, more than anyone else, helped me to become an American . . . This man I have chosen to call my American 'Big Brother' " (217).

Although this specific troping strategy may seem like proffering one's readers the blade of a double-edged sword instead of a warmly extended hand—so ambiguously resonant is Panunzio's figural choice—this type of exquisitely literary strategy is very common amongst immigrant and ethnic autobiographers, who often feel the need to dress up in a uniform of Americanism in order to leave their local enclaves of cultural difference and mimetically enter the homotopic territory of national circulation. In his *Autobiography,* for example, John Cournos's young protagonist quickly enough learns that he must mime those industrious, go-getting, ever-ready Horatio Alger types who hawk their latest editions on city street corners in order to rise in the world, "for in those days I . . . strove with all my heart and soul, with all the power I could muster, to become like the rest" (113).

As regards the type of intertextual reflexivity so generally overlooked in ethnic autobiographies, Cournos is even retroactively concerned to identify the master trope which helps to codify both his and a major American author's autobiographical texts, of course to his own advantage: "Years before the publication of *The Education of Henry Adams* I characterized the conflict as one between the Daemon and the Dynamo" (124). Instead of Adams's Virgin, Cournos's daemon inhabits the Russian woods of his childhood. It will be what he has to offset the machine age's condition of chaos, multiplicity, and specialization.

Troping in ethnic autobiographies, in other words, can work both ways at once, as an apparent confirmation of already canonic texts and as an act of cultural and literary criticism.

In Mary Antin it is the topos of the public school which facilitates the protagonist's *Bildung*: "Having traced the way an immigrant child may take from the ship through the public schools, passed on from hand to hand by the ready teachers; through free libraries and lecture halls, inspired by every occasion of civic consciousness; . . . seeking, in American minds, the American way, and finding it in the thoughts of the noble, . . . having traced the footsteps of the young immigrant almost to the college gate, the rest of the course may be left to the imagination" (359–60). What often happens in the summarizing strategies of such autobiographies is that the narrator uses a well-chosen master trope to smuggle in a rich and unforgettably dramatic variety of previously unedited cultural scenarios usually considered outside of normal and normative American space. The end result is frequently a finely balanced ambiguity in which the reader—and it depends which reader—is not sure if the narrator meant him or her to notice the system of guiding stars in the American cultural firmament or the mysterious and menacing black holes disseminated in their midst. The black holes, in this case, are the Chinatowns, the Little Italys, the Hester Streets, the barrios, and the Afro-American neighborhoods that make up those extra-territorial cultural zones within the political boundaries of the nation. The guiding stars are not only the textbook ideals that make en ethos possible but also the rhetorical scaffolding that mainstream autobiographers use to give their narrative a form of closure.

Of course the choice of a troping strategy is itself a maieutic act of cultural perspectivism. Again and again, immigrant autobiographers in particular will inscribe their episodic rambles across mainstream American culture with a deliberately footloose Whitmanian gaiety. The "son of Mannahatta" becomes a perfect pretext for naturalizing a series of heterotopic experiences which often yield to conceptual alignment only through a considerable imaginative leap or an uncommon act of interpretive trust. As figural prototype for the self's textualization, the Whitmanian artifice evidently allows our autobiographical narrators to interpret surfaces without having to verify in-depth if correspondences between public ideals and firsthand experience are actually forthcoming. Thus, in *A Walker in the City* (1951) Alfred Kazin models his ethnic self on the poetic stance of "Crossing Brooklyn Ferry" (Eakin, 227f.).

On the other hand, in *The Autobiography of Emanuel Carnevali* (1967) the Whitmanian trope ultimately betrays the narrator's initial project by leading him into but not beyond the urban multiverse. Carnevali's

autobiographical self breaks down under the burden of his own Pro-
mothean desire not only to contain but also to interpret multitudes.
Others, like Louis Adamic in *Laughing in the Jungle* (1932), explicitly in-
tend their troping probe as a means of cultural criticism (Christian). In
the opening chapter, "'Amerikanci' in Carniola," returned emigrant
Peter Molek shows the narrator a copy of Upton Sinclair's *The Jungle*
(1906). When Adamic the young boy intimates, "Some day I am going
to America," Molek explains to him what *dzhungla* means:

A jungle is a wild place, a great forest, all tangled up with vegetation, everything
growing crisscross, almost impenetrable, mysterious and terrible, infested with
beasts and snakes, and spiders bigger than my fist. . . . This is a book about the
United States, although there are no jungles in the United States, so far as I
know. But the whole of America is a jungle. This is a story about people like
me—foreigners—who go there and are swallowed by the jungle. Understand?"
(Adamic, 16, 17).

It is interesting to see how Adamic uses this borrowed perspective to
collect and connect the various stories of his Bohemian characters'
fragmented lives.

It is not until chapter 6, "The Jungle," that the sixteen-year-old boy,
now alive and not so well in New York, remembers the book Peter Molek
had spoken to him about five years earlier. After going to the local public
library—that omnipresent topos for alluding to possible uses of the *déjà
lu* in immigrant and ethnic autobiographies—and then poring through
it overnight, he is finally illuminated: "So *this* was America! For a few
days I felt a sharp hatred for the whole country" (79). The point is, as
Adamic notes in his concluding pages, "I had come to experience
America, to explore the great jungle, to adventure in understanding—
and here I was" (325–26). Due primarily to his reading, which included
a strong dose of Mencken as well, he could now dramatize his own interpretive adventure in a confidently idiosyncratic way, but only after
structuring it still further according to the format of Theodore Dreiser's
Twelve Men (1919). The fictional mold of Adamic's self and the readability
of his immigrant story are thereby guaranteed. A little more than a
decade later, Philippine writer Carlos Bulosan would model his own
autobiography *America Is in the Heart* (1946), with its strong socialist
slant, after Richard Wright's fictionally explored protest vision.

This intertextual going beyond simple forms of referentiality is also
true of the constitutive play of descent and consent (as Werner Sollors
has referred to it), which equally informs the making of immigrant and
ethnic autobiographies. In my own work I have tried to reveal the type
of semiotic activity that results from this cultural dynamic of consent

and descent partially because Henry James's ethnic question and Henry Adams's own preoccupations over the American self are not only symbiotically related to each other but are also intrinsic to any attempt to understand centripetal processes of cultural modeling. As Sollors notes, the interplay between descent and consent constitutes one of the basic conflicts of American culture. While attempts to legitimate the self and establish its identity usually involve one in issues of race, consanguinity, genealogy and ancestral pride—all descent issues—part of the newness of American identity derives from the fact that it is supposedly self-made, self-determined, contractual, and independent. Americans pride themselves on being a mobile, no-strings-attached, road people.

Identity as cultural fusion is the vaunted model of a "consent-focused culture" (Sollors, 37). The program of fusion and consent points explicitly to the sought-after goal of cultural homogeneity. In turn the achievement of such a goal was historically to be the natural outcome of the leveling processes of the modern democratic state, with its hyperspace of rational bureaucracy, secularization, advanced market economy, endless progress, and unlimited opportunity. On the basis of this model, there should, at least theoretically, be no further need to cultivate such potential factors of descent as local traditions, religious customs, Old World languages, and a sense of local place. By its very activity, an enlightened state would naturally standardize (modernize) life, while imposing a single order, law, and culture; in short, a single global space symbolically characterized by the technics of money circulation. Indeed, this very process of circulation, which also calls for a highly mobile population to keep it going, is itself apparently a compelling mechanism of cultural homogenization.

What Sollors and myself have tried to do with the two vectors of consent and descent, however, is to treat them as cultural constructs, as two structurally related ways of encoding identity and interpreting it in situational contexts. The terms themselves, in other words, prove most helpful as tools of cultural analysis when they are understood as pragmatic principles rather than as categories that yield a definable and easily measurable set of substantive traits. There is a great deal of *symbolic* play going on in the cultural dynamics of descent/consent, and it is perhaps the proper historical moment to reexamine its processes in a new light (Boelhower, *Through a Glass Darkly*). As costructuring terms for interpreting autobiographical identity, they can best be appreciated for the type of semiotic space they produce and the positions of reading they allow. In this context, relational fluency, or the positive ability to move back and forth between the two different semiotic intentionalities of descent and consent, is foremost.

The concern for specific cultural contents and their semantic defin-
ability will easily follow. It is, after all, one thing to identify the system
of representational practices responsible for generating individual
ethnic autobiographies and quite another to reduce the latter to a bare
inventory of represented facts. For the latter approach there seems to
be no room for troping strategies in a text-type which has traditionally
been written off as aesthetically poor. Evidently, our set of autobiographers did not know how to play with, let alone interpret, their lives.
But it must not be forgotten that immigrant and ethnic types were active
participants in the modernist condition; they could not shake off cultural complexity any more than other inhabitants of the new century.
And if they often used forms of cultural primitivism in their narratives
with the same gusto as the new masters of the burgeoning science of
anthropology, immigrant and ethnic autobiographers also knew how to
apply the distancing pincers of quotation marks to their folkloric finds.

By the end of the first decade of the twentieth century, it must have
become peremptorily evident to guardians of the republic that any new
inventory of American identity would have to follow James and Adams
in their attempt to grasp the totally unpredictable autobiographical consequences implied in the huge urban amassing of new immigrant sur-
names. Such lives were unpredictable because the names themselves
were not only new to the American scene but also contributed to making
that scene radically new. And the concomitant shift in American dwelling from a rural to a predominantly urban population and from a homo-
geneously to a heterogeneously perceived culture certainly prepared
the way for a recategorization and a new *paideia* of traditional autobiographical identities, just as it prepared the way for the climate of regi-
mentation which, at the port of entry, resulted in the mutilation of the
immigrant names themselves.

As one moved through successive waves of immigration, it was increasingly less true that the reconstruction of immigrant autobiographical sequence would lead one predictably to the author's legitimate
name and to a consoling understanding of the person behind it. Nor
did having the name necessarily lead one to the master code of a narratively policeable identity. Such apparent loss of interpretive control,
registered even stylistically in certain pertinent passages of stunned
prose by Adams and James, is very much due to a generalized crisis in
how to proceed with the old substantive issue of American identity now
that the context had become one of relational fluidity. James himself
reflected the change by converting Hawthorne's allegorical house of the
seven gables—a nice analogue for the traditional house of American
dwelling—into a new cosmopolitan house of modern fiction built to

accommodate the incoming multitudes, "the effect of which is so to multiply the possibilities, so to open, by the million, contingent doors, and windows . . . " (121–22).

Thus, the source of the major problems of American identity during the high period of immigration lies in the central pattern of an unfolding cultural pluralism, while the very existence of ethnic subjects can only be formulated in the broader definitional terms of a dominating pantheon of American identities. Perhaps the best example of what Moses Rischin called "biographical sociology" (Haphood, xxx) is still W. I. Thomas and Florian Znaniecki's *The Polish Peasant in Europe and America.* On the other hand, as I have already suggested, a typical reworking of American identity codes can be found in Mary Antin's blatantly consent-oriented *The Promised Land* or John Cournos's conscious dialogue with Adams's *Education.* In short, autobiographical relations are fluid indeed.

It is, at any rate, the strong ritual requirements of American behavioral codes in these early, nativist decades that elicit the rhetoric of consent which so often imbues the type of autobiographies under consideration. These requirements are spelled out on the rebound as immigrant/ethnic narrators rhetorically heed the pressure to pledge their allegiance to American ideals as they develop their identities. The rigid and stereotypical narrative pattern that generally emerges can be read as a negative of the liturgically sustained model self of Anglo-Saxon origin. In her autobiographical account "Mostly About Myself," which she included in her book *Children of Loneliness* (1923), Anzia Yezierska nicely captures a fundamental truism about this subgenre in its nascent years: "Critics have said that I have but only one story to tell and that I tell that story in different ways each time I write" (18). The infinite variations of ethnic autobiography are always on a single theme— a hyphenated self's attempt to make it in America. Still, it is perhaps too easy to forget that ethnic sign production is actually the result of the double dynamic of consent and descent developed in the preceding discussion. Strategies of consent lead the immigrant/ethnic self to a stance of alleged cultural homogeneity, while those of descent claim an inevitable cultural difference. The subgenre's narrative tension lies precisely in this type of code-switching. Furthermore, since most Americans cannot seem to forget their ancestors were immigrants to begin with (or in the case of Afro-Americans, brought over from Africa as prisoners), they often express political and cultural dissent through a rhetoric of ethnic descent.

At the center of ethnic autobiography, of course, is the gnawing absent presence of an Old World heritage, or in the case of Native

American texts, of a culturally intact and non-European past. It is this critical factor that ultimately originates not only a politics of descent but also converts American identity and topology into a very self-reflexive set of metaphors. Through a strategy of reconstruction, autobiographical interpretation defamiliarizes actual self and place by converting them into *figurae*, or tropes, which defer to an alternative cultural scenario. In this regard, it is easy to see why immigrant autobiographies in particular, with their built-in topological system of juxtaposed cultures (Boelhower, *Immigrant Autobiography*), represent the full narrative elaboration which most ethnic autobiographies only invest in elliptically. The kind of metaphorization I am speaking of is nicely exemplified by Louis Adamic when he notes that "immigrants were Americans before they landed," for "they were part of the same movement, the same surge toward freedom, that brought over the Puritans" (Laurence, 163). Such a system of idealistic appeal leads to a new—and descent-originated—reading of what Bercovitch called America's national script. Immigrants (and ethnics too) have something hopelessly utopian about them, which easily spills over into Adamic's sort of self-reflexive worrying.

Indeed, Yezierska could go so far as to say, "What, after all, is America, but the response to the demands of immigrants like me, seeking new worlds . . . " (27). The original difference of Europe, Asia, or Africa in other words, allows the immigrant/ethnic self to put America in parentheses, to treat it as so many letters of the alphabet. It is this indelible, other-worldly epicenter of ethnic autobiography that allows the American as ethnic to live simultaneously inside and outside of American culture and to express a double allegiance. Such shifting pertinence implicates the autobiographical narrator in a type of ethnic framing that fits well with possible world theory. It should be added, however briefly, that for such theory the old positivist distinction (according to which symbolic worlds do not really exist, whereas the so-called real world does) appears insufficiently responsive to a highly technological and mass-media-oriented twentieth century. In the age of simulation, the two—symbolic and real—are simply different kinds of representation, both semiotically productive.

For the immigrant, America is first of all, in Abraham Cahan's words, "a figment of the imagination" (215), a "strange world" (243). By adopting a representational strategy of similitude, wherein lies the energy of ethnic transcultural seeing, Cahan can arrive in the heart of New York and say without blinking an eye, "It looks just like Vilna" (209). The overturned version is Antin's "America is not Polotzk" (193). But she gives a definition of the unique perspectival mechanism of immigrant/ethnic autobiographical seeing when she writes in the introduction to her autobiography, "I was constantly referring my new world to the old for comparison, and the old to the new for elucidation" (287). On the other hand, the difference between the immigrant and ethnic moments of autobiographical narration is largely one of charting the process of transformation from an old world topology to Antin's "What happened next was Dover Street" (287). Even ethnic seeing is historically and genealogically grounded in an originating ethnic territory.

As Thomas and Znaniecki discovered in their monumental study, it is best to consider the ethnic self not only as the result of its environment but also as an independent source of cultural production. What the latter implies is what few ethnic encyclopedias care to admit; namely, that there is an aleatory force in ethnic sign production that makes the ethnic self and its activity definitionally ineluctable and unpredictable, able to transcend any rigid cultural semantics—a particularly modern self ready to switch roles and adopt a different identity at the snap of a finger. At least this is what I presume James so brilliantly meant when he said that the ethnic self is an "illegible word . . . belonging to no known language" (121–22). Who is American and who is not the alien; "where does one put a finger on the dividing line," he asks (124). Given American mobility and the fact that many ethnics become quickly deterritorialized—no longer living in a specific ethnic neighborhood—there is no longer any way to control the ethnic subject or ethnic interpretation. In short, the elements of ethnic diversity, difference, and discontinuity can surface at any moment, making the ethnic self a truly catastrophic subject. As Constantine Panunzio confesses in his autobiography, "No matter how much he is at heart American, he [the ethnic] is still different and will forever remain so" (328). Nor must he forget that the verses from Kipling which head chapter 16 of *Soul of an Immigrant* apply to all Americans, especially when they wonder about origins: "The Stranger within my gates,/ He may be true and kind,/ . . . /But I cannot tell what powers control—/ What reason sway his mood;/Nor when the gods of his far off land/ Shall repossess his blood."

The Riises, Antins, Panunzios, and Yezierskas are always doubling back, no matter how much they protest their 100 percent Americanness. There is even a good example of this strategy in so ideal a cultural ambassador as Edward Bok. After some four hundred pages of arguing his Americanization, the disturbing scruple of character is brought to light: "The question now naturally arises . . . : To what extent, with his unusual opportunities of fifty years, has the Americanization of Edward Bok gone? How far is he to-day, an American?" (433). What shocks here, for those acquainted with the classical texts of American mainstream autobiography, is his presumption that the question is "natural," even if we are talking about the year 1923. After all, he is not Ludwig Lewisohn, who in the early 1900s could not find a university teaching position because of "my dark hair, my melancholy eyes, my unmistakenly Semitic nose" (143). The point is, whether Bok wills it or not, his question responds to one of the informing conventions of ethnic autobiography: namely, the procedure of appealing to a double audience or, more specifically, to a structurally insecure American self. Depending on context and the perspective one chooses to adopt, one's interpretive stance can convert anything into an ethnic or a mainstream sign, can switch from a consent to a descent pragmatics, or even choose to play it both ways at once. The base of such structural insecurity in ethnic autobiography is partially clarified, I think, by the strategy to which Marcus Ravage feels he must resort, "In America . . . I had sometimes found it expedient to keep my origin to myself" (310). As a result, he finds himself saying, "I was, indeed, a man without a country" (264) and then, two pages later, "I was an American" (266).

Such a defining convention of ambiguity, which is part and parcel of the consent/descent dynamic, suggests a slight but significant aesthetic twist to Philippe Lejeune's use of real proper names as a test of verification, his "petite pragmatique du nom réel," for the genre of autobiography (25). Indeed, there is no apparent reason to take special note of Adolfo Rossi's remark that in coming to America he feels "like a character from a novel;" "I played over in my mind the marvellous story of the first voyages" (17). This stance, though, may be given broader implications if put in the real immigrant/ethnic context of proper names.

For example, everybody knows from the book cover that the author of *The Promised Land* is Mary Antin, but by page 188 we learn that her Hebrew name is Maryashe ("Mashke for short"), which was then "Russianized into Marya." By playing on names, ethnic autobiography is able to multiply referential systems. Revealing one of her aesthetic strategies, the author can say at one point, "I, Mashke, the granddaughter of Raphael the Russian" (197). Or, in a telling revision of James's Isabel Archer story in *The Portrait of a Lady*, she can say, "The heir of the ages am I" (251), thus opening up a domain of shifting interpretation. Her various identities coexist; she both is and is not "Mary" Antin. Like Edward Bok and the others already mentioned here, she is, as ethnic autobiographer, in a position constantly to make and unmake her American self.

The essential way in which the ethnic autobiographer interrogates American reality is by drawing facts into a system of ethnic interpretation through a politics of memory. In this way facts become what they actually are: constructions. The system itself is usually elaborated as a genealogical narrative program. Thus, Antin says she is a "pilot on the seas of memory" (78); and certainly ethnic interpretation draws its special kind of author-ity from a practice of ancestral return. Here "return" often implies an ethnic savoir-faire that is faced with a disestablished ancestral world and a deterritorialized ethnic community. But precisely because there is a radical discontinuity between the ethnic American self and its cultural tradition, the autobiographical narrator sets about producing a strategy of perspectival comparison and contrast. Indeed, the ethnic autobiographer's peculiar semiosis derives from this form of attention, by which one's tradition (or ethnic encyclopedia, if you will) becomes itself a hermeneutical object, the signifying source that allows for a descent strategy of cultural pertinence. The more one's local ethnic encyclopedia is disestablished, the more its semiotic nowhere becomes a cultural everywhere, with the ethnic subject now forced into a floating practice of genealogical ordering and interrogation. It is easy to see why ethnicity remains a perennial cultural option in American culture and one way of handling the condition of twentieth-century modernism.

As Anzia Yezierska puts it, "All those dumb generations back of me, are crying in every breath of every word that itself is struggling out of me" (10). This way of falling through the present is, of course, one with the attempt to heed an altogether different inferencing system; not so much to summon up a different set of objects, subjects, and events but a different perspective for realigning and reusing those already charged with organizing and maintaining a culturally homogeneous "American" reality. To the extent that the autobiographical self invests in this type of strategy, to that extent will it produce ethnic interpretation and write an ethnic autobiography.

Not contents, but ethnic framing and intention are what count. Thus, George Grimm's autobiographical account, *Pluck*, published in 1911, would read like a Horatio Alger story, like a stereotypical repetition of Benjamin Franklin's autobiography, were it not for this determining remark in the preface: "In preparing this narrative, my constant earnest wish has been to awaken a slight pride of blood in the hearts of our foreign born citizens—particularly our German-Americans—which will cause them to cling to the good traits of their ancestors." In other words, the story of his successful rise in America is ambiguously a double-edged hermeneutical sword of consent and descent, of looking backward in order to go narratively forward. His spatial route is ultimately ordered by his German roots.

It is by virtue of this new genre, pushing to achieve institutional status

by its very popularity, that we have what is perhaps the first inside articulation of a vision of multiple ethnic worlds, a narrative way for ad-
mitting to Adams's multiplicity and James's sense of multiplication in
a positive light. New doors and windows would be added to the house
of American autobiography. This is culturally possible because the new
subjects were in part both the cause and the expression of the modern,
insubstantial, even serial self. Ethnic autobiography, therefore, is very
much an act of higher criticism and an instrument of cultural construction in a way that Adams's and James's texts are not. By "higher criticism" I am referring to the hermeneutical implications in the sustained
cultural work of juxtaposing different cultural models or spaces. In
terms of narrative procedure, this means that ethnic semiosis is
specifically used to open up to the autobiographical self reversible
routes of interpretation.

Cournos, for example, tropes the Russian woods of his childhood as
a hypothetical elsewhere to American mechanization: "The woods
served as a kind of invulnerable mirror faithfully reflecting all that
followed: whether the urban life I had grown to know or the Machine
with all its implications of a civilization which has developed an involved, complex, contradictory, anarchic vision, no longer seeing directly, simply and clearly, but, as it were, in a series of refractions, serving,
in spite of separate intensities, to confuse, to create chaos within oneself . . . " (124). Again and again, he relies on a politics of memory to
criticize the cultural impasse of modernism. But even more importantly,
by constantly introducing heterotopic spaces within mainstream culture, ethnic autobiographical semiosis cannot but generate as part of
its narrative logic a deconstructive dynamic.

Given the generalized mobility of American life, it is not at all surprising that through ethnic pragmatics, Americans are accustomed to
an intercultural field of experience both within and outside of national
boundaries; so that such a serialized and functional version of the self—
in harmony with the requirements of modernist simulation practices—
cannot be decodified as a single, substantial entity. In fact, as a genre,
ethnic autobiography systematically set about undoing and redoing the
so-called American self by creating new American types and new narrative perspectives. This introduction of cultural difference as a contribution to American autobiographical identity is explicitly discussed
by Adamic at the very end of his autobiography and is worth quoting
in full:

Podgornik, when I considered him symbolically, was to me a promise of a possible spiritual and intellectual awakening and flowering of America. I believed
that, if such an awakening occurred, it probably would begin with the immigrants and their children—the Hunkies, the Jews, the dagoes, the Germans,

and others. The early American stock . . . was, I feared, emotionally, spiritually, and intellectually flat. For generations the old stock had been pickled in the sour juices of Puritanism, or dried over the sacrificial fires on the altars dedicated to the great god Work. . . . The nation would have to be bumped and jarred out of itself. Then, with luck, perhaps, there would be a long period of awkward groping after new spiritual and intellectual values. . . . Thinking about Mrs. Tanasich, Steve, Lenard, and the others, I decided that eventually I would put them all in a book, along with myself (325).

This passage, I think, speaks for itself. I might only add that it took the ethnic renaissance of the 1960s to begin the canonic process of charting the rise of a distinct generic way of handling the epistemological explosion set off by books like Adamic's.

The particular kind of ethnic architectonics I am talking about is, after some eighty years, now well known, though no better understood semiotically; and nobody better than Cahan explains why this paradox is bound to persist: "The building at 165 East Broadway was full of meeting halls and rooms. But in the season of the High Holidays, all meeting rooms, dance halls and other gathering places in the Jewish quarter were turned into places of worship" (300). As an inhabitant of possible worlds, ready to meet the challenge of dwelling among multiplying screens of reality, the ethnic autobiographer is at ease among the chaos of signs. After all, the immigrant heart of the matter has taught the ethnic writer to handle America with parenthetical pincers to begin with; hence the utopian residue one almost inevitably finds radiating from the ethnic autobiographical self. The preceding commitment by Adamic to write his autobiography exemplifies rather well what I mean. Indeed, the ethnic self is at times so idealistically charged that Edward Bok, after having dropped the rhetorical bomb of his dubious loyalties, goes on to use his not-so-latent Dutch heritage to launch a searing criticism of the American character.

Of course, Bok would argue that real (that is, ideal) America is nothing but the invention of immigrants anyhow. And surely Israel Zangwill's David Quixano would agree, he too dreaming utopian dreams, but only because "stinking" hopelessly of foreign things. At least his melting pot ideal is a nice immigrant project, compared to Adams's bad dream. The shift, therefore, that was taking place in American culture in the period between 1880 and 1910 had found in ethnic autobiography its corresponding new text-type, which proved to be not only the most suitable vehicle for presenting new and exquisitely modern versions of the American self, but also a lens for interpreting the complex structural tensions that would lead to the closing of the golden doors in 1924.

NOTES

1 The passages in English from Rossi's *Un italiano in America* are my own translations.
2 Of course, there are earlier samples of ethnic autobiography—those of Frederick Douglass and Booker T. Washington, for example—but there was as yet no systematic proliferation of this text-type and no institutional recognition of its status.

WORKS CITED

Adamic, Louis. *Laughing in the Jungle*. New York: Harper & Bros., 1932.
Adams, Henry. *The Education of Henry Adams*. [1907]. Boston: Houghton Mifflin, 1974.
Antin, Mary. *The Promised Land*. New York: Houghton Mifflin, 1912.
Bercovitch, Sacvan. "The Ritual of American Autobiography: Edwards, Franklin, Thoreau." *Revue Française d'Etudes Américaines* 14 (1982): 139–50.
Boelhower, William. *Immigrant Autobiography in the United States*. Verona, Italy: Essedue, 1982.
Boelhower, William. *Through a Glass Darkly. Ethnic Semiosis in American Literature*. New York: Oxford University Press, 1987.
Bok, Edward. *The Americanization of Edward Bok*. New York: Charles Scribner's Sons, 1923.
Bulosan, Carlos. *America Is in the Heart. A Personal History*. [1946]. Seattle: University of Washington Press, 1973.
Cahan, Abraham. *The Education of Abraham Cahan*. [1926]. Trans. Leon Stein, Abraham Conan, and Lynn Davison. Philadelphia: The Jewish Publication Society of America, 1969.
Carnevali, Emanuel. *The Autobiography of Emanuel Carnevali*. Ed. Kay Boyle. New York: Horizon, 1967.
Christian, Henry. "Beyond Dreiser: Louis Adamic's *Laughing in the Jungle*." In *The Future of Modernism: Ethnic Writing Between the Wars*. Ed. William Boelhower. Amsterdam: University of Amsterdam Press, 1990.
Cournos, John. *Autobiography*. New York: G. P. Putnam's Sons, 1935.
Eakin, Paul John. *Fictions in Autobiography*. Princeton: Princeton University Press, 1985.
Grimm, George. *Pluck*. Monroe, WI: Vaughan, 1911.
Hapgood, Hutchins. *The Spirit of the Ghetto*. [1902]. Cambridge: Harvard University Press/Belknap, 1967.
James, Henry. *The American Scene*. [1907]. Bloomington: Indiana University Press, 1968.
Laurence, Elwood. *The Immigrant in American Fiction, 1890–1920*. Western Reserve University: Ph. D. diss., 1943.
Lejeune, Philippe. *Moi aussi*. Paris: Editions du Seuil, 1986.

Lewisohn, Ludwig. *Up Stream*. New York: The Modern Library, 1926.

Panunzio, Constantine. *The Soul of an Immigrant*. [1928]. New York: Arno, 1969.

Ravage, Marcus. *An American in the Making*. [1917]. New York: Dover, 1971.

Riis, Jacob. *The Making of an American*. New York: Macmillan, 1924.

Rossi, Adolfo. *Un Italiano in America*. Milan: Fratelli Treves Editore, 1892.

Sayre, Robert. "Autobiography and the Making of America." In *Autobiography: Essays Theoretical and Critical*. Ed. James Olney. Princeton: Princeton University Press, 1980.

Sollors, Werner. *Beyond Ethnicity*. New York: Oxford University Press, 1986.

Spengemann, William, and L. R. Lundquist. "Autobiography and the American Myth." *American Quarterly* 17 (1965): 501–19.

Staeuble, Irmingard. *Critica della psicologia sociale*. Trans. Maria Magrini. Milan: Feltrinelli, 1977.

Steffens, Lincoln. *The Autobiography of Lincoln Steffens*. [1931]. New York: Harcourt, Brace & World, 1958.

Steiner, Edward. *From Alien to Citizen*. New York: Fleming H. Revell, 1914.

Wald, Lillian. *The House on Henry Street*. [1915]. New York: Henry Holt, 1938.

Yezierska, Anzia. *Children of Loneliness*. New York: Funk & Wagnalls, 1923.

Zangwill, Israel. *The Melting Pot. Works of Israel Zangwill*. [1909]. New York: The American Jewish Book Company, 1921.

Znaniecki, Florian, and William Thomas. *The Polish Peasant in Europe and America*. Chicago: The University of Chicago Press, 1918–20.

CHAPTER 6

Immigrant Autobiography: Some Questions of Definition and Approach

SAU-LING CYNTHIA WONG

INTRODUCTION

Just as immigrants are often seen as less than fully American, immigrant autobiography has been customarily assigned to the peripheries of American autobiographical scholarship.[1] Of the many studies based implicitly or explicitly on the premise that autobiography is a characteristically American genre, few dwell at length, if at all, on works written by immigrants.[2] This state of affairs, which seems oddly incongruent with the widely acknowledged centrality of the immigrant experience in American history, has only recently been challenged by William Boelhower in *Immigrant Autobiography in the United States: Four Versions of the Italian American Self* (1982). Employing a heavily structuralist apparatus with a deconstructive twist, he makes a case for regarding immigrant autobiography as nothing less than a genotype of American autobiography. Boelhower's work is significant because it is, thus far, the only existing book-length study devoted to immigrant autobiography and attempting a coherent theoretical account of it. The following essay uses Boelhower's study as a focus to explore some fundamental questions on how immigrant autobiography is to be defined and read.

BOELHOWER'S MODEL OF IMMIGRANT AUTOBIOGRAPHY

"The Brave New World of Immigrant Autobiography" is the title of the first chapter in William Boelhower's *Immigrant Autobiography*. The author's palpable excitement for his theoretical model can be under-

142

stood if one reviews existing criticism on the subject. The one study devoted exclusively to Boelhower's topic, Neidle's unpublished dissertation, "The Foreign-Born View America," is a descriptive survey classifying the authors' stated reactions to the immigrant experience. Most scholars who treat immigrant autobiographies in some detail give scant consideration to immigrant autobiography as a distinct entity and do not share Boelhower's theoretical ambitions. A common practice is to subsume immigrant autobiography under ethnic autobiography. Holte, whose "The Representative Voice: Autobiography and the Ethnic Experience" appeared in the same year as *Immigrant Autobiography*, covers some of Boelhower's territory and even makes some generalizations similar to Boelhower's. However, he does not distinguish immigrant autobiography from ethnic autobiography. His recent sourcebook, *The Ethnic I*, likewise groups immigrant autobiographers with native-born ones. Abramson's introductory overview, *The Immigrant Experience in American Literature*, while placing the immigrant experience in the foreground, does not consider possible differences between autobiography and fiction. Other critics confine their attention to individual authors or titles, or else to specific ethnic groups or themes.[3] Demirturk's dissertation on immigrant autobiography, though cross-cultural, deals specifically with female identity, excluding male authors. Bergland's recent theoretical work, "Rethinking the Ethnic Subject,"[4] which redefines the subject in ethnic autobiography in a postmodernist context, cites some immigrant autobiographers but does not discuss in full all three parameters of Boelhower's study: *American, immigrant,* and *autobiography*.

Yet even a casual look at America's history suggests that immigrant autobiography—a body of works frequently "classified as non-texts, . . . written covertly, out of culturally invisible rooms" (Boelhower, 18)— could very arguably take center stage in the study of American autobiography. Except for Native Americans, everyone in America is from or has ancestors from "somewhere else." Obviously immigration is not the only means by which people from "somewhere else" have ended up in the United States. Slavery brought the ancestors of most Afro-Americans. As for Mexican-Americans, the history of annexation makes their situation unique, even though the continued immigration from Mexico, expecially since 1965, conforms to a larger pattern of Third-World immigration (Reimers, 131–37). Despite these important qualifications, one may safely generalize that immigration has played, and will continue to play, an essential role in the making of America. As Oscar Handlin puts it in his famous introduction to *The Uprooted*, "Once I thought to write a history of the immigrants in America. Then

I discovered that the immigrants *were* America" (3). It stands to reason, therefore, that immigrant autobiography may illuminate the meaning of being American as well as, if not better than, autobiography by the native-born.

On precisely such a rationale rests Boelhower's *Immigrant Autobiography*, which has antecedents in such work as Bercovich's concept of "auto-American-biography," defined as a celebration of the representative American self embodying a "prophetic universal design" (*Puritan Origins*, 136; qtd. in Bergland, 3), or Sollors's emphasis on Biblical typology as a source of American literary ethnicity ("Literature and Ethnicity," 649–53). What makes Boelhower's thesis particularly thought-provoking for students not only of autobiography but of ethnic literature in general is the boldness of its claims and the potential scope of its applications.

Boelhower sketches out a "macrotext, . . . a single story" (30), in which all immigrant autobiographies are presumed to participate. Beginning with a mythic moment of "dream anticipation" (28), the protagonist undertakes a journey from the Old World to the New and engages in a series of contacts and contrasts (40). During a process of "transformation" or "Americanization," the protagonist is "forced to confront the utopian grammar of the New World for what it actually represents," so that immigrant autobiography must "organize *two* cultural systems, a culture of the present and the future and a culture of memory, into a single model" (29; italics in original). The narrative possibilities are diagrammatically represented in figure 6.1:

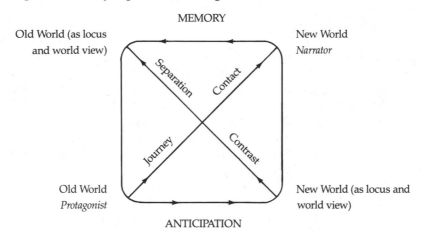

Reversing the historical banishment of immigrant autobiographies to the outermost reaches of American literature, Boelhower asserts that the model he propounds "can serve as the real epicenter for the larger category of ethnic autobiographies" (21–22). Further, he sees the theoretical implications of his work extending beyond the autobiographical genre, to challenge the commonsensically assumed ontological basis of American culture itself. Boelhower suggests that an analysis of immigrant autobiography may help uncover the "original metaphorical status" of the nation's reigning "monocultural paradigm": "the explicitiation [sic] of [the] marginal text [of the multiethnic paradigm] entails the deconstruction of the foundations of monocultural theory" (221). No matter how naturalized the dominant society's myths have been, how securely accorded the official status of history, "the multiethnic paradigm is necessarily copresent as a countertext and cancels the representational pretensions of monocultural theory" (226). Far from being the academic equivalent of political special-interest groups, therefore, ethnic literary scholarship, in Boelhower's view, assumes a centrality and dignity equal to, if not exceeding, that traditionally accorded mainstream literary scholarship.[5]

As the subtitle of his book indicates, Boelhower's model is derived from four Italian-American works covering the first half of the twentieth century: Panunzio's 1922 *The Soul of an Immigrant*; D'Angelo's 1924 *Son of Italy*; *The Autobiography of Emanuel Carnevali*, compiled by Kay Boyle and published in 1967 (Carnevali lived from 1897 to 1941); and Mangione's 1942 *Mount Allegro*. Despite the small number of texts on which he bases his theory, however, Boelhower is a committed believer in "narrative constants" and a common perspective (18): "It is understood that what is true of one text is true of all, though with varying degrees of intensity" (32). He maintains that the range of cultural strategies exemplified in the four Italian-American works—confirmation, variation, negation, and substitution of the codes of the dominant culture—could just as easily have been illustrated by other ethnic groups (20). Moreover, Boelhower adds in a footnote, "by its very paradigmatic nature . . . the model's applicability can be, should be able to be, extended backward and forward in time" (29, n.9).

This necessarily brief paraphrase of Boelhower's arguments makes his thesis more homogenizing than it is. He is careful to point out that "there are as many varieties as there are ethnic groups" and "in no way does the macrotext exhaust the . . . microtexts" (31). True to his deconstructive bent, he maintains that the American mythic language itself, as adopted by immigrant autobiographers, may serve a subversive rather than celebratory function:

The immigrant actant, welcomed in on the basis of his appeal to a mythic language, actually smuggles into the house of American autobiography a Pandora's box of uncontrollable textual variants. As one passes from macrotext to microtexts, he finds that the actant fragments into actors of all races. . . . Through a deconstructive process, immigrant autobiography uses the cultural patterns on which the typology of American selves is based in order to shift the American cultural text towards the pole of diversity (50, 51).

There is no denying, however, that *Immigrant Autobiography* intends its schema to be all-encompassing, capable of shedding light on details from highly diverse textual sources.

Such claims of universality across ethnic and period lines could have potentially far-reaching ramifications. If Boelhower's model of American immigrant autobiography is valid, it forces a radical reevaluation of current critical practice in ethnic literature, which has proceeded largely on the assumption that the works embody group-specific experiences. The "group-by-group approach" to ethnic literature (Sollors, "Critique," 256) has come under attack recently for being exclusionary, static, unhistorical, and timid in spirit (Sollors, "Nine Suggestions"; "Critique," especially 250–58, 273–79; *Beyond Ethnicity,* 11–19). It would be interesting to read Boelhower's *Immigrant Autobiography* in the light of this methodological debate, in order to see if it offers a successful example of a transethnic approach to American ethnic literature.

Accordingly, I will attempt to assess Boelhower's typology by testing its claims of broad applicability across generational, ethnic, and period boundaries, with Chinese-American immigrant autobiographies as my main sources.[6] My aims are to clarify the definition of American immigrant autobiography, whose distinctness Boelhower has labored to establish in his book, and to explore ways to approach autobiographies by immigrant authors from diverse backgrounds. Does the term *immigrant autobiography* adequately address the different historical experiences of both first- and second-generation ethnics, as Boelhower apparently intends it to? How does the immigrant autobiography "macrotext" hold up against "microtexts" from an ethnic group which is barely mentioned in *Immigrant Autobiography*[7] but has been in the United States for some 140 years of the nation's history? Do immigrants of all ethnic groups and all periods share, in some profound sense, a collective American experience? Does immigrant autobiography constitute a clearly marked subgenre of American autobiography? How useful is the concept of immigrant autobiography for scholars of ethnic literature?

THE FOREIGN-BORN AND THE AMERICAN-BORN

In a way, *Immigrant Autobiography* is a misnomer: only three of the four exemplary Italian-American autobiographies cited by Boelhower are written by immigrants. The author of *Mount Allegro*, Jerre Mangione, is a son of immigrant parents, as is Gerlando Amoroso, the narrator-protagonist of the book.[8] Boelhower seems to believe that the *immigrant* experience is shared by the second (that is, first *American-born*) generation, and that his model of immigrant autobiography is broad enough to cover works by both immigrants and their immediate descendants.

According to common usage, Chicano autobiographies are autobiographies written by Chicanos, black autobiographies, by blacks, and so on. It would seem reasonable to expect immigrant autobiographies to be written by immigrants. In fact, compared to ethnic labels, the word *immigrant* admits of few definitional disputes, for it is a denotative term based on a documentable physical and legal event. (My initial reaction, upon noting the apparent discrepancy, was to attempt to sneak in Mangione's work by rephrasing the definition as "autobiographies written by and about immigrants." But of course, except in an explicitly "as-told-to" situation, one cannot have an *auto*-biography written by one's child.) Obviously, it cannot be merely an oversight or a concern for economy of expression alone that has led Boelhower to delineate the subject of his study as *immigrant autobiography*. What does the phrase imply about the way he conceptualizes his subject?

To me, Boelhower's omnibus term *immigrant autobiography* signals a conceptually problematic telescoping of first and second generations into a single "immigrant experience." It suggests that the generational positioning of the narrator and the historical particulars of his life are relatively insignificant as long as the interactions between Old World and New are embodied in his narrative. In other words, while the immigrant generation actually spans the Old World and the New, the American-born may also be said to experience the "confrontation" of the two cultural systems—an indispensable element in Boelhower's schema—by having been born into a family with an Old World culture.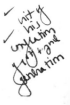

Mount Allegro, Boelhower notes, "is only superficially concerned with the protagonist's *bildung*," and "the narrator gives his protagonist a very small quantum of individuality" (187). Rather, the focus of the book (and presumably Boelhower's rationale for straining the nomenclature) is the Sicilian immigrant community's "collective 'ethnos'": "there is a structuring narrator only because there is a preceding structuring transindividual subject" (187). The tacit assumption is that Gerlando,

Mangione's American-born narrator, could have portrayed the "preceding structuring transindividual subject" just as accurately as his immigrant parents. Through a long "ethnic apprenticeship" (204) Gerlando gains grammatical competence (207) in "the Sicilian Way" as opposed to "The American Way" (213). In Boelhower's analysis, then, the *auto* in autobiography may be interchangeable between generations inasmuch as it serves primarily as a mouthpiece for one of the four possible modes of response to the Old World/New World confrontation. It does not seem to matter that the second generation's *autobiography* can never contain an autobiography, only a *biography*, of the first generation. When we reach the "Finale" of *Mount Allegro* (especially 298–300), written decades after the main body of the book, we realize—for Mangione now realizes—that there is in fact an interiority to the parents' lives that cannot be tidily subsumed under their role as representatives of Old World ways or components of a "group-biography" (Boelhower, *Immigrant Autobiography*, 192). To adequately articulate their own subjectivity as immigrants caught in the Old World/New World confrontation, they would in fact need to write their own autobiographies.

Boelhower's inclusion of a second-generation autobiography under the rubric of *immigrant autobiography* raises some interesting theoretical questions. For example, to what extent can the macrotext be stretched to accommodate intractable details in microtexts? How far can symbolic import be allowed to overshadow the historicity of a physical act? When does a variant stop being a variant and turn into a separate entity? Boelhower considers Gerlando's visit to Sicily a variant of the immigrant parents' voyage to America: it "[reverses] the typical journey paradigm of immigrant autobiography" (216). By this means, *Mount Allegro* is kept within a schema set up to deal with what is normally meant by *immigration*. Certainly there *is* a pleasing symmetry to noting reversals of this nature: American-born ethnics visiting their ancestral lands for the first time are often motivated precisely by a desire to complete the circle of geographical movement. However, Boelhower's identification of the opposite of X as a variant of X, when this X is not merely a cipher in a symbolic order but an actual historical event, is at the very least counter-intuitive.

It seems to me that whereas directions on arrows can be manipulated in a diagram and matrices can be filled in to complete a set of theoretical possibilities, the historically-situated voyage that transforms foreign nationals into American immigrants separates the first and second generations quite drastically.[9] As a result, in spite of obvious biological and cultural continuities, first- and second-generation ethnics cannot be said to experience and perceive "Americanization" in the same way;

to say that their autobiographies manifest an identical deep structure presupposes a rather static concept of culture.

Several arguments support a more scrupulous use of the term *immigrant autobiography*. To begin with, the American-born do not have direct memories of the Old World; their understanding of Old World culture is necessarily mediated by their parents, who themselves undergo inevitable transformations as a result of permanently relocating to the United States. This is not to say that the immigrants are always aware of how American they have become—such a realization can be psychologically threatening and is often resisted—or that, in front of their children, they don't gladly assume the authority of authentic representatives of the culture of origin. Moreover, immigrants and their children frequently do experience their family conflicts *in the form of* cultural confrontation; to that extent they are most likely incapable of deconstructing the rhetoric they use, and to that extent they can be said to share a common metaphor. Nevertheless, as critic, Boelhower could have gone through with (and beyond) *his* deconstructive analysis more rigorously, to reach an acknowledgment of different historical placements of the generations and the dynamic nature of cultural formation.[10] After all, autobiographies are often most fascinating to analysts when the protagonists think and say they are doing something but provide ample clues to the contrary.

Boelhower runs through various combinations of "Old World," "New World," "ideal" and "reality" as if they were pieces in a chess game. Closer to the truth, probably, is the more organic view that a new ethnic American culture has silently emerged even as its makers think they are busy with this or that end of a binarism, so that second-generation ethnics have to contend with three, not two, systems: "ideal" Old World values as presented (by parents who fancy themselves guardians of a beleaguered culture), "real" Old World values as actually mediated (by these same parents, Americans by adoption, who are rooted enough in America to produce children), and "real" New World values as seen from the vantage point of Americans by birth.

Evidence for mediation and transformation of the ethnic culture is in fact quite plentiful in second-generation autobiographies. Gerlando, in *Mount Allegro*, discovers only in later years that many words he used to consider Sicilian dialect are in truth Americanisms understood only in the immigrant community (251); his Rochester relatives, clearly oblivious to the extent of their own Americanization, must have believed they were simply passing on Sicilian Italian to the protagonist. Examples can also be found in Chinese-American autobiography. In *Father and Glorious Descendant* (1943), Pardee Lowe, aware as he is of

Chinatown's cultural practices, cannot but remember that he and his siblings have been named by his father after prominent American politicians (17–19); at the same time that the father insists on Pardee's remaining a "son of Tang," he himself has cut off his queue and assumed an American demeanor (34). The father's matter-of-factness about taking Pardee to social gatherings where prostitutes are present (43–50) reflects social attitudes of a largely "bachelor society" caused by American immigration restrictions against the Chinese.[11]

Jade Snow Wong, author of *Fifth Chinese Daughter* (1945), couches her *bildung* in terms of a rebellion against Old World values, yet the book abounds in details that show a more complex struggle. Her father, relentless traditionalist that he is in Jade Snow's eyes, speaks against foot-binding and in favor of treating women as individuals with rights; subjectively, he feels no disjunction between word and deed, his deep-seated Confucianism having been selectively fused with Western ideas (74–75). Jade Snow's mother reads "The Katzenjammer Kids" (73) and points out how Chinatown funeral practices have been altered to suit American conditions (78). The "after-hours" Chinese language school Jade Snow attends is an institution unknown in China proper, developed to meet the special cultural needs of Chinese on American soil.[12]

Finally, Maxine Hong Kingston's *The Woman Warrior* (1975) thematizes this very cultural dynamism.[13] The protagonist eventually realizes that she has no access to so-called genuine Chinese tradition, her mother's cultural mediations having been idiosyncratic, arbitrary, partial, and confusing. As a child, though, Maxine is capable only of posing a Chinese system against an American system: when aunt Moon Orchid goes mad, drawing curtains and locking doors against invisible enemies, Maxine and her siblings erroneously conclude, "Chinese people are very weird" (183). Such is the danger of a model premised on binary oppositions.

To echo Boelhower's terminology in the diagram, the Old World is both "locus" and "world view" for the immigrants prior to their relocation, but it has never been their children's "locus," and as "world view" it pervades the life of the latter in both a presented and a mediated form. In second-generation autobiography there is no "Old World protagonist" upon whom a "New World narrator" looks, for both narrator and protagonist are situated in the New World. The "culture of memory" of the foreign-born is not the same as the "culture of memory" of the American-born. All in all, a great deal of conflating appears to have taken place to make the elegance of Boelhower's model possible; in the process, some important historical realities have been obscured.

Two other ways in which the generations may experience and perceive "Americanization" differently—a difference inscribed in their autobiographies—can only be dealt with briefly here. America confers citizenship automatically on the native-born, whereas the foreign-born must naturalize (if, that is, the law allows them to).[14] The two groups do not really share the same expectations about the kind of place they can make for themselves in America. Expecting to find the streets of "gold mountain" paved with gold is not the same as expecting to be able to become President of the United States or to be given equal opportunity in hiring (notions of which young Pardee Lowe has to be rudely disabused) (Lowe, 137, 145–47). Naïveté from misinformation is not naïveté from indoctrination, though both may go under the name of "dream anticipation" in Boelhower's theory.

And if, as Boelhower implies, confirmation, variation, negation, and substitution of dominant cultural codes are adopted by both groups, the choice of strategy and its materialization are unavoidably affected by one's horizon of expectations. Historian M. L. Hansen has suggested a "principle of third generation interest" ("Problem," 9) to explain the evolution of cultural attitudes seen in immigrant families.[15] He notes that, typically, the immigrants often become "Americanized" simply as "a treaty of peace with society"; their children want "to lose as many of the evidences of foreign origin as they [can] shuffle off"; and then, by the third generation, "what the son wishes to forget the grandson wishes to remember" ("Third Generation in America," 494, 495). While this "principle" may be an oversimplification,[16] it does dramatize how generational positioning cannot be ignored in any consideration of cultural strategies.[17]

Secondly, immigrants, except for those from Anglophone areas, start out with an ethnic mother tongue and use English as a second language; on the other hand, their children, who may be bilingual to varying degrees, have an expected (if often frustrated) claim to the language of the nation unshared by the parents. Many second-generation ethnics have been brought up virtually English-monolingual, while others are not proficient enough in the mother tongue to compose in it with confidence. As a result of language shift, immigrant writers who compose in English tend to do so by choice; the American-born, by right and necessity. In Chinese-American literature, at least, there exists a fairly substantial body of immigrant autobiographies in the ethnic language, which suggests the possibility that immigrants who write their autobiographies in English are perhaps already predisposed to orient themselves to the dominant society in certain ways.[18]

Thus, prior to constructing a taxonomy of cultural responses from the content of immigrant autobiographies, the critic would do well to reckon with another important response capable of functioning as an epistemological and ideological filter: choice of language. Choice of language already presupposes a relationship—"speaking terms," if nothing else—to the intended audience, regardless of the ideological views stated within the autobiography. As is made clear in a recent ethnic autobiography, Richard Rodriguez's *Hunger of Memory* (1981), loss of the mother tongue and acquisition of English may fundamentally alter the second generation's alignments with both the ethnic culture and Anglo culture (see especially "Aria," 11–40). Pending more extensive investigation of native-language works, a theorist seeking patterns in the depictions of "Americanization" in immigrant autobiography should at least entertain choice of language as a possible determinant.

To conclude this part of my inquiry, I find Boelhower's comprehensive usage of the term *immigrant autobiography* more misleading than helpful. This is not to say that second-generation autobiographies should never be grouped together with first-generation ones in any kind of theoretical analysis; such insistence would lead to an infinite proliferation of categories that would make meaningful generalizations difficult. The point is that to use *immigrant*—a term so imbued with historicity—with the kind of liberty Boelhower desires calls for more justification than his structuralist schema can provide. I suspect that *autobiography of Americanization*—autobiography in which the Americanization process is explicitly in the foreground—may be a more appropriate description of Boelhower's subject matter, and I propose reserving *immigrant autobiography* for autobiography written by immigrants. (This distinction will be observed in the rest of the essay.) A change of name may catalyze a reconfiguration of Boelhower's many insightful ideas; of itself, however, it cannot resolve the issues of ahistorical and reductionist conceptualization that I have raised.

READING IMMIGRANT AUTOBIOGRAPHIES ACROSS ETHNIC AND PERIOD BOUNDARIES

Having clarified the term *immigrant autobiography*, I will now turn to questions of approach. How valid are the claims of transethnic and transhistoric applicability that Boelhower makes for his theoretical model? How are we to read immigrant autobiographies from widely divergent backgrounds and historical periods, all of them products of American experiences of one kind or another? By matching several major constitutive features of Boelhower's macrotext against Chinese-

American microtexts, we may be able to test the usefulness of a universal interpretive grid for immigrant autobiography.

Boelhower identifies three "fabula moments" for immigrant autobiography which are indispensable ingredients of the macrotext: "anticipation" ("Old-World reality vs New-World ideal"), "contact" (New-World ideal vs New-World reality"), and "contrast" ("Old-World reality vs New-World reality"). The seminal moment is that of "dream anticipation": "America was an idea before it was a geographical reality" (222).[19] Without the impetus of dream anticipation, there would be no journey; without the journey, no movement from the realm of myth to the realm of history; and without this movement, no "metacultural perspective" (29) which allows for cultural contrast. To Boelhower, "it is myth that has tended to construct history and not vice versa" (27).

Boelhower's analysis can readily be supported not only by the four exemplary Italian-American texts but also by a number of autobiographies by other European ethnics, such as Mary Antin's *The Promised Land* (1912), Edward Steiner's *From Alien to Citizen* (1914), Edward Bok's *The Americanization of Edward Bok* (1920), Louis Adamic's *Laughing in the Jungle* (1932), and Abraham Cahan's *The Education of Abraham Cahan* (1969), all of which are cited in the first chapter of *Immigrant Autobiography*. The language used in these autobiographies to evoke the dream image of America is heavily Biblical: "Edenic" and "Garden of Eden" (27, 41), "exodus" (33), the "heavenly city" or "sacred city" (33), and naturally, "the Promised Land." Of course, Boelhower quotes this language not to endorse it but rather to expose its instrumentality in constructing a fictive "monocultural paradigm" (221). Nevertheless, one might say his theory of immigrant autobiography depends on the idea that immigrant autobiographers celebrate, allude to, trope upon, challenge, subvert, or reject the dominant American myth: every time a new immigrant lands, the archetypal American drama of spiritual renewal that brought over the Puritans is supposed to be reenacted.

Are there immigrant autobiographies that are simply *indifferent* to this myth: works in which the requisite "fabula moments" are exhibited either not at all, or in so weak a form that they cannot convincingly be described as variants? If so, how would one account for them?

I have found a number of Chinese immigrant autobiographies that exhibit major deviations from the pattern proposed by Boelhower: "anticipation" is minimal, "contact" with the "utopian grammar" of America and its consequences hardly portrayed, and cultural "contrast" either not drawn or drawn more to enlighten Anglo readers than to map the protagonist's own "Americanization." Instead, the majority of the autobiography is devoted to the protagonist's pre-immigration life in China. In this category can be included Lee Yan Phou's *When I Was a Boy in China* (1887),[20] Helena Kuo's *I've Come a Long Way* (1942), Buwei Yang Chao's *Autobiography of a Chinese Woman* (1947), Su-ling Wong (pseud.) and Earl Herbert Cressy's *Daughter of Confucius* (1952), Katherine Wei and Terry Quinn's *Second Daughter* (1984), and Nien Cheng's *Life and Death in Shanghai* (1986). In none of these autobiographies have I found the kind of almost rhapsodic dreaming about America or meditation on an abstract idea of the New World that forms the basis of Boelhower's formulation in "The Brave New World of Immigrant Autobiography."[21] This is particularly striking in view of the Christian faith expressed (Wong and Cressy) or missionary schooling described by some of the autobiographers (Kuo; Wong and Cressy; Wei and Quinn).

Among another group of works that do devote more space to life in America than in China—Huie Kin's *Reminiscences* (1932),[22] No-Young Park's *Chinaman's Chance* (1940),[23] and Anna Chennault's *The Education of Anna* (1980)—the majority also do not appear to take part in the symbolic discourse outlined by Boelhower. The closest thing to "dream anticipation" is found in Huie Kin's *Reminiscences*: the young boy had been so excited by relatives' reports of overnight fortunes in America that once, delirious with fever, he "talked of nothing else but wanting to go to Chinshan [Gold Mountain]" (18). His arrival in San Francisco in 1868 is described thus: "I wonder whether the ecstasy before the Pearly Gate of the Celestial City above could surpass what we felt at the moment we realized that we had reached our destination" (24). It is worth noting, however, that America is mentioned along with Australia, also associated with gold and also a destination for nineteenth-century Cantonese emigrants (18);[24] and that the Pearly Gate figure did not occur to the young Huie at the time of his arrival in America, for he converted to Christianity only later. The mythic rhetoric, therefore, is retrospectively applied, an overlay on an experience which at the time was felt in secular and psychological terms.

Huie's example points to a possible explanation of why Boelhower's macrotext fits Chinese-American microtexts so poorly: the historical situation of Chinese immigrants and their relationship to the Judaeo-Christian tradition are different from those of Italian, Jewish, and other European immigrants on whose autobiographies Boelhower builds his case. Thus the meaning of America may differ quite considerably for the two groups. A lost Golden Age or lost Eden to be recovered, a new Adam to be reborn, the Old World renewed, the New Jerusalem, the City on a Hill—these are European-origin fictions. For those coming from the real Orient, it would be impossible to think of America as

"a type of fabulous new Orient" (Boelhower, 19). The mysterious
✓ Cathay to which the European explorers sought passage was, to early
Chinese immigrants, simply home. The kind of symbolic formula Boelhower establishes for Italian immigrant autobiography—"Panunzio =
Columbus = America-as-idea" (73)—would not work when extended
to the literature of non-Europeans who were the victims rather than
emissaries of an (at heart) imperialistic myth.

One must bear in mind how relatively recent an import Christianity
is in China: although records of Christian activity date as far back as
the eighth century, it wasn't until the nineteenth century that missionaries found a wider audience in China, along with other Western
influences.[25] Contact with Christianity in China before the 1949 Communist Revolution was a function of, among other things, missionary
activity (different nations and denominations in different spheres of
influence, different styles of proselytization), geographical location (the
southern and coastal provinces, the cities), and social class, (the severely disenfranchised or the socially ambitious who understood the advantages of consorting with the privileged missionaries) (Latourette,
825–31, 774, 479–80; Varg, 226–29).[26] For many of the Chinese immigrant autobiographers, the effects of a missionary education are limited
to proficiency in English, familiarity with Western customs, association with foreigners in China which facilitated study abroad or emigration, and a general inclination to accept things Western. One's world
view may or may not be recast.[27] The preponderance of Christianized
authors among Chinese immigrant autobiographers stems from complex historical interactions between colonialism, religious institutions,
emigration, and perhaps not the least, the American publishing industry and reading public.[28] It does not bespeak the kind of total immersion in the Judaeo-Christian tradition that informs Boelhower's
cited works.

Overall, I detect a pragmatic, matter-of-fact attitude toward the idea
of going to America on the part of Chinese immigrant autobiographers.
America is one, albeit a particularly attractive one, of many destina-
tions for Chinese emigrants, in a global scattering over a long period
that some scholars call the Chinese diaspora.[29] Gold has few alchemic
connotations for them, and fleeing war and upheaval does not necessarily spell conversion to the Enlightenment political ideals upon which
the American nation was founded. Moreover, the Chinese were the first
racial group to be singled out for exclusion from immigration, so that
subterfuges had to be resorted to by many immigrants entering after
1882 and before 1965.[30] The Chinese exclusion period (1882–1943)
overlapped and outlasted the period of great European immigration

(1880–1920).[31] Chinese immigrants had no "passcard," comparable to Panunzio's reminder that the American myth originated in Europe (Boelhower, 74), to present in defense of their difference. In such a historical context, it would hardly be surprising to find the "utopian grammar" of America exerting so negligible a structuring influence on Chinese immigrant autobiography.

Of course, Boelhower does acknowledge the existence of a cluster of symbolic equivalences operating alongside or beneath the theological language:

geographical (Old-World vs New-World, closed space vs open space); economic (poverty vs wealth, static condition vs opportunity); psychological (despair vs hope); religious and political (oppression vs freedom, racial discrimination vs racial equality). (42)

As theorist, he is less interested in real motives than cultural pieties, in sociological analysis than semiological speculations. But it is precisely the paucity of even *allusion* to American myths in Chinese immigrant autobiographies to which I wish to draw attention. (That the actual fate of minorities belies the governing pieties of the land is no news.) In a very broad sense, no one can deny that even for Chinese immigrants "America was an idea before it was a geographical reality"; this much can be said for any destination chosen by any emigrant for any reason. The Judaeo-Christian overtones of "idea" therefore admit of little dilution in Boelhower's theory, and I stress them advisedly.

Not only is "anticipation" weakly represented in Chinese immigrant autobiography, but whatever cultural "contact" and "contrast" take place appear to differ in kind from those found in the works cited by Boelhower. In Boelhower's model, the voyage is the turning point in the immigrant's life that makes the "juxtaposition of cultural spaces" (39) possible. "The journey literally breaks the immigrant autobiographical text in two" (39–40), at times into almost equal halves (151), with the arrival marking the beginning of Americanization. With those Chinese immigrant autobiographies whose center of gravity lies squarely in China, however, the journey is usually hastily narrated, while Americanization takes up a very small fraction of the textual space at the end.[32] In other words, while Boelhower implies *immigrant autobiography* and *autobiography of Americanization* to be more or less synonymous in a typological sense, a structurally recognizable cluster of Chinese immigrant autobiography indicates otherwise. Once again, the divergence is so marked that it would be far-fetched to call these Chinese works variants of the macrotext.

Several hypotheses on the Chinese counterexamples may be offered. To begin with, to immigrants who bore witness to the upheavals in recent Chinese history, the promise of America may mean simply a resting point, a clean, neutral space from which to look back on and take stock of their harrowing past. The autobiographies of Wei and Quinn and Cheng fit this pattern. Even though, in some minimalist sense, they have indeed come to America for a new beginning, these autobiographers are not particularly interested in an American fable of renewal attended by prospects of further questionings and struggles.

A second plausible explanation lies in the social class and educational background of many of the Chinese immigrant autobiographers, who learned English and became conversant in American ways *before* undertaking the journey (Kuo, Chao, Wong and Cressy, Wei and Quinn, Chennault, Cheng). An early immigrant from rural China like Huie fits more closely Boelhower's picture of the representative, early 1900s autobiographer: a "pre-metropolitan self" witnessing the birth of a modern, American self (17) and undergoing a movement from myth to history, "from an agricultural valley to the industrialized metropolis" (108). In contrast, many of the post–World War II Chinese immigrants fleeing Japanese invasion, civil war, the Communist Revolution, and the Cultural Revolution are already Americanized products of the metropolis, have already acquired what Boelhower calls a "metacultural" perspective. Physical relocation to America merely continues cultural "contact" begun in China.

This leads us to consider a third hypothesis: these Westernized autobiographers probably knew that the American reading public would not be very interested in their lives after immigration. (Their publishers almost certainly knew this.) It is traditional China (later, Communist China) that excites the American imagination, evokes mystery and alienness, and requires the service of knowledgeable insiders to explain terminology, kinship, manners, social organization, cultural practices, political ideology, . . . *differences.* Chao, whose autobiography was written in Chinese and rendered into English by her husband, explains in her foreword: "When I do publish the Chinese, it will not be the same book either. For, to a Chinese reader, there would be no point in telling what weddings and funerals are like in China" (x).[33]

To return to Boelhower's paradigm, no doubt a great deal of cultural "contrast" takes place in this kind of Chinese immigrant autobiography, but not in the form of "Old-World reality vs New-World reality." Rather, it is "Old-World reality vs New-World readers' expectations": what the audience wants to know, may misunderstand, may find incomprehen-

sible, and so forth. If the Old-World account has a "folkloric" (105) element to it, it is <u>anthropological instead of mythological</u>. One observation provides ancillary evidence for this reading of China-centered
Chinese immigrant autobiography: Huie, Park, and Kuo were all at one
time or another paid lecturers on Chinese subjects, Park having been
successful enough to be a regular on the Chautauqua circuit. (Huie
writes of his Midwestern tour: "China was then little known among
American people and Chinese lecturers were a rarity. So our tour was
quite a success. Incidentally, my Oriental garb lent local color to my talks
helping to fill the halls and churches in the towns and villages we visited,
and, in turn, filling our pockets in a way beyond our expectations" [39]).
May it not be that the writing of autobiography for them is a kind of
fixing in print of a sustained lecture?[34] If so, the autobiographer's New
World self is more a guide than an adventurer, more an interpreter than
a discoverer.[35] The narrative elaboration of life in China and extreme
foreshortening of life in America are a structural reflection of this function of the immigrant autobiographer.

   If the intended audience could be a powerful shaper of narrative, one
needs to revise the concept of the autobiographical project as an individual's negotiation of cultural forces. The audience's role has been
taken into account only minimally in Boelhower's model (21, on "implied model reader"; 61, on Panunzio as cultural diplomat). On the
whole, he assumes "contrast" to originate in a (culturally structured)
private impulse to attain understanding and coherence in the form of
a constructed American identity. (The enterprise's eventual outcome
is irrelevant to Boelhower's basic scenario.)

The problem of identity springs from [the] displacement process, for [the immigrant autobiographer's] function is to personify, to map out, the cultures he
journeys through while seeking his identity. (37)

Boelhower's emphasis on the tensions within the individual psyche can
be seen in his choice of two poet figures (D'Angelo and Carnevali) as
versions of a new American self. It can also be seen in his positing an
inverse relationship between "anticipation" and "memory"; that is, if
the American dream comes true for the immigrant protagonist, memory
of the Old World tends to be weak, whereas a nightmarish New World
would enhance memory (36). The China-centered autobiographies
show, however, that what gets retrieved and presented as memory may
be colored by what the autobiographer feels to be attractive to Anglo
readers. In that sense, these texts are subtly "sponsored"; certainly they
are not as self-authorized and inward-looking as one would be led to
believe by Boelhower's theory.

CONCLUSION

There is strong evidence that the Chinese-American deviations from Boelhower's typology analyzed above are in fact characteristic of other Asian-American immigrant autobiographies.[36] While a handful of the latter, such as Buaken's *I Have Lived with the American People* (1948), may fit Boelhower's macrotext, the majority do not—for good historical reasons. The absolute number of Asian-Americans, especially before immigration reforms lifted racially based restrictions in 1965, has been small; geographically Asians have been concentrated on the west coast, ✓ away from the publishing centers of the east. These factors may have encouraged the writing of immigrant autobiographies set mostly in "exotic" Asia. Further, given the fact that Asians have traditionally been excluded from the American mainstream as "unassimilable aliens," upper-class, English-speaking, Christianized (or at least Westernized) immigrant autobiographers may have served as culture brokers.[37] ✓ Such a role would eclipse any effort to fashion the representative American self—to answer Crevecoeur's famous question, "What then is the American, this new man?"—which is commonly said to inform American autobiography. Sociologist Blauner, author of the theory of "internal colonialism," notes that because nineteenth-century Asians entered the United States under conditions ranging from the "colonial" (Filipinos) to the "semicolonial" (Chinese, Japanese), and because their group size and status were rigidly controlled, "it is misleading to equate the Asian experience with the European immigration pattern. . . . Even when, later on, some third world peoples were able to immigrate, the circumstances of the earlier entry affected their situation and the attitudes of the dominant culture toward them" (55).[38] As immigrant experiences differ, so must immigrant autobiographies.

The above investigation suggests that Boelhower's allegedly universal paradigm of immigrant autobiography is implicitly Eurocentric, derived as it is from a small corpus of works by European immigrants steeped in the Judaeo-Christian tradition, most of whom came during the great waves of immigration at the end of the nineteenth and the beginning of the twentieth century. When matched against immigrant autobiographies from a non-European, non-Christian ethnic group or a different historical period, Boelhower's macrotext proves inadequate, for his structuralist assumptions have foreclosed understanding of how profoundly historical realities may affect consciousness. To him, the autobiographers' situatedness in history pales before the mythic roles they incarnate and the symbolic drama their lives enact. Generational positioning, ethnic membership, historical period, and social class are little more than wrinkles on some pre-existing deep structure. The result of reasoning from axioms (one of Boelhower's favorite words) is a static if elegant model of limited applicability.

Rather than seeking some totalizing system in which autobiographers speak from a priori fixed positions and follow a finite set of trajectories, I believe it is less confining and more productive to conceive of multiple, provisional *axes of organization*: different salient features are revealed when an autobiography is read with different intertexts. In this approach, grouping autobiographies by immigrant status is only one of many possible strategies for eliciting insights; grouping them by treatment of Americanization is another. In Boelhower's case, despite the theoretical difficulties created by their conflation, both have yielded some fascinating observations. One could also group autobiographies by ethnicity, social class, gender, historical period, narrative point of view, or any number of other promising criteria (thematic options are numerous).[39] If there is truth in Bergland's proposed redefinition of the "I" of autobiography—"a speaking subject inscribed by multiple discourses, positioned in multiple subjectivities and situated in multiple historical contexts" (Bergland, 5)—then *immigrant autobiography* can no longer be conceived of as an unalterably demarcated segment of reality with a single set of inherent features. The term merely highlights a few of the many discourses, subjectivities and historical contexts in which immigrant autobiographers find themselves embedded.

Because of the critical role played by immigration in the making of America and the enduring potency of the immigrant myth of renewal in shaping the American imagination, the autobiographer's nativity may indeed, as Boelhower's innovative work gives us cause to hope, be an especially serviceable axis of organization. Boelhower has forced us to reassess the relevance of what appears to be a marginal literary concern, thence to rethink the nature of ideological myth itself. He has also demonstrated how the concept of immigrant autobiography can help reveal the lines of force that pattern "the American," much like a magnet drawn under a tray of iron filings. Provided that the critic exercises care in conceptualizing the "immigrant experience," employs a textually grounded rather than a schema-inspired approach, and pays attention to the historical particularities of various ethnic groups, the concept of immigrant autobiography should continue to be a fruitful one for the study of American autobiography.

A final remark: choice of reading strategy can be motivated as much politically as intellectually—as well it should be. This is actually a corollary of Boelhower's statement on the potential subversiveness of immigrant autobiography—the "Pandora's box of uncontrollable textual variants" smuggled into the "house of American autobiography"—

though it is never fully explored in his book. (Ironically, in his own critical practice, Boelhower has underestimated the unruly diversity of the contents of the "Pandora's box.") To return to the methodological questions raised earlier about the implications of Boelhower's theoretical venture: when Sollors deplores the current state of ethnic literary studies, he seems unaware that premature adoption of a transethnic approach, before the uniqueness of each group's historical situation and its manifestations in literature are adequately understood, can be as static and ahistorical as any mechanically applied "group-by-group approach." So much for my intellectual objection to Sollors's critique. The political one is obvious: reading by ethnicity is a necessary act of tradition- and identity-building for those whose literatures have been rendered invisible by subsumption; this is true even for the reading of autobiography, a genre which often appears to oppose the personal to the political.

NOTES

I am grateful to Gloria Chun, King-Kok Cheung, Paul John Eakin, Giulia Fabi, Him Mark Lai, Kathy Lo, Brian Niiya, Michael Omi, Shelley Wong, and Judy Yung for their help in the writing of this essay.

1 Following customary usage (Easterlin, 5), the term *immigrant* is used here to refer to those entering the United States after its establishment as an independent nation, even though, relative to Native Americans, the colonists could also be considered immigrants.

2 Little discussion of immigrant autobiography is found in studies that ponder the distinctiveness and continuities of the American autobiographical tradition beyond the colonial period, such as (in chronological order) Sayre (*Examined Self*), Spengemann and Lundquist, Cox, Cooley, Blasing, Couser, Sayre ("Autobiography and the Making of America"; "Proper Study"), Stone ("Autobiography in American Culture"), Bercovitch ("Ritual"), Stone (*Autobiographical Occasions*), and Taylor.

3 A few examples must suffice to illustrate these approaches, which as a rule are employed in article-length studies: Rubin focuses on the style and meaning of a single work, Mary Antin's *The Promised Land*; Fried examines Riis in terms of the theme of "quest for community." The immigrant experience is covered in a chapter in Yudkin's *Jewish Writing and Identity in the Twentieth Century*. DiPietro and Ifkovic's sourcebook, *Ethnic Perspectives in American Literature*, touches on immigrant autobiographies in a group-by-group survey of European ethnic literature.

4 Some of the ideas in Bergland's paper are developed more fully in her forthcoming dissertation, "Reconstructing the Self in America: Patterns of Im-

migrant Women's Autobiography" (University of Minnesota). Like Demirturk's study, Bergland's is limited to women.

5   The idea that ethnic literature is prototypically American informs current
    scholarship on ethnic literature; Sollors (*Beyond Ethnicity*, 8) briefly traces
    the evolution of this idea in American studies.

6   Excluded from discussion are first-person works presented as sketches or
    impressions (e.g., Y. Chiang; Sze); autobiographies of "returned students"
    for whom sojourn in the United States was clearly a brief interlude (e.g.,
    M. Chiang); and autobiographies by Chinese-Americans written in Chi-
    nese, such as those listed in Lai (*A History Reclaimed*, 85–105). The issue
    of choice of language is discussed in the text of this essay.

7   Boelhower briefly mentions Chinatowns in his introduction (*Immigrant
    Autobiography*, 52).

8   For the limited purposes of this essay, I accept, without challenge, Lejeune's
    identification of author, narrator, and protagonist as a criterion for defin-
    ing the autobiographical genre. Elbaz (6–9) summarizes some theoretical
    objections to this view.

9   There are always "gray areas" qualifying any generalization; those who
    immigrate in early childhood, those of mixed blood, those with one immi-
    grant and one American-born parent, and other borderline cases must be
    left out of our discussion.

10 Sumida provides an interesting example of such deconstructive reading
    in his analysis of the conflict between first- and second-generation Japanese
    Americans portrayed in Murayama's story of Hawaiian plantation life, *All
    I Asking for Is My Body* [sic].

11 A policy of exclusion against the Chinese was in effect from 1882 to 1943;
    laborers, "aliens ineligible for citizenship" (Chinese included), as well as
    Chinese wives of U.S. citizens were all denied entry. Chinese-American
    communities became "bachelor societies" with extremely unbalanced
    male-female ratios and hardly any family life to speak of. See Chen (144–71)
    and Lyman (86–92) for brief accounts of this history.

12 See S. C. Wong (212–16) for a brief account of the "after-hours" Chinese
    language school as an evolving institution in America.

13 The generic ambiguity of this well-known work is a subject of great con-
    troversy within the Chinese-American community. In a forthcoming essay,
    "Autobiography as Guided Chinatown Tour? Maxine Hong Kingston's
    The Woman Warrior and the Chinese American Autobiographical Debate,"
    to appear in *American Lives: Essays in Multicultural American Autobiography*,
    ed. James Payne (Knoxville: Tennessee University Press), I have treated
    this complex matter at some length. The publication and widespread ac-
    ceptance of *The Woman Warrior* as an autobiography are by now historical
    facts which have led to extensions of the concept of autobiography.

14 Ueda reviews legislation on naturalization and citizenship from the colo-
    nial period to the present. Note, in particular, various restrictions against
    the naturalization of Chinese as well as other ethnic groups judged unlikely
    or unwelcome candidates for assimilation (125–37). Lesser examines Su-

preme Court naturalization rulings affecting Asian-Americans, tracing the role of race in legal definitions of the undesirable "other."

15 I am indebted to Michael Omi for referring me to Hansen's work.

16 Hansen's principle does not take into account factors like age at immigration, mixed parentage, socioeconomic background, and so forth.

17 In this connection, I wonder why Boelhower has found second-generation *Mount Allegro* a better exponent of the substitution strategy than any other first-generation account. Could it be that Gerlando, more secure than his parents in the American mainstream, can afford the luxury of celebrating his ethnic culture as a "counter-cultural alternative" (Boelhower, *Immigrant Autobiography*, 20)?

18 Under "Biographies and Travel Accounts" Lai (*A History Reclaimed*, 85–105) lists a number of autobiographies in Chinese; life in America is depicted to various extents in these works.

19 An elaboration of this idea can be found in a section on cartography in Boelhower's recent *Through a Glass Darkly* (44–79).

20 Lee Yan Phou has retained the Chinese practice of placing the surname before the given name, as have other early immigrant writers discussed in this essay, such as Huie Kin and Yung Wing. (See notes 22 and 28.) Korean author New Il-Han (see note 37) follows a similar practice.

The basis for regarding Lee as an immigrant rather than a visitor can be found in LaFargue (14–18, 50–54). This evidence overrides the suggestion in X. Li (56–60) that Lee might have returned to China when his sponsoring organization, the Chinese Education Mission founded by Yung Wing, was closed down.

21 The single reference to the "Promised Land" that I found in Wei and Quinn (9) is more a cliché than part of an extensive network of mythic references.

22 Altough Huie returned to and died in China (Yang, 53), he spent the majority of his life working and raising a family in the United States (Huie, 114). I think we may safely classify him as an American immigrant and his *Reminiscences* as an immigrant autobiography.

Boelhower himself includes the repatriated Carnevali in his discussion; to me, the practice is considerably more justifiable than combining the second generation with the first. Among immigrants, the subjective sense of belonging and the objective fact of residence do not always coincide, and intention and circumstances are always open to change, so that the sojourner-settler distinction cannot be absolute. Repatriation was common even during the "Great Wave" of European immigration; the 1911 Dillingham Commission Report estimated that two-fifths of the new immigrants returned to Europe after a relatively short time (Portes and Bach, 31).

23 Park's parents were Korean, but he was raised in Manchuria as a Chinese and later wrote of Chinese matters as a Chinese. For the purposes of this essay I consider *Chinaman's Chance* a Chinese-American autobiography. Cheung and Yogi's bibliography of Asian American literature, organized on the basis of ethnic origin alone, lists Park under "Korean-American writers."

24 One indication of the parallel perceptions of Australia and America can be seen in the Chinese names for San Francisco and Melbourne: *Old Gold Mountain* and *New Gold Mountain*. I am indebted to Chinese-American historian Him Mark Lai for this information.

25 According to Latourette, although missionary activities were recorded in China as early as the eighth and ninth centuries, it wan't until the Qing, or Manchu, Empire began its precipitous decline in the mid-nineteenth century that Christianity penetrated Chinese culture to any significant degree. The civil war and Japanese invasion of the 1930s and 1940s, the establishment of the Communist regime on the mainland in 1949, and periodic crackdowns by the Communists on organized religion all curtailed the spread of Christianity. See Brown for an account of the church since 1949. All in all, despite the church's continued presence in Taiwan and recent signs of religious revival on the mainland, the cumulative impact of Christianity on the life and thought of the majority of Chinese must be deemed extremely limited.

26 Gender may also have been a significant factor (Latourette, 449–51; Varg, 117).

27 Wei and Quinn (158–62) provide a vivid example of how Christian doctrine may be viewed by the Chinese simply as an inconvenience attached to an elite Western education. See also Latourette (683–84) and Varg (320). Note that even as partisan a Christian apologist as Latourette has to contend seriously with the criticism that "beyond aiding in the initial stages of the introduction of Western civilization, especially of the newer education, missions have made little impression upon the country as a whole" (831).

28 Chin, in "This Is Not an Autobiography," asserts that there is a Christianized or missionary tradition in Chinese-American literature, exemplified by autobiography and starting with Yung Wing's *My Life in China and America*, which has been disproportionately favored by white publishers.

29 Lai (*A History Reclaimed*, 17–22) lists sources that document the global presence of Chinese as well as their current status.

30 See, for example, Lyman (110–11) and Lai, Lim, and Yung (20, 22) for an account of the "paper son" system. Other fraudulent means of entry were also used. Immigration laws were liberalized in 1965 to eliminate previous biases in favor of Northwestern European immigrants (Bernard, 103–105).

31 These dates are approximate but generally accepted. 1924 saw the passage of the restrictive Johnson-Reid Act which, among other provisions, set up a "national origins" system curtailing the entry of southern and eastern Europeans (Bernard, 96–98), who constituted the majority of immigrants in the 1890s. See Easterlin (11–18) for figures and trends in European immigration.

32 In Lee, the account of life in China up to departure for the United States takes up 98 out of 105 pages; in Wong and Cressy, 365 out of 379 pages; in Wei and Quinn, 232 out of 241 pages; in Cheng, 530 out of 533 pages.

33 According to Lai (*A History Reclaimed*, 86, 90, 95), Chennault, M. Chiang, and Chao have published autobiographical accounts in Chinese as well.

It would be interesting to compare the Chinese and English versions to see what modifications, if any, the authors have made to accommodate different audiences.

34 Elbaz's thesis that the practice of autobiography is based on a concept of the self as "a commodity with an exchange value" (152) or "the exclusive property of its owner" (153) may be relevant here.

35 These terms allude to Boelhower's description of the "double self" in immigrant autobiography: "The protagonist-narrator is both emigrant and immigrant, exile and discoverer, and both these aspects enroll him under the sign of the voyager, the hero-adventurer" (*Immigrant Autobiography*, 37). My forthcoming essay, cited in note 13, discusses the "tour guide" function of the ethnic autobiographer in greater detail.

36 Brian Niiya, personal communication, 2 Feb. 1989. This section of my essay relies heavily on Niiya's work on Asian-American autobiography for a master's thesis at the University of California, Los Angeles.

37 Kim (25–26) notes that Lee's *When I Was a Boy in China* and New Il-Han's *When I Was a Boy in Korea* were solicited by D. Lothrop Company of Boston as part of a series of books by young men from various lands. Kuo (344–45) writes of her meeting with American publishers to size up the market and the competition for first-person interpretations of Chinese culture after the manner of Lin Yutang. See Hsu and Palubinskas (10) and Chin et al. (xxiii–xxiv) for an analysis of the "publishability" of Asian-American autobiographies in a racial context.

38 I am indebted to Michael Omi and Brian Niiya for pointing out the relevance of Blauner's work to my thesis.

39 For example, if Mangione's *Mount Allegro*, Lowe's *Father and Glorious Descendant*, and Sone's *Nisei Daughter*, by children of immigrants from different ethnic groups, are read together, we might detect in their humorous tone an effort to fuse ridicule of and affection for the parents' Old World ways; this may lead to an inquiry into the cultural balancing strategies of second-generation autobiographers.

Second-generation autobiographies from the same ethnic group, Chinese, might show another kind of similarity: *Father and Glorious Descendant*, *The Woman Warrior*, and L. Li's *Life Is for a Long Time* share an uncertainty of focus, in that the autobiographical label sometimes seems a cover for telling the immigrant generation's stories.

Titles like *Daughter of Confucius* (foreign-born), *Fifth Chinese Daughter* (American-born), and *Second Daughter* (foreign-born) should alert us to the importance of gender in Chinese-American autobiography. Almost all the autobiographies by women that I have cited in this essay allude to the author's awareness of the disadvantages of her sex, accompanied by an account of how she has come to be educated: an enlightened father or a wise grandmother or mother, the good fortune to be given the chance to acquire literacy, or to go to college, or to study English. From this one might make a leap across ethnic boundaries, contrasting the importance of literacy in the autobiographies of Chinese women and of blacks.

WORKS CITED

Abramson, Edward A. *The Immigrant Experience in American Literature.* BAAS
    Pamphlets in American Studies 10. Durham, England: British Associa-
    tion for American Studies, 1982.
Adamic, Louis. *Laughing in the Jungle: The Autobiography of an Immigrant in Amer-*
    ica. New York: Harper & Bros., 1932.
Antin, Mary. *The Promised Land.* Boston: Houghton Mifflin, 1912.
Bercovitch, Sacvan. *The Puritan Origins of the American Self.* New Haven: Yale
    University Press, 1975.
Bercovitch, Sacvan. "The Ritual of American Autobiography: Edwards, Frank-
    lin, Thoreau." *Revue Française d'Etudes Américaines* 14 (1982): 138–50.
Bergland, Betty. "Rethinking the Ethnic Subject: Submerged Narratives and
    Autobiographies of Immigrant Women." Paper delivered at the MELUS
    Convention. Amherst, MA, 14–16 April, 1988.
Bernard, William S. "A History of U.S. Immigration Policy." In Easterlin et al.,
    75–205.
Blasing, Mutlu Konuk. *The Art of Life: Studies in American Autobiographical*
    Literature. Austin: University of Texas Press, 1977.
Blauner, Robert. *Racial Oppression in America.* New York: Harper & Row, 1972.
Boelhower, William. *Immigrant Autobiography in the United States: Four Versions*
    of the Italian American Self. Verona, Italy: Essedue Edizioni, 1982.
Boelhower, William. *Through a Glass Darkly: Ethnic Semiosis in American*
    Literature. 1984. New York: Oxford University Press, 1987.
Bok, Edward. *The Americanization of Edward Bok: The Autobiography of a Dutch*
    Boy Fifty Years After. New York: Charles Scribner's Sons, 1920.
Buaken, Manuel J. *I Have Lived with the American People.* Caldwell, ID: Caxton,
    1948.
Brown, G. Thompson. *Christianity and the People's Republic of China.* Rev. ed.
    Atlanta: Knox, 1986.
Cahan, Abraham. *The Education of Abraham Cahan.* Trans. Leon Stein, Abraham
    P. Conan, and Lynn Davison. Philadelphia: Jewish Pub. Soc. of America,
    1969.
Carnevali, Emanuel. *The Autobiography of Emanuel Carnevali.* Comp. Kay Boyle.
    New York: Horizon, 1967.
✓ Chao, Buwei Yang. *Autobiography of a Chinese Woman.* [1947]. Trans. Yuenren
    Chao. Westport, CT: Greenwood, 1970.
Chen, Jack. *The Chinese of America.* San Francisco: Harper & Row, 1981.
Cheng, Nien. *Life and Death in Shanghai.* 1986. New York: Penguin, 1988.
Chennault, Anna. *The Education of Anna.* New York: Times, 1980.
Cheung, King-Kok, and Stan Yogi. *Asian American Literature: An Annotated*
    Bibliography. New York: Modern Language Association, 1988.
Chiang, Monlin. *Tides from the West: A Chinese Autobiography.* New Haven: Yale
    University Press, 1947.
Chiang, Yee. *The Silent Traveller in New York.* New York: Day, 1950.
Chin, Frank. "This Is Not an Autobiography." *Genre* 18 (1985): 109–30.

Chin, Frank et al. "An Introduction to Chinese- and Japanese-American Literature."[1974]. In *Aiiieeeee! An Anthology of Asian-American Writers.* Ed. Frank Chin et al. Washington, DC: Howard University Press, 1983, xxi–xlviii.

Cooley, Thomas. *Educated Lives: The Rise of Modern Autobiography in America.* Columbus: Ohio University Press, 1976.

Couser, G. Thomas. *American Autobiography: The Prophetic Mode.* Amherst: University of Massachusetts Press, 1979.

Cox, James M. "Autobiography and America." *Virginia Quarterly Review* 47 (1971): 252–77.

D'Angelo, Pascal. *Pascal D'Angelo, Son of Italy.* New York: Macmillan, 1924.

Demirturk, Emine Lale. "The Female Identity in Cross-Cultural Perspective: Immigrant Women's Autobiography." *DAI* 47 (1987): 2584-A.

DiPietro, Robert J., and Edward Ifkovic, eds. *Ethnic Perspective in American Literature.* New York: Modern Language Association, 1983.

Easterlin, Richard A. "Economic and Social Characteristics of the Immigrants." In Easterlin et al., *Immigration*, 1–34.

Easterlin, Richard A.; David Ward; William S. Bernard; and Reed Ueda. *Immigration.* Dimensions of Ethnicity: A Series of Selections from the Harvard Encyclopedia of American Ethnic Groups. Ed. Stephan Thernstrom, Ann Orlov, and Oscar Handlin. Cambridge: Harvard University Press, 1982.

Elbaz, Robert. *The Changing Nature of the Self: A Critical Study of the Autobiographic Discourse.* London: Croom Helm, 1988.

Fried, Louis. "Jacob Riis and the Jews: The Ambivalent Quest for Community." *American Studies* 20 (1979): 5–24.

Handlin, Oscar. *The Uprooted: The Epic Story of the Great Migrations That Made the American People.* Boston: Little, Brown, 1951.

Hansen, M. L. "The Problem of the Third Generation Immigrant." Augustana Historical Society Publications. Rock Island, IL: 1938.

Hansen, M. L. "The Third Generation in America: A Classic Essay in Immigration History." *Commentary* 14 (1952): 492–500.

Holte, James Craig. "The Representative Voice: Autobiography and the Ethnic Experience." *MELUS* 9 (1982): 25–46.

Holte, James Craig. *The Ethnic I: A Sourcebook for Ethnic American Autobiography.* New York: Greenwood, 1988.

Huie, Kin. *Reminiscences.* Peiping: San Yu, 1932.

Hsu, Kai-yu, and Helen Palubinskas. "Chinese American Literature." In *Asian-American Authors.* Ed. Kai-yu Hsu and Helena Palubinskas. Boston: Houghton, Mifflin, 1972, 7–12.

Kim, Elaine H. *Asian American Literature: An Introduction to the Writings and Their Social Context.* Philadelphia: Temple University Press, 1982.

Kingston, Maxine Hong. *The Woman Warrior: Memoirs of a Girlhood Among Ghosts.* 1976. New York: Random-Vintage, 1977.

Kuo, Helena. *I've Come a Long Way.* New York: Appleton-Century-Crofts, 1942.

LaFargue, Thomas E. *China's First Hundred.* Pullman, WA: State College of Washington Press, 1942.

Lai, Him Mark, comp. *A History Reclaimed: An Annotated Bibliography of Chinese Language Materials on the Chinese of America*. Ed. Russell Leong and Jean Pang Yip. Los Angeles: Resource Development and Publications, Asian American Studies Center, University of California, 1986.

Lai, Him Mark; Genny Lim; and Judy Yung. *Island: Poetry and History of Chinese Immigrants on Angel Island, 1910–1940*. San Francisco: HOC DOI Project, 1980.

Latourette, Kenneth Scott. *A History of Christian Missions in China*. New York: Macmillan, 1929.

Lee, Yan Phou. *When I Was a Boy in China*. Boston: Lothrop, 1887.

Lejeune, Philippe. *Le pacte autobiographique*. Paris, Seuil, 1975.

Lesser, Jeff H. "Always 'Outsiders': Asians, Naturalization, and the Supreme Court." *Amerasia Journal* 12, no. 1 (1985–86): 83–100.

Li, Ling-Ai. *Life Is for a Long Time: A Chinese Hawaiian Memoir*. New York: Hasting, 1972.

Li, Xisuo. *Jindai Zongguo de liuxue sheng* [*Chinese Students Abroad in Recent History*]. Beijing: Renmin, 1987.

Lowe, Pardee. *Father and Glorious Descendant*. Boston: Little, Brown, 1943.

Lyman, Stanford M. *Chinese Americans*. New York: Random House, 1974.

Mangione, Jerre. *Mount Allegro: A Memoir of Italian American Life*. [1942]. New York: Columbia University Press, 1981.

Murayama, Milton. *All I Asking For Is My Body*. San Francisco: Supa Press, 1975.

Neidle, Cecyle S. "The Foreign-Born View America: A Study of Autobiographies Written by Immigrants to the United States." Ph.D. diss. New York University, 1964.

New, Il-Han. *When I Was a Boy in Korea*. Boston: Lothrop, 1928.

Olney, James. ed. *Autobiography: Essays Theoretical and Cultural*. Princeton: Princeton University Press, 1980.

Panunzio, Constantine M. *The Soul of an Immigrant*. New York: Macmillan, 1922.

Park, No-Yong. *Chinaman's Chance: An Autobiography*. Boston: Meador, 1940.

Portes, Alejandro, and Robert L. Bach. *Latin Journey: A Longitudinal Study of Cuban and Mexican Immigrants in the United States*. Berkeley and Los Angeles: University of California Press, 1985.

Reimers, David M. *Still the Golden Door: The Third World Comes to America*. New York: Columbia University Press, 1985.

Riis, Jacob. *The Making of an American*. New York: Macmillan, 1924.

Rodriguez, Richard. *Hunger of Memory: The Education of Richard Rodriguez*. Boston: Godine, 1981.

Rubin, Steven J. "Style and Meaning in Mary Antin's *The Promised Land*: A Reevaluation." *Studies in American Jewish Literature* 5 (1986): 35–43.

Sayre, Robert F. *The Examined Self: Benjamin Franklin, Henry Adams, Henry James*. Princeton: Princeton University Press, 1964.

Sayre, Robert F. "Autobiography and the Making of America." In Olney, *Autobiography*, 146–68.

Sayre, Robert F. "The Proper Study: Autobiographies in American Studies." In *The American Autobiography: A Collection of Critical Essays*. Ed. Albert E. Stone. Englewood Cliffs, NJ: Prentice-Hall, 1981, 11–30.

Sollors, Werner. "Literature and Ethnicity." In *Harvard Encyclopedia of American Ethnic Groups*. Ed. Stephan Thernstrom, Ann Orlov, and Oscar Handlin. Cambridge: Harvard University Press, 1980, 647–65.

Sollors, Werner. "Nine Suggestions for Historians of American Ethnic Literature." *MELUS* 11 (1984): 95–96.

Sollors, Werner. "A Critique of Pure Pluralism." In *Reconstructing American Literary Theory*. Ed. Sacvan Bercovitch. Cambridge: Harvard University Press, 1986, 250–79.

Sollors, Werner. *Beyond Ethnicity: Consent and Descent in American Culture*. New York: Oxford University Press, 1986.

Sone, Monica. *Nisei Daughter*. [1953]. Seattle: University of Washington Press, 1979.

Spengemann, William C., and L. R. Lundquist. "Autobiography and the American Myth." *American Quarterly* 17 (1965): 501–19.

Steiner, Edward A. *From Alien to Citizen*. New York: Fleming H. Revell, 1914.

Stone, Alfred E. "Autobiography in American Culture: Looking Back at the Seventies." *American Studies International* 19 (1981): 3–14.

Stone, Alfred E. *Autobiographical Occasions and Original Acts: Versions of American Identity from Henry Adams to Nate Shaw*. Philadelphia: University of Pennsylvania Press, 1982.

Sumida, Stephen H. "First Generations in Asian American Literature: As Viewed in Some Second Generation Works." In *Issues in Asian and Pacific American Education*. Ed. Nobuya Tsuchida. Minneapolis: Asian/Pacific Learning Resource Center, University of Minnesota, and National Association for Asian and Pacific American Education, 1986, 64–70.

Sze, Mai-mai. *Echo of a Cry: A Story Which Began in China*. New York: Harcourt, Brace, 1945.

Taylor, Gordon O. *Chapters of Experience: Studies in 20th* [sic] *Century American Autobiography*. New York: St. Martin's, 1983.

Ueda, Reed. "Naturalization and Citizenship." In Easterlin et al., *Immigration*, 106–154.

Varg, Paul A. *Missionaries, Chinese, and Diplomats: The American Protestant Missionary Movement in China, 1890–1952*. Princeton: Princeton University Press, 1958.

Wei, Katherine, and Terry Quinn. *Second Daughter: Growing Up in China, 1930–1949*. Boston: Little, Brown, 1984.

Wong, Jade Snow. *Fifth Chinese Daughter*. [1945]. New York: Harper-Perennial, 1965.

Wong, Sau-ling Cynthia. "The Language Situation of Chinese Americans." In *Language Diversity: Problem or Resource? A Social and Educational Perspective on Language Minorities in the United States*. Ed. Sandra Lee McKay and Sau-ling Cynthia Wong. Cambridge: Newbury, 1988, 193–228.

Wong, Su-ling [pseud.], and Earl Herbert Cressy. *Daughter of Confucius: A Personal History*. New York: Farrar, Straus, and Giroux, 1952.

Yang, Qizhuang. "Xu Qin Mushi Zhuanlue" ["A Brief Biography of Huie Kin"]. In *The 100th Anniversary of the Founding, 58th Anniversary of the Naming of the First Chinese Presbyterian Church of the City of New York, 1868–1968*. New York: First Chinese Presbyterian Church, 1968.

Yudkin, Leon Israel. *Jewish Writing and Identity in the Twentieth Century*. London: Croom Helm, 1982.

Yung, Wing. *My Life in China and America*. New York: Henry Holt, 1909.

CHAPTER 7

Native American Autobiography and the Synecdochic Self

ARNOLD KRUPAT

Although studies of Native American autobiography have become more numerous of late, no one of them has yet taken as a central focus the matter that has perhaps more than any other occupied students of Western autobiography: the nature of the self presented in these texts. This is not to indicate an error or omission; on the contrary, inasmuch as the centrality of the self in Western autobiography finds no close parallel in Native American autobiography, any immediate orientation toward the self would inevitably have seemed ethnocentric, or at the least premature. But to say that the typical Western understanding of the self is neither prioritized nor valorized in Native American autobiography is not to say that all modes of subjectivity are, therefore, absent or unimportant in these texts. Whether or not Paul Heelas is correct in his sweeping suggestion that "the autonomous self is universal" (48), it is very likely the case that some sense of self—perhaps Amelie Rorty's "reflective, conscious subject of experience, a subject that is not identical with any set of its experiences, memories or traits, but is that which *has* all of them" (11)—is indeed to be found universally, and therefore also present among Native American people.

The problem is that every term in Rorty's (or any other) description is culturally inflected, determined in its meaning by the specific codes according to which we differentially "have," as historically and geographically situated men and women, our similar "experiences" as human beings.[1] What, after all, does it mean for the Koya to be "reflective," for the Yaqui to be "conscious," for the Talensi to be a "subject," for the Ilongot to "remember"? Humans are or do all of these things,

171

and we are or do them in the same ways—differently. Considerations of this sort have animated work in the ethnography of the self, from its rudimentary and initially "anti-psychological"[2] beginnings in the form of "culture and personality" studies from about 1910 on, to its current existence in the form of a decidedly "psychological anthropology." Yet for all of this work, we are still far from any conceptual and terminological consensus about how to speak of the *self*, the *individual*, or the *ego*, the *I*, or *me*, the *modal personality*, the *model of identity*—or, indeed, the *subject*,—where each of these terms signals not only a personal preference, a research interest or emphasis, but also, as Paul Smith has recently shown, a disciplinary affiliation (*subjects* coming more or less from philosophy, *selves* from the humanities, *egos* and *modal personalities* from the social sciences, etc.).[3] Even to the extent that we do know how these terms apply to the West, we know less well how they apply (or don't apply) to the rest, whose thought on such matters is reduced (or elevated) to the level of "indigenous psychologies."[4]

Studies of this sort are barely a century old, so that it would be premature to abandon, as a certain postmodernist strain of thought would urge, further efforts in the direction of some greater accuracy of description and explanation. Yet it is necessary to acknowledge here a practical rather than a theoretical problem certain to beset advances along these lines, one akin to a problem that Freud posited for the general prospects of psychoanalysis.[5] I refer to the fact that while it is a fairly simple matter to convince people that their eating or greeting habits are cultural rather than natural, it is considerably more difficult to convince them that the ways in which they think and deeply feel about themselves are also more nearly culturally than biologically determined. And modern, Western concepts of the self are so thoroughly committed to notions of interiority and individualism that even anthropologically sophisticated Westerners tend to construct their accounts of the varieties of selfhood as evolutionary narratives, telling stories of a progression from the social and public orientation of ancient or "primitive" self-conception (the self as social "person") to the modern, Western, "civilized," egocentric/individualist sense of self.[6]

This tendency may be responsible for the comic plot of Marcel Mauss's 1938 essay, most recently translated as "A Category of the Human Mind: The Notion of Person; the Notion of Self." This classic piece tells a story which has as its happy ending the emergence of the *moi*, the Western postromantic self as veritably "sacred," a construction that surpasses the *personnage* models of the Native Americans, Mauss's chief illustrative example, and the *personnalité* models of ancient and/or non-Western peoples generally. For Mauss, Native American self-consciousness was minimal, or, better, defined by the etymology of the word *person* (*personne, personnage*), from Latin *persona, per sonare,* as this referred to the mask through which the actor spoke his role in public. Not an individual with rights and responsibilities before the law (this must await the Roman addition of the right to a personal *praenomen,* or "forename," and the Christian invention of "the moral person"), the Indian was rather the representative of his ancestor or his clan, an actor who merely performed his appointed character. He (*she* was rarely at issue) knew nothing of that consciousness which is self-consciousness as "an act of the 'self,'" which, from Fichte on, saw "the revolution in mentalities . . . accomplished" (Mauss, 22). The modern *moi,* I will suggest, may be seen at its apogee in such texts as Gerard Manley Hopkins's "As kingfishers catch fire, dragonflies draw flame," where the inward self appears both as actor "in God's eye," and unique romantic consciousness. For Hopkins,

> Each mortal thing does one thing and the same:
> Deals out that being indoors each one dwells;
> Selves—goes itself; *myself* it speaks and spells,
> Crying *What I do is me: for that I came* (51).

But this lovely indoor self, in Mauss's tale, unfortunately was never present to the poor outdoor Indian.

In his ultimate celebration of the inward self, Mauss, as a number of commentators have noted, seems to renege on his initial promise to "leave aside everything which relates to the 'self' (*moi*), the conscious personality as such," and to focus instead on the "social history" (3) of the person, the category of prime concern to Mauss's uncle and *maître,* Emile Durkheim, as it was to the major but—at least in literary circles—somewhat obscure figure, George Herbert Mead. Mead's "social theory of the self," as Stephen Lukes has remarked, sought "to explain how it can be, in all societies and cultures, that [in Mead's words, now]

all selves are constituted by or in terms of the social process, and are individual reflections of it [yet] every individual self has its own peculiar individuality, its own unique pattern (Lukes, 287).

In this regard, any attempt to privilege the sacred inviolability of the self by setting it in opposition to society or culture, standard Western bourgeois practice at least since Fichte, involves a significant loss of understanding. To avoid just such a loss, indeed, to achieve some gain in understanding, we get, in the forties and fifties, a redescription of the Native American sense of self by such writers as Dorothy Lee and George Devereux, among others, in ways that seek not to make it seem

"primitive" and retrograde, but progressively wiser than the West in
its comprehension of the dynamics of self and society: here is comedy
once again, only with a different protagonist.[7] It was Devereux's opinion that for the Native Americans, "maximum individuation and maximum socialization go hand in hand" ("From Anxiety to Method," 291),
while Lee concluded that Lakota cultures demonstrate "autonomy and
community in transaction" ("Autonomy," 41). Of the Wintu self, Lee
noted (her generalizations supported by impressionistically selective
citations from Wintu grammar and diction), that it is

> not clearly opposed to the other, neither is it clearly identical with or incor-
> porated in the other. On most occasions it participates to some extent in the
> other, and is of equal status to the other . . . ("Conception of the Self," 137).

Wintu know "society" more easily than the "self," the reverse of our
Western knowledge, but most of all, Wintu seem to have found a way
to reconcile what often appears to Euro-Americans as an opposition
between self and society.[8]

In any event, insofar as we would attempt to generalize about the
Native American self from the available studies, that self would seem
to be less attracted to introspection, integration, expansion, or fulfil-
ment than the Western self appears to be. It would seem relatively un-
interested in such things as the "I-am-Me" experience,[9] and a sense of
uniqueness or individuality. More positively, one might perhaps instan-
tiate an I-am-We experience as descriptive of the Native sense of self,
where such a phrase indicates that I understand myself as a self only
in relation to the coherent and bounded whole of which I am a part (e.g.,
the preceding quotation from Lee above). Here, Jane Fajans's distinction between the "*person* as a bounded entity invested with specific
patterns of social behavior, normative powers, and restraints, and the
individual as an entity with interiorized conscience, feelings, goals,
motivations, and aspirations" (370; my emphasis) is useful. Native
Americans (along with most of the world's people, it would seem) tend
to construct themselves not as individuals but as persons, who, because
of their sensitivity to social "restraints," may well feel more nearly
"under control," in Andrew Lock's term, rather than "in control" (28ff),
the sense of self more typical of Western "individuals" oriented toward
interiority. It needs to be said that this subjective sense of the matter
does not mean that Native American "persons" are, in point of objective fact, more "controlled" than Euro-American "individuals," nor that
their sense of operative "restraints" corresponds closely to what the
Western bourgeois individual would understand by such terms.

At this point it would be possible to proceed with readings of several Native American autobiographies in order to determine whether their authors do or do not seem to conceive themselves in the ways suggested by the available anthropological and psychological literature. The danger is that such readings inevitably tend to become not actually "readings" at all, but, instead, tautological exercises in the "discovery" of literary "evidence" for psychological or anthropological "truths" already found elsewhere, as if autobiography were no more than a museum of the self where one could peer through language as through the transparent glass of a case. To avoid such vulgar reductionism, it is tempting to adopt, instead, the purely formalist position of someone like Paul de Man, who insists that autobiography is no more than a figure of reading, an effect of language, and as such, can provide no reliable information about selves—or about anything else.[10] In de Man's view, autobiographical writing is entrapped within an infinitely regressive specular structure whose only legitimate terminal point is the silence of death, the end of self. This position forecloses the possibility of ever knowing another self in autobiography while opening— what it takes as abundant recompense—the possibility of an endless play of linguistic signification.

How, then, to navigate between the Scylla of a purely realistic/referential reading and the Charybdis of a purely linguistic/figural reading? How satisfy a thoroughly reputable interest in the subject of autobiography as biographical existent, and as cultural and historical agent, while centering one's commentary on what autobiographical texts present linguistically, the actual words from which any sense of self must be inferred? For, to speak now only of Native American autobiographies, one finds little or no explicit mention of who-I-am, little or no mention at all of the self as the object of conscious and developed concern.

Let me propose as one approach—and as an attempt at mediating the two positions—that we appropriate terms for the figures of language as applicable to some facts of life. I want to suggest that the West's traditional fourfold rhetorical division of *elocutio* and *poeisis* into metaphor, metonymy, synedoche, and irony (antiphrasis), a division intended to name linguistic relations, may be taken metaphorically as naming relations of an actual/"realistic" type between the person/individual and others (or society) and so may provide terms for a theory of self-conception and self-situation *as these appear in the texts we call autobiographies.* If, for example, there are indeed peoples who actually do conceive of themselves as in some very real sense interchangeable with their ancestors and their posterity (Geertz's Balinese, perhaps?[11]), then we might expect any stories they tell about themselves to show a *metaphorical* conception of the self, one that constructs identity paradigmatically, along the vertical axis of selection. Metonymy and synecdoche involve relations of part-to-part and part-to-whole. Thus, where personal accounts are marked by the individual's sense of herself predominantly in relation to other distinct individuals, one might speak of a *metonymic* sense of self; where narration of personal history is more nearly marked by the individual's sense of himself in relation to collective social units or groupings, one might speak of a *synecdochic* sense of self, both of these constructing identity syntagmatically, along the horizontal axis of combination.

While I am ignorant of specific instances of an *ironic* sense of self elsewhere in the world, I would suggest that the "modernist" sense of self in the West may be usefully categorized as ironic. The exemplary texts here (I cite novelistic examples for the purer types that fiction can construct; autobiographical near-equivalents may readily enough be found) are, at the earliest, Dostoevsky's story of the "underground man," and then a whole library of modern "characters": T. S. Eliot's fragmented voices out of "the waste land," Robert Musil's "man without qualities," Kafka's "arrested" and metamorphosed men, Virginia Woolf's disembodied monologists in *The Waves*, right on to Samuel Beckett's portrayals of the self as contingent to the point of virtual dissolution. In these texts there is neither the metaphorical sense of the cosmic interchangeability of persons, nor the metonymic sense of the specific uniqueness of otherwise comparable individuals, nor the synecdochic sense of personal representation of an abstract collective entity. Rather there is only the sense of self-identity as fact-with-no-meaning: I-am-I, but so what. Or, in the specifically antiphrastic form, I am not like him, not like her, certainly not like them, that's not me, nor that, nor am I much like anything at all.[12]

From the perspective of a rhetorical hardliner like de Man, the procedure I have outlined represents no more than a categorical error: one cannot cross the line from language to life, inasmuch as it is the very essence of figures to signify *only* linguistically and *not* realistically. That is to say, if one takes the standard illustration of synecdoche, *fifty sail* for *fifty ships*, it is obvious that the figure makes no sense realistically:[13] although one *can*, of course, visualize fifty unattached *sails* coming across the water, the image itself is unlikely to refer to anything one might actually see. Literally, it makes no sense. The same is true for "he is all heart" (e.g., visualizing "him" as an assemblage of arteries, auricles, ventricles, etc.). Nonetheless, I am making the assumption that the part-to-whole relation named by the term *synecdoche* and the part-to-part relation named by the term *metonymy,* along with the relations termed *metaphoric* and *ironic* as these are posited in language, can usefully be applied to relations we experience in life, in particular the relation of the individual, self, or subject to other individuals, selves, or subjects and to collectively constituted groups.

I am assuming, to put it in the phrase of George Lakoff and Mark Johnson, that there are, indeed, "metaphors we live by" and that, as M. Brewster Smith has written, "the metaphorical texture of our views of self is part and parcel of our metaphorical construction of the world" (74). I tend to believe that there is not a radical epistemological break between the use of metaphor in life, as in Lakoff and Johnson's sense that metaphor quite unself-consciously and unambiguously involves "*understanding and experiencing* one kind of thing in terms of another" (5 my emphasis), and the use of metaphor in texts, as in Gerard Genette's sense of the figure precisely as "a sense of figure, . . . [whose] existence depends completely on the awareness that the reader has, or does not have of the ambiguity of the discourse that is being offered him" (54). For all that the former emphasizes the sense-constructing possibilities of figures while the latter asserts the sense-deconstructing possibilities of figures, I take the difference as a matter of emphasis rather than one of opposition.[14] Thus, I will suggest that the theory of tropes has value for a theory of self-conception, and that its usefulness resides most particularly in its giving us a way of speaking of the self as it is actually presented textually, in autobiography. I shall further suggest that cultural techniques of information transmission—oral as differentiated from written techniques—also correlate with particular figural preferences and particular conceptions of self.

In a provocative article, Stephen Tyler has attempted to place the "Standard Average European"[15] preference for seeing as a way of knowing and for writing as a way of conveying what is known against the backdrop of an ignored or undervalued non-Western preference for doing and speaking. Evading the formalist-structuralist distinction between metaphor and metonymy that, at least since Roman Jakobson's famous essay on "Linguistics and Poetics," has become a virtual staple of poetics—"the irreplaceable bookends of our own modern rhetoric," in Gerard Genette's phrase (107)—Tyler focuses on a distinction between metonymy and synecdoche, not so much as parallel terms concerned with relations of contiguity, contact, or correspondence (syntagmatic relations as opposed to the paradigmatic relations of substitution definitive of metaphor, or the antiphrastic relations of negation definitive of irony), but as terms differentiable by the *kinds* of relation with which they are concerned. For Tyler—and I have already accepted his account of these matters in my preceding remarks—metonymy is concerned with part-part relations while synecdoche is concerned with part-whole relations.[16] Here I want to propose that while modern Western autobiography has been essentially metonymic in orientation, Native American autobiography has been and continues to be persistently synecdochic, and that the preference for synecdochic models of the self has relations to the oral techniques of information transmission typical of Native American culture. Let us (briefly) take this second matter first.

Traditionally, the autobiographical forms (such as they were) that existed among Native American peoples—the *coup* story on the Plains foremost, and accounts of dreams or mystic experiences—were communicated orally—Indians of the present-day United States not having developed alphabetic writing—and (therefore) publicly as well.[17] One did not tell of one's war honors in private, to one's wives or best friends, but to assembled members of the tribe, an audience that included eyewitnesses to the events narrated who were duty-bound to object to or deny any false claims. In the same way, we know that the most powerful visions (e.g., the celebrated visions of Black Elk at ages five and nine) were often enacted tribally, dramatically performed in public so that their full effect, which is to say their collective effect, might be experienced ("done," as Tyler might say).[18] I win honors, then, not only for me (most assuredly for me, however, particularly on the Plains, but elsewhere as well), but for us, the tribe; I am granted a vision, but the vision is not just for me: nor is any of it usable or functional until it is spoken, even performed publicly. This sense of personal eventfulness and this manner of communicating the personal orally, dramatically, performatively, in public, to the extent that they inform any written text of an Indian is very clearly more likely to privilege the synecdochic relation of part-to-whole than the metonymic relation of part-to-part. Speech always assumes a present listener as opposed to writing, where the audience is absent to the author, the author absent to the audience.

It is the part-to-part relation, however, that seems to mark Western autobiography—itself marked by writing. Consider, as evidential shorthand, that *locus classicus* of modern autobiography, Rousseau's *Confessions*. "I understand my own heart," Rousseau writes, "and understand my fellow man. But I am made like no one in the whole world. I may be no better, but at least I am different" (17). The units compared are precisely that, units, one to one, man to man, part to part. Rousseau does not see himself as an aberration, one who cannot accurately be classified among the genus, Man; rather, he is specifically different from other individual men, from each and every one of them, one by one.

If we turn to Thoreau, writing half a century after Rousseau, we find much the same sort of thing.[19] Addressing his "neighbors," in the headnote to *Walden*, Thoreau promises (or threatens) to "wake" them up; addressing his "readers" in the book's second paragraph, he promises to answer their questions "concerning [his] mode of life." In every case, "the *I* or first person . . . will be retained" in his book, for it is "always the first person that is speaking" in writing. What Thoreau would provide is what he himself

require[s] of every writer . . . a simple and sincere account of his own life, and not merely what he has heard of other men's lives; some such account as he would send to his kindred from a distant land; for if he has lived sincerely, it must have been in a distant land to me (1).

"Perhaps," Thoreau continues,

these pages are more particularly addressed to poor students. As for the rest of my readers, they will accept such portions as apply to them. I trust that none will stretch the seams in putting on the coat, for it may do good service to him whom it fits (1–2).

It seems reasonable to read these remarks metonymically: Thoreau's model of proper speech-in-writing images the individual man addressing other individual men (there remains the problem of what women were to do with these constructions), who, while they certainly make up the generalized categories of "neighbors," or "readers," or "writers," or "students," must finally read as he writes, in the "first person," each individually "putting on the coat" to assess its fit. This metonymic construal of the individual autobiographer asserting his or her individuality against or with the individuality of others persists into the twentieth century—when, as I have noted, it begins to dissolve. "I am I because my little dog knows me" (64), Gertrude Stein wrote—but in a book she ironically called *Everybody's Autobiography.*

When we turn to Native American autobiography, the situation is rather different. Native American autobiography, a post-contact phenomenon, as I have detailed the matter elsewhere,[20] exists in two forms, the Indian autobiography and the autobiography by an Indian. The first of these is constituted as a genre of writing by its original, bicultural, composite composition, the product of a collaboration between the Native American subject of the autobiography, who provides its "content," and its Euro-American editor, who ultimately provides its "form" by fixing the text in writing. Autobiographies by Indians, however, are indeed self-written lives; there is no compositeness to their composition, although inasmuch as their subject, in order to *write* a life, must have become "civilized" (in many cases Christianized as well), there remains the element of biculturalism. In both sorts of texts, let me claim, we find a privileging of the synecdochic relation of part-to-whole over the metonymic relation of part-to-part.[21]

At this point, the reader may well expect some illustrative demonstration of a synecdochic nature to make its entrance, a detailed reading of a single text being offered as representative of a larger body of autobiographical work; nor will I fail to conform to such expectation. I have chosen to consider an autobiography by an Indian rather than an Indian autobiography for two reasons. First, every aspect of the Indian autobiography, including the particular sense of self conveyed, is at least theoretically ascribable to its non-Native editor as much as to its Native subject. This fact raises questions it would be too cumbersome to deal with just here. More importantly, to work with the autobiographies of traditional, tribal persons—and Indian autobiographies are almost exclusively focused on this sort of person—and then to show that they are indeed traditionally tribal, relationally synecdochic, courts even a greater circularity than such exercises must inevitably involve. As noted, Indians who write their own life stories must first have learned to write and, at least to that extent, been influenced by the dominant Euro-American culture. To see whether their autobiographical presentations of self, therefore, have also been influenced by the dominant culture—whether they have, in my terms, tended to move from synecdochic to metonymic senses of the self—seems the more interesting tack to take. I proceed now to consider the autobiographical work of the Reverend William Apes (1798–1837).

One of the very first autobiographies by an Indian is *A Son of the Forest* (1829) by the mixed-blood Pequot and Methodist preacher, the Reverend William Apes.[22] This text was followed in 1833 by Apes's the *Experiences of Five Christian Indians of the Pequod Tribe*, the first chapter of which, the "Experience of the Missionary," offers a second brief autobiography by Apes ("the Missionary"). This makes no reference to *A Son of the Forest* but instead promises a further autobiographical volume, "a book of 300 pages, 18mo. in size; and there, the reader will find particulars respecting my life" (4). Apes was never to write such a book, although his further publications—*Indian Nullification of the Unconstitutional Laws of Massachusetts, Relative to the Marshpee Tribe* (1835), in part an account of political work on behalf of the Mashpees which landed him in prison, and *Eulogy on King Philip* (1836), a fierce attack on the Puritan origins of American racism—are both intensely personal. All of his texts, I would suggest, may fruitfully be read as pieces of an extended autobiography.

By 1798, the year of William Apes's birth, Pequot cultural integrity was at a low point. This is to say that aboriginal lands had been usurped or heavily encroached upon by whites, so that traditional ecological economies and cultural practices were severely disrupted where they were not entirely destroyed. Disease, alcoholism, and Christianity served as further agents undermining tribal coherence and cultural competence, with predictable effects on Native self-conception— although Apes came to view Christianity as part of the solution, rather than part of the problem. Apes did not live long with his parents, who tended to move about considerably. Placed with his grandparents, Apes was so cruelly treated—at the age of four, his arm was broken in three places (*Son of the Forest*, 12) as the result of a drunken beating administered by his grandmother—that he eventually was sent to live "among good Christian people" (13). Their goodness did not prevent them from "selling" (31) him to a judge who worked him and "sold" (35) him to someone else. I will not detail Apes's life-adventures further[23]; suffice it to say that he eventually became a convert to evangelical Methodism, attaining to the position of licensed Methodist "exhorter," (111) although the license to preach which he desired was still, at the conclusion of *A Son of the Forest*, withheld from him.

At this point in his life, Apes seems to see himself as something like Mauss's Christian "'moral person,'" virtually "a metaphysical entity" (19). Although Mauss reads the Christian stage of Western self-conception as a step on the way toward (these are, of course, my terms, not those of Mauss) metonymic construals of self, it needs to be said that this is by no means the only reading possible. Christian tradition gives us abundant instances of solitary individuals seeking relation foremost with God (e.g., the early desert fathers, medieval mystics, Louis Dumont's "outworldly" Christian individuals), but it also gives us abundant images of individuals defined foremost by a sense of commonality and community (Dumont's post-Calvinist "inwardly" Christians). For every "I" focused exclusively on "Thou"; for everyone trying to love her particularized neighbor, there are also those who are committed to doing unto *all* others as they would be done to themselves; those committed to what William Bradford called "the church or commonwealth" (39), made up of persons who believe that (I return to Dumont) "we should embody that other world in our determined action upon this one" (116).

It is this latter sense of Christian self-definition that is important to Apes, nor does he fail to grasp its political implications. Towards the close of *A Son of the Forest*, Apes writes

I feel a great deal happier in the *new* [Methodist Society] than I did in the *old* [Methodist Episcopal] church—the government of the first is founded on *republican*, while that of the latter is founded on *monarchial* principles . . . (115).

And Apes "rejoice[s] sincerely in the spread of the principles of civil and religious liberty—may they ever be found 'hand in hand' . . . " (115). He believes that

If these blessed principles prevail . . . the image of God in his members will be a sufficient passport to all Christian privileges; and all the followers of the most high will unite together in singing the song of praise, *Glory to God in the highest, &c.* (115).

In this way Apes seeks to replace the lost paradise of the Pequot—what he called in the first paragraph of his autobiography, "the goodly heritage occupied by this once peaceable and happy tribe" (7)—with the paradise regained in Christ. The tribe to which he would now belong, defining himself by his membership, is that of "the followers of the most high." Obviously enough, "*all* the followers of the most high" (my emphasis) must include Indians—at least those Native "members" of the saved in whom "the image of God" is to "be a sufficient passport to all Christian privileges." "Look brethren," Apes exhorts in his penultimate paragraph,

at the natives of the forest—they come, notwithstanding you call them "*savage*," from the "east and from the west, the north and the south," and will occupy [because the last shall be first?] seats in the kingdom of heaven before you (116).

Yet for all that Christian Indians will share equally with Christian whites a heavenly heritage in the future, those same Indians, now, in the present, are abused and discriminated against by whites. Nor is it Indians only, as Apes came increasingly to understand, but blacks and all people of color[24] who suffer from American racial prejudice. Here, the incompatibility of Christianity and racism emerges as a major theme of William Apes's subsequent writing (as it would, of course, become a theme of Frederick Douglass and the abolitionists). I shall try to say in a moment how this bears on the question of his synecdochic self-definition.

Consider, in these regards, Apes's second brief autobiography, "The Experience of the Missionary." Addressed to the "youth," "those poor children of the forest, who have had taken from them their once delightful plains, and homes of their peaceable habitations . . . " (*Experience of Five Indians*, 3), Apes's account of his life here places a particular emphasis on those aspects of his suffering that occurred because of race prejudice. In a text of only seventeen pages, Apes's increased awareness of the problem of color in America is indicated by such phrases and sentences as "Had my skin been white . . . " (8); "Now, if my face had been white . . . " (9), "I would ask the white man, if he thinks that he can be justified in making just such a being as I am . . . unhappy . . . because God has made us thus . . ." (17); "I was already a hissing-stock and a by-word in the world, merely because I was a child of the forest . . ." (19); and so on.

In these regards, consider also that the cover of the first edition of *The Experience*, gives its full title as *The Experiences of Five Christian Indians: or The Indian's Looking Glass for the White Man*. But *The Indian's Looking Glass* . . . is not merely an alternate title for the collection of autobiographies, but the title of a pamphlet or sermon that appears after the fifth "Experience," at the end of the book. This is a brilliant and violent attack on racism. I will quote its first sentences; they indicate, I believe, a new strength and stylistic assurance.[25] Apes begins,

Having a desire to place a few things before my fellow creatures who are travelling with me to the grave, and to that God who is the maker and preserver both of the white man and the Indian, whose abilities are the same, and who are to be judged by one God, who will show no favor to outward appearances, but will judge righteousness. Now I ask if degradation has not been heaped long enough upon the Indians (53)?

The *or* in the compound title—*or*, that is, instead of *and*—on the cover would seem to urge that the whole of Apes's book be taken as providing a "looking glass" for the white man. And what that looking glass reflects above all are the "national crimes" (56) of white Americans. Here is the extraordinary passage in which this phrase occurs; I believe it is worth quoting at length:

Assemble all nations together in your imagination, and then let the whites be seated amongst them, and then let us look for the whites, and I doubt not it would be hard finding them; for to the rest of the nations, they are still but a handful. Now suppose these skins were put together, and each skin had its national crimes written upon it[26]—which skin do you think would have the greatest? I will ask one question more. Can you charge the Indians with robbing a nation almost of their whole Continent, and murdering their women and children, and then depriving the remainder of their lawful rights, that nature and God require them to have? And to cap the climax, rob another nation to till their grounds, and welter out their days under the lash with hunger and fatigue under the scorching rays of a burning sun? I should look at all the skins, and I know that when I cast my eye upon that white skin, and if I saw those crimes written upon it, I should enter my protest against it immediately, and cleave to that which is more honorable. And I can tell you that I am satisfied with the manner of my creation, fully—whether others are or not (56).

Apes's next work (the *Indian Nullification*) continues his concern with racism, announcing it explicitly as central to his life. Writing in the third person, Apes announces in his Introduction that the author

wishes to say in the first place, that the causes of the prevalent prejudice against his race have been his study from his childhood upwards. That their colour should be a reason to treat one portion of the human race with insult and abuse has always seemed to him strange; believing that God has given to all men an equal right to possess and occupy the earth, and to enjoy the fruits thereof, without any such distinction (10).

Apes now sees himself quite self-consciously as the prophet of color-blind Christianity, and this bears upon the question of self-definition inasmuch as it would seem he can be fully himself only as an Indian member of the tribe of the nonracist saved. It is the part-to-whole relation in which the self as such is validated only in its social-collective (Christian) personhood that is important to Apes. But let us come finally to William Apes's last known text, the *Eulogy on King Philip*.

Apes's turn to King Philip is rather a return, for the initial sentence of his first work, *A Son of the Forest*, had described its author as "a native of the American soil, and a descendant of one of the principal chiefs of the Pequod tribe, so well known in that part of American history called King Philip's Wars" (7). It was Philip's defeat in war which initiated the Pequots' loss "of the[ir] goodly heritage," and so it may come as no surprise to discover that a vindication of Philip, the narrative reconstitution of his "defeat" as a victory, now becomes for Apes the necessary condition for any recuperation of that "goodly heritage." The *Eulogy* proclaims Philip "the greatest man that was ever in America" (55–56), providing a revisionist history of the Pilgrim invasion: "the seed of iniquity and prejudice was sown in that day" (21), when the Pilgrims invaded these shores, Apes writes. Speaking to the descendants of the Pilgrims and Puritans in Boston, Apes would yet say,

Let the children of the pilgrims blush, while the son of the forest drops a tear, and groans over the fate of his murdered and departed fathers. He would say to the sons of the pilgrims, (as Job said about his birth day,) let the day be dark, the 22d of December, 1622; let it be forgotten in your celebration, in your speeches, and by the burying of the Rock that your fathers first put their foot upon. For be it remembered, although the gospel is said to be glad tidings to all people, yet we poor Indians never have found those who brought it as messengers of mercy, but contrawise. We say therefore, let every man of color wrap himself in mourning, for the 22d of December and the 4th of July are days of mourning and not of joy (20).

And so, Apes continues, "while you ask yourselves, what do they, the Indians, want? you have only to look at the unjust laws made for them, and say they want what I want," which is that "all men must operate under one general law" (59). That law is to be, as Apes had earlier written, both "civil and religious," (*Son of the Forest*, 115), for it is the implication of Christianity as Apes understands it that the "image of God in his members," be the "sufficient passport to all Christian privileges" (*Son of the Forest*, 115), not only in Heaven but here on earth as well—and, as he says, "first, in New England" (*Eulogy*, 59).

Curiously—amazingly?—Apes's *Eulogy* was sufficiently popular to warrant a second edition in 1837, after which year, as I have noted, no more is known of the Reverend William Apes. So far as his writings may be taken as formally and informally autobiographical, it seems reasonable to suggest that they show him as engaged in a very particular form of synecdochic self-definition. Recalling from the first a lost tribal identity and a "goodly heritage" in which all share together, he attempts with increasing self-consciousness to reconstitute and redefine his "tribe" and its "heritage" in Christian terms as a means of constituting and defining himself—this latter process, in typical Native American fashion, hardly self-conscious at all. The tribe to which Apes will ultimately belong must finally be made up not so much of Pequots or Puritans, not even only of Christians, "but [of] men" (*Eulogy*, 59). In the end, Apes is simply an Indian member of the color-blind saved, one of those nonracist Christians who, like most Indians traditionally, are usually more interested in their integration within a principled community rather than in their unique or "sacred" individuality.

Apes's synecdochic presentation of self finds parallels in a great many autobiographies by Indians. I would instance first Sarah Winnemucca Hopkins's *Life Among the Paiutes: Their Wrongs and Claims* (1883), whose very title proclaims her individual life as comprehensible foremost in relation to the collective experience of her tribe. Then there is Charles Alexander Eastman's *From the Deep Woods to Civilization: Chapters in the Autobiography of an Indian* (1916) with its conclusion, "I am an Indian. . . . I am an American" (195). Approaching the present, there is Leslie Marmon Silko's *Storyteller* (1981) which, as I have described it elsewhere,[27] conceives of individual identity only in functional relation to the tribe. Silko, as a contemporary Laguna "storyteller," takes her place in a line of "storytellers as far back as memory goes" ("Dedication," n.p.); she is what she does to sustain her community. Finally, we may look to the ongoing autobiographical projects of the Minnesota Chippewa novelist and critic, Gerald Vizenor, who, in his recent "Crows Written on the Poplars: Autocritical Autobiographies," invokes the "mixedblood," the trickster, and the author as categories in relation to which he may define himself. Inasmuch as "mixedbloods loosen the seams in the shrouds of identity" (101), they have a ready relation to tricksters—those jokers, shape-changers, and limit-challengers—and to writers of fiction, poetry, or criticism who are all, if true to their vocation, focused on the powers of the imagination. And Vizenor will define himself as one of the mixed-bloods, tricksters, and writers—for all that these each take self-definition as a loose and impermanent thing.

For all of this, I would not want to be understood as claiming that all autobiographies by Indians must necessarily be unimpressed by varieties of individualism, nor that all autobiographies by Native people must take synecdoche as their defining figure. The autobiographies by the much-acclaimed N. Scott Momaday, a Kiowa, seem to me as metonymic in their orientation as those by Rousseau and Thoreau, for example.[28] In the same way, Western autobiography is hardly constrained to metonymic strategies. Some autobiographical writing by Western women and certain forms of Christian autobiography, as I have noted above, are quite likely to adopt synecdochic types of self-identification, as are the autobiographies of writers whose deep commitment to political egalitarianism works to structure their self-conception in a part-to-whole manner: I think here, for example of Prince Peter Kropotkin, Emma Goldman, and, more recently, Assata Shakur.[29] For all that, so far as one may generalize, it nonetheless seems true that Native American autobiography is marked by the figure of synecdoche in its presentation of the self.

NOTES

I would like to thank Dell Hymes, Roy Harvey Pearce, and most particularly Paul John Eakin for their valuable comments on earlier drafts of this essay.

1 If not another "problem," another consideration is that while *some* sense of self may be universal, that sense of self, whatever it may be, does not receive cultural validation. As we shall see, not selfhood, hallmark of "individualist" society, so much as personhood, hallmark of the "holist" society (Dumont, *passim*), is what is found among most of the world's people.

2 Clyde Kluckhohn, quoted by A. I. Hallowell ("The Self," 387n). I would not be quite so certain as Marsella, DeVos, and Hsu, writing at the meridian of Reaganism, that "The Self has returned!" (n.p.), nor so unequivocally cheered if that were indeed the case. Nevertheless, it does seem to be true that psychological anthropology, for better or worse, is currently on an upswing and that its focus of study is whatever name we choose to give to the unitary male's or female's own sense of him- or herself as a unit entity. Almost by definition, a strictly conceived *psychological* anthropology tends to privilege the individual perception of self, projecting a Western

bourgeois bias. For a tough, ideologically-inflected account of the early culture and personality movement, see Harris. Although culture-and-personality studies may be dated from as early as 1910, their influence, through Benedict, Mead, and others (cf. n. 7, below) is more nearly a matter of the thirties. Hsu is particularly hostile to *personality* as the reference term for this type of study, which may account for the title of his co-edited text, *Culture and Self*. Thomas Williams lists over a hundred and twenty references that permit the interested reader to trace the historical trajectory from culture and personality to psychological anthropology in his "The Development of Psychological Anthropology," the introduction to a collection of essays on the subject. For the "continuities" between the two orientations, see also the study by Philip K. Bock. Victor Barnouw's textbook, in its fourth edition as of 1985, still adheres to the older nomenclature for its title. The introduction by John Kirkpatrick and Geoffrey M. White to their *Person, Self, and Experience: Exploring Pacific Ethnopsychologies* offers a particularly sophisticated and thoughtful account of these matters. The journal, *Ethos*, published by the American Society for Psychological Anthropology was founded in 1973.

3   See Smith, *Discerning the Subject.*

4   See, for example, Heelas and Lock, eds., *Indigenous Psychologies.*

5   Sigmund Freud, "One of the Difficulties of Psychoanalysis."

6   Paul Heelas, who develops practical applications of Andrew Lock's distinction between concepts of the self as "in control" or "under control," according to what he calls "idealist" or *"passiones"* models (39ff), quotes Edward Tylor, Lucien Levy-Bruhl, and C. Hallpike in ways that would seem to indicate their attachment to a Western view for all their (rudimentary, in Tylor's case) commitment to versions of cultural relativism.

7   But there is a complicated history here, which, although it is beyond the scope of this paper, is very well worth detailing. The background involves Ruth Benedict's prescriptive "descriptions" in *Patterns of Culture* of Native American personality clusters; Margaret Mead's Pacific excursus in *Coming of Age in Samoa*; and Erik Erikson's intervention culminating in detailed accounts in *Childhood in Society* of *correlations* (Erikson being quite careful to deny any claim to statements of a directly causal nature) between Yurok and Sioux childrearing practices and adult character structures. The work of Anthony Wallace with the Tuscarora and A. I. Hallowell with the Ojibwa also deserves mention, as does that of George Spindler and the "rorschachists." George Devereux's important invention, as it were, of ethnopsychoanalysis, commences with the practical demonstration of his *Reality and Dream: the Psychoanalysis of a Plains Indian*, and achieves full theoretical statement in *From Anxiety to Method*. Current work along a variety of these lines, as I have noted above, is abundant. Still, the conclusions of Richard Shweder's recent three-part essay, "Rethinking Culture and Personality Theory," is that "Most of the postulates of the culture and personality school . . . worked out in the 1940s and 1950s . . . do not weather well under empirical and conceptual scrutiny" (I:255–6). Shweder's own positions are

"worked out" in his "Does the concept of the person vary cross-culturally?" (co-authored with Edmund J. Bourne).

8   To the extent this is true, it might then be said that some Native American cultures seem to have reconciled the apparently antithetical implications of the English words *subject* and *individual*, for all that these are often used as synonyms. As Raymond Williams has usefully pointed out, the etymology of the first, from the Latin *sub-* and *jactum* (p.p.), to be thrown under or beneath, persists in the senses of being subject to, the subject of, subjected, and so forth (e.g., Lock's self "under control"). The etymology of *individual*, however, continues to carry with it the original sense of "indivisible," as if one were fully present to oneself and uniquely empowered as causal agent (e.g., Lock's self "in control"). This sense of the individual, espoused ahistorically by a certain vulgar humanism in the fifties, called forth an equivalently vulgar antihumanism in the sixties and after (as, e.g., in much of Foucault), with no place whatever for the active force of human agency. For a fine account of these matters, see Kate Soper's *Humanism and Anti-Humanism*.

9   For the "I-am-me" experience, see Eakin (217–9).

10 See Paul de Man "Autobiography as De-Facement." The figure specified by de Man is prosopopeia. For an excellent brief discussion see Eakin, (184–91), whose own view is rather different. Paul Smith comments on de Man's essay as well (105ff).

11 For a sketch of the Balinese "self" as well as some others, see Geertz's " 'From the Native's Point of View': On the Nature of Anthropological Understanding."

12 The typical affective response to such a sense of self in modernist literature is the feeling of alienation and anxiety. The postmodern self, it should be said, is also constructed ironically and rhetorically presented by the figure of *catachresis*, "abusive" or absurd usage. Its affective response is what Fredric Jameson has referred to as schizophrenic "euphoria." See Jameson's "Postmodernism, Or the Cultural Logic of Late Capitalism." For *catachresis*, see my "Modernism, Irony, Anthropology: the Case of Franz Boas."

13 Granted, it makes *surrealistic* sense, but "surrealistic sense" I take as a textual effect. Surrealistic *speech* by definition cannot have ordinary or normative force.

14 Lakoff and Johnson rather casually take the figure of metaphor as a master trope (all other figures are taken as kinds of metaphors) and assume that what is understood and experienced in the natural-language and ordinary-usage examples on which they exclusively base their argument (they are totally unconcerned with metaphors in writing) is always clear and unambiguous. There is a kind of extraordinary complacence in asserting categorically, as they do, for example, that "UNKNOWN IS UP," and "KNOWN IS DOWN" (137), without (say) taking into account the "metaphor" of "consciousness raising." To have one's consciousness raised, whatever this may indicate in terms of "understanding and experiencing," would seem to move up toward knowing. But even if I am wrong—if, that is, a "better"

interpretation of the "metaphor" bears out the unknown/up, known/down interpretation—clearly there is at least the possibility of a certain ambiguity. In the same way, for all that a Genette, a de Man, or a Derrida can always show the persistence in any apparently plain statement of some further possibility of signification and so the possibility of some further ambiguation, that does not prevent us from "understanding and experiencing" some relatively clear meaning. I offer these remarks in support of my contention that the textual and ordinary uses of metaphor are different versions of the same.

15 "Standard Average European" is a category Tyler takes from Benjamin Whorf, whose work he specifically praises in some polemical notes.

16 See, for example, the study of Lynne Woods O'Brien.

17 See *Black Elk Speaks*.

18 The link between metonymic self-conception and the primacy of textual communication is affirmed by Rousseau:

> I know nothing of myself till I was five or six. I do not know how I learnt to read. I only remember my first books and their effect upon me; *it is from my earliest reading that I date the unbroken consciousness of my own existence* . . . (19, my emphasis).

Scenes of reading and/or writing, as I have noted elsewhere ("American Autobiography"), are central to the eastern American tradition of autobiography and even before Thoreau. It remains to add what recent feminist criticism has solidly established: that orality (speech, the voice, and the *mother* tongue) and textuality (writing and the *father's* pen(is)) are, indeed, perceived as gender related in the West, where men tend toward metonymic presentations of self, and women—in this like Indians and traditional peoples generally—tend toward synecdochic presentations of self.

19 That *Walden is* an autobiography is assuredly open to question. Given the current sense of the broadness of the autobiographical genre, I will simply take it as such without further comment.

20 See my *For Those Who Come After*.

21 Gerard Genette quotes an early text of Mauss, the 1902 *Esquisse d'une theorie de la magie* [*Sketch of a Theory of Magic*] to the effect that "The simplest form [of association by contiguity] is the identification of the part with the whole" (108). Thus Mauss's early sense of the simple or primitive nature of synecdoche would seem to accord with his late sense of the simple or primitive nature of *personnage* concepts of self.

22 Apes was preceded as an autobiographer by the Reverend Samson Occom, a Mohegan, who wrote a brief account of his life in 1762, and by Hendrick Aupaumut, generally referred to as a Mahican, who produced a text in 1792 that at least contained a good deal of autobiographical material. The *Memoir of Catherine Brown, a Christian Indian of the Cherokee Nation*, as edited by the missionary Rufus Anderson, appeared in the same year, 1829, as Apes's text. The very brief life history of Paul Cuffe, like Apes, a Pequot, appeared in 1839. By that time the first Indian autobiography, J. B. Patterson's *Life of Black Hawk* (1833) had been published. For further references, see the

indispensable annotated bibliography by David Brumble (*An Annotated Bibliography*) and its "Supplement," as well as Brumble's recent full-length study, *American Indian Autobiography*. My own book (*For Those Who Come After*), as well as the introduction to Swann and Krupat, may also prove helpful.

23 A further account of Apes's life and work, most particularly in relation to the Bakhtinian concern with the plural elements of "individual" speech appears in my "Monologue and Dialogue in Native American Autobiography."

24 This includes the Jews, who, as Apes writes in *The Indian's Looking Glass*, "are a colored people, especially those living in the East, where Christ was born . . . " (60)!

25 The grammar, to be sure, is questionable, the two sentences properly constituting but a single sentence. But it should be remembered that Apes's written style is very much the transcription of an oral manner. Whatever he may or may not have known and remembered of aboriginal orality, his commitment to a Christian tradition of "exhorting" and "preaching" provides a continuity with Native modes of communication. It is fitting, therefore, that his final work is "only" the text of what was orally "pronounced at the Odeon."

26 I find it difficult not to think of Kafka's "In the Penal Colony," just here. Apes's image of corporeal criminal inscription resonates with a good deal of contemporary theoretical work.

27 See my "Monologue and Dialogue."

28 See Momaday, *The Way to Rainy Mountain* and *The Names*, and my discussion in the study cited in note 27.

29 See Kropotkin, *Memoirs of a Revolutionist*; Goldman, *Living My Life*, and Shakur, *Assata*. Shakur's use of lowercase *i* within sentences (she capitalizes *I* at the beginning of sentences, where all letters equivalently get to appear in uppercase) seems a gesture in the interest of bringing the individual ego back to proper scale as simply an existant among others.

WORKS CITED

Apes, William. *A Son of the Forest: The Experience of William Apes, a Native of the Forest*. New York: Published by the Author, 1829.

Apes, William. *The Experience of Five Christian Indians of the Pequod Tribe; or the Indian's Looking-Glass for the White Man*. Boston: James B. Dow, 1833.

Apes, William. *Indian Nullification of the Unconstitutional Laws of Massachusetts, Relative to the Marshpee Tribe: or, The Pretended Riot Explained*. Boston: Jonathan Howe, 1835.

Apes, William. *Eulogy on King Philip, as Pronounced at the Odeon in Federal Street, Boston, by the Rev. William Apes, an Indian, January 8, 1836*. [Boston: 1836]. Reprint. Brookfield, MA: Lincoln A. Dexter, 1985.

Aupaumut, Hendrick. *A Narrative of an Embassy to the Western Indians, from the Original Manuscript of Hendrick Aupaumut, with Prefatory Remarks by Dr. B. H. Coates.* [1791]. *Pennsylvania Historical Society Memoirs* 2, pt. I (1827): 61–131.

Barnouw, Victor. *Culture and Personality.* Homewood, IL: Dorsey, 1985.

Benedict, Ruth. *Patterns of Culture.* [1934]. New York: Mentor, 1946.

Black Elk. *Black Elk Speaks.* [1932]. Ed. John G. Neihardt. Lincoln: University of Nebraska Press, 1979.

Black Hawk. *Black Hawk: An Autobiography.* [1833]. Ed. Donald Jackson. Champaign-Urbana: University of Illinois Press, 1964.

Bock, Philip K. *Continuities in Psychological Anthropology.* San Francisco: W. H. Freeman, 1980.

Brown, Catherine. *Memoirs of Catherine Brown a Christian Indian of the Cherokee Nation.* Ed. Rufus B. Anderson. Philadelphia: American Sunday School Union, 1824.

Brumble, David. *An Annotated Bibliography of American Indian and Eskimo Autobiographies.* Lincoln: University of Nebraska Press, 1981.

Brumble, David. "A Supplement to *An Annotated Bibliography of American Indian and Eskimo Autobiographies.*" *Western American Literature* 17(1982): 242–60.

Brumble, David. *American Indian Autobiography.* Berkeley: University of California Press, 1988.

Carrithers, Michael; Steven Collins; and Steven Lukes, eds. *The Category of the Person.* Cambridge: Cambridge University Press, 1985.

Cuffe, Paul. *Narrative of the Life and Adventures of Paul Cuffe, Pequot Indian: During Thirty Years at Sea, and in Travelling in Foreign Lands.* Vernon [?]: Horace N. Bill, 1839.

de Man, Paul. "Autobiography as De-Facement." *Modern Language Notes* 94 (1979): 919–30.

Devereux, George. *From Anxiety to Method in the Behavioral Sciences.* The Hague: Mouton, 1967.

Devereux, George. *Reality and Dream: Psychotherapy of a Plains Indian.* [1951]. Garden City, NY: Anchor, 1969.

Dumont, Louis. "A Modified View of Our Origins: The Christian Beginnings of Modern Individualism." In Carrithers, Collins, and Lukes, eds., *Category,* 93–122.

Eakin, Paul John. *Fictions in Autobiography.* Princeton: Princeton University Press, 1985.

Eastman, Charles Alexander. *From the Deep Woods to Civilization: Chapters in the Autobiography of an Indian.* [1916]. Lincoln: University of Nebraska Press, 1977.

Erikson, Eric. *Childhood and Society.* [1950]. New York: W. W. Norton, 1963.

Fajans, Jane. "The Person in Social Context: The Social Character of Baining 'Psychology'." In White and Kirkpatrick, eds. *Person, Self, and Experience,* 367–400.

Freud, Sigmund. "One of the Difficulties of Psychoanalysis." In *Collected Papers of Sigmund Freud.* Vol. 4. Trans. Joan Riviere. London: Hogarth, 1925, 347–56.

Geertz, Clifford. " 'From the Native's Point of View': On the Nature of Anthropological Understanding." In *Local Knowledge: Further Essays in Interpretive Anthropology.* New York: Basic Books, 1983, 55–72.

Genette, Gerard. *Figures of Literary Discourse.* Tr. Alan Sheridan, New York: Columbia University Press, 1982.

Goldman, Emma. *Living My Life.* 2 vols. [1931]. New York: Dover, 1970.

Hallowell, A. I. "The Self and Its Behavioral Environment." In *Culture and Experience.* Philadelphia: University of Pennsylvania Press, 1955, 75–111.

Harris, Marvin. *The Rise of Anthropological Theory.* New York: Crowell, 1968.

Heelas, Paul. "The Model Applied: Anthropology and Indigenous Psychologies." In Heelas and Lock, eds., *Indigenous Psychologies,* 39–64.

Heelas, Paul, and Andrew Lock, eds. *Indigenous Psychologies: The Anthropology of the Self.* London: Academic, 1981.

Hopkins, Gerard Manley. A Selection of His Poems and Prose. Ed. W. H. Gardner, Baltimore: Penguin, 1953.

Hopkins, Sarah Winnemucca. *Life Among the Piutes: Their Wrongs and Claims.* [1883]. Ed. Mrs. Horace Mann. Bishop, CA: Chalfant Press, 1969.

Jakobson, Roman. "Concluding Statement: Linguistics and Poetics." In *Style in Language.* Ed. Thomas A. Sebeok. Cambridge: The MIT Press, 1960, 350–77.

Jameson, Fredric. "Postmodernism, or the Cultural Logic of Late Capitalism." *New Left Review* 146(1984): 53–93.

Kropotkin, Peter. *Memoirs of a Revolutionist.* [1899]. Gloucester, MA: Peter Smith, 1967.

Krupat, Arnold. "American Autobiography: The Western Tradition." *Georgia Review* 35(1981): 307–17.

Krupat, Arnold. *For Those Who Come After: a Study of Native American Autobiography.* Berkeley and Los Angeles: University of California Press, 1985.

Krupat, Arnold. "Monologue and Dialogue in Native American Autobiography." In *The Voice in the Margin: Native American Literature and the Canon.* Berkeley: University of California Press, 1989.

Krupat, Arnold. "Modernism, Irony, Anthropology: the Case of Franz Boas." In *Modernism and Anthropology.* Ed. Marc Manganaro. Princeton: Princeton University Press, 1990.

Lakoff, George, and Mark Johnson. *Metaphors We Live By.* Chicago: University of Chicago Press, 1980.

Lee, Dorothy. "The Conception of the Self Among the Wintu Indians." *Freedom and Culture.* Englewood Cliffs, NJ: Prentice-Hall, 1959, 131–140.

Lee, Dorothy. "Autonomy and Community." In *Valuing the Self: What We Can Learn from Other Cultures.* Prospect Heights, IL: Waveland, 1986, 28–41.

Lock, Andrew. "Universals in Human Conception." In Heelas and Lock, eds., *Indigenous Psychologies,* 19–38.

Lukes, Steven. "Conclusion." In Carrithers, Collins, and Lukes, eds., *Category,* 282–301.

Marcella, Anthony J.; George DeVos; and Francis L. K. Hsu, eds. *Culture and Self: Asian and Western Perspectives.* New York: Tavistock, 1985.

Mauss, Marcel. "A Category of the Human Mind: The Notion of Person; the Notion of Self." [1938]. Trans. W. D. Halls. In Carrithers, Collins, and Lukes, eds., *Category*, 1–25.

Mead, Margaret. *Coming of Age in Samoa*. [1928]. New York: Mentor, 1953.

Momaday, N. Scott. *The Way to Rainy Mountain*. [1969]. New York: Ballantine, 1973.

Momaday, N. Scott. *The Names*. New York: Harper & Row, 1976.

O'Brien, Lynne Woods. *Plains Indian Autobiographies*. Boise, ID: Boise State College Press, 1973.

Occom, Samson. "A Short Narrative of My Life." In *The Elders Wrote: An Autobiography of Early Prose by North American Indians, 1768–1931*. [1762]. Ed. Bernd Peyer. Berlin: Dietrich Reimer Verlag, 1982, 12–18.

Rorty, Amelie O. *The Identities of Persons*. Berkeley and Los Angeles: University of California Press, 1976.

Rousseau, Jean-Jacques. *The Confessions*. [1781]. Trans. J. M. Cohen. Harmondsworth, England: Penguin, 1953.

Shakur, Assata. *Assata*. Westport, CT: Lawrence Hill, 1987.

Shweder, Richard A. "Rethinking Culture and Personality Theory." Part I. "A Critical Examination of Two Classical Postulates." *Ethos*. 7(1979): 255–78.

Shweder, Richard A. "Rethinking Culture and Personality Theory." Part II. "A Critical Examination of Two More Classical Postulates." *Ethos*. 7 (1979): 279–311.

Shweder, Richard A. "Rethinking Culture and Personality Theory." Part III. "From Genesis and Typology to Hermeneutics and Dynamics." *Ethos*. 8(1980): 60–94.

Shweder, Richard A., and Edmund J. Bourne. "Does the Concept of the Person Vary Cross-Culturally?" In *Culture Theory: Essays on Mind, Self, and Emotion*. Ed. Richard A. Shweder and Robert LeVine. Cambridge: Cambridge University Press, 1984, 158–99.

Silko, Leslie Marmon. *Storyteller*. New York: Seaver Books, 1981.

Smith, M. Brewster. "The Metaphorical Basis of Selfhood." In Marsella, DeVos, and Hsu, eds., *Culture and Self*, 56–88.

Smith, Paul. *Discerning the Subject*. Minneapolis: University of Minnesota Press, 1988.

Soper, Kate. *Humanism and Anti-Humanism*. London: Hutchinson, 1986.

Spindler, George D., and Louise S. Spindler. "American Indian Personality Types and Their Sociocultural Roots." *Annals of the American Academy of Political and Social Science*. 311(1957): 147–57.

Stein, Gertrude. *Everybody's Autobiography*. New York: Random House, 1937.

Swann, Brian, and Arnold Krupat, eds. *I Tell You Now: Autobiographical Essays by Native American Writers*. Lincoln: University of Nebraska Press, 1987.

Thoreau, Henry David. *Walden*. [1854]. New York: W. W. Norton, 1966.

Tyler, Stephen. "The Vision Quest in the West, or What the Mind's Eye Sees." *Journal of Anthropological Research*. 40(1984): 23–40.

Vizenor, Gerald. "Crows Written on the Poplars: Autocritical Autobiographies." In Swann and Krupat, eds., *I Tell You Now*, 99–109.

Wallace, Anthony. "The Modal Personality Structure of the Tuscarora Indians as Revealed by the Rorschach Test." *Bureau of American Ethnology Bulletin No. 150.* Washington, DC: Smithsonian Institution, 1952.

White, Geoffrey M., and John Kirkpatrick. "Exploring Ethnopsychologies." In White and Kirkpatrick, eds., *Person, Self, and Experience,* 3–34.

White, Geoffrey M., and John Kirkpatrick, *Person, Self, and Experience: Exploring Pacific Ethnopsychologies.* Berkeley and Los Angeles: University of California Press, 1985.

Williams, Raymond. *Keywords.* New York: Oxford University Press, 1976.

Williams, Thomas R., ed. *Psychological Anthropology.* The Hague: Mouton, 1975.

CHAPTER 8

African-American Autobiography Criticism: Retrospect and Prospect

WILLIAM L. ANDREWS

It may be a little surprising as well as instructive to begin this discussion by noting that the first book-length study of African-American autobiography in the United States was published a generation earlier than its ground-breaking counterpart in American autobiography. Yet, as Robert F. Sayre candidly admits in his new introduction to the 1988 reprint of *The Examined Self: Benjamin Franklin, Henry Adams, Henry James* (1964), he "knew little or nothing" about black autobiography when he wrote his pioneering book. More than likely he had also not heard of Rebecca Chalmers Barton's *Witnesses for Freedom: Negro Americans in Autobiography* (1948), the first major critical analysis of African-American—and thus, one might argue, of American—autobiography. To offer this observation is not to fault Sayre. It is rather to suggest that unless we regard African-American autobiography as somehow distinct from American autobiography, we cannot escape the fact that the history of American autobiography criticism begins not with a study of the classics of what academe used to call "the American experience" but with an examination of what Barton called "the Negro point of view" (xi). *Witnesses for Freedom* may not have quickened the scholarly interest in white American autobiography that emerged in the 1960s. Nevertheless, to historicize American autobiography criticism without noting the precedence of Barton's book would deny us something crucial, namely, an awareness of black autobiography's prior claim to the agenda of American autobiography criticism.

"The problem of the Twentieth Century is the problem of the color line," prophesied W. E. B. Du Bois in *The Souls of Black Folk* (1903). When

195

the United States finally started to come to grips with these words in
the post-World II era, Rebecca Chalmers Barton marshaled the autobiographies of twenty-three American blacks to interpret the significance
of and possible solutions to what Gunnar Myrdal called *An American
Dilemma: The Negro Problem and Modern Democracy* in 1944. As she read
African-American autobiography from Frederick Douglass's *Life and
Times* (1892) to Era Bell Thompson's *American Daughter* (1946), Barton
found a variety and richness of matter and manner that refuted stereo-
types about black experience, attitudes, and capabilities. She found in
black autobiography "literary merit" commensurate with the "vigor
and versatility of expression" that, she claimed presciently, "guarantees
them [the autobiographies] an integral place in American letters" (274).
Yet to Barton these texts "achieve their final importance by their special
insights into the complexities of race" (274). Thus *Witnesses for Freedom*
ends with a didactic chapter entitled "Values for Intergroup Living,"
in which the author extrapolates from modern black autobiography certain intellectual and ethical standards that would facilitate, in her view,
the integration of American society. "The Negro Americans who come
to life in these pages display the same variety of taste, temperament,
and purpose as any other segment of the population" (282), Barton concludes. She goes on to urge that whites accept the "like-mindedness"
of modern black autobiographers as the key to "an improved social
order." Should white America continue to refuse to recognize like-
mindedness between blacks and whites, Barton warns of dire consequences. The "militancy" of recent black autobiographers whom she
classifies as "Protesters for a New Freedom"—writers like Angelo Hern-
don, Du Bois, and Richard Wright—is "no chance occurrence" (281).
Because "suppressed people will not remain so," the rising voices of
militant black autobiographers "point to danger signals on the social
horizon. Let him who will not heed become chaff on the wind" (281).

Barton's anticipation of an accelerating militancy in modern black
autobiography was borne out in the 1960s when figures like Malcolm
X and Eldridge Cleaver forged their first-person narratives in the political flame of Black Power. More articulately and cogently than any book
before it, *The Autobiography of Malcolm X* (1964) exemplified the concept
of black identity as necessarily distinct from and morally superior to
the corporate white identity that dominated the cultural and socio-
political ethos of America. This concept of blackness as the *sine qua non*
of African-American identity in the 1960s inspired a new generation of
self-styled black revolutionaries to give voice to their own life stories
and political opinions, which liberal white America, highly sensitized
by the Civil Rights Movement, bought, read, and reviewed assiduously.

Cleaver's *Soul on Ice* (1968), H. Rap Brown's *Die Nigger Die* (1969), George Jackson's *Soledad Brother* (1970), Julius Lester's *Search for the New Land* (1970), and Bobby Seale's *Seize the Time* (1970) were among the best-selling of the revolutionary narratives of the 1960s. Scholars and critics of American literature felt challenged to account for these seemingly unprecedented works of black rage and radical political consciousness. Where did these autobiographies belong in the history of American—or African-American—literature, assuming one could speak of them as literature at all?

Responding to this question led scholars in two directions. Barely two years after Malcolm's *Autobiography* was published, Robert Penn Warren became the first of several distinguished critics, including Carol Ohmann, Warner Berthoff, and Barrett John Mandel, to try to locate the most widely read black autobiography of the sixties in relation to well-established white literary traditions such as the Alger myth, the Benjamin Franklin success story, and the narrative of conversion exemplified by St. Augustine's *Confessions*.[1] To those who were unsatisfied with this kind of domestication of literary blackness, however, the antebellum slave narrator seemed a more likely progenitor of Malcolm X and his successors. In *Studies in Black Literature*, *Phylon*, and other journals open to the controversial discipline of Black Studies, some of the earliest scholarship on the slave narrative and its largely unacknowledged importance to American literary history was first published.[2] This criticism depended heavily on the pioneering research of Marion Wilson Starling and Charles H. Nichols, in whose dissertations (completed in 1946 and 1948, respectively) the first extensive literary study of the slave narrative appears.

After publishing in the 1950s a series of articles based on his research, Nichols was able to get his dissertation published in 1963 under the auspices of the Amerika-Institüt of the Free University of Berlin. *Many Thousand Gone: The Ex-Slaves' Account of Their Bondage and Freedom* was designed primarily to let the slaves have their say on a subject that had become of central concern to American historians by the early 1960s— the nature of slavery and its effect on African-Americans. Rather than concentrate on the merits of a few autobiographies, Nichols chose to create a composite portrait of the slave experience by blending the life stories of many former slaves into a single overarching narrative pattern. The result was more of a summary and a celebration of the message of the slave narrators than a critical analysis of the means by which they achieved their rhetorical goals. Yet Nichols was among the first to use the slave narratives as a necessary corrective to the plantation myth of Southern literature and history and to suggest the historical continuity between Frederick Douglass and Martin Luther King, Jr. Nichols's research pointed the way for those who believed that the antebellum slave narrators were the literary and political antecedents of the revolutionary black autobiographers of the 1960s and early 1970s.

It is not coincidental that during the 1960s the *Narrative of the Life of Frederick Douglass, an American Slave* (1845) began its rise to preeminence among all black American autobiographers of the nineteenth century. The persona and rhetorical posture that Douglass assumed in his first autobiography strongly appealed to the mood of the sixties and to the search for a useable past that impelled Black Studies scholars into the slave narrative in the first place. In 1960 Benjamin Quarles, anticipating this need, rescued the *Narrative* from decades of out-of-print oblivion and edited it for the Belknap Press of Harvard University. Soon paperback reprints of the *Narrative* appeared, closely followed by reprints of Douglass's second and third autobiographies, *My Bondage and My Freedom* (1855) and *Life and Times of Frederick Douglass* (1892). By the end of the 1960s, the inclusion of Quarles's brief essay on the *Narrative* in Hennig Cohen's *Landmarks of American Writing* (1969) indicated that the *Narrative* was well on its way to inclusion in the canon of American literature.

The 1960s also saw the reprinting of dozens of long out-of-print black autobiographies, especially slave narratives, by numerous reprint houses, such as the Arno Press of the *New York Times* and Negro Universities Press. Some of these reprints were ably introduced by noted scholars such as Arna Bontemps, Larry Gara, and Robin Winks. Gilbert Osofsky's "Puttin' on Ole Massa: The Significance of Slave Narratives," which introduces *Puttin' on Ole Massa* (1968), Osofsky's edition of the narratives of Henry Bibb, William Wells Brown, and Solomon Northup, is the most detailed and valuable of the criticism that appeared in connection with reprinted texts. Unfortunately, few of the nineteenth-century slave narratives brought into print with the wave of interest in Black Studies during the 1960s remain in print today. Thanks to the herculean effort of George P. Rawick, however, the entirety of the more than two thousand interviews with ex-slaves conducted by the Federal Writers' Project between 1936 and 1938 have been compiled and reprinted in *The American Slave: A Composite Autobiography* (1972).

By the end of the 1960s, the primary texts of African-American autobiography were back in print, in some cases for the first time in many decades. Not surprisingly, the most important criticism of the 1970s attempted to create literary histories of black autobiography in America using the recent celebrities and newly reprinted texts of the 1960s as their touchstones. Stephen Butterfield's *Black Autobiography in America*

(1974) is the first and still the most comprehensive literary history of African-American autobiography. In an often trenchant and vigorously polemical analysis of about fifty autobiographies published between 1830 and 1972, Butterfield set a standard for those who wished to take seriously the rhetorical art and literary import of black autobiography. Beginning with "the Slave Narrative Period, 1831–1895," Butterfield offers sustained analyses of point of view, irony, parody, and the influence of white autobiographical discourse on the slave narrators. He singles out Frederick Douglass's *Narrative* and *Life and Times* as epitomizing, in both subject matter and style, the strength of the first era of black autobiography.

Butterfield detects a certain malaise in many texts from the second era of black American autobiography, the "Period of Search," which extends from 1901, when *Up from Slavery* first appeared, to 1961, when James Baldwin's *Nobody Knows My Name* signaled the advent of a new consciousness and sense of identity among black autobiographers. The search was for a viable sense of identity for blacks in a new era, when the blandishments of the "Negro bourgeoisie" and the "white American mainstream" lure the successful black person away from the "black masses" and hence, in Butterfield's view, away from the only valid source of identity for blacks who desire a historically meaningful existence. The end of this search took black autobiographers of the middle period into a renewed sense of black pride, which led black autobiography "back into direct political struggle" (107), the theme of the third part of Butterfield's book, "the Period of Rebirth," treating autobiographies of the 1960s and early 1970s. Here Butterfield celebrates "the growth of a new radicalism" in Baldwin and "the revolutionary self" in the work of Malcolm X, Cleaver, Jackson, Lester, Brown, and Seale. Butterfield also devotes a chapter to the contributions of Ida B. Wells, Maya Angelou, and Anne Moody to the tradition, although he has difficulty reconciling the sense of self represented in Angelou and Moody to the "revolutionary self" that he offers as a paradigm of the new generation of black autobiographers. He concludes that the "strongest books" of the contemporary period—*Soul on Ice, Search for a New Land,* and *Soledad Brother*—are those "that most successfully assimilate and unify personal narrative and political message" (274).

As both a literary history and a work of polemic, *Black Autobiography in America* reads almost like a period piece today. No scholar since Butterfield has attempted to put the history of African-American autobiography between the covers of a single book. The politics of canon-formation, which would certainly have problematized Butterfield's enterprise, does not demand his attention, nor does the problematic

nature of historical reconstruction itself trouble him—Butterfield did
his work before these theoretical concerns came to the fore in autobiography criticism. One can almost be thankful that Butterfield was not
inhibited by these issues, since his sense of freedom allowed him to explore and map a literary frontier with singular clarity, conciseness, and
confidence. Yet to enforce his sense of historical progression and
political relevance in black autobiography, Butterfield had to submit
each text of this tradition to an ideological test. He candidly acknowledges his preference for works that seem to him "revolutionary narratives." He declares that "the appeal of black autobiographies is in their
political awareness" (3) first and foremost. What Butterfield means by
"political awareness" is never specified in his book, but one thing seems
clear. Any autobiography that could be classified as a "middle-class success story" is *ipso facto* not politically aware. In keeping with the tenor
of the 1960s, Butterfield's book argues that black autobiographers who
did not take a stand against the American Dream usually were co-opted
by it, though in their self-portraits one can find evidence of interior
struggles with this condition. The problem with this dismissive attitude
toward the many "middle-class success stories" of African-American
autobiography is that it fails to recognize the political, and indeed,
sometimes the revolutionary, significance of the black middle-class
autobiographer, who proudly laid claim to a status that American
racism denied him and her and whose historical role of leadership in
the battle for racial integration made middle-class autobiographies
potent texts in the black community.

   Sidonie Smith's *Where I'm Bound: Patterns of Slavery and Freedom in
Black American Autobiography* (1974) is less comprehensive but also less
tendentious than Butterfield's book. Smith is interested in the patterns
that structure the plots of ten black autobiographies, beginning with
the antebellum slave narrative of William Wells Brown and concluding
with Claude Brown's *Manchild in the Promised Land* (1965). She finds in
the slave narrative a pattern of breaking "*away from* an enslaving community" in search of the chance to "break *into* a community that allowed
authentic self-expression and fulfillment in a social role" (ix). Since the
antebellum era, she argues, black autobiographies have manifested
these patterns of flight and immersion in increasingly complex ways,
depending on the autobiographer's sense of whether authentic self-
expression is possible in communal roles. In the autobiographies of
Cleaver, Angelou, Horace Cayton, and Claude Brown, Smith percep-
tively analyzes the function of the act of autobiography-writing itself
in the search for liberation beyond communal identification and social
roles. Unlike Butterfield, who regards the achievement of individual

black identity and fulfillment apart from the black community as an impossibility, Smith argues cogently that many black autobiographies suggest that "the ultimate place of freedom lies within the self, which alone must be content to create its own 'free' consciousness" (75).

Since 1974, the trend of black autobiography criticism has been more in the direction of Smith's concept of the significance of the autobiographical act rather than Butterfield's. Many critics who address the knotty problem of what constitutes "freedom" in black autobiography have taken seriously Smith's analysis of the importance of highly subjective, individualistic acts of writing as means of achieving and expressing an elusive sense of liberation. Butterfield grants that the "subjective experience" and street-wise expressiveness of a Malcolm X or a Rap Brown is an index to the progress of the revolution, but only in the service of black militancy does an individual autobiographical act take on positive significance. A more flexible concept of the relationship between individual and community in black first-person narratives appears in Elizabeth Schultz's discussion of "the blues genre" in African-American autobiography, in which she probes the cultural traditions that enable black autobiographers to transmit the social significance of their experience through a process of creating and articulating a sense of self that draws on both the style and substance of the blues.[3]

1974 saw the publication of a third major book on African-American autobiography, Russell C. Brignano's *Black Americans in Autobiography,* an annotated bibliography of autobiographical writing since the Civil War. Revised and updated in 1984, Brignano's bibliography is the best bibliographical work ever done on black American autobiography. It not only provides reliable information on the publishing circumstances and history of 424 black autobiographies; it also offers a brief comment on the subject matter of each text and lists the libraries in the United States that possess a copy of each text. In addition Brignano lists more than 200 "autobiographical books" by blacks, in which the author's life story is treated in sufficient detail to warrant attention from students of autobiography. Although *Black Americans in Autobiography* only lists modern reprints of antebellum autobiographies, it can be supplemented by the more thorough bibliographies that append the work of Davis and Gates (1985) and Andrews's *To Tell a Free Story* (1986). In combination, these bibliographies constitute a virtually definitive inventory of African-American autobiography. For bibliographies of black autobiography criticism, researchers have had to wait until the 1980s, when Gregory S. Sojka's checklist of works on the slave narrative and Joe Weixlmann's thoroughgoing bibliographical study of twentieth-century African-American autobiography began the process of mapping the intellectual terrain.[4]

The black autobiography that received the most scholarly attention in the 1970s was Richard Wright's *Black Boy*. Three timely books on Wright, Dan McCall's *The Example of Richard Wright* (1969), Edward Margolies's *The Art of Richard Wright* (1969), and Michel Fabre's *The Unfinished Quest of Richard Wright* (1973), offered early readings of Wright's autobiography in light of his achievements in fiction. McCall and Margolies confess to a certain disappointment with the rhetoric of *Black Boy*, though they try to offer explanations for what they regard as the stylistic inadequacy of the book. Fabre's biographical approach to *Black Boy* makes a more lasting contribution to scholarship. Fabre judiciously notes some of the differences between the image of Wright's childhood in *Black Boy* and the facts of his youth and family situation as the biographer's research revealed them. Since Fabre's identification of these discrepancies, one of the chief topics of criticism on *Black Boy* has been the significance of discrepancies between the life and perspective of Richard Wright and that of the "black boy" whose story is not necessarily Wright's, nor perhaps even intended by Wright to represent him alone. From Claudia Tate's "*Black Boy*: Richard Wright's 'Tragic Sense of Life'" (1976) and James Olney's "Some Versions of Memory/Some Versions of *Bios*: The Ontology of Autobiography" (1980) to the chapter in Timothy Dow Adams's recent book, *Telling Lies in Modern American Autobiography* (1990), critics have attempted to articulate the relationship of Wright to the "black boy" persona whose status as a representative of and commentator on southern black culture has proved persistently controversial. What critics have come to agree on, however, since the early 1970s, is that *Black Boy* is a highly self-conscious and carefully crafted work that displays considerable attention to narrative technique. Moreover, critics of the last ten years have increasingly emphasized the centrality to *Black Boy* of the narrator's desire to become a writer and his identification with language as his ultimate means of transcending that which inhibits self-realization in and beyond the text.

While the 1970s saw the growth of an increasingly sophisticated critical literature devoted to some of the most famous texts of the black autobiographical tradition, the decade also gave its attention to books that did not easily conform to the male-centered tradition exemplified in *Black Boy* or *The Autobiography of Malcolm X*. Feminist criticism in the late 1970s, particularly essays focussing on Maya Angelou's *I Know Why the Caged Bird Sings* (1970), forecast a major redirection of black autobiography criticism.

George Kent's 1975 article, "Maya Angelou's *I Know Why the Caged Bird Sings* and Black Autobiographical Tradition," while no more specifically feminist than the discussion of Angelou's first autobiography in the books by Butterfield and Smith, argues cogently for the importance of *I Know Why* as a kind of model in which two traditions—those of black religion and the blues—that seem to be at odds in texts like *Black Boy* find "a just balance." One can hardly imagine a better way for scholarship on black women's autobiography to be launched. Kent neither accommodated Angelou to a male-defined tradition nor suggested that her uniqueness and success as an autobiographer were to be evaluated apart from the cultural traditions of black America that she so intimately knew. Instead, he prepared the ground for many subsequent studies of Angelou's work that probe the extent to which and/or the means by which Angelou achieves the sort of "balance" that Kent ascribes to her.

Although Angelou's work attracted most of the attention that black women's autobiography received in the 1970s, criticism and research on the first-person writings of Zora Neale Hurston,[5] along with a revived interest in black women's narratives of the slavery era, especially Harriet Jacobs's *Incidents in the Life of a Slave Girl* (1861),[6] demonstrated that there was no shortage of writing in this tradition to be revived and examined. Two useful essays from the end of the decade, Mary Burgher's "Images of Self and Race in the Autobiographies of Black Women" (1979) and Regina Blackburn's "In Search of the Black Female Self: African-American Women's Autobiographies and Ethnicity" (1980), outlined for the first time the thematic range of black women's autobiography from the antebellum era to the 1970s and thus offered the first tantalizing glimpses of the breadth and diversity of this hitherto unrecognized tradition.

At the end of the 1970s, the study of the slave narrative received major impetus from the publication of two books, Frances Smith Foster's *Witnessing Slavery: The Development of Ante-bellum Slave Narratives* (1979) and a collection of essays edited by Dexter Fisher and Robert B. Stepto entitled *Afro-American Literature: The Reconstruction of Instruction* (1979). Foster's book represents the first literary history of the antebellum slave narrative in the United States. She divides this history into two eras— the first from 1760 to 1807, the second from 1831 to 1865—and argues that the principal difference between the two lies in the increased concentration on the outrages of slavery and the humanity of blacks in narratives of the second era. That Foster is correct in this overall view of the slave narrative's development is unquestionable. What is most important, indeed unprecedented, in her work is her fundamental contention, backed by cogent argumentation and extensive citation from the little-known as well as the better-known texts, that the slave narrative was not a monolithic entity, but rather a dynamic and ever-evolving genre of black self-expression. Persuasive arguments have been written to the contrary,[7] but through her careful historizing of the slave narrative, Foster's case for its "development" has held its ground. One testimony to the importance of Foster's study is the publication, two years after her book, of Marion Wilson Starling's *The Slave Narrative: Its Place in American History*, her pioneering 1946 Ph. D. dissertation. Starling's research anticipates that of Foster, and the two critics, when read together, base the study of the slave narrative in the 1980s in impeccable traditional literary historical scholarship.

The major contribution of *Afro-American Literature: The Reconstruction of Instruction* to autobiography criticism stems from the collective import of three essays on Douglass's 1845 *Narrative* included in the volume. In the first, "Narration, Authentication, and Authorial Control in Frederick Douglass's *Narrative* of 1845," Robert B. Stepto suggests a dramatic new way of understanding the text of a narrative like Douglass's by calling attention to the interplay between the narrative proper and the authenticating documents that enclose it. Stepto goes on to examine the rhetoric of Douglass's narrative as an index to the narrator's attempt to gain control over the signifying potential of his text. This essay has had a considerable impact on subsequent criticism primarily by challenging assumptions about textual form in black autobiography and by offering a critical language in which to discuss the crucial problem of self-authorization in black autobiography.[8] Following Stepto's essay, Robert O'Meally's "Frederick Douglass' 1845 *Narrative*: The Text Was Meant to Be Preached," treats the relationship of the written text to the oral tradition, particularly that of black preaching, to which Douglass's eloquence owes so much. Like Stepto, O'Meally emphasizes the formal art of Douglass's narration and attributes much of it to his black oral resources. Critics before O'Meally had emphasized the relationship of slave narratives like Douglass's to white literary models, but no one had made such an effective or suggestive argument for the formal and substantive influence of black oral culture on Douglass.[9]

Finally, Henry Louis Gates's "Binary Oppositions in Chapter One of *Narrative of the Life of Frederick Douglass an American Slave Written by Himself*" proposes a third, and specifically structuralist method, of investigating the formal dynamics of this autobiography. Gates's analysis of the opening of the *Narrative* reveals that Douglass understood the slaveocratic worldview to be premised on a fundamental binary opposition between "the absolute and the eternal," with which the culture of slavery endowed itself, and the "mortal and the finite," which the culture of slavery assigned to the slave and to nature. Gates then shows how Douglass plays the trickster with these oppositions by reversing their application, thus exposing their purely arbitrary, "humanly-imposed not divinely ordained" status in southern discourse. This essay is the first in black autobiography criticism to show the influence of continental critical models. It problematizes the dimension of meaning in the slave narrative by suggesting that reference in black autobiography is never "natural" but always culturally determined, that texts like the *Narrative* lure the critic into accepting and using uncritically the very oppositional discourse that Douglass actually aims to discredit. Gates's essay anticipates a central concern of the increasingly theoretical black autobiography criticism of the 1980s: the development of a critical vocabulary and analytic method that will allow scholars to recognize *how* black autobiography signifies, what it does with and to the structures of discourse that it inherits from both white and black culture, and what those linguistic operations say about once-privileged notions of the "blackness" of African-American autobiography as well as the very notion of racial or self-representation in the form of what is called today (with unprecedented lack of confidence in the term) *autobiography*.

At least two things are remarkable about African-American autobiography scholarship in the 1980s. First, the largest proportion of that scholarship was devoted to the antebellum slave narrative; second, some of the most thoughtful criticism on black autobiography seems to have gravitated toward the slave narrative because of its priority as the site of the African-American's first recorded confrontation with "the prison-house of language," to use Fredric Jameson's often-cited term. While a number of sensitive and productive readings of slave narratives have been published in essay collections and monographs of the 1980s,[10] the most far-reaching work on this genre of black autobiography appears in a handful of books, notably Houston A. Baker's *Blues, Ideology, and Afro-American Literature* (1984), William L. Andrews's *To Tell a Free Story* (1986), and Gates's *The Signifying Monkey* (1988). Different as the books obviously are, each one may be read as a response to a problem first explicitly posed by Baker in remarks on Douglass's *Narrative* published in *The Journey Back* (1980). After arguing that the *Narrative* demonstrates Douglass's adoption of "a public version of the self—one molded by the values of white America" (39), Baker goes on to wonder "where in Douglass's *Narrative* does a prototypical black American self reside?" (43). His answer is skeptical, in keeping with the posture of much black autobiography criticism of the 1980s: "The voice of the unwritten self, once it is subjected to the linguistic codes, literary conventions, and audience expectations of a literate population, is perhaps never again the authentic voice of black American slavery. It is, rather, the voice of a self transformed by an autobiographical act into a sharer in the general public discourse about slavery" (43).

Baker's doubts about the "authentic voice" of the slave narrative, and by implication of any African-American autobiography that employs the language and discursive conventions of the Anglo-American literary tradition, have had a salutary effect on black autobiography criticism. While never denying the inevitable accommodations that black autobiography must make to its white discursive milieu, critics such as Andrews and Gates, and even Baker himself, have argued that, however one wishes to code the voice of black autobiography, that voice is not ultimately dominated by its discursive circumstances; it makes of its encounter with discourse, its narrated scenes of reading and writing, a metaphor of the autobiographer's determination, in the words of Andrews, not just to attain freedom but to "tell a free story" about that all-consuming aim. By viewing freedom as not just the theme but the *sign* of the best of the slave narratives as well as of black autobiography as a whole, criticism of the 1980s seems to have become sensitized anew to the formal, stylistic, and rhetorical richness of African-American autobiography as a narrative tradition.

In *Blues, Ideology, and Afro-American Literature*, Baker homes in on "blues moments" in African-American discourse when the "trained" voice translates into metaphorical and formal terms the "unrestrained mobility and unlimited freedom" of the railroad, the focal and aural symbol of black vernacular expression in this country. To read and hear the blues in this extended fashion is to suggest that freedom plays through African-American narratives in ways hitherto unimagined, despite and because of black autobiography's awareness of what Baker terms "the economics of slavery" and racial oppression. Thus when he takes up Douglass's *Narrative*, Baker posits a tension of voices in that text: one acculturated and inauthentic in the ways argued in *The Journey Back*, the other much more self-consciously aware of its economic conditions and conditioning. In the latter stages of the *Narrative*, the Douglass who takes "a fully commercial view of his situation" (48) repossesses himself through marriage, "*individual* wage earning," and eventually employment as a "*salaried* spokesman" for antislavery. The result is a "convergence of the voices" that emerge from the *Narrative* and a reconciliation of "literacy, Christianity, and revolutionary zeal in an individual and economically profitable job of work" (49). Baker goes on to explain how Harriet Jacobs's *Incidents in the Life of a Slave Girl* articulates "a sense of *collective*, rather than individualistic, black identity" (55), in marked contrast to Douglass's autobiography and that of his male compatriots in the slave narrative. Jacobs also negotiates the economics of oppression, Baker concludes, on her way to attaining a voice that invokes "sisterly communion by imaging a quite remarkable community of black women" (56).

In *To Tell a Free Story*, Andrews echoes some of Baker's criticism of Douglass's *Narrative*, which he identifies as part of the tradition of the American jeremiad, so ably reconstructed by Sacvan Bercovitch. As an American Jeremiah, Douglass was free to excoriate his country for its failure to live up to its ideals, as stated in the Declaration of Independence. However, the rhetorical posture of the jeremiad also required Douglass to celebrate the American Dream, to affirm the middle-class consensus about how to achieve it, and thus to endorse the ideology of "true Americanism" even as he denounced those who threatened that ideal with their perverted or "false Americanism." Andrews then goes on to discuss how Douglass equates the Southern slaveocracy with false Americanism, only to whitewash the racism and economic oppression he experienced in the North by embodying in the *Narrative*'s charming images of New Bedford the "true Americanism" of capitalist-industrial prosperity. By comparing to the *Narrative* what Douglass had been saying in his speeches and writing in private about his life in the North, Andrews suggests that Douglass did not feel free to express fully his sense of alienation from the American ideals that he seems so fully to endorse in the *Narrative*. Like Baker, Andrews believes that Douglass eventually did find his way to greater expressive freedom, but Andrews argues that Douglass's second autobiography, *My Bondage and My Freedom* (1855), signals this movement. Also reminiscent of Baker's approach is Andrews's comparison of *My Bondage and My Freedom* to *Incidents in the Life of a Slave Girl* as culminating texts of multiple autobiographical traditions whose evolution and import it is the burden of *To Tell a Free Story* to delineate.

In *The Signifying Monkey*, Gates calls signifyin(g)[11] "the trope of tropes" in African-American oral culture and written literature. Gates goes on to show that the essence of this trope is to parody, destabilize, invert, or otherwise make free with sign, signified, and indeed, the person who plays the role of the signifier. The persistence of signifyin(g) throughout black American literary history testifies to the priority of what Gates call the "speakerly text" in African-American writing, as contrasted to Roland Barthes's notion of the "writerly text" in the dominant Western discourse since the Renaissance in Europe. Gates emphasizes that African-American writers signify on both the texts of Western discourse and the texts (both verbal and written) of their own tradition. In fact, Gates's very idea of African-American literary tradition is grounded in the image of black writers as revisionists of texts and participants in a vast, as yet largely uncharted, intertext of signification in which presumed absences assume verbal presence, imbalances of power are linguistically redressed, and rhetorical spaces are repeatedly being cleared out, occupied, and then displaced by the play of black voices. Where does this revisionist tradition begin? In a brilliant discussion of five black texts from the late eighteenth and early nineteenth centuries, Gates locates the literary wellspring of the entire signifyin(g) tradition in the autobiographical narrations of James Gronniosaw, John Marrant, Ottobah Cugoano, Olaudah Equiano, and John Jea. Citing the presence in all these texts of "the trope of the talking book," and then brilliantly analyzing the revisions of that trope in each successive text, Gates makes a strong case for the earliest black narrators in English as masters of signifyin(g), fully engaged in the international debates of their era concerning the relationship of racial identity, linguistic performance, and ontological status in the Great Chain of Being. *The Signifying Monkey* attests to the literary complexity of early black autobiography more convincingly than any work of criticism before it, while it also adds compelling evidence of the primacy of the autobiographical tradition to the evolution of both the verbal artistry and the thematic substance of all subsequent narrative forms in African-American literature.

Looking to the 1990s, it is hard to imagine that critics and scholars of black American autobiography will veer sharply away from the interests and concerns that preoccupied criticism of this genre in the 1980s. The idea of black autobiography as a site of formal revisionism and the free play of signification may, we might hope, lead to a fresh examination of texts and traditions in the genre's history that have up to now received little attention. For instance, although the antebellum slave narrative has enjoyed high visibility in attempts to reconstruct the history of black autobiography, only slight research has been done on the postbellum slave narrative, not to mention the proliferation of autobiographies in the late nineteenth and early twentieth centuries that espouse ideological points of view apparently at variance with those of Douglass's *Narrative* or *The Autobiography of Malcolm X*. A large gap of knowledge about black American autobiography from 1865 to 1940 still exists in criticism,[12] and one may hope that the 1990s will find us better informed about this complex period of African-American literary history.

Another undeniable need in black autobiography criticism is for increased research on black American women's autobiography. With the publication of scholarly editions of Hurston's *Dust Tracks on a Road* (1984) and Jacobs's *Incidents in the Life of a Slave Girl* (1987), along with *Sisters of the Spirit* (1986), Andrews's edition of three early spiritual autobiographies, and the sixteen first-person narratives in the Schomburg Library of Nineteenth-Century Black Women's Writing, under the general editorship of Henry Louis Gates, the texts of the black female tradition in autobiography are rapidly returning to currency in American literary scholarship. While Frederick Douglass and Richard Wright remained the most often-discussed African-American autobiographers in the 1980s, Jacobs and Hurston attracted unprecedented critical attention during that decade too, a fact all the more striking in the face of the largely dismissive attitude of earlier autobiography critics toward *Incidents* and *Dust Tracks*. In "Race, Gender, and Cultural Context in Zora Neale Hurston's *Dust Tracks on a Road*," Nellie Y. McKay explains how the marginal position of Hurston as autobiographer positioned between black and white cultures and readerships shaped the problematic status of *Dust Tracks* and helped turn it into a textual "statue" of selfhood (to use Hurston's own metaphor) rather than the flesh-and-blood self-representation that many readers have expected to find in the book. McKay goes on to show that previous evaluators of *Dust Tracks*, particularly those disturbed by its evidently accommodationist politics, have failed to apprehend the politics of its author's identification with southern black culture and the linguistic strategies by which black women writers have affirmed their literary autonomy even at the expense of literal authenticity. The idea that Hurston's own concept and interpretation of black folk culture is itself the best model of how *Dust Tracks* should be conceptualized and understood is further elaborated in Françoise Lionnet's study of Hurston's autobiography in *Autobiographical Voices*. What Lionnet terms "autoethnography," a process of defining one's subjectivity as inevitably mediated through language, history, and ethnographical analysis, provides a new lens through which critics in the 1990s can reconsider not only black women's autobiography but texts by any African-American whose autobiography aims at elucidating selfhood through an articulation of ethnic ties and cultural roots.[13]

A third direction in which the study of black autobiography may profitably move is towards comparatist studies of the pan-African dimensions of this genre. As he has done so often in autobiography studies in general, James Olney has pointed this direction in particular in his essay, "The Value of Autobiography for Comparative Studies: African vs. Western Autobiography" (1979), in which *Black Boy* is compared to Camara Laye's *L'Enfant Noir* (1953) to suggest that African works in this genre tend to be "autophylographical," that is, concerned with the tribal self, whereas African-American autobiographies tend to be predicated on the idea of individualized self-expression. Such a contrast, however, may be more typical of male than of female-authored black autobiographies on the international scene. In any event, criticism in the 1990s will be much enriched by extensions of this sort of cross-disciplinary inquiry into the fullest intertextual dimensions of what an African heritage and a sense of African identification has meant to black autobiography.

What is most needed, and what is most to be anticipated, in future African-American autobiography criticism, ultimately, are books that reconstruct the history of this genre and/or offer theories of analysis and criticism that bring into play the full panoply of cultural, social, and historical research that has been done in the last thirty years on African-Americans. While no one is likely to attempt a study on the scale of Butterfield's survey of the entire genre, a number of scholars are currently researching and writing books on important traditions within the larger tradition. The ongoing work by Sandra Pouchet Paquet, Alice Deck and Nellie Y. McKay, and William L. Andrews on West Indian autobiography, African-American women's autobiography, and the history of African-American autobiography from 1865 to 1940, respectively, will continue to open new vistas on black American literary, cultural, and intellectual history. The value of this kind of work is attested by the enthusiastic response generated by the publication (since this essay's composition) of Joanne M. Braxton's *Black Women Writing Autobiography*, the first history of African-American women's autobiography. One of Braxton's basic theses—summed up in the subtitle of her book, *A Tradition within a Tradition*—is that there is no single tradition, myth, or representative voice in or for African-American autobiography. Even within the tradition Braxton chronicles, the "outraged mother" and the "visionary" engage in a creative dialogue, if not an outright dialectic, revealing in "the Afra-American experience" that "many streams converge, improvising, dancing and playing, together and with the rivers from which they emerge" (208). No more apt metaphor could be applied to African-American autobiography as a whole, or to the criticism that students of this genre may look forward to in the years ahead.

NOTES

1   Warren found Malcolm X an Algeresque hero in his *Yale Review* essay of 1966, while in their essays of the early 1970s, Ohmann read Malcolm as deliberately parodying the Franklin tradition, and Mandel saw in Malcolm's story

an exemplar of the spiritual conversion narrative. Readings of modern black autobiography in a white literary context continued in Michael G. Cooke's "Modern Black Autobiography in the Tradition" (1973), which argues that the autobiographies of Richard Wright, Malcolm X, and Eldridge Cleaver achieve "happy resolutions of an autobiographical paradox" that demands individuality and universality at the same time. Thomas Couser's *American Autobiography: The Prophetic Mode* (1979) emphasizes the debt owed by both Frederick Douglass and Malcolm X to the conversion narrative tradition while noting the importance of the conversion experience to the development of both men as "prophets"—that is, critics of the status quo in the name of some transcendental ideal—in their autobiographies. Albert E. Stone has done the most extensive study of black autobiography's role in the creation of what he calls "versions of American identity" in *Autobiographical Occasions and Original Acts* (1982). Stone's pairings of Du Bois with Henry Adams, Richard Wright with Louis Sullivan, along with a discussion of the collaborative autobiographies of Ossie Guffy, Nate Shaw, and Malcolm X, have yielded the most productive analyses yet of the integral contribution of black and white autobiography to American self-consciousness in the twentieth century.

2 See, for instance, the essays of Edward Margolies and Phyliss R. Klotman. H. Bruce Franklin's early essays on the slave narrative as the "first literary genre" in the United States and on the importance of black autobiography to a genre he calls American "prison literature" are collected in his *The Victim as Criminal and Artist*.

3 The first critic to link the blues tradition to a peculiar comic and lyric quality in African-American autobiography was Ralph Ellison in his essay "Richard Wright's Blues."

4 I am much indebted to Weixlmann's excellent research in the preparation of this essay.

5 See, in particular, the chapter on Hurston's *Dust Tracks on a Road* (1942) in Hemenway's critical biography, *Zora Neale Hurston*.

6 Perhaps the first critic to give Jacobs's narrative a serious reading was H. Bruce Franklin, in the opening chapter of his book *The Victim as Criminal and Artist*.

7 See, for instance, Olney, "'I Was Born': Slave Narratives."

8 Published in the same year as his essay, Stepto's *From Behind the Veil: A Study of Afro-American Narrative* pursues the implications of his approach to Douglass's *Narrative* in subtle analyses of *Up from Slavery* and *Black Boy*. What Stepto calls "the contrapuntal and dialectical" interplay between these texts enables him to chart the formal evolution of African-American narrative in a way that gives unprecedented importance to the manner, as well as the matter, of black autobiographical discourse.

9 It is worthwhile to note that Houston A. Baker, in his chapter on Douglass's 1845 *Narrative* in *Long Black Song*, claims the *Narrative* as an expression of a peculiarly black folk culture, although he does not pursue this relationship to the depth or with the specificity of O'Meally.

10   See, for instance, Sekora and Turner, eds., *The Art of Slave Narrative* and
     Davis and Gates, eds., *The Slave's Narrative*. Note also Costanzo, *Surpriz-
     ing Narrative*, for a study of the eighteenth-century slave narrative, and
     Valerie Smith, *Self-Discovery and Authority in Afro-American Narrative*, for
     an analysis of the importance of the slave narrative to the black American
     novelistic tradition.
11   The parentheses around the *g* remind the reader that in black vernacular
     usage, to which Gates is greatly indebted for his examples of the oral prac-
     tice of "signifyin," the *g* is elided.
12   For a brief overview of some of the texts and traditions of this period in the
     history of black American autobiography, see Andrews, "Forgotten Voices
     of Afro-American Autobiography, 1865–1930." See also Andrews, "The
     Representation of Slavery and the Rise of Afro-American Literary Realism,
     1865–1920."
13   For further insight into the notion of "cultural autobiography" in connec-
     tion with African-American women writers, see Bernice Johnson Reagon,
     "My Black Mothers and Sisters, or On Beginning a Cultural Autobiog-
     raphy."

WORKS CITED

Adams, Timothy Dow. *Telling Lies in Modern American Autobiography*. Chapel
     Hill: University of North Carolina Press. 1990.
Andrews, William L. "Forgotten Voices of Afro-American Autobiography,
     1865–1930." *a/b: Auto/Biography Studies* 2 (1986–87): 21–27.
Andrews, William L. *Sisters of the Spirit: Three Black Women's Autobiographies of
     the Nineteenth Century*. Bloomington: Indiana University Press, 1986.
Andrews, William L. *To Tell a Free Story: The First Century of Afro-American Auto-
     biography, 1760–1865*. Champaign-Urbana: University of Illinois Press,
     1986.
Andrews, William L. "The Representation of Slavery and the Rise of Afro-
     American Literary Realism, 1865–1920." In Deborah E. McDowell and
     Arnold Rampersad, eds. *Slavery and the Literary Imagination*. Baltimore:
     Johns Hopkins University Press, 1989, 62–80.
Baker, Houston A. *Long Black Song*. Charlottesville: University Press of Virginia,
     1972.
Baker, Houston A. *The Journey Back*. Chicago: University of Chicago Press, 1980.
Baker, Houston A. *Blues, Ideology, and Afro-American Literature*. Chicago: Univer-
     sity of Chicago Press, 1984.
Barthes, Roland. *The Pleasures of the Text*. Trans. Richard Miller. New York: Hill
     & Wang, 1975.
Barton, Rebecca Chalmers. *Witnesses for Freedom: Negro Americans in Autobiog-
     raphy*. New York: Harper & Bros., 1948.

Blackburn, Regina. "In Search of the Black Female Self: African-American Women's Autobiographies and Ethnicity." In *Women's Autobiography: Essays in Criticism*. Ed. Estelle C. Jelinek. Bloomington: Indiana University Press, 1980, 133–48.

Braxton, Joanne M. *Black Women Writing Autobiography: A Tradition within a Tradition*. Philadelphia: Temple University Press, 1989.

Brignano, Russell C. *Black Americans in Autobiography: An Annotated Bibliography of Autobiographies and Autobiographical Books Written since the Civil War*. [1974]. Rev., expanded ed. Durham, NC: Duke University Press, 1984.

Burgher, Mary. "Images of Self and Race in Autobiographies of Black Women." In *Sturdy Black Bridges: Visions of Black Women in Literature*. Ed. Roseann P. Bell, Bettye J. Parker, and Beverly Guy-Sheftall. Garden City, NY: Anchor, 1979, 107–22.

Butterfield, Stephen. *Black Autobiography in America*. Amherst: University of Massachusetts Press, 1974.

Cooke, Michael G. "Modern Black Autobiography in the Tradition." In *Romanticism*. Ed. David Thorburn and Geoffrey Hartman. Ithaca, NY: Cornell University Press, 1973, 255–80.

Costanzo, Angelo. *Surprizing Narrative: Olaudah Equiano and the Beginnings of Black Autobiography*. Westport, CT: Greenwood, 1987.

Couser, G. Thomas. *American Autobiography: The Prophetic Mode*. Amherst: University of Massachusetts Press, 1979.

Davis, Charles T., and Henry Louis Gates, Jr., eds. *The Slave's Narrative*. New York: Oxford University Press, 1985.

Douglass, Frederick. *Narrative of the Life of Frederick Douglass an American Slave*. Ed. Benjamin Quarles. Cambridge, MA: Belknap Press, 1960.

Ellison, Ralph. "Richard Wright's Blues." *Antioch Review* 5 (1945): 198–211.

Fabre, Michel. *The Unfinished Quest of Richard Wright*. Trans. Isabel Barzun. New York: William Morrow, 1973.

Fisher, Dexter, and Robert B. Stepto, eds. *Afro-American Literature: The Reconstruction of Instruction*. New York: Modern Language Association, 1979.

Foster, Frances Smith. *Witnessing Slavery: The Development of Ante-bellum Slave Narratives*. Westport, CT: Greenwood, 1979.

Franklin, H. Bruce. *The Victim as Criminal and Artist*. New York: Oxford University Press, 1978.

Gates, Henry Louis. "Binary Oppositions in Chapter One of *Narrative of the Life of Frederick Douglass an American Slave Written by Himself*." In Fisher and Stepto, eds., *Afro-American Literature*, 212–32.

Gates, Henry Louis, general ed. *The Schomburg Library of Nineteenth-Century Black Women Writers*. 30 vols. New York: Oxford University Press, 1988.

Gates, Henry Louis. *The Signifying Monkey: A Theory of Afro-American Literary Criticism*. New York: Oxford University Press, 1988.

Hemenway, Robert E. *Zora Neale Hurston*. Champaign-Urbana: University of Illinois Press, 1977.

Hurston, Zora Neale. *Dust Tracks on a Road*. Ed. Robert E. Hemenway. 2nd ed. Champaign-Urbana: University of Illinois Press, 1984.

Jacobs, Harriet. *Incidents in the Life of a Slave Girl*. Ed. Jean Fagan Yellin. Cambridge: Harvard University Press, 1987.

Kent, George E. "Maya Angelou's *I Know Why the Caged Bird Sings* and Black Autobiographical Tradition." *Kansas Quarterly* 7, no. 3 (1975): 72–78.

Klotman, Phyliss R. "The Slave Narrative and the Western: Popular Literature of the Nineteenth Century." *North Dakota Quarterly* 41 (1973): 40–54.

Lionnet, Françoise. *Autobiographical Voices: Race, Gender, Self-Portraiture*. Ithaca: Cornell University Press, 1989.

Mandel, Barrett John. "The Didactic Achievement of Malcolm X's Autobiography." *Afro-American Studies* 2 (1972): 269–74.

Margolies, Edward. *The Art of Richard Wright*. Carbondale: Southern Illinois University Press, 1969.

Margolies, Edward. "Ante-bellum Slave Narratives: Their Place in American Literary History." *Studies in Black Literature* 4 (1973): 1–8.

McCall, Dan. *The Example of Richard Wright*. New York: Harcourt, Brace, & World, 1969.

McKay, Nellie Y. "Race, Gender, and Cultural Context in Zora Neale Hurston's *Dust Tracks on a Road*." In Bella Brodzki and Celeste Schenk, eds. *Life/Lines: Theorizing Women's Autobiography*. Ithaca: Cornell University Press, 1988, 175–188.

Nichols, Charles H. *Many Thousand Gone: The Ex-Slaves' Account of Their Bondage and Freedom*. Leiden: E. J. Brill, 1963.

Ohmann, Carol. "*The Autobiography of Malcolm X*: A Revolutionary Use of the Franklin Tradition." *American Quarterly* 22 (1970): 131–49.

Olney, James. " 'I Was Born': Slave Narratives, Their Status as Autobiography and as Literature." In Davis and Gates, eds., *The Slave's Narrative*, 148–174.

Olney, James. "The Value of Autobiography for Comparative Studies: African vs. Western Autobiography." *Comparative Civilizations Review* 2 (1979): 52–64.

Olney, James. "Some Versions of Memory/Some Versions of *Bios*: The Ontology of Autobiography." In *Autobiography: Essays Theoretical and Critical*. Ed. James Olney. Princeton: Princeton University Press, 1980, 236–67.

O'Meally, Robert G. "Frederick Douglass' 1845 *Narrative*: The Text Was Meant to Be Preached." In Fisher and Stepto, eds., *Afro-American Literature*, 192–211.

Osofsky, Gilbert, ed. *Puttin' On Ole Massa*. New York: Harper & Row, 1969.

Quarles, Benjamin. "*Narrative of the Life of Frederick Douglass*." In *Landmarks of American Writing*. Ed. Hennig Cohen. New York: Basic Books, 1969, 90–100.

Rawick, George P. *The American Slave: A Composite Autobiography*. 19 vols. Westport, CT: Greenwood, 1972.

Reagon, Bernice Johnson. "My Black Mothers and Sisters, or On Beginning a Cultural Autobiography." *Feminist Studies* 8 (1982): 81–95.

Sayre, Robert. *The Examined Self: Benjamin Franklin, Henry Adams, Henry James*. [1964]. Reprint. Madison: University of Wisconsin Press, 1988.

Schultz, Elizabeth. "To Be Black and Blue: The Blues Genre in Black American Autobiography." *Kansas Quarterly* 7, no. 3 (1975): 81–96.

Sekora, John, and Darwin T. Turner, eds. *The Art of Slave Narrative.* Macomb: Western Illinois University, 1982.

Smith, Sidonie. *Where I'm Bound: Patterns of Slavery and Freedom in Black American Autobiography.* Westport, CT: Greenwood, 1974.

Smith, Valerie. *Self-Discovery and Authority in Afro-American Narrative.* Cambridge: Harvard University Press, 1987.

Sojka, Gregory S. "Black Slave Narratives—A Selected Checklist of Criticism." In Sekora and Turner, eds., *The Art of Slave Narrative,* 135–47.

Starling, Marion Wilson. *The Slave Narrative: Its Place in American History.* Boston: G. K. Hall, 1981.

Stepto, Robert B. *From Behind the Veil: A Study of Afro-American Narrative.* Champaign-Urbana: University of Illinois Press, 1979.

Stepto, Robert B. "Narration, Authentication, and Authorial Control in Frederick Douglass' *Narrative* of 1845." In Fisher and Stepto, eds., *Afro-American Literature,* 178–91.

Stone, Albert E. *Autobiographical Occasions and Original Acts.* Philadelphia: University of Pennsylvania Press, 1982.

Tate, Claudia. "*Black Boy*: Richard Wright's 'Tragic Sense of Life.' " *Black American Literature Forum* 10 (1976): 117–19.

Warren, Robert Penn. "Malcolm X: Mission and Meaning." *Yale Review* 56 (1966): 161–71.

Weixlmann, Joe. "Black American Autobiography in the Twentieth Century: A Bibliographical Essay." (Work in progress).

CHAPTER 9

Nineteenth-Century Autobiographies of Affiliation: The Case of Catharine Sedgwick and Lucy Larcom

CAROL HOLLY

Confident and clear rings the note of the white male self from many classical texts of nineteenth-century American literature. Emerson intones the value of manly individualism in "Self-Reliance," and *Walden* and "Song of Myself" relate their narrators' quests for self-awareness and poetic inspiration apart from the mundane constraints of American life. "These mid-nineteenth-century classics are all autobiographical and all illustrations of the manifold ways of using personal experience in American literature," says Robert Sayre, not only of the narratives by Whitman and Thoreau, but also of Hawtorne's preface to *The Scarlet Letter*, "The Custom-House" sketch (*Examined Self*, 42). But who are the nineteenth-century women who are included in an autobiographical tradition that, according to Sayre, reaches back to Franklin's *Autobiography* and forward to Adams' *Education* and Henry James's three-volume autobiography? Like many studies on American autobiography in the sixties and seventies, Sayre's effort to define the boundaries of the genre in the nineteenth century stops short of discussing—sometimes even of mentioning—the contributions by nineteenth-century literary women.[1]

In 1986 the publication of Estelle Jelinek's *The Tradition of Women's Autobiography* began to correct this omission by devoting no fewer than three chapters to the autobiographies of nineteenth-century American women, both black and white, and several pages in the third of these chapters to the autobiographies of literary women.[2] But the models of identity she employs in the process of categorizing and interpreting these autobiographies present problems of conceptualization rather than omission.

Drawing on the work of Karl Weintraub and other theorists, Paul John Eakin uses the phrase "model of identity" to refer to the "example of selfhood or character that a given culture offers for imitation" to groups of individuals at given points in time ("Self and Culture," 2). We see such models not only in the concept of individuality developed in European culture in the late sixteenth and early seventeenth centuries but also in the radically different concept of "the Dinka of the southern Sudan, who . . . have 'no firm basis for thinking of themselves as selves'" (36–37). Moreover, in many cultures, models of identity are constructed "in literature" as well as "in life," and self-consciously so in the literature we call autobiography (45). "When it comes to self," says Eakin, ". . . autobiography is doubly structured, doubly mediated, a textual metaphor for what is already a metaphor for the subjective reality of consciousness" (45).

Autobiography, then, is a "construct of a construct," and, to be properly understood, individual autobiographies need to be read in terms of the constructs, or "models of identity," available to autobiographers for imitation in writing (Eakin, "Self and Culture," 45). And, to create a certain extent, Jelinek does just that: she uses a nineteenth-century model when she defines as autobiographies of childhood an impressive selection of texts by Margaret Fuller, Grace Greenwood, Lucy Larcom, and Catharine Sedgwick. After all, childhood as a subject for autobiographical reflection may have been informed by the fact that, as Richard Chase suggests, "one of the careers open to women" in the nineteenth century was "that of perpetual childhood" (quoted in Rich, 166).[3] It may also have been informed by the nineteenth century's tendency to privilege childhood as a time of spiritual transcendence and poetic inspiration. But Jelinek goes on to interpret these autobiographies from another, more questionable model when she explains that, "consciously or not, these literary women" concentrated "exclusively on their girlhood" in order to avoid discussing their literary "careers" (*Tradition*, 90).

The problem with this observation is that, in a stroke, Jelinek has focused our attention on what is absent, what is missing, from the texts to which she is introducing us. To be sure, "neither self-affirmation nor social acceptance of aesthetic pursuits by women existed" in the nineteenth century, "as they would a century later" (*Tradition*, 90). Women writers did not think of themselves primarily as artists, nor did they find sanction in their culture for public expression of professional identity.[4] But however accurate her assessment of the attitude of literary women toward the public definition of their careers, however suggestive her linking of childhood reminiscences to the cultural silencing of professional identities for women, Jelinek's approach to literary women's autobiography moves too easily from the descriptive to the dismissive. By employing a model of identity unavailable to nineteenth-century women writers, she addresses the gaps and the absences in a large and significant subgenre of women's autobiography. And she suggests that the childhood reminiscences of literary women are not so significant, not so authentic perhaps, as later narratives in which women began to discuss their careers.[5]

I would like to suggest a different and, I hope, more fruitful approach to these autobiographies of childhood by considering a model of identity that *was* available to nineteenth-century female autobiographers, that of " 'affiliation' rather than 'achievement.' " According to Nancy Cott, the "cardinal goal" of nineteenth-century women "was to establish positive affective relationships. Didactic works on sex-roles and marriages from the late eighteenth through the nineteenth century named a woman's 'stations' in life according to her personal relationships as daughter, sister, loved one, wife, and mother, not in terms of her discrete individual status or aims" (165). There was, of course— and still is—a painfully exploitative dimension to the culture's expectation that women define themselves in relation to others. As many critics and historians have shown, nineteenth-century women were often victims of an ideology that relegated them to the role of domestic caretakers "in order to serve men's view of social utility and order" (Cott, 197).[6] Yet the ideology of separate spheres also created the social space for women to exert some control in defining themselves and shaping their lives. Carroll Smith-Rosenberg argues, for example, that "some nineteenth-century women channeled their frustration with women's restricted roles combined with a sense of superior righteousness legitimized by the Cult of True Womanhood into the reform movements of the first half of the nineteenth century" (*Disorderly Conduct*, 109). Both Smith-Rosenberg and Cott, moreover, have described the strong network of female friendships that developed in the nineteenth century as a result not only of the shared experiences of women but also of the belief in women's privileged capacity for empathetic relationship. Here, says Cott, "woman's sphere" is seen "as the basis for a subculture among women that formed a source of strength and identity and afforded supportive sisterly relations"; here "ideology's tenacity owed as much to women's motives as to the imposition of men's or 'society's'

wishes" (197).[7] Here too women constructed female discourses that offered "clear" and empowering "alternative[s] within the dominant bourgeois discourse" that demarcated woman's sphere (Smith-Rosenberg,
"Writing History," 51).

To consider women's identities in terms of "affiliation" instead of
"accomplishment," relationship rather than career, is to invite consideration of what is present—not what is absent—in the autobiographies
of the literary women who, according to Jelinek, avoid discussion of
careers.[8] It is to invite consideration of the ways in which literary
women structure their narratives and, accordingly, restructure themselves. It also opens our thinking to the ways in which they define the
nature and purpose of the autobiographical act. Of course there are
theorists who deny the possibility of female presence in traditional
female texts. Sidonie Smith argues that when a woman's " 'story' shapes
itself . . . around the fluid, circumstantial, contingent responsiveness
to others that, according to patriarchal ideology, characterizes the lives
of women," the woman autobiographer produces what is in effect "a
nonstory, a silent space, a gap in patriarchal culture" (*Poetics*, 50). But
if it is possible to affirm that nineteenth-century women shaped the
ideology of separate spheres to reflect their own interests and priorities,
then it is likewise possible to see women writers as using the cultural
mandate for female other-directedness to shape autobiography into a
form that constructs "female discourses," that "rescues female priority"
from a culture that otherwise reflects the priorities of men (Smith-
Rosenberg, "Writing History," 37–8; Kolodny, 127).[9] In Catharine
Sedgwick's "Recollections of Childhood" and Lucy Larcom's *A New
England Girlhood*, in fact, the autobiographer's sense of affiliation not
only structures her narrative but structures it so as to promote relationship apart from the strictures of marriage. And her language of affiliation creates a sense of relationship with her audience—her largely
female audience, that is—that posits the autobiographical act as an ex-
pressly intimate, interactive, and female event.

Take, as the first example, the autobiography of Catharine Maria
Sedgwick, one of our first and, to nineteenth-century readers, one of
our most renowned American novelists (1789–1867). Writing intermit-
tently between 1853 and 1860, Sedgwick set down in a private notebook
a series of personal reflections that cover the first fourteen years of her
life. In 1871, these "Recollections of Childhood" were published by
Mary E. Dewey, a close friend of the Sedgwick family, along with a
selection of the novelist's letters.[10] In her Preface to *The Life and Letters*,
Dewey claims that the "story" of Sedgwick's life relates "the gradual
unfolding and ripening amid congenial surroundings of a true and

beautiful soul, a clear and refined intellect, and a singularly sympathetic social nature" (10). She suggests, in other words, that "Recollections" focuses on Sedgwick's development somewhat in the fashion of the autobiographies of individuality that, according to Karl Weintraub, began to be written by such male autobiographers as Franklin, Goethe, and Rousseau at the end of the eighteenth and the beginning of the nineteenth century. But Sedgwick herself considered the project as much a family history as a story of her life. Writing in 1853 to her grandniece Alice, the audience and intended recipient of the narrative, she begins:

MY DEAR LITTLE ALICE,—About two years since your father wrote me an eloquent note persuading me to write for you some memorial of my life, and what I knew of your forbears and mine. If you live to be an old woman, as I now am, you may like to rake in the ashes of the past, and if, perchance, you find some fire still smouldering there, you may feel a glow from it. It is not till we get deep into age that we feel by how slight a tenure we hold on to the memories of those that come after us, and not till then that we are conscious of an earnest desire to brighten the links of the chain that binds us to those who have gone before, and to keep it fast and strong (13).

In this letter Sedgwick clearly signals the extent to which her sense of family affiliation in general and her relationship with Alice in particular shape her conception of the autobiographical act. In the first place, the decision to write this "memorial" comes at the suggestion of her nephew, Alice's father, and the narrative, she reveals, is intended for Alice herself. In a metaphor comparing the autobiographical act to the tending of a fire in a hearth—a domestic metaphor clearly befitting the nature of her project—Sedgwick admits to the satisfaction or "glow" she finds in discovering what still lives for her in memories, or "ashes of the past." But she does so by imagining Alice, not herself, as the autobiographer who at some future date will "rake in the ashes of the past" and discover the "fire still smouldering there." In the final sentence, she further downplays her own autobiographical impulse by attributing it to those of "us"—and this includes the Alice of the future—who feel in old age "by how slight a tenure we hold on to the memories of those that come after us." This impulse is motivated for Sedgwick by the desire not only to forge a link between herself and her descendents, Alice in particular, but to sustain and strengthen the links between themselves and their ancestors as well.

Continually throughout this brief but suggestive passage, then, Sedgwick not only positions herself in the midst of her family—its past, present, and future—but also defines herself as a typical "old woman" who recovers her memories for the family's benefit. She also wishes to serve as a model for Alice to imitate in the future, but because she blurs the distinction between herself and her grandniece, because she speaks not of "I" but of "we," she does so less by setting an example than by imaginatively sharing with Alice the role of family chronicler and sustainer of family ties. Indeed, as we have seen, Sedgwick partly defines herself in terms not of her own identity but of the future identity of Alice and thereby reflects the mutuality or "relational self-definition" that Elizabeth Abel suggests is characteristic of relationships between women (414). Written by an older for a younger woman of the family, Sedgwick's "Recollections" thus reflect a woman's orientation towards others and an interactive sense of female relationship.

What follows Sedgwick's opening letter to Alice is a fragmented, discontinuous narrative typical, some critics believe, of women's autobiographical form.[11] In "Recollections," this sense of fragmentation is created by the fact that, writing over a period of seven years, Sedgwick does not attempt to sustain chronological or obvious thematic unity in her narrative. She focuses specifically on family history in her first entry from May, 1853, for example, but determines to reflect on changes in village life in her entry from 1854. This lack of narrative continuity persists even within the sections written during a distinct compositional period. In the long May, 1853, entry, for example, Sedgwick not only moves within the space of thirty pages from the portrait of one family member to another, but she often quotes from the memoirs or letters written by family members or friends to provide further insight into the lives of her ancestors or members of her immediate family. By thus piecing together bits of family biography, family legend, family letters, testimony from friends, and reflections on family traditions, "Recollections" embodies in its mosaic form the collective life of her family. Even her commentary on the changes in village mores, inspired as it was in May, 1854, by the annual visit from Alice's parents, is simultaneously a reflection on the Sedgwick family's participation in the life of the community.

Sedgwick's personal history is, of course, virtually indistinguishable from the story of her family, as she suggests in the following passage from May, 1853: "But I am far enough off from our family history, or rather my own story, which I began with; but fearing, dear Alice, that you would never know how I came here, I have, and shall transmit to you all that I know of my progenitors" (22). In fact, Sedgwick has given next to nothing of her "own story" by this point in the narrative; the circumstances of her own birth and early years do not appear until much later, after she has touched on the histories of her grandparents and parents. And even then, when she does recall her earliest memories and discusses her early education, she does so to recover, say, her earliest association with her father (39), or her memories of other people, her nurse in particular, who were instrumental in forming her character (40–41), or her sense of the educational value of their exceptional home life (46–47). As the syntax of her sentence suggests, in other words, her "own story" becomes "family history," and "family history" tells her "story." Moreover, the direct yet intimate address to "dear Alice," an address we encounter throughout the narrative, serves to include her niece in this interfamilial, historical design. Once again a term like *relational* identity or *self-in-relationship* describes the way in which through a variety of means—narrative design, statement of intent, relationship with audience—Sedgwick articulates the impossibility of defining herself apart from others (Abel, 411, 417). So too does her absolute silence about her career as a writer suggest that, as she once wrote in a letter, "My *author* existence has always seemed something accidental, extraneous, and independent of my inner self" (Sedgwick, 249).

That she defined her life as inextricable from that of her family does not imply that Sedgwick was unaware of the dangers inherent in the self-sacrificial role that nineteenth-century women were expected to play in marriage. "Sedgwick believed," says Mary Kelley, "that the role of wifehood and motherhood was the most appropriate for woman, and yet she was equally adamant in her refusal to adopt legally that role for herself. She wanted to feel the embrace of familial intimacy without yielding her total self. She wanted intimacy *and* autonomy" ("Woman Alone," 211). Her "Recollections" suggest, moreover, that her decision to remain single was related to the domestic fate of her mother and sisters. Of her sister, Frances, she writes, "Her marriage was not a congenial one. She endured much and heroically" (71). Of her sister Eliza's marriage, a marriage that produced twelve children, she cries, "Oh dear Sister! what a life of toil, of patient endurance, of sweet hopes, heavenly affections, keen disappointments, harsh trials, acute sorrows, and acute joys then opened upon you!" (69). Throughout her "Recollections," she likewise makes continual reference to the "two or three turns of insanity" that, due to "the terrible weight of domestic cares," afflicted her mother throughout Sedgwick's childhood (28–29). Indeed, her discussion of the relationship between her mother and father, a relationship characterized by her father's expectation of female submissiveness and his wife's compliance in her domestic role, provides an unintentional but nonetheless powerful critique of nineteenth-century marriage.

It also provides a compelling endorsement of a different way of defining woman's sense of affiliation or relational identity. As I have shown, Sedgwick's narrative focuses on family relationships but, given her status as a single woman and her consciousness of domestic unhappiness, it tends to privilege relationships outside of marriage. Moreover, though she professes deep affection for her father and brothers—though, in fact, biographical studies reveal an intense dependence on her male relatives[12]—Sedgwick reserves her language of deepest affiliation and identification for her relationships with women. Her destiny was "mingle[d]" with that of Aunt Susan (55); the "tenderest union, the most unwavering confidence subsisted between" Sedgwick and Eliza, the sister who addressed Catharine as her " 'sister-mother-child-friend' " (70). And she continually highlights her relationship with her grandniece Alice, the daughter of her favorite niece or "surrogate" daughter, Kate, through her awareness of Alice not only as audience of her "Recollections" but also as heir to her role as family chronicler or sustainer of family ties (Kelley, "Woman Alone," 220).[13] Through her network of relationships with the family in general and with women in particular, Sedgwick challenges the patriarchal prescriptions for womanhood by redefining the relational boundaries for women. Through her textual embodiment of self-in-relation and her intimate, almost interactive sense of her female audience, moreover, she charts the possibilities of a woman-centered autobiography as well.

The pattern of affiliation that informs Sedgwick's private "Recollections" on the level of tacit assumption becomes in Lucy Larcom's *A New England Girlhood* a clearly articulated ground for an autobiography written for a public yet intimate audience of women. Published in 1889, four years before Larcom's death, *A New England Girlhood* traces the events of Larcom's life from her early years in Beverley, Massachusetts, through the death of her father and the family's move to Lowell, through the years in which Larcom worked in the Lowell textile mills and the following six-year period in which, living with her sister's family in Illinois, she both taught and attended school. The story ends with her return to Massachusetts in 1852. Because of Larcom's depiction of New England culture, *A New England Girlhood* has long been available to twentieth-century readers as "an illuminating document in the cultural history of nineteenth century America" (Davis, vi). But it has been ignored as an autobiography shaped by Larcom not only to present the pattern of a woman's life, interwoven with the lives of others, but also to reflect her thinking about the aims and identities of women.

Larcom begins *A New England Girlhood* with a preface which posits a distinctly relational approach to personal identity. "None of us can think of ourselves as entirely separate beings," she says; we each have a "debt to the lives around us for whatever of power or beauty has been poured into ours" (6). Somewhat later, however, she celebrates the "individuality" of "every child [who] comes into the world" in order to

identify her lifelong need to cultivate her love for poetry (10). But in Larcom's thinking, individuality is never achieved at the expense of relationship, autonomy at the expense of connection. The definition of
poetry she develops for her reader blends her recognition of individuality—of personal talents, proclivities, aspirations—with her sense of
relationship with others: "As I grew up and lived on, friendship became
to me the deepest and sweetest ideal of poetry. To live in other lives, to
take their power and beauty into our own, that is poetry *experienced*,
the most inspiring of all" (10–11).

The story of personal development that Larcom tells in the autobiography proper—a story that includes the development of her poetic sensibility and her life as a working girl—likewise reflects this balance
between autonomy and relationship. From her beginnings with her
large family and the people of her neighborhood in chapter 1 to her relationships with her sisters and other mill-girls in later chapters, Larcom
portrays her life as having been continuously intertwined with and
dependent upon the lives of others. Larcom says of her Aunt Lucy, for
example, "her beautiful character was just such an illumination to my
young life as I should most desire mine to be to the lives of others" (27).
And again she comments on the influence of family life on her early
development: "We understand ourselves best and are best understood
by others through the persons who came nearest to us in our earliest
years" (27). Even by the end of her narrative, where her younger self
has begun to develop a distinct sense of individuality, "a certain Myself
who was always starting up with her own original plan or aspiration
before me" (156), Larcom continues to insist that she cannot "illustrate
my own early experience, except by the lives around me which most
influenced mine" (205). Indeed, she explains in another portion of the
narrative, following an account of her attachment to her sister, "I am
not sure but self-reliance and dependence really belong together. They
do seem to meet in the same character, like other extremes" (258). When
she compares the relationships among mill-girls to "the webs of cloth
we saw woven around us," Larcom thus provides a metaphor for the
patterning of self and other that her narrative both embodies and
depicts. "That we are entirely separate, while yet we entirely belong
to the Whole," she concludes, "is a trust that we learn to rejoice in . . ."
(184–85).[14]

Like Sedgwick, Larcom never married, and her sense of affiliation
is primarily expressed through her relations with other women. Indeed,
Larcom claims that "the first duty of every woman" is to "recognize the
mutual bond of universal womanhood" (200). As if to make her theory
fit her practice, Larcom's recognition of the "mutual bond" of woman-

hood provides a basis not only for her autobiographical narrative and the language of identity that informs it but for her sense of audience as well. She dedicates the book to "To My Girlfriends in General; and in Particular to my Namesake-Niece, Lucy Larcom Spaulding," and, at the beginning of her preface, she defines her audience as essentially female or female-identified: "My audience is understood to be composed of girls of all ages, and of women who have not forgotten their girlhood. Such as have a friendly appreciation of girls—and of those who write for them—are also welcome to listen to as much of my narrative as they choose. All others are eavesdroppers, and, of course, have no right to criticize" (5–6).

When she goes on in her preface to discuss her understanding of the autobiographical act, Larcom depends for that understanding on the sympathy and trust she believes to exist between herself and her predominantly female audience. "To many," she begins, "the word 'autobiography' implies nothing but conceit and egotism," nothing but the attempt to focus on and glorify the autobiographer herself. "But these," she suggests, "are not necessarily its characteristics." What she believes to be a true or "complete autobiography" must honestly acknowledge the author's relationship to other lives—and to the "One Infinite Life"— of which she is part. If, in other words, we refuse to "think of ourselves as entirely separate beings," we will see that such terms as "conceit and egotism" no longer apply to the act of self-revelation. "Indeed," she continues, "there may be more egotism in withdrawing mysteriously into one's self, than in frankly unfolding one's life-story, for better or worse. There may be more vanity in covering one's face with a veil, to be wondered at and guessed about, than in drawing it aside, and saying by that act, 'There! you see that I am nothing remarkable'" (6).

We might take Larcom's reformulation of egotism in autobiography as a somewhat spurious justification of her autobiographical act if, soon after, she did not explicitly discuss "the relation that exists between writer and reader" in this process of "unfolding one's life-story." Larcom defines this relation to be one of "mutual friendship," and the purpose of friendship to be mutual self-revelation or exchange. "Friends naturally like to know each other in a neighborly way"; indeed we are "all willing to gossip about ourselves, sometimes, with those who are really interested in us. Girls especially are fond of exchanging confidences with those whom they think they can trust" (6–7). Within this context, then, the act of withholding one's life story would be tantamount to refusing to share oneself with a friend, to betraying a mutual understanding or trust between women. But the fact that she likens the autobiographical act to the "exchanging of confidences" between girls suggests not only that Larcom trusts her female audience the way girls trust their friends but also that, by virtue of the trust, she *en*trusts or turns over to her sympathetic readers a part of herself. Autobiography, by this account, becomes a mingling or fusion of selves between female autobiographer and reader, and the reader, no less than Larcom, her sisters, and her friends, becomes part of the network or weave of female affiliation that *A New England Girlhood* both celebrates and portrays. The "bonds of universal womanhood," in Larcom's hand, thus define the boundaries of a woman-centered autobiography, an autobiography that, even as it privileges a sense of relational identity and loyalty to women, invites women to interact with the conversation or confidences of the text. In so doing Larcom has publicly posited what is privately enacted in Sedgwick's "Recollections": a "dialogic" or interactive relationship between herself and her reader that is foreign to the more detached, autonomous, and self-consciously authoritative narrators of the autobiographical writings of Franklin, Whitman, Adams, and Thoreau. [15]

That women pattern their life stories to reflect their sense of relationship with others is, of course, one of the reigning generalizations put forth by recent critics. Ann Walters writes that because women tend "toward involvement" with others "as opposed to separation," they are accordingly "more likely to explore the self in relation to others" in their autobiographical acts (86). Susan Friedman insists that women's autobiography is possible when "the individual does not feel *herself* to exist outside of others, and still less against others, but very much *with* others in an independent existence that asserts its rhythms everywhere in the community" (38). [16] And, throughout these pages, I have argued that women's sense of affiliation in nineteenth-century America, particularly their affiliation with women, provided two women autobiographers with the terms with which to structure their narratives, determine their audiences, even to define the autobiographical act itself. It is true that, to the extent that they ignore or undervalue literary careers, Sedgwick's and Larcom's autobiographies of affiliation reflect the prescriptions for true womanhood determined by patriarchal culture. But through patterns of affiliation organized around the autobiographer as single woman, they also subvert patriarchal prescriptions by presenting a distinct sense of female priority or presence. Perhaps they present a unique form of women's autobiography as well.

It is important to note, however, that to make such claims about a small selection of texts is not to posit an overarching theory about all women's autobiography in nineteenth-century America; nor is it to suggest that the model of identity which enabled single, white, middle-class literary women to write such autobiographies was necessarily available—or available in the same form—to black or working-class women, or to other white women writers.[17] Although an interest in others structures her *Recollections of My Childhood* (1854), for example, Grace Greenwood neither portrays the sense of female affiliation we see in Sedgwick and Larcom nor articulates a sense of her autobiographical act as predicated on a female audience. In "Looking Back on Girlhood" (1892), Sarah Orne Jewett credits her father with cultivating the interest in people that so richly informs her fiction, and in *Chapters From a Life* (1897), Elizabeth Stuart Phelps not only attributes her development to the influence of both of her parents but devotes a good portion of her narrative to her relationships with literary men. In the veiled autobiographical anecdote that appears in *Woman in the Nineteenth-Century* (1845), the story of Miranda, Margaret Fuller likewise attributes to her father the education and encouragement that enabled her to develop a "dignified sense of self-dependence" (39). Yet in the unfinished sketch of her youth that appears in the *Memoirs* (1852), Fuller portrays her former self as a lonely and disturbed child who suffered not only from the death of a younger sister but also from her father's exacting approach to her education.

What these counter-examples suggest is that the effort made here to read two neglected texts with more detail and more attention to nineteenth-century models of identity than we have been given to date is but a step toward the needs of the future: comprehensive, contextual study of nineteenth-century autobiography by literary women, indeed by all nineteenth-century American women.[18] We need to establish not only the economic, social, and historical contexts in which these autobiographies were written but the literary and biographical contexts as well.[19] As we undertake each of these tasks, moreover, we must chart the similarities and differences between models of identity that have shaped the autobiographies of *all* American women—white women and women of color. And we must do so with an eye to the political implications of our theories, methodologies, and conclusions.[20] The scholarly and critical work left to be done in these areas is both important and immense.

NOTES

I wish to thank Susan Albertine, Dale Bauer, and Pamela Schwandt for their helpful comments on an earlier draft of this essay.

1 Other autobiography critics who focus all or a good portion of their attention on nineteenth-century American autobiographers (most of whom are

male) are Blasing, Buell, Cooley, Couser, Cox, Fendelman, Sayre ("Autobiography and America"), and Spengemann and Lundquist.

2   Among the many other studies of women's autobiography to have emerged
in the eighties are articles, books, and collections of essays written and/or
edited by Adams, Anderson, Andrews, Benstock, Brée, Brodzki, Bunkers,
Carby, Foster, Fox-Genovese, Gwin, Heilbrun, Hoffman, Jelinek, Lionett,
Mason, Peterson, Reagon, Sanders, Smith, Spacks, Spender, Stanton,
Stone, Walters, Watson, and Yellin. In addition, the nine volumes of *The
Schomburg Library of Nineteenth-Century Black Women Writers* that are devoted
to autobiographical writing include critical introductions by William An-
drews, James Olney, Valerie Smith, Brenda Stevenson, and others.

3   In *The Female Experience*, Gerda Lerner suggests another reason why
nineteenth-century women might limit their autobiographies to reminiscences of childhood when she notes that "more frequently than the boy,"
a nineteenth-century girl "would experience growing up as a loss, a con-
finement, a decrease of freedom" (5).

4   For further discussion of literary women's approach to their professional
identities, see Baym (30–33) and Kelley, *Private Woman, Public Stage*.

5   Other critics who have similarly commented on the tendency of women
autobiographers to ignore their careers, to downplay their public importance, are Conway (quoted in Heilbrun), Heilbrun, Jelinek ("Paradox and
Success"), and Spacks ("Selves in Hiding").

6   For further discussion of nineteenth-century prescriptions for womanhood
in America, see Epstein, Welter, Smith-Rosenberg, and Woloch.

7   See also Cott 190 and Smith-Rosenberg, "The Female World of Love and
Ritual" in *Disorderly Conduct* (53–76).

8   In *Revolution and the Word*, Cathy Davidson cautions that "schooled as we
may be in decoding silences (and especially through recent reassessment
of the possibilities of criticism) we have too often also been schooled in
dismissing presence" (3).

9   In her provocative, closely-argued *Poetics of Women's Autobiography*, Smith
argues that, for all the "energy, intelligence, and courage" she showed in
rejecting "the silenced life demanded of most women in their times," the
pre-twentieth-century female autobiographer seeks "to appropriate the
story of man in a culture that would condemn her to its sentence." She is
the product of the "margin who desire[s] access to the father country" (62).
I posit the contrasting view that, for some nineteenth-century American
women, to write from the "margin" of woman's sphere was to create in autobiography the empowering female discourses that Smith-Rosenberg discovers in the writings of women reformers.

10 The two notebooks in which Sedgwick wrote her recollections are housed
at the Massachusetts Historical Society, Boston, Massachusetts (Catharine
Maria Sedgwick Papers). My examination of the original manuscript reveals
that, in editing the "Recollections" for publication, Mary Dewey made
several alterations or adjustments in the text: the occasional rephrasing of
a sentence, the omission of a passage probably considered too personal

for public consumption, and, in what appears to be an effort to lend greater formal coherence to the narrative, the occasional grouping-together of passages that are thematically or chronologically related. Because none of these changes affects or challenges my interpretation of the "Recollections," I quote not from the original manuscript, inaccessible to most readers, but from the published version available in Dewey. Because Sedgwick appears not to have provided a title for her autobiography, I have used Dewey's title, "Recollections of Childhood," as well. Professor Mary Kelley, Dartmouth College, is currently preparing an anthology of Sedgwick's prose writings that will soon make an authoritative version of Sedgwick's "Recollections" available to interested readers.

11   See, for example, Jelinek (*Women's Autobiography*, 17) and Walters (87).

12   See Kelley ("Woman Alone") and Mintz (151–71).

13   Another example of the intimate language Sedgwick uses to describe her relationships with women comes from the 1834 diary entry she made after a meeting with Fanny Kemble: "I do not believe that men can even feel so pure an enthusiasm for women as we can feel for one another—ours is nearest to the love of angels" (quoted in Cott, 189). In keeping with Sedgwick's "enthusiasm for women" were the intimate friendships with Kemble and the female relatives who, according to Foster, formed the "inner circle" of Sedgwick's social life in Stockbridge, Massachusetts (35).

14   For a similar use of the weaving metaphor, see Larcom's poem, "Weaving" (95).

15   I take my definition of the "dialogic" relationship between writer and reader from Patrocinio Schweickart's provocative discussion of female modes of reading woman-authored texts. Schweickart claims that the female or "dialogic" mode, governed by the "drive 'to connect' " or experience intimacy with the female author, grows out of women's tendencies to "define and experience themselves in terms of their affiliations and relationships with others" (54–55). What is so striking about Larcom's discussion of her autobiographical intentions is her desire as *author* to develop a "dialogic" or interactive relationship with her reader.

16   I first encountered these views in Germaine Brée's generous summary in "Autogynography" of a draft of Friedman's essay, "Women's Autobiographical Selves: Theory and Practice." The essay itself, recently published in Benstock's *The Private Self*, includes both a useful summary of the concepts of female selfhood in the work of Sheila Rowbotham and Nancy Chodorow and an illuminating application of these concepts to the autobiographical writings of twentieth-century women. Taken together, our findings suggest that there is a good deal of overlap not only between nineteenth- and twentieth-century models of female identity but also between their embodiments in women's diaries and in autobiographies. Other essays that explicitly address the issue of the other-directedness of women's autobiography are those by Mason and Watson.

17   See, for example, Smith and Valenze's discussion of collectivity among nineteenth-century working-class women in England, and Andrews and

Carby's analyses of Harriet Jacobs' *Incidents in the Life of a Slave Girl* (*Free Story*, 239–41 and 247–58; *Reconstructing*, 40–61).

18   Friedman, as summarized by Brée (see note 16), supports the idea of the contextual study of women's autobiography: "the formal characteristics of the autobiographic text are inseparable from the concepts of self held by the writer. And these are in turn determined by the circumstances of women's and men's lives. Their significance and the forms they take cannot be understood apart from their socio-historical context" (174).

19   In his recent essay, "Henry James's 'Obscure Hurt': Can Autobiography Serve Biography?", Paul John Eakin addresses the importance of conceptualizing the writing of autobiography as a "primary biographical event" in the present life of the autobiographer (679).

20   The first chapter of Hazel Carby's *Reconstructing Womanhood* provides an excellent discussion of some of the issues that must be faced by black and white feminist critics who seek to reconstruct the literary history of women.

WORKS CITED

Abel, Elizabeth. "(E)Merging Identities: The Dynamics of Female Friendship in Contemporary Fiction by Women." *Signs* 6 (1981): 413–35.

Adams, Timothy Dow, and Rebecca Hogan, eds. *Studies in Women's Autobiography*. Special Issue of *a/b: Auto/Biography* 4 (1988).

Anderson, Linda. *Women and Autobiography*. New York: St. Martin's. (Forthcoming, 1990).

Andrews, William, ed. *Sisters of the Spirit: Three Black Women's Autobiographies of the Nineteenth Century*. Bloomington: Indiana University Press, 1986.

Andrews, William. *To Tell a Free Story: The First Century of Afro-American Autobiography, 1760–1865*. Champaign-Urbana: University of Illinois Press, 1986.

Baym, Nina. *Woman's Fiction: A Guide to Novels by and about Women in America, 1820–1870*. Ithaca: Cornell University Press, 1978.

Benstock, Shari, ed. *Feminist Issues in Literary Scholarship*. Bloomington: Indiana University Press, 1987.

Benstock, Shari, ed. *The Private Self: Theory and Practice in Women's Autobiographical Writings*. Chapel Hill: University of North Carolina Press, 1988.

Blasing, Mutlu. *The Art of Life: Studies in American Autobiographical Literature*. Austin: University of Texas Press, 1977.

Brée, Germaine. "Autogynography." In Olney, ed. *Studies*, 171–79.

Brodzki, Bella, and Celeste Schenck, eds. *Life/Lines: Theorizing Women's Autobiography*. Ithaca: Cornell University Press, 1989.

Buell, Lawrence. "Transcendental Self-Examination and Autobiographical Tradition." *Literary Transcendentalism: Style and Vision in the American Renaissance*. Ithaca: Cornell University Press, 1973, 265–83.

Bunkers, Suzanne. "Midwestern Diaries and Journals: What Women Were (Not) Saying in the Late 1880s." In Olney, ed., *Studies*, 190–210.

Carby, Hazel. *Reconstructing Womanhood: The Emergence of the Afro-American Woman Novelist*. New York: Oxford University Press, 1987.

Cooley, Thomas. *Educated Lives: The Rise of Modern Autobiography in America*. Columbus: Ohio State University Press, 1976.

Cott, Nancy. *The Bonds of Womanhood: "Woman's Sphere" in New England, 1770–1835*. New Haven: Yale University Press, 1977.

Couser, Thomas. *American Autobiography: The Prophetic Mode*. Amherst: University of Massachusetts Press, 1979.

Cox, James. "Autobiography and America." *Virginia Quarterly Review* 47 (1971): 53–66.

Davidson, Cathy. *Revolution and the Word: The Rise of the Novel in America*. New York: Oxford University Press, 1986.

Davis, Charles T. "Introduction." In *A New England Girlhood*. Ed. Charles T. Davis. New York: Corinth Books, 1961, v–ix.

Dewey, Mary E. Preface. *Life and Letters of Catharine M. Sedgwick*. Ed. Mary E. Dewey. New York: Harper, 1871, 9–11.

Eakin, Paul John. "Henry James's 'Obscure Hurt': Can Autobiography Serve Biography?" *New Literary History* 19 (1988): 675–92.

Eakin, Paul John. "Self and Culture in Autobiography: Models of Identity and the Limits of Language." In *Autobiography as a Referential Art*. (Forthcoming, Princeton University Press).

Epstein, Barbara. *The Politics of Domesticity: Women, Evangelism, and Temperance in Nineteenth-Century America*. Middleton, CT: Wesleyan University Press, 1981.

Fendelman, Earl. "Toward Walden Pond: The American Voice in Autobiography." *Canadian Review of American Studies* 8 (1977): 11–25.

Foster, Edward. *Catharine Maria Sedgwick*. New York: Twayne, 1974.

Foster, Frances Smith. "Adding Color and Contour to Early American Self-Portraitures: Autobiographical Writings of Afro-American Women." In Pryse and Spillers, eds. *Conjuring*, 25–38.

Fox-Genovese, Elizabeth. "To Write Myself: The Autobiographies of Afro-American Women." In Benstock, ed., *Feminist Issues*, 161–80.

Friedman, Susan Stanford. "Women's Autobiographical Selves: Theory and Practise." In Benstock, ed. *Private Self*, 34–62.

Fuller, Margaret. *Memoirs of Margaret Fuller Ossoli*. 2 vols. Boston: Phillips, Sampson, 1852.

Fuller, Margaret. *Woman in the Nineteenth-Century and Kindred Papers Relating to the Sphere, Condition and Duties, of Woman*. [1855]. New York: W. W. Norton, 1971.

Gates, Henry Louis, Jr., ed. *The Schomburg Library of Nineteenth-Century Black Women Writers*. 30 vols. New York: Oxford University Press, 1988.

Greenwood, Grace. *Recollections of My Childhood and Other Stories*. Boston: Ticknor, Reed, and Fields, 1854.

Gwin, Minrose C. "Green-eyed Monsters of the Slavocracy: Jealous Mistresses in Two Slave Narratives." In Pryse and Spillers, eds., *Conjuring*, 39–52.

Heilbrun, Carolyn G. "Woman's Autobiographical Writings: New Forms." In *Modern Selves: Essays on Modern British and American Autobiography*. Ed. Philip Dodd. London: Frank Cass, 1986, 14–28.

Hoffmann, Lenore, and Margo Culley, eds. *Women's Personal Narratives: Essays in Criticism and Pedagogy*. New York: Modern Language Association, 1985.

Jelinek, Estelle. "Introduction: Women's Autobiography and the Male Tradition." In *Women's Autobiography: Essays in Criticism*. Ed. Estelle Jelinek. Bloomington: Indiana University Press, 1980, 1–20.

Jelinek, Estelle. "The Paradox and Success of Elizabeth Cady Stanton." In Jelinek, ed., *Women's Autobiography*, 71–92.

Jelinek, Estelle. *The Tradition of Women's Autobiography; From Antiquity to the Present*. New York: Twayne, 1986.

Jewett, Sarah Orne. "Looking Back on Girlhood." In *Uncollected Short Stories of Sarah Orne Jewett*. Ed. Richard Cary. Waterville, ME: Colby College Press, 1971, 3–7.

Kelley, Mary. "A Woman Alone: Catharine Maria Sedgwick's Spinsterhood in Nineteenth-Century America." *New England Quarterly* 51 (1978):209–25.

Kelley, Mary. *Private Wonan, Public Stage: Literary Domesticity in Nineteenth-Century America*. New York: Oxford University Press, 1984.

Kolodny, Annette. "The Influence of Anxiety: Prolegomena to a Study of the Production of Poetry by Women." In *A Gift of Tongues: Critical Challenges in Contemporary American Poetry*. Ed. Marie Harris and Kathleen Aguero. Athens: University of Georgia Press, 1987, 112–41.

Larcom, Lucy. *The Poetical Works of Lucy Larcom*. Boston: Houghton Mifflin, 1884.

Larcom, Lucy. *A New England Girlhood*. Ed. Charles T. Davis. New York: Corinth Books, 1961.

Lerner, Gerda. *The Female Experience: An American Documentary*. Indianapolis: Bobbs-Merrill, 1977.

Lionnet, Françoise. *Autobiographical Voices: Race, Gender, Self-Portraiture*. Ithaca: Cornell University Press, 1989.

Mason, Mary G. "The Other Voice: Autobiographies of Women Writers." In Olney, ed., *Autobiography*, 207–35.

Mintz, Steven. *A Prison of Expectations: The Family in Victorian Culture*. New York: New York University Press, 1983.

Olney, James, ed. *Autobiography: Essays Theoretical and Critical*. Princeton: Princeton University Press, 1980.

Olney, James, ed. *Studies in Autobiography*. New York: Oxford University Press, 1988.

Peterson, Linda. "Gender and Autobiographical Form: The Case of the Spiritual Autobiography." In Olney, ed., *Studies*, 211–22.

Peterson, Linda. "Martineau's *Autobiography*: The Feminine Debate Over Self-Interpretation." In *Victorian Autobiography: The Tradition of Self-Interpretation*. New Haven: Yale University Press, 1986, 120–55.

Phelps, Elizabeth Stuart. *Chapters From a Life*. Boston: Houghton Mifflin, 1897.

Pryse, Marjorie, and Hortense J. Spillers, eds. *Conjuring: Black Women, Fiction, and Literary Tradition*. Bloomington: Indiana University Press, 1985.

Reagon, Bernice Johnson. "My Black Mothers and Sisters on Beginning a Cultural Autobiography." *Feminist Studies* 8 (Spring 1982): 81–95.

Rich, Adrienne. *On Lies, Secrets, and Silence: Selected Prose 1966–1978*. New York: W. W. Norton, 1979.

Sanders, Valerie. *The Private Lives of Victorian Women: Autobiography in Nineteenth-Century England*. New York: St. Martin's Press, 1989.

Sayre, Robert. "Autobiography and the Making of America." In Olney, ed., *Autobiography*, 146–68.

Sayre, Robert. *The Examined Self: Benjamin Franklin, Henry Adams, Henry James*. Princeton: Princeton University Press, 1964.

Schweickart, Patrocinio P. "Reading Ourselves: Toward a Feminist Theory of Reading." In *Gender and Reading: Essays on Readers, Texts, and Contexts*. Ed. Elizabeth A. Flynn and Patrocinio P. Schweickart. Baltimore: Johns Hopkins University Press, 1986, 31–62.

Sedgwick, Catharine Maria. "Recollections of Childhood," *Life and Letters of Catharine M. Sedgwick*. Ed. Mary E. Dewey. New York: Harper, 1871, 13–78.

Smith, Ruth L., and Deborah M. Valenze. "Mutuality and Marginality: Liberal Moral Theory and Working-Class Women in Nineteenth-Century England." *Signs* 13 (1988): 277–98.

Smith, Sidonie. "The Impact of Critical Theory on the Study of Autobiography: Marginality, Gender, and Autobiographical Practice." *a/b: Auto/Biography Studies* 3 (1987): 1–12.

Smith, Sidonie. *A Poetics of Women's Autobiography: Marginality and the Fictions of Self-Representation*. Bloomington: Indiana University Press, 1987.

Smith-Rosenberg, Carroll. *Disorderly Conduct: Visions of Gender in Victorian America*. New York: Oxford University Press, 1985.

Smith-Rosenberg, Carroll. "Writing History: Language, Class, and Gender." In *Feminist Studies/Critical Studies*. Ed. Teresa de Lauretis. Bloomington: Indiana University Press, 1986, 31–54.

Spacks, Patricia M. "Reflecting Women." *Yale Review* 63 (1973): 26–42.

Spacks, Patricia M. "Women's Stories, Women's Selves." *Hudson Review* 30 (1977):29–46.

Spacks, Patricia M. "Selves in Hiding." In Jelinek, ed., *Women's Autobiography*, 112–32.

Spender, Dale, ed. *Personal Chronicles: Women's Autobiographical Writings*. Special Issue of *Women's Studies International Forum* 10 (1987).

Spengemann, William C., and L. R. Lundquist. "Autobiography and the American Myth." *American Quarterly* 17 (1965): 501–19.

Stanton, Domna C., ed. *The Female Autograph: Theory and Practice of Autobiography from the Tenth to the Twentieth Century*. Chicago: University of Chicago Press, 1984.

Stone, Albert E. *Autobiographical Occasions and Original Acts*. Philadelphia: University of Pennsylvania Press, 1982.

Walters, Ann. "Self Image and Style: A Discussion Based on Estelle Jelinek's
    The Tradition of Women's Autobiography From Antiquity to the Present. In
    Spender, ed., *Personal Chronicles*, 85–93.
Watson, Julia. "Shadowed Presence: Modern Women Writers' Autobiographies
    and the Other." In Olney, ed., *Studies*, 180–89.
Weintraub, Karl J. "Autobiography and Historical Consciousness." *Critical In-
    quiry* 1 (1975): 821–48.
Welter, Barbara. *Dimity Convictions: The American Woman in the Nineteenth Cen-
    tury*. Athens: Ohio University Press, 1976.
Woloch, Nancy. *Women and the American Experience*. New York: Alfred A. Knopf,
    1984.
Yellin, Jean Fagan. "Introduction." In Harriet A. Jacobs, *Incidents in the Life of
    a Slave Girl Written by Herself*. Ed. Jean Fagan Yellin. Cambridge: Harvard
    University Press, 1987, xiii–xxxiv.

CHAPTER 10

Speaking Her Own Piece: Emma Goldman and the Discursive Skeins of Autobiography

BLANCHE H. GELFANT

"I was woven of many skeins, conflicting in shade and texture."

Emma Goldman

"Oh, the tangle of human life!"

Theodore Dreiser

"They live harmoniously and cordially and quietly and happily and gayly and actively."

Nikolai Chernyshevsky

It was August 1889. A young woman boarded a train for Chicago. She was eighteen years old, full of the illusions of youth and hopeful, though she had only four dollars, a small trunk and cheap imitation alligator satchel, a purse, and a scrap of paper with an address. As the train clacked on its way, the threads that bound her to family and home were irretrievably broken.

It was August 1889. A young woman was arriving in New York, having boarded the cheapest train out of Rochester. She was twenty years old, eager to enter the strange and terrifying new world before her, though she had only five dollars, a small hand-bag, a sewing-machine, and three local addresses. As she set foot in the city, all that had happened to her was left behind—cast off like a worn-out garment.

On the train, the first young woman met a man who would alter the course of her life; and on her first day in the city, the other woman meets the man with whom her destiny, shaped in great part by their relationship, will be forever linked. Then, as August 1889 recedes into the past, resemblances between the two women begin to fade but not to disappear entirely. Both find themselves welcomed coldly by their relatives, a sister and an aunt. Both are told that times are hard and they must get a job to pay for their board. Both will leave their relatives, one more quickly than the other, and each will assume a relationship with the man she met on her first day in the big city. By that time, both will have worked in factories for less than five dollars a week and responded, each in her own way, to the immense disparities they saw between the mansions of the rich and the meager lives of the poor. Both will move from place to place, assuming new names in new situations. Meanwhile, however, their ways will separate and diverge. Carrie Meeber will become an actress, her electrified image emblazoning Broadway while she, the young woman, sits in her rocking chair, gazing out her window and wondering whether she will ever be happy. Emma Goldman will also assume the stage, but not to mouth the words of others that she had memorized. Rather, she would electrify audiences with her impassioned oratory as America's most famous and notorious anarchist.

Different as their destinies will be, the stories of their lives as told in Theodore Dreiser's novel *Sister Carrie* (1900) and Emma Goldman's *Living My Life* (1931), a two-volume autobiography, resemble each other in ways that should not remain unremarked, for they are neither insignificant nor coincidental.[1] Nor are they, as might be thought, signs of intertextual influence or of a coalescence of fiction and autobiography as narrative forms.[2] Rather they represent a coalescence of the complex narrative designs of two subversive writers seeking to gain acceptance for their unacceptable social views. Their strategy was one of rhetorical overdetermination. Both Dreiser and Goldman counted upon the confusion and profusion inherent in their literary forms to obscure and yet reveal their ideological alienation from established social norms. As writers, they could seem to be conforming, if only to the standards of literary genre, because these standards allowed for, and indeed demanded, deviation and variety, freedom of rhetorical choice. Unexpected similarities in their texts emerge thus less from thematic agreement than from similarities between literary forms that contain inchoate and indeterminant elements. These overlapping elements blur the boundaries between the naturalistic novel and (women's) autobiography and between the discursive modes of either genre and those of history, journalism, philosophy, myth, melodrama, romance, apologias and confessions, and propaganda.[3] Instead of selecting a single predominant discourse, Dreiser and Goldman conflated the various modes available to them, as though hoping that rhetorical excess would make their unacceptably radical social criticism seem cogent, logical and, as expressed in familiar literary conventions and clichés, acceptable.[4]

This strategy of over-determination was at once defensive and aggressive, an attempt to prevent rejection and to overpower the reader with the sheer redundancy of a text's rhetorical assaults. Neither writer succeeded in lulling public suspicion. Dreiser's readers knew that his novel violated literary conventions as flagrantly as his heroine transgressed the bounds of conventional society. As even Carrie dimly perceived, transgressions were entangling as well as liberating; they could disorder a character's life. They could also produce disarray in a writer's style. Dreiser's style in *Sister Carrie* has been called confused, clumsy, and clichéd—a tangled web of discursive skeins that (in Goldman's words) conflicted "in shade and texture." Goldman's autobiographical style, a melee of incompatible styles, has been similarly criticized, as has the "clumsy and awkward" prose of an extraordinary novel to which Goldman explicitly refers: Nikolai Chernyshevsky's *What Is To Be Done?* (1886).[5]

The suggestion that *Living My Life* is an autobiographical redaction of *What Is To Be Done?* is supported by Goldman's claim that literature, and this novel in particular, shaped her life.[6] Goldman said she had patterned her self upon Chernyshevsky's feminist heroine, Vera Pavlovna, and she might have patterned her prose upon that of a writer whose revolutionary vision and rhetorical purposes she shared, one as didactic as she and as desirous of avoiding interdiction. However, Goldman believed she had to translate her anarchism, clearly traceable to foreign revolutionaries, into an American idiom, for she wanted her autobiography to establish her as a citizen worthy of readmission to the United States. As an exiled radical alien, she had much at stake in her style, which by discursive variety and profusion might accrete enough persuasive force to effect an ideological reconciliation with her American readers. She hoped her story, told in language modulating from didacticism to indictment and sentimentality to passion, would represent a multifaceted woman admirable for her honesty and humane ideals. Goldman may have been an aging and unwanted exile, but through writing she could appropriate a traditional American role by beginning with a young girl's entry into the city of her dreams, a conventional novelistic beginning, used famously in *Sister Carrie*. Immediately, she would by typified as an American, a newcomer arriving at a new world. It was, of course, the world of perennial opportunity and freedom—and freedom was America's sign and Goldman's aspiration. Strategically, Goldman began the story of her life, as Dreiser began

Sister Carrie, with a traditional scene that would appeal to American readers whatever their political persuasion because it epitomized a mythic American experience. A young innocent enters a great American city, her new world, and seeks in its lavish and alluring excess the fulfillment of a heart's desire. Carrie's vague but incremental desire was for happiness; Goldman dreamt of independence and freedom—and of revolution.

In 1928, when the fifty-eight-year-old Goldman was inscribing her hopeful, if hackneyed, opening scene, she had been living in exile for almost ten years. She was disillusioned with Soviet Russia, a refuge she had by now rejected as she rejected all coercive states (and to her all states were coercive). She was tired of wandering. She wanted to return to the United States, the country she considered home. Since she had been deported because of ideas the government considered politically dangerous, she needed to place her anarchism within a context that would demystify it without attenuating its social and moral urgency. She would not deny her revolutionary past—she could not, since she considered fidelity to the "Ideal" of anarchism the essence of her life. But she would try to dispel fears her anarchism aroused by contextualizing it within a historical process of conflict and change. Centering herself within this process, she described her actions as consistently furthering the cause of freedom. This was, she noted, a quintessentially American cause. It was also a universal dream, for all revolutionary ideas of liberty—including those of Thoreau and Emerson, whom she considered early American anarchists—flowed together, she believed, in a historic ideological stream coursing toward freedom.[7]

As Goldman faced the task of writing herself into history—while, conversely, personalizing history by writing it into her life-story—she had to resolve problems other than those usually attributed to women autobiographers (and to women writers in general). She did not have to overcome a fear of speaking in her own voice or displaying herself upon a public stage. She had not lived a private, silenced, and covertly rebellious life. On the contrary, like other radical women of her time—Mother Jones, Elizabeth Gurley Flynn, Charlotte Perkins Gilman, and Margaret Sanger, all of whom wrote autobiographies—Goldman shattered the stereotype of woman as private, selfless, and submissively conforming to social expectations she sought secretly to subvert.[8] Goldman's rebellion was overt, her stage public, and her voice, heard by thousands, respected and feared. In 1917, when she was ordered by a United States Marshal not to speak in public, she had an audience stomping and screaming as she appeared on stage with a handkerchief stuffed in her mouth. Even gagged, she could not be silenced. Nor could she be domesticated. Her autobiography recounts her life-long resistance to men who wanted her to marry, bear children, and stay at home as wife and mother. She defied her father, whose physical violence and emotional abuse blighted her young years; and she refused her lovers, who wanted her to relinquish her political ideals and public persona. Though autobiography, one might think, was generically different from propaganda, Goldman would not mute or mutate her political discourse because she would not misrepresent the woman it had taken her a lifetime to create. On the other hand, simply to restate her ideology would have been redundant and inexpedient. Autobiography permitted her to recontextualize her much-rehearsed social criticism within the personal story of a woman's life, while at the same time, it allowed her to reidentify the woman with her ideas. "E. G. the woman and her ideas are inseparable," she wrote (1:268).

Goldman realized that creating the autobiography implied an act of self-appropriation that placed her in a politically contentious position, for she was in effect challenging a public image of Red Emma, the notorious demagogue who could, presumably, persuade a naive listener to violence, even to assassination. Like other public women in American history, Elizabeth Cady Stanton and Charlotte Perkins Gilman, for instance, Goldman believed she had to confront a factitious image created by the public to serve interests often antithetical to her own. Like these women, she proposed to modify and correct, or erase, a portrait painted by admirers as well as adversaries. Autobiography would permit her to reclaim her image from the public and redefine herself.[9] She defined also her own recuperative strategies, different from those of other radical women. Stanton, for example, tried to modify a public perception of her as an extraordinary person by emphasizing her ordinary daily activities; the story of her private life as wife, housekeeper, and mother, she wrote, might "amuse" and "benefit" her readers.[10] Gilman, on the other hand, stressed her debilitation, calculating for her reader the productive years she might have enjoyed had she not been incapacitated by recurrent episodes of depression (97–104). At the same time that these women were disavowing their public images, they reiterated their ideological positions, so that their autobiographies reinscribed an impression that, ostensibly, they wished to revise. Even as they revealed their ordinariness or inadequacy (usually equated with conformity or debilitation), they emerged as extraordinary women, strong and contentious, and threatening to the established social order from which, for all their attempted reconciliations, they remained alienated.[11] Goldman's need for an ideological reconciliation with her readers was more urgent than that of Stanton and Gilman because her

situation was more critical. And her motives were more conflicted than
theirs, her discursive modes more diverse and entangled. She wanted
to assert her Americanism, but she could not resist advertising her
alienating (and alienated) political views. Her complicated and perhaps
duplicitous design was to persuade her readers that alienation itself was
an American strain—an indigenous tension and ideological identification. As an unregenerate revolutionary, she could be an American and
a prodigal American daughter returning home.

Goldman's efforts to revise Red Emma's tabloid image tested her
rhetorical powers as a writer. She knew she possessed the power of
speech. Indeed, if she had been less persuasive as a speaker, less public
and publicized and, of course, less sweepingly revolutionary, she might
not have marshaled against her the full power of the United States
government. Now she needed the power of the written word to create
a self-portrait that would show everyone that E. G. and her ideas were
benignly conceived and morally sound. As she knew, Red Emma per-
sonified two ideologies unacceptable to the American public: anarchism
and radical feminism. Both were perceived, as she herself perceived
them, as forces that would destroy society's founding institutions: marriage and the state. To Goldman, both were inherently oppressive. As
a woman who had not only advocated but also acted out a woman's right
to economic and sexual independence—and sought to subvert accepted
views of family life, motherhood, and education—Goldman now faced
formidable obstacles in creating a portrait of herself that would validate
her politics and her person.

In an oblique way, Goldman outlined a strategy for creating such a
portrait in her prefatory essay entitled "In Appreciation." These few
pages suggest a theory of autobiography that implies a reciprocity between self and style, each revealing in the other conflicting elements
that could coalesce to form a self inseparable from social history, and
an autobiography thematically unified by interactions between society and the self. In this "appreciation," an acknowledgment of her indebt-
edness to others, Goldman wrote about writing her life as though,
strangely, the life she was writing about was not her own. To begin with,
she projected the desire to write upon anonymous others, describing
herself as the passive recipient of suggestions that "came" to her unin-
vited. This self-effacement, uncharacteristic of Goldman, may represent a proleptic denial of the charge of egotism she anticipated as a
woman autobiographer. It may also be a conciliatory gesture towards
the convention that women writers should approach self-expression
reluctantly, with an appropriate sense of modesty; and, indeed, Goldman had justifiable misgivings about self-exposure. Nevertheless, she

produced a two-volume work in which (contrary to contemporary views that she hid her personal self) she revealed startling secrets that might never have been told.[12] The occasion for writing also "came" to her (through the unwelcome leisure of exile), its timing fortuitous, since she was old enough to have lived a life, but not so old that her powers of recall and recreation were impaired. Goldman felt hindered, however, by a lack of documentary materials she considered essential to the autobiographer as archivist of an historical past as well as a private life. Since all her private papers and files had been confiscated in a federal raid of her office, she had lost historical documents (including those she had created, like issues of *Mother Earth*) that could testify to the "truth" of her autobiography, its fidelity to fact. Fortunately, public documents were retrievable, but not documents of another kind needed to recreate the "personal atmosphere" of her past. How could she retrieve the hundreds of unduplicable love letters she had written under the sway of passions she intended to reveal? Her "appreciation" expresses her gratitude to friends and former lovers who found the documents she wanted and supported her "research"—an odd but pointed term that implies a claim to scientific objectivity. As Goldman added secretarial help, editorial assistance, and financial support to her list of prerequisites, she implicated many others in the making of her autobiography, so that *Living My Life* seems, finally, the artifactual product of a large cooperative effort. Even the title—in which the possessive pronoun declares her autonomy or, at least, her desire to resist appropriation—came from someone else, her lifelong friend and fellow anarchist, Alexander Berkman. Thus, in describing the genesis of her text, Goldman was already creating a woman she wanted the public to see as inspiring people to work together in voluntary cooperation. Such cooperation, she would show in the text, was the ideal end of anarchism. Goldman's introduction, appreciative of her friends, somehow impersonalized her relationship to this text. It set standards that seemed unsuited to autobiography as a genre: distance and detachment; historical exposition; objective documentation, even of personal feelings—an effect of impersonality. These are criteria that historians and biographers have established for their narratives and that novelists like Theodore Dreiser prescribed for the realistic novel.

Neither in her preface nor her text did Goldman express doubt that she had a self who existed prior to the act of writing about her and apart from the language that was creating an autobiographical "I."[13] Indeed, she believed that the documents she had retrieved—newspaper reports, proceedings of her court trials, issues of *Mother Earth*—proved the existence of this self. As a woman, she may have been conflicted and complex—"woven of many skeins," she wrote. She knew she was elusive to others and, sometimes, to herself. But even when she admitted that she had "never been able to unearth" the "real" Emma Goldman (2:529), she was implicitly affirming the existence of a continuous and authentic identity. The problems she encountered in translating Emma Goldman or E. G. into an autobiographical "I" were rhetorical and emotional, rather than ontological; and she resolved them by casting Goldman the writer in a variety of authorial roles. Writing as a revisionist historian, she interjected long expository descriptions of the background for her political actions, authenticating her accounts of the past with verifiable dates, places, and names. Just as Dreiser had interpolated a passage on a Chicago department store ("established about 1884") in order to preserve "an interesting chapter in the commercial history of our nation" (22), so Goldman devoted chapters to American labor history and, as the setting of her story changed, to the early years of the Russian revolution. In describing the Haymarket Affair that had converted her to anarchism, she recounted historical events she had heard reported; in writing about the Hempstead strike—which linked her destiny indissolubly with that of Alexander Berkman, the young anarchist she had met on her first day in New York—she revealed how her actions created history. Her historical excursus are appropriately framed about herself as central character of her story, just as Dreiser's were framed about his heroine. Carrie looks for a job in a Chicago department store; Goldman recalls her young, impressionable self listening to the socialist Johanna Greie tell of the 1886 riot in Haymarket Square (1:7–9).

In describing how the Haymarket Affair had converted her to anarchism, Goldman's narrative strategy was complexly involuted, as were her autobiographical designs—her intentions and her narrative form. Almost fifty years after the Haymarket riot, Goldman still wanted to assert the innocence of the convicted anarchists and to justify her commitment to their cause, a definitive, lifelong commitment that was to transform her from a young immigrant woman into the Red Emma of tabloid notoriety. Goldman recalls that Johanna Greie had beckoned the awed young Goldman to her and prophesied that some day she would make the Haymarket anarchists' cause her own (1:9). The prophecy, the speech, and the "cause" are framed as the memory of a memory. Goldman begins by remembering her first night in New York. She is excited and sleepless, having just heard a stirring "denunciation of American conditions" by the anarchist orator Johann Most. Then, as she tosses about, she once more "live[s] through the events of 1887" (1:6)—events that had taken place in Rochester almost two years ago and that recapitulated still earlier events now irrefrangibly part of American history and Goldman's past. Thus Goldman links her past, as she is remembering herself remembering it, to the American scene, tracing her feelings as well as her future to a flashback of Johanna Greie's impassioned speech. This involuted chronology coalesces time and the historical times. It places historical events in the past, while it makes history immediate in the living narrator (Greie) present before Goldman; simultaneously, it foreshadows the future by prophesying the execution of the Haymarket anarchists and Goldman's conversion to their cause. As this framing suggests, Goldman was violating the chronology of events in order to rationalize her radicalism as a justifiable response to what she believed were acts of flagrant injustice. She was also giving her life an inherently dramatic structure by beginning her story at a climatic moment of conversion that decides her to set out for the city in quest of a new life. Then, through intermittent flashes of memory, she recovers her childhood and past.[14] Unlike the autobiographies of activist women that begin with the moment of birth—"I was born in the city of Cork, Ireland," writes Mother Jones, and Elizabeth Gurley Flynn begins, "By birth I am a New Englander"— Goldman's autobiography opens with a memory of herself at the age of twenty hopefully arriving in New York, a strange "new world."[15]

Goldman's fractured chronology allows her to present historical events like the Haymarket Affair as self-contained and didactic passages of exposition and as crucial moments of self-revelation that expose the genesis of desire. Just as Dreiser's historical account of the department store served to explain the origin of Carrie's desire for the trinkets and clothes on display before her (each item "dainty," "delicately frilled," and "dazzling," making her feel its "claim" and "all touch[ing] her with individual desire"), so Goldman's recapitulation of historical events provided an origin for the desire that Goldman said determined the course of her life. Though Carrie made money and material things her object of desire, and Goldman, social revolution—radically different objects, each subversive of the other—both women are described as pursuing an elusive, ever-receding idea.[16] Like Carrie, who was to find "neither surfeit nor content" (369), Goldman would never realise her "great ideal," though it remained the only permanent element in her life (1:343). Thus, her story thematized an irrefragable contrast between aspiration and history, between the permanence of human desire and life's disappointing transitoriness. This contrast is reflected in Goldman's rhetorical vacillations as she moved from an inviolable and ideal "Cause" to the various causes into which she was thrust by the vicissitudes of history. While she depended upon the hard cogency of facts to assert the necessity behind these causes, she represented human aspiration through a romantically elusive image—that of humanity reaching for the stars. The image became muddled in its spatial designations when Goldman's aspiration signified sexual, rather than political, desire; then it described her "soaring high" (towards the stars) in a desire to experience the "depths" of passion. As in time the object of Goldman's sexual passion changed, each lover receded into the past to become part of her history, but her yearning for sexual fulfillment (like Carrie's yearning for happiness) never abated. Personal love began to seem as elusive to Goldman as her political ideals, and as enduringly desirable. However, though the end of one affair after another led her to question whether a woman's public life inevitably destroys private happiness, she never questioned or abandoned her ideals in order to keep her lovers.

Though Goldman's revolutionary ideal remained as inviolably fixed as the stars, her views on violence, as the means to an end, underwent revision. The change is an integral part of her autobiography as it traces the conception and reconception of ideas with which she was associated. Although Goldman knew as she wrote that she would disavow a position she was presenting as tenable, if not irresistible, she offered no clue to her subsequent reversals. Her dramatic denunciation of her idolized mentor, Johann Most, for example, was unforeshadowed and startlingly violent: she beat him with a horsewhip in front of a huge audience. Years later, she reconsidered her action, which she had justified as a righteous reaction to Most's disavowal of Berkman's attempted assassination of Henry Clay Frick. Most's disaffection had infuriated her as a betrayal of the anarchist cause as well as of Berkman. Later, she would feel betrayed by Berkman when he repudiated Leon Czolgosz, McKinley's assassin, for the same reason Most had condemned him: that his action lacked "social necessity." (1:324).[17] Most's condemnation had enraged her; Berkman's evoked despair. For his difference with her left her totally rejected and alone. She believed that she had lost more than her beloved Sasha—as, for his sake, she had lost Most, her "teacher" and "inspiration": she lost confidence in her ability to stand alone. Reviled by friends and foes because of her sympathy for Czolgosz, a young man she believed haplessly misguided, Goldman felt abandoned and beaten. She saw her faith in the transformative processes of history betrayed, and human endeavor turned into a "cruel, senseless farce" (1:324).

Unusual in its revisions, in effect Goldman's admissions of the serious mistakes she had made, *Living My Life* is extraordinary in its revelation of Goldman's part in a plot to assassinate Henry Clay Frick, the Chairman of Carnegie Steel Company. His "inhumanity" to workers he had locked out of the Homestead steel-factories and evicted from company homes aroused Goldman's revolutionary passion—and Berkman's incendiary rhetoric. Berkman denounced Frick as "the symbol of wealth and power, of the injustice and wrong of the capitalistic class, as well as personally responsible for the shedding of the workers' blood." Accordingly, he and Goldman plotted a political assassination or *Attentat* that would "stir terror in the enemy's ranks and make them realize that the proletariat of America had its avengers" (1:85–88). In his autobiography, *Prison Memoirs* (1912), Berkman never mentioned Goldman by name, alluding to her only as *the Girl*, and her role in the assassination plot remained unknown and unsuspected. If autobiographies are somehow self-serving, then *Living My Life* served, among other functions, as the confession of a secret Goldman found too burdensome, too guilt-ridden, to protect. At the time of Berkman's fateful attempt on Frick's life, the call to violence had seemed to them, she recalled, unequivocal and commanding, "the psychological moment for an *Attentat*." This was the moment for which the young Berkman had waited: "this sublime moment to serve the Cause, to give his life for the people" (1:87). In melodramatically ringing tones, Berkman declared his intention "to die by my own hand" after he had killed Frick; he wanted "to live [only] long enough to justify his act . . . , so that the American people might know that he was not a criminal, but an idealist" (1:87). Even an involutedly plotted melodrama would not have produced the ironies that ensued from the young anarchists' action. Frick lived; Berkman was convicted as a criminal; and the "great suffering people" for whom he was sacrificing his life denounced Berkman and the assassination. An aftermath, congruent with melodrama, was Goldman's guilty secret and a need to expiate her guilt that autobiographical confession may have at last satisfied. Convinced that "they" were going to kill Berkman, Goldman wanted to share his fate. Her desire seems coercive as she reiterates the word *must*: "I must pay the same price as he—I must stand the consequences—I must share the responsibility" (1:96). She never did. Her participation in the assassination remained secret—until her autobiography.[18]

By confessing to violence, Goldman placed herself in a position to repudiate it as a legitimate means for an anarchist. As she watched while Berkman worked on the bomb he planned for Frick, Goldman questioned their right to endanger the lives of innocent people: "What if anything should go wrong—but, then, did not the end justify the means? Our end was the sacred cause of the oppressed and exploited people. . . . What if a few should have to perish?—the many would be free. . . . Yes, the end in this case justified the means" (1:88). Goldman's questions were fundamental to her ideology, and the answers she gave at the time would later produce in her feelings of "paralyzing horror" (2:536). She came to see violence as incompatible with her ideals, and both the confession and repudiation of her willingness to bomb and kill seemed to her essential to her autobiography. For underlying all her motives as autobiographer was a desire to educate. This desire took precedence over self-interest. If she had hoped the autobiography would help her return to the United States, then a confession of complicity in an infamous assassination plot would be self-defeating. However, if she wished to defend the principles of anarchism, then a confrontation with the issue of violence, equated with anarchism in the public mind, was essential.[19]

The Frick affair called forth Goldman's most flamboyant rhetoric. Goldman describes events leading to Berkman's departure for Pittsburgh in a series of dramatically heightened scenes: a horrifying moment when she reads of police shooting strikers' families; a sudden decision to rush to Homestead; a tense experiment with bomb-making; Berkman's departure as assassin and human sacrifice; and, finally, Goldman standing alone at the railway station, her arms outstreched toward the receding train that is carrying away her lover. These rapidly moving cinematic scenes end abruptly in a tableau of loss: "I ran after the vanishing train, waving and calling to him: 'Sasha, Sashenka!' The steaming monster disappeared round the bend and I stood glued, straining after it, my arms outstreched for the precious life that was being snatched away from me" (1:91). This was a moment Goldman would recall fifteen years later as she stood at another railroad station awaiting Berkman's return. Melodramatically, the figures before her grow faint and blurred, the past rises out of the depths, she stretches out her arms, crying frantically, "Sasha! Sasha!"—and then, in a cinematic flash, the present reappears as she hears her name called, "Emma! Emma! The train is in" (1:383). The exclamations, tears, and confusion, the physical details signifying panic and desire as Goldman describes her numb feet, clutching hands, throbbing heart, and burning brain—not to mention Berkman's "deathly white" face, outstretched hand, and pathetic gaze— show Goldman appropriating the language of melodrama and sentiment to express the pathos of two idealists (and lovers) who are sacrificing all for a transcendent Cause.

The morning after Berkman's departure, Goldman awakened to feel the anguish of a fictional heroine who had been tormented by the need to save her loved ones. She could see this distraught character lying in her bed, her face turned to the wall, her shoulders twitching, and she "could almost feel the same way" (1:91). Goldman had now melded into Dostoevsky's Sonya Marmeladov, the self-abnegating prostitute of *Crime and Punishment* who saves Raskolnikov's soul. Indifferent to the absurdity of identifying herself, a Jewish atheist, with a saintly Christian, Goldman followed Sonya's example by deciding to sell her body for the money she needed to join Berkman. Melodrama merges with farce as Goldman faint-heartedly parades the streets and finally attracts a man. He surveys her with an experienced eye and declares: "You haven't got it, that's all there is to it" (1:93). Goldman fails at prostitution, but farce blends into fantasy as the mysterious stranger gives her ten dollars and sends her home with honor unsullied. In recounting this incredible sequence of events, Goldman violates the secrecy she considered vital at the time. Always didactic, she had wanted to give the stranger an impromptu lecture on the economic causes of prostitution (which she would delineate in her essay "The Traffic in Women"), but she silenced herself to keep "a juicy story" from the press (1:93). Now, however, she reveals the long-kept secret, ennobling her attempt at prostitution by identifying herself with a suffering and self-sacrificing woman—or, to be precise, with a fictional character created by a novelist who abhorred anarchism (and the Nihilist Chernyshevsky, Goldman's hero) with an intensity bordering on obsession.[20]

A coalescence of literature with life is one of Goldman's rhetorical strategies of self-ratification. When she described moments of heightened emotions, she typically merged her character with those of fictional heroines and often spoke her piece in the clichéd language of sentimental or romantic novels. The effect was self-subverting, since she simultaneously enhanced and diminished an image of herself as an exemplary woman of her times—enhanced by imbuing herself with the emotional intensity of self-sacrificing and self-aggrandizing heroines like Dostoevsky's Sonya and Chernyshevsky's Vera Pavlovna, and diminished by equating her own reality with that of merely imagined or unreal women. She seemed untroubled by discrepancies between herself as a "real" person and literary characters, or between women characters created by writers whose ideologies were diametrically opposed. However, literary characters could create trouble between her and her lovers. She tells, for example, how Ben Reitman, to whom she felt passionately enslaved, abruptly left her after reading D. H. Lawrence's novel, *Sons and Lovers*; like Lawrence's hero, Reitman was obsessed with his mother and he projected his emotional conflicts upon a character torn between sexual and maternal love.[21] She lost another lover, Edward Brady, because of Nietzsche. Brady's denunciation of Goldman's intellectual idol seemed to her more than a philosoplical disagreement; it signified, she said, an intolerable violation of her freedom, "more precious to [her] than life." Following their quarrel over Nietzsche, she accused Brady of "binding" her "body" and her "spirit" and (in ascending order of insult) of trying to "tear" her away from "the movement," her "friends," and "the books I love" (1:194–95).

Usually, however, a shared love of books mediated Goldman's relationship with men. *What Is To Be Done?* immediately established a rapport with Berkman, her lifelong companion. When Goldman first met the young anarchist, she confided to him her dream: "I wanted to have time for reading," she told him, "and later I hoped to realize my dream of a co-operative shop. 'Something like Vera's venture in *What's to be Done?*'" A brief quarrel ensued when Berkman could hardly believe that this young woman had read a prohibited Nihilist novel. Goldman resented having her word or independence of mind questioned: "I repeated angrily that I had read the forbidden book and other similar works, such as Turgeniev's *Fathers and Sons*, and *Obriv* (*The Precipice*) by Gontcharov," she said, citing her reading as proof of her political and personal liberation. The books she named created a bond between the two young anarchists.[22] They also recalled scenes of violence Goldman had seen as a girl in Russia and the novels (*Fathers and Sons* and *What Is To Be Done?*) that had articulated her inchoate feelings of sympathy for Nihilists executed by the Tsar—sympathies later conferred upon the Haymarket anarchists (1:26–28).

As the autobiography reveals, men who gave Goldman books became her political idols and her sexual partners, the list of her readings expanding with that of her lovers: Jacob Kershner, her feckless husband, whose "interest in books . . . had first attracted her" (1:20); the anarchist Johann Most, who supplied her "with a list of books" that grounded her in revolutionary theory (1:35); Edward Brady, who introduced her "to the great classics of English and French literature," to Rousseau, Voltaire, Goethe, and Shakespeare (1:115); Stefan Grossman, who taught her to admire "the new literature—Friedrich Nietzsche, Ibsen, Hauptmann, von Hoffmansthal" (1:172); and Max Baginski, who engaged her in "exquisite" discussions of Gottfried Keller, Strindberg, Wedekind, Gabriele Reuter, Knut Hamsun, and her philosophical idol, Nietzsche (1:239).[23] Goldman's literary prototype in this discipleship was Chernyshevsky's heroine Vera Pavlovna, who entered the world of ideas through books given to her by her brother's tutor, subsequently her rescuer and husband.[24] Ironically, prison offered Goldman the luxury of time to read; she always carried a book with her when she thought she might be arrested (she mentions, for example, *A Portrait of the Artist as a Young Man*). One of the prison reforms she effected was to win library privileges for women inmates.

Among the books Goldman remembered reading as a schoolgirl were popular romances—especially those of the nineteenth century German writer Eugenie Marlitt—that had made her "grow tearful over the unhappy heroines" (1:116). These romances left an indelible impression. Years later she recalled their trite sentimental images as she wrote about her own love affairs, the "ecstasy" and unhappiness that, like their romantic heroines, she too experienced. Clearly, Goldman adjusted her discursive mode to her immediate subject, changing from the journalistic, or didactic, or caustic style that described historical events to a murkily melodramatic language for romance. From popular novels she appropriated the prose she considered suitable to sexual passions she believed herself politically obligated to reveal. As an anarchist and a feminist, she wanted to dramatize through her own life a woman's freedom to love as she desired. She advocated frankness as an ideological principle; and in her autobiography she would describe her erotic yearnings, her passionate responses, and her abjectness toward lovers she knew were not her equals, particularly Ben Reitman, with whom she had a ten-year liaison. After all, if she was going to humanize Red Emma, she needed to show that she had experienced weakness and humiliation, as well as fulfillment, in her relationship with men. She told how she endured Reitman's obsessive infidelities, his boorishness, desertions, demands, and even his dishonesties and betrayals—and she was honest enough to suggest ulterior motives. For as her manager, "travelling companion," and "helpmate," Reitman relieved her of the burdensome details of her lecture tours and significantly enlarged her audiences (1:433). As her "lover," he caught her in a "torrent of elemental passion" and she "responded shamelessly to its primitive call" (1:420). Goldman knew that Berkman and other friends deplored her dependence upon a man inferior to her in intellect and conscience, but she turned to Reitman because, she wrote, he satisfied her "great hunger for someone who could love the woman in me and yet who would also be able to share my work. I had never had anyone who could do both" (1:432). He fulfilled also her fantasy of experiencing in life the passions she had felt vicariously through literature. Indeed, as she described Reitman's "primitive" sexual appeal, she recreated him as the "savage" male considered generic to the naturalistic novel.[25] The story of his chaotic life, as she recounts his telling it, drew her to him because he "came from a world so unlike mine": "I was enthralled by this living embodiment of the types I had only known through books, the types portrayed by Dostoyevsky and Gorki" (1:420).[26] Later, she refers to him passingly as Raskolnikov because he was "always stealing back to the scene of his old crimes" (2:650).

Given Goldman's explicitness about her love affairs, one would think the issue of frankness irrelevant to her autobiography. Nevertheless, critics have raised it by asking pointedly, "What did she want to hide?"[27] According to a recent study of her love-letters to Reitman, she hid the profoundly erotic desires she allowed herself to express in the private coded language of her love-letters.[28] Such language supports a commonsensical view of autobiography as a self-interested account of a life which, in the act of revealing, inevitably selects, omits, and conceals. Contemporary critics trace the omissions in Goldman's life story to women's socially conditioned reticence; but a demand that Goldman tell all, especially about her love life, is not only unrealistic but sexually discriminating, since as we know, elisions in men's autobiographies are commonplace and commonly considered generic.[29] Given the times and circumstances in which Goldman wrote and the purposes she hoped to achieve, her frankness, rather than her omissions, seems anomalous. To ask, as modern critics do, what she was hiding is to assume a total congruence between the living woman and the autobiographical "I" (a naive assumption for contemporary theorists) and to overlook all that Goldman did reveal: an enslaving passion for Reitman inappropriate to her as an independent woman; desire for younger men that she could satisfy only by risking humiliating rejections; and (highly damaging to her image of herself as a feminist), constant need for support—moral and intellectual backing, money, and admiration—that she sought and received from men. She did not hide the fact that men bought her beautiful clothes and that (like Dreiser's Carrie) she wore them with pleasure.

More significantly, she did not hide her doubts about the psychological motives underlying her political commitments. She repeatedly stated her suspicions that work may have represented an escape from the emptiness of her life, as though her work and her life were discrete and not, as she also stated, interwoven. She did not hide her fear of nihilism. She referred recurrently to a sense of inner void she identified with her empty womb; and she wondered if her desire to care for humankind was a displaced expression of her desire for motherhood.[30] Her equation of personal feelings with socially conditioned views of woman as biologically determined—as influenced in temperament and desire by her womb—subverted her feminist declarations of freedom. Nevertheless, she did not hide her sense of subservience to biological forces. Nor did she hide her periods of depression. She admitted her violent temper, her irascibility, her weaknesses, and her sexual wildness. Given her hope that the autobiography might present her favorably enough to allow her readmission into the United States, she was remarkably candid about her private life and admirably loyal to her anarchist beliefs. She never disavowed her social and political principles or attenuated her revolutionary purposes. She never hid opinions she knew would alienate her fellow revolutionists. Late in life, she paid dearly for her criticism of Soviet Russia, just as she had, years ago, for her expressions of sympathy for President McKinley's assassin.[31] But she considered herself morally obligated to criticize a regime that she believed subverted the principles and purposes of social revolution. She might have hidden views she knew were unpopular with radical audiences she depended upon for support, but instead she insisted upon advertising them, and she devoted almost half of the second volume of *Living My Life* to a chronicle of disillusioning discoveries about the revolution that had been her visionary ideal. She might have tried to protect this ideal by hiding the facts as she knew them, but though her secrecy would have been undetected, since few at the time had the access to Russian life that she did, she refused the safety of silence.

Speaking out and speaking her own piece constituted her integrity and the identity Goldman created for herself in life and in her autobiography. She shared with other radical woman orators a claim to autonomy in speech that Elizabeth Gurley Flynn epitomized in her retort to David Belasco, the impresario who, in 1906, had offered her a part in a play: "I don't want to be an actress! I want to speak my own words and not say over and over again what somebody else has written. I'm in the labor movement and I speak my own piece!"[32] Apparently Flynn never wondered whether her freedom to speak her own piece might be constrained by the political movements to which she was successively committed, labor unionism, socialism, and communism, or by the structures of language itself. Nor did Goldman. She too insisted she would speak her own piece, and though she made her first public appearances as a disciple of the anarchist Johann Most, lecturing on subjects he had chosen in a style he rehearsed, she soon saw "the need of independent thought" (47). In time, she condemned the "meaningless prattle" she had appropriated from Most: "I realized I was committing a crime against myself and the workers by serving as a parrot repeating Most's views" (52). Margaret Sanger expressed the determination of all these activist women when she wrote in her autobiography: "I *would* be heard. No matter what it should cost. I *would be heard*" (56, original emphasis).

As such declarations attest, the issue in autobiographies of radical public women was not only women's claim to their own voice, but also their insistence upon self-possession: upon the "I" reiterated in their statements—"I" four times in succession in Flynn's self-appropriating words and Goldman's emphatic "I," "I," and "myself." Their pronouns signified their opposition to others, women and men, who presented them with social scenarios, as though they were derivative speakers, merely actresses reciting someone else's piece. Set beside Goldman's self-appropriation, as she refused to speak another's lines, the capitulation of Dreiser's Carrie Meeber to the lure of the theater reveals that for her success entailed denying the possibility of her own speech. Dimly as Carrie understood the forces about her, she knew she could attain money and fame by commodifying herself—by making herself into a representation of what others desired and could buy with a theater ticket. On a Broadway stage at last, before a large, paying audience, Carrie pronounces herself a public property. Asked by the company's male star, "Well, who are you?," she answers with uncharacteristic pointedness, "I am yours truly" (314). Her "I" has collapsed in the "your" that Goldman had resisted as the sign of society's appropriation of women.[33]

In 1906, speaking her own piece on the corner of Broadway and 38th Street, Elizabeth Gurley Flynn was arrested. As a result of this arrest, she writes in her autobiography, she met Theodore Dreiser, the managing editor of *Broadway Magazine*, the journal in which Dreiser would publish his sketch of Flynn as "An East Side Joan of Arc" (Flynn, 54). "I am very proud to have had a fleeting glimpse of this great American in his youth," Flynn writes, approving his "many struggles for American democratic rights" and his enlistment in 1945 in the Communist Party (55). Charlotte Perkins Gilman also records her encounter with Dreiser, now editor of the *Delineator*, from whom she sought advice on how to have her essays published. According to her account, Dreiser said "gloomily," "You should consider more what the editors want" (304). But like Flynn and Goldman, Gilman wanted to speak her own piece, even though she knew that all of her "principal topics were in direct contravention of established views, beliefs and emotions" (304). She sought to publish her views precisely because they were subversive; and she resisted, even resented, Dreiser's advice as pressuring her to the conformity and silence that, she implied, had driven her to madness in her first marriage. Unlike Gilman, Goldman placed Dreiser in a position of authority in her autobiography, implicitly sanctioning her right to tell the story of her life because of his words. Goldman reports Dreiser telling her to write the autobiography: " 'You must write the story of your life, E. G.,' he urged; 'it is the richest of any woman's of our century. Why in the name of Mike don't you do it?' " (2:986). For Goldman, as for other radical women autobiographers, the authorizing male writer of their times was Theodore Dreiser.[34]

Goldman's frequent references to supportive men, including those who encouraged her autobiography, attentuates her claim to independence—or more precisely, to a desire for independence sometimes thwarted by her complex needs as a woman "woven of many skeins." Early in the autobiography Goldman drew upon images of piecing and weaving (activities that contemporary feminists consider characteristically "feminine") to describe her difference from the men she considered her counterparts. "I knew that the personal would always play a dominant part in my life," she wrote; "I was not hewn of one piece, like Sasha [Alexander Berkman] or other heroic figures. . . . I was woven of many skeins, conflicting in shade and texture. To the end of my days I would be torn between the yearning for a personal life and the need of giving all to my ideal" (1:153). The image of herself as "woven" while men are "hewn" suggests Goldman's susceptibility to metaphors that reinforce gender differences her autobiography was seeking to deny— and did. For Goldman's lifelong devotion to her "ideal" showed that she was as much hewn of one piece as Berkman or any other man she considered heroic. In describing how an anarchist leader like Johann Most longed for, even wept for, love and marriage, she erased the differences by which she rationalized her sexual needs. Indeed, Berkman, Most, and every radical man she mentioned (as well as radical women like Voltairine de Cleyre) could be considered woven of conflicting skeins, if conflict implied desiring personal as well as public gratification, love as well as political power. Though she projected upon Berkman her desire for total commitment to a cause and idealized him as the personification of selflessness, she complained about his intransigent single-mindedness. At the same time she revealed that for him, too, life was complicated by inner conflicts he could not resolve.

As she teased out and studied the diverse strands of her personality, Goldman drew upon various discursive modes, weaving them together into a literary style as mixed and inchoate as the conflicting skeins she considered intrinsic to her self. Though each discourse, whether of politics, romance, or propaganda, brought to mind its own clichés, an overlapping occurred, so that a public lecture became, like love, an "esctatic song" (1:51, 120). Thus, discourses sometimes merged indiscriminately, and yet if samples of Goldman's variegated autobiographical style(s) were set side by side, they would seem the product of different sensibilities working at cross-purposes. In this respect, *Living My Life*, seems an inchoate and discursively tangled as *Sister Carrie*.

If Goldman's text may be considered exemplary of a subgenre of women's autobiography—of those written by influential vocal and radical public women—then one might conclude that women who announce a desire to speak their own piece and represent themselves as doing so in their autobiographies speak (as perhaps we all do) various pieces at the same time, gathering threads from different and incongruous skeins of discourse and weaving them together to create a pattern characterized by contrasts and contradictions. Of the radical women autobiographers of her time, Emma Goldman created the most synthetic and most original piece. Like Elizabeth Gurley Flynn, Mother Jones, Margaret Sanger, and Charlotte Perkins Gilman, she defended radical views she presented as her own even as she traced them to their sources in political thinkers, social movements, and contemporary events. She traced them also to books, particularly and perhaps surprisingly, to novels. Each source offered its own discursive mode, whether expository, polemic, reportorial, didactic, melodramatic, sentimental, or romantic. Her autobiography modulated from one to the other, and her readers selected one or the other to admire or criticize, just as today, they select from among her various causes a particular social view to reinforce, by its historical precedence, one of their own.[35] Her most consistent theme was freedom, and when her beloved Berkman criticized her for dancing with "reckless abandon" at an anarchist party, she "grew furious" because she believed her freedom had been constrained and their "Cause" falsified—"a Cause which stood for a beautiful ideal, for anarchism, for release and freedom from conventions and prejudice" (1:56). She declared her personal freedom as a woman emblematic of an ideal of freedom that included all humankind. As she said, "I want freedom, the right to self-expression, everybody's right to beautiful, radiant things" (1:56). She aestheticized her politics by making "beautiful" an epithetic qualifier of "freedom," "ideal," and, even more elusively, all "things" to which she believed everyone entitled. As she described her quest for freedom, she implied that her life exemplified an historical process in which woman represented the future. This was Chernyshevsky's explicit claim for his heroine Vera Parlovna, whose ringing words in *What Is To Be Done?* inspired Goldman. "I wish to be independent and live in my own fashion," Vera Pavlovna had cried; "I wish to act after my own fancy; let others do the same. I respect the liberty of others, as I wish them to respect mine" (35).

Though she declared a desire for independence and implied that it foreshadowed sweeping revolutionary change, Goldman candidly revealed her dependence upon men who were her political mentors, financial supporters, managers and promoters, lawyers, disciples, and lovers. If as many modern theorists claim, language represents a legacy of patriarchal power, then she depended upon men, above all, for the very possibility of speaking her own piece. She did not attempt to create a language of her own, though she might not have lacked the ambition if she had lived at a time when the notion of such originality was current.[36] She conceived of her autobiographical writing as a weaving together of the different and conflicting skeins of her personality and her politics. Unlike Theodore Dreiser, who in his great first novel *Sister Carrie* also wove strands from various and incongruous discursive skeins, Goldman did not end her story with a vision of life as a tangle. "Oh, the tangle of human life!," Dreiser wrote at the end of *Sister Carrie.* Emma Goldman's life may have been knotted and tangled with diverse historical events, social and political ideas, and conflicting personal desires, but her vision remained clear and simple—and so wishful it seems dreamlike. It was a vision of a happy ending that would result from a revolution in consciousness and in society. It is expressed in its naïveté and hopefulness by a single sentence from Chernyshevsky's *What Is To Be Done?*: "They live harmoniously and cordially and quietly and happily and gayly and actively." Of all the discursive skeins in Emma Goldman's *Living My Life,* the most vulnerable to criticism is the idyllic and utopian. It is also the most enduringly appealing.

NOTES

1 Volume and page references to *Living My Life* are given in parentheses. The Pizer edition of *Sister Carrie* contains background and source material that shows a relationship between sections of the text and Dreiser's journalistic writings.

2 Paul de Man makes the issue of generic coalescence moot by arguing that "the distinction between fiction and autobiography is not an either/or polarity[;] . . . it is undecidable" (921). The essay itself is decisive in its view of autobiography as a "figure of reading" rather than as a genre or a mode. "Empirically as well as theoretically," de Man writes, "autobiography lends itself poorly to generic definition; each specific instance seems to be an exception to the norm; the works themselves always seem to shade off into neighboring or even incompatible genres" (920). In referring to "*the* norm," de Man implies, one assumes, a generic definition based upon the practices of male autobiographers. While genre is at issue to de Man, gender, a concern of many contemporary critics, is absent from his considerations. The view that autobiography is generically "an instrument of reading, not primarily a formula for writing" is reiterated by Gunn (21).

3 In discussing the naturalistic novel as a genre—with *Sister Carrie* as "an exemplary case" (41)—Howard enumerates the different narrative strategies

the genre deploys and the "different generic discourses" these strategies introduce into a single text. "Naturalist novels frequently incorporate conventional elements from popular literary genres like the adventure story and the domestic novel" (142). In her discussion of *Sister Carrie*, Bowlby disagrees with Petrey's view of Dreiser's " 'two styles'—the simple narrative and the prosy moralizing which has [sic] earned him epithets like 'cloddish,' 'clumsy,' 'elephantine' " (64–65).

4   The tenacity of clichés and, of course, the ease with which they come to mind also explain their frequency in the texts of the two writers, both of them more concerned with social ideas than with style, though clearly both were striving for a style that could evoke intense emotions as well as explain, argue, persuade, philosophize, and convert. In their vision of themselves as cultural critics, one more sweeping and radical than the other, both developed, I believe, similar strategies of rhetorical indifference—that is, both used all stylistic means they saw available and were indifferent to their generic origins. Goldman's text gives little evidence, explicitly or formally, that she was writing in a literary tradition particular to women—or that she thought there was such a tradition for her to follow. Clearly, gender was central to many of Goldman's anarchist arguments, but if genre implies formal design, as distinct from thematics, then the relationship between gender and genre seems to me difficult to discern in her autobiography. This is not to deny that "there is a literary tradition in which women write autobiography that is different from men"—Jelinek's conclusion (preface to *Women's Autobiography: Essays in Criticism*, xi–xii). Rather it is to suggest that Goldman's rhetorical strategies resemble those of her contemporary (male) novelists who held subversive views of society and of literary realism.

5   Nikolai Chernyshevsky's *What Is To Be Done?* (1886) was written while the author was in prison, under a life-long sentence, for his politically subversive ideas. Its serial publication in 1863 in *The Contemporary* (a journal Chernyshevsky had edited) has been attributed in part to its "turgid prose," which presumably the censors thought would "discredit Chernyshevsky among the young intelligentsia" (ix). This, at least, is what Kathryn Feuer reports in her introduction to a recent edition of the novel. A new and detailed study of the novel confirms that its style was considered "atrocious" in its own time and still strikes the modern critic as "clumsy and awkward" (Paperno, 26). I have read the three English versions of the novel cited below. In a prefatory note to the Ardis edition, Feuer says there are "distortions, bordering on deceptions" in the Virago edition (xxxvi). Page references in this essay are to Tucker's 1886 edition. I might add that in a chapter entitled "Goldman as Rhetor," Solomon describes Goldman's autobiographical style as "straightforward" and "dull" (143) and her prose in general as "clear and vivid" but "also heavy and graceless" and often "turgid" (145). Turgidity and vividness seem difficult to reconcile, and yet they appear together commonly, as is well-known, in criticism of Dreiser's style, as well as in that of Chernyshevsky.

6 A work of considerable influence in Russian intellectual history, *What Is To Be Done?* provided Goldman with a theoretical basis for her revolutionary beliefs, and its famous feminist heroine, Vera Pavlovna (to whom Goldman explicitly refers), prefigured practical ways for her to achieve independence. Like Vera Pavlovna, Goldman starts a liberated new life with a sewing machine, and like her, she relies upon the tutelage and ideas of men while she pursues her ideal of woman's autonomy. Drinnon has noted the importance of Chernyshevsky's novel in shaping Goldman's life as a revolutionary woman. Though Drinnon called the novel "artistically inferior" (a failing that apparently did not attentuate its influence upon contemporary readers), he pointed out that "a large part of her [Goldman's] later life was consciously patterned after Vera Pavlovna, the heroine of *What Is To Be Done?*" (10). Elsewhere, enumerating specific ways Goldman emulated Vera Pavlovna, Drinnon stated (in language Goldman might have used): "Emma soaked in the ideas of Chernyshevsky as rain is soaked in by the desert sands" (25). I find more parallels between Goldman and her fictional prototype than Drinnon, among them her triangular love affair with men who were best friends, her venture with them into a cooperative form of production, her marriage of convenience (made late in life), and her ambition, admittedly short-lived, to become a doctor. In her autobiography Goldman stressed her love of gaiety, parties, good food, and dancing, an enjoyment of life she shared, almost programmatically, with Chernyshevsky's heroine.

7 In defining what is American about American radicalism, DeLeon has focussed upon anarchism, an inveterate American "resistance to institutional authority" (the hallmark of Goldman's anarchism), which he traces to indigenous cutural conditions and self-consciously native writers like Emerson and Thoreau. DeLeon points out that "American symbolism" was "prominent" in Goldman's social commentary (95–96). In her autobiography Goldman describes her encounters with American anarchists and her realization that Americans were capable of the idealism and sacrifices demanded of anarchists in their struggle for freedom (1:155 and *passim*).

8 This view of women as writers, in particular as writers of their own life stories, is summarized and reiterated in the essays of *Women's Autobiography*. Currently, feminist critics have begun to question or coalesce the polarities used to define differences between women and men as literary figures—specifically, polarities between private and public realms, between silence and speech, otherness or alterity and selfhood, emotionality and intellect, covertness and assertion, and, formally, between fragmentation and linearity, and openness and closure—in short, between feminine and masculine as culturally defined antinomies. See, for example, the theorizing about women's autobiography in Stanton; in Smith, whose study begins by putting "into question its own terms"—private and self; and Watson, who describes a collapse of the "Other" into the autobiographical "I" (180–89). A collapsing of these particular binaries is adumbrated in Renza's essay, "The Veto of the Imagination: A Theory of Autobiography"; and in

Autobiographical Acts, Bruss concludes that a common generic tendency was "toward discontinuous structures . . . with disrupted narrative sequences and competing foci of attention"—formal markers that Jelinek and others find characteristic of women's narrations. In a startling declaration that patriarchy is now extinct in the Western world, Badinter says "a different world order is coming into being" that will dispel the patriarchal forms of sexual "complimentarity" which have, historically, related men and women in "a power system that places the One above the Other" (xi, xiv). Instead of inequality based upon claims of difference, she sees "democratic societies currently generating a completely new model: *the resemblance between the sexes*" (xiv, original emphasis). Though her prediction that "a cultural mutation" will equalize the sexes carries her far beyond issues of gender differences in literary genres, it is germane in suggesting a belief among some contemporary theorists that meaningful differences between women and men are erasable, or as Badinter would have it, have already been erased in the Western world.

9   Bruss points out that one deliberate (and legitimate) use of autobiography may to "to rebut" a writer's "public character" (12).

10   Griffin speculates that Stanton may have chosen "to appear more commonplace in an effort to have more in common with her readers, to convert them by an ordinary example rather than to inspire them with extraordinary accomplishments. As she [Stanton] asserted in the preface, she was just a 'wife . . . housekeeper . . . and the mother of seven children' " (207–8). Jelinek believes that Stanton's subject in her autobiography was her "public career," her purpose to "convert" her reader to the women's suffragist movement, and her strategy "to omit anything that might cast a negative light on her achievements" (*Women's Autobiography,* 74).

11   To cite an example from a later period, Eleanor Roosevelt—who believed, obviously, in ameliorative rather than revolutionary change—repudiated a common and comic public view of her as ubiquitously intrusive by claiming that her public life was the result of chance rather than her choices or competencies. Her autobiography would have value, she said, if others could learn from her mistakes: "perhaps my very foolishness may be helfful!" (xvii).

12   What Goldman hid and whether hiding is a characteristic mark of gender in women's autobiography are issues discussed later in this essay.

13   In "The Veto of the Imagination," Renza states that "the autobiographer must come to terms with a unique pronominal crux: how can he [sic] keep using the first-person pronoun, his sense of self-reference, without its becoming—since it becomes, in the course of writing, something other than strictly his own self-referential sign—a de facto third-person pronoun?" (9). After kindly reading this manuscript on *Living My Life,* Professor Renza asked me whether Goldman's reference to herself as "E. G." (quoted above) is a "trope of familiarity, of self-demystification . . . or of social resistance"— a shedding of the name by which society identifies the self? Since Goldman quotes Dreiser as referring to her, in her presence, as "E. G.," this third-

person abbreviation might pose additional questions about the naming and the splitting of the self in autobiography. (I might add that occasionally Goldman refers to herself as "Emma Goldman.") In the context of her use of "E. G.," Goldman seems to me involved in self-repossession rather than self-demystification; she was appropriating her self from others (male financial benefactors) who are telling her how to behave. Dreiser's address may signify his appropriative attempt to familiarize (or diminish) Goldman so that *he* can tell what she "must" do; he assumes authority as he directs a depersonalized (and degendered) "E. G." to write. I am grateful to Professor Renza for helping me "blend out," as he put it, some of the tensions within my account of Goldman's self-representation.

14 Though *Sister Carrie* begins with Carrie as a young adult, it never refers to her past, as though she had no childhood. Like the trains that take Carrie first to Chicago and then to Montreal and New York, her life moves in one direction, inexorably forward towards a future that Dreizer envisions as an evolutionary unfolding. Goldman's story of her life shuttles back and forth, from present to past, action to memory. The past, as personal and social history, is crucial to Goldman's rationalization or ratification of her life.

15 The discovery of "a new world" as a metaphor for conversion to a social cause, while particularly appropriate to Goldman as an immigrant, appears in the autobiographies of other public women. Sanger, for example, describes her decision to speak out for birth control as an "illumination" that reveals "a new day" and "a new world" (56).

16 Given the initial similarities between Carrie's story and Goldman's, the differences that ensue are diametric and irreconcilable. If modern interpretations of *Sister Carrie* are correct, then the novel (perhaps unintentionally) endorses capitalism and its values, while *Living My Life* is a testament to a revolutionary ideal that would demolish all capitalistic institutions. See, for example, Howard; Kaplan, 140–60; and Michaels, 31–58. In his recent biography of Dreiser, Lingeman notes in passing that "Carrie is a sister of a generation of remarkable women carving out a place in the world— Jane Addams, Emma Goldman, Margaret Sanger, Alice Hamilton, and others." But differences between Carrie and Goldman as "sisters" seem more salient than similarities, since Lingeman has just described Carrie as passive, materialistic, and uneducated, traits that clearly do not relate her to Goldman (256).

17 In a letter written to Berkman in 1928, more than a quarter of a century after the act, Goldman said she still could not forget or forgive Berkman's intractable rejection of Czolosz's attack upon President McKinley, a response she found "as absurd now as I did then" (Drinnon and Drinnon, 95).

18 Advised by an attorney friend to omit her involvement in the Frick affair because it might jeopardize her chances of readmission to the United States, Goldman replied that she "would rather never again have the opportunity of returning than to eliminate the very essence of my book."

Her "connection with Berkman's act" was, she said, "the pivot around which my story is written" (Drinnon and Drinnon, xix–xx).

19 Goldman tells of committing various acts of violence, all of them, like the horsewhipping of Most, melodramatic gestures of outrage. She threw a pitcher of water at a woman who insulted the Haymarket anarchists and a glass of water at a detective who suggested she spy for the police. She also threw a Bible at a prison matron, furiously swept a tray of jewelry to the floor, and attacked her lover with a chair. Ironically, Goldman describes others seeing her as pacific and benign. "I don't believe you could hurt a fly," she reports a prison doctor saying to her, "A fine inciter you would make!" (1:137). Because of their public image as incendiary figures, radical women often surprised those they met in private (including each other) by their pleasant appearances—as Elizabeth Gurley Flynn, Mother Jones, and Margaret Sanger indicate in their autobiographies. See, for example, Flynn's reaction on first meeting the "fiery agitator" Emma Goldman (39). Goldman mentions Flynn's imprisonment for expressing pacifist views during World War I (2:640) and Mother Jones's "deportation" from the scene of a miners' strike (2:521); she considers both women victims of society rather than threats. Writing about women anarchists from 1870–1920, Marsh points out that they were commonly accused of fomenting public violence, but Marsh denies that Goldman "incited her hearers to riot." Rather, she says, "Goldman used the tactics of nonviolent confrontation to assert her right to speak." Nevertheless, the "fantasy" of anarchist violence persisted (110–12).

20 Dostoyevsky created Lebeziatnikov of *Crime and Punishment* and the narrator of *Notes from Underground* as vitriolic parodies of Russian Nihilists (anarchists). His opposition to Chernyshevsky was specific and profound, as pointed out by Paperno, who suggests that "Dostoevsky was trying to refute Chernyshevsky not just by attacking his initial premise and final conclusion, but also by attacking his pattern of reasoning itself: the logical sequence of cause and effect" (202). Paperno goes on to say that "Dostoevsky's objections to Chernyshevsky rested on ethical, epistemological, and psychological considerations," as well as on religious grounds (203–4)— which leaves little room for negotiation between the two.

21 On Ben Reitman's reading, see *Living My Life*, 2:518.

22 Like Goldman, the idealistic ideologue Alexander Berkman had seen his future projected in Chernyshevsky's characters, with whom he associated himself immediately in his own autobiography, *Prison Memoirs* (6, 7, 9). In the most portentious moment of his life, when he arrives in Pittsburgh to assassinate Frick and immolate himself as a revolutionary hero, Berkman registers in a hotel under the name Rakhmetov, man of the future and hero of *What Is To Be Done? Prison Memoirs* unintentionally introduces a comic note when it describes the police interrogation that follows Berkman's capture. A detective tells Berkman, "I know a good deal more about you than you think. We've got your friend Rak-metov" (41). *Prison Memoirs* has been highly praised for its "masterful artistry," and Berkman's "adroit handling

of a variety of literary styles" has been compared in "caliber" to that "found only in the most finely wrought fiction" (Doherty, 99).

23 Throughout the autobiography, Goldman continues to add to her list of readings as friends, usually men, introduce her to books and writers she had not known. One friend, Alexander Harvey, gave her "several volumes of Greek plays in English translation" and, as a supreme compliment, compared her to Antigone. In an ironic reply, she asked him "to explain the existence of slavery in his beloved old [Greek] world" (2:682). She always enlarged her reading when she traveled, at home and abroad, and when she was (comparatively briefly) in prison. She met many American and English writers of her time and established friendships with some of them, like Frank Harris, whose novel *The Bomb* she both praised and criticized, and Rebecca West, who tried to help her when she was being denounced for her anti-Soviet views.

24 In Dreiser's novel, Carrie begins to perceive the possibility of ideals beyond the dream of money and fashion when the exemplary male character Ames derides the popular book she enjoys. He recommends Balzac, and when last seen, Carrie is reading *Père Goriot*. I have described Carrie as a reader and the city as her text in an essay called "Sister to Faust: The City's 'Hungry Woman' as Heroine." Goldman could be considered a "hungry" woman reader, though I use the term to define a literary type.

25 Howard has described the "brute" or savage in the naturalistic novel as a generic character who embodies atavism. He represents also a process of proletarization or social decline that may produce a social victim, a criminal, or (particularly pertinent to Goldman's lover, Reitman) a tramp. Though Reitman was a doctor, he had taken up the life of a tramp and affiliated himself in his wanderings with criminals, prostitutes, and the poor, the underworld of American society. An intense and almost obsessive sexuality also characterized Reitman, as it does Howard's "brute" (36–103).

26 Clearly, Goldman knows she is coalescing life and fiction and reversing their usual relationship by valuing a "real" living person because he resembles literary "types" (underworld types that seemed to her exotic because their marginality was different from hers as a radical woman immigrant). Goldman had studied Shakespeare's plays, and in describing her seduction through stories, she may having been casting herself, however inappropriately, as Desdemona listening to Othello's exotic tales.

27 Quoted from Rosenberg, 380. Spacks relates "hiding" to gender in her essay, "Selves in Hiding." Spacks conceded that in the context she has hypothesized, "Emma Goldman presents something of an anomaly" (118); nevertheless, she tries to fit Goldman into the pattern of self-abnegation and reticence she considers typical of public women's autobiographies. Though Goldman described her slavish infatuation with Reitman (and included photographs of him in the autobiography), Jelinek declares that "Goldman excludes her ten-year relationship with Ben Reitman out of fear that her public image will be even more tainted or devalued by intimate disclosures" (*The Tradition of Women's Autobiography*, 129). In fact, Goldman

refused to listen to friends' advice that she omit her love affairs; she considered women's sexual freedom crucial to her anarchistic ideal, and she would not compromise this ideal by eliding her sexual passion and needs. Goldman's affairs did disturb some contemporary radical women, like the journalist Dorothy Day, who wrote in her autobiography that she was "revolted" by Goldman's "promiscuity" and would not read *Living My Life* "because I was offended in my sex" (60). Day surrounds her comments on Goldman with expressions of doubt about her own commitment to the social causes she served (and with sexist remarks).

28 Falk has described her extraordinary discovery of the love letters and reproduced many of them in *Love, Anarchy, and Emma Goldman*.

29 As we know, Henry Adams omitted twenty years from his famous autobiography and mentioned his wife only once. Dreiser wrote several volumes recounting the story of his life, and omitted more than he revealed— understandably, when one sees what he might have told if he had transferred information (mainly on sex and money) from his private records to his autobiographies. Dreiser's private papers are in the Van Pelt Library of the University of Pennsylvania.

30 Goldman's views on motherhood were complex and contradictory. She considered herself deprived of the joys of motherhood, which she wanted the reader to believe she had sacrificed to her ideal. On the other hand, she described motherhood as "that blind, dumb force that brings forth life in travail, wasting woman's youth and strength, and leaving her in old age a burden to herself and to those to whom she has given birth" (1:340). Contrary to critical views that women's autobiography reveals strong mother-daughter ties, Goldman's "life" describes estrangement between her and her mother. Her half-sister Helena acted as her surrogate mother, lavishing upon her the love denied by her parents.

31 Characteristically, Goldman refused to "be gagged on the question of Bolsheviki." "I had kept silent long enough," she writes, and she determined "to speak out" and to speak her own piece (2:936). When her criticism of the Bolsheviks appeared in American newspapers, a political ally called for communist volunteers "to burn E. G., at least in effigy." Goldman's comment typifies her hyperbolic, caustic style: "What a picture! The chairlady intoning the *International*, and the audience holding hands in an orgiastic dance round the flames licking Emma Goldman's body to the tune of the liberating song" (2:938).

32 Flynn reports this interview in *I Speak My Own Piece* (53). Goldman was actually prepared to do an "act" in Oscar Hammerstein's theater, but once backstage she was appalled at the prospect and fled (2:536).

33 Dreiser may have appropriated Goldman for his portrait of Ernita in *A Gallery of Women*, as Lehan claims (172), but if he did, he has so thoroughly changed or disguised her that his representation distorts her life and politics. Unlike the exiled Goldman, Ernita moves voluntarily from America to the Soviet Union; once there, her acceptance of the revolutionary regime, and in particular of Lenin (*A Gallery of Women*, 1:346), has little in common with Goldman's critical appraisal.

34 Sanger included Dreiser in her list of "distinguishing men" who supported the cause of birth control during "the dark early days of the movement" (202–3). While Sanger named many men as her supporters, some of whom did little more than give her verbal assent, she carefully omitted Goldman's active role in the birth control movement. Kennedy discusses the strategic usefulness of this omission to Sanger and the image of herself she wished to project in her autobiography (18–20). Goldman, on the other hand, was generous in assigning credit for the birth control movement in America to others. "Neither my birth-control discussion nor Margaret Sanger's efforts were pioneer work," she wrote; then she listed the men and women (comparatively unknown today) whom she considered the "pioneers and heroes of the battle for free motherhood" (2:553).

35 An example is Shulman's strong emphasis upon Goldman's feminism (*To The Barricades* and *Red Emma Speaks*). In her autobiography Goldman confessed that she had difficulty maintaining friendships with women (particularly articulate and activist women like Voltairine De Cleyre), that she was drawn into divisive political rivalries with women who advocated the same cause (like Margaret Sanger), that she lacked sympathy for and belief in the suffragist movement, and that suffragists and other women reformers considered her a "man's woman." Like Goldman, the labor organizer Mother Jones expressed her belief that women did not need the vote in order to raise political "hell." In her autobiography Mother Jones recalls that at a labor meeting, a woman had protested that she could not freely speak her piece as long as women "haven't a vote." Mother Jones replied, "I never had a vote. . . . and I have raised hell all over this country! You don't need a vote to raise hell! You need convictions and a voice!" (203–4). Though Sanger considered women's welfare her cause, she too rejected women's suffrage as an effective means to her end—that of eradicating society's "negative attitude toward women" and securing women's control of their "generative" functions (74).

36 Jelinek concludes her survey of women's autobiography with an accolade to experimental American women writers who are "enriching and expanding the genre's possibilities." She cites in particular "creative" and ethnic woman—for example, Maxine Hong Kingston, Maya Angelou, Annie Dillard, Ntozake Shange, Lillian Hellman, and Judy Chicago (*The Tradition of Women's Autobiography*, 189–90). Smith finds the "most radical promise of difference" for women's autobiography articulated, not surprisingly, by French feminists who believe in the possibility of a language yet to be written by women yet to be liberated from "the phallologocentric *écriture* of Western culture" (58). Smith herself sees the possibility of new de-centered forms emerging from the margins that, she believes, women and women writers usually inhabit; she too considers Maxine Hong Kingston an exemplary figure in the development of a woman's autobiographical tradition, and points to others like Gertrude Stein, Virginia Woolf, and Anaïs Nin for whom "the masculine autobiographical mode is passé" (175).

WORKS CITED

Badinter, Elisabeth. *The Unopposed Sex: The End of the Gender Battle.* Trans. Barbara Wright. New York: Harper & Row, 1989. (Published originally in 1986 in France by Editions Odile Jacob as *L'un est l'autre.*)
Benstock, Shari, ed. *The Private Self: Theory and Practice of Women's Autobiographical Writings.* Chapel Hill: University of North Carolina Press, 1988.
Berkman, Alexander. *Prison Memoirs of an Anarchist.* New York: Mother Earth, 1912.
Bowlby, Rachel. *Just Looking: Consumer Culture in Dreiser, Gissing, and Zola.* Chapel Hill: University of North Carolina Press, 1985.
Bruss, Elizabeth W. *Autobiographical Acts: The Changing Situation of a Literary Genre.* Baltimore: Johns Hopkins University Press, 1976.
Chernyshevsky, Nikolai. *What Is To Be Done? A Romance.* Boston: Benj. R. Tucker, 1886.
Chernyshevsky, Nikolai. *What Is To Be Done? Tales About New People.* Expanded by Cathy Porter. Intro. by E. H. Carr. London: Virago, 1982.
Chernyshevsky, Nikolai. *What Is To Be Done?.* Trans. N. Dole and S. S. Skidelsky. Intro. by Kathryn Feuer. Ann Arbor, MI: Ardis, 1986.
Day, Dorothy. *The Long Loneliness: The Autobiography of Dorothy Day.* New York: Harper & Bros., 1952.
de Man, Paul. "Autobiography as De-Facement." *Modern Language Notes* 94 (1979):919–30.
DeLeon, David. *The American as Anarchist: Reflections on Indigenous Radicalism.* Baltimore: Johns Hopkins University Press, 1978.
Doherty, Thomas P. "American Autobiography and Ideology." In *The American Autobiography: A Collection of Critical Essays.* Ed. Albert E. Stone. Englewood Cliffs: Prentice-Hall, 1981, 95–108.
Dreiser, Theodore. *Sister Carrie.* [1900]. Ed. Donald Pizer. New York: W. W. Norton, 1970.
Dreiser, Theodore. *A Gallery of Women.* New York: Horace Liveright, 1929, 1: 288–358.
Drinnon, Richard. *Rebel in Paradise: A Biography of Emma Goldman.* Chicago: University of Chicago Press, 1961.
Drinnon, Richard, and Anna Maria Drinnon, eds. *Nowhere At Home: Letters from Exile of Emma Goldman and Alexander Berkman.* New York: Schocken Books, 1975.
Falk, Candace. *Love, Anarchy, and Emma Goldman.* New York: Holt, Rinehart and Winston, 1984.
Flynn, Elizabeth Gurley. *I Speak My Own Piece: Autobiography of "The Rebel Girl."* New York: New Masses and Mainstream, 1955.
Gelfant, Blanche, H. "Sister to Faust: The City's 'Hungry Woman' as Heroine." *Novel: A Forum on Fiction,* 15, no. 1 (Fall 1981): 23–38.
Gilman, Charlotte Perkins. *The Living of Charlotte Perkins Gilman: An Autobiography.* New York: Arno Press. 1972. (Published originally in 1935 by D. Appleton-Croft.)

Goldman, Emma. *Living My Life*. 2 vols. New York: Dover, 1970. (Published originally in 1931 by Alfred Knopf.)

Griffin, Elizabeth. *In Her Own Right: The Life of Elizabeth Cady Stanton*. New York: Oxford University Press, 1984.

Gunn, Janet Garner. *Autobiography: Towards a Poetics of Experience*. Philadelphia: University of Pennsylvania Press, 1982.

Howard, June. *Form and History in American Literary Naturalism*. Chapel Hill: University of North Carolina Press, 1985.

Jelinek, Estelle, ed. *Women's Autobiography: Essays in Criticism*. Bloomington: Indiana University Press, 1980.

Jelinek, Estelle. "The Paradox and Success of Elizabeth Cady Stanton." In Jelinek, ed., *Women's Autobiography*, 71–82.

Jelinek, Estelle. *The Tradition of Women's Autobiography: From Antiquity to the Present*. Boston: Twayne, 1986.

Kaplan, Amy. *The Social Construction of American Realism*. Chicago: University of Chicago Press, 1988.

Kennedy, David M. *Birth Control in America: The Career of Margaret Sanger*. New Haven: Yale University Press, 1970.

Lehan, Richard. *Theodore Dreiser: His World and His Novels*. Carbondale: Southern Illinois University Press, 1969.

Lingeman, Richard. *Theodore Dreiser: At the Gates of the City, 1871–1907*. New York: G. P. Putnam's Sons, 1986.

Marsh, Margaret S. *Anarchist Women: 1870–1920*. Philadelphia: Temple University Press, 1981.

Michaels, Walter Benn. "*Sister Carrie*'s Popular Economy." In *The Gold Standard and the Logic of Naturalism*. Berkeley and Los Angeles: University of California Press, 1987.

Mother Jones. *Autobiography of Mother Jones*. Ed. Mary Field Parton. Chicago: Charles H. Kerr, 1925.

Paperno, Irina. *Chernyshevsky and the Age of Realism: A Study in the Semiotics of Behavior*. Stanford, CA: Stanford University Press, 1988.

Petrey, Sandy. "The Language of Realism, the Language of False Consciousness: A Reading of *Sister Carrie*." *Novel: A Forum on Fiction* 10 (1977): 101–13.

Renza, Louis A. "The Veto of the Imagination: A Theory of Autobiography." *New Literary History* 9 (1977–78): 1–26.

Roosevelt, Eleanor. *The Autobiography of Eleanor Roosevelt*. Abbreviated edition. New York: Harper and Bros., 1961.

Rosenberg, Karen. "An Autumnal Love of Emma Goldman." *Dissent* 30, no. 3 (Summer 1983): 380–83.

Sanger, Margaret. *My Fight For Birth Control*. New York: Farrar & Rinehart, 1931.

Shulman, Alix. *To the Barricades: The Anarchist Life of Emma Goldman*. New York: Thomas Y. Crowell, 1971.

Shulman, Alix, ed. *Red Emma Speaks: An Emma Goldman Reader*. New York: Schocken Books 1983.

Smith, Sidonie. *A Poetics of Women's Autobiography: Margnality and the Fictions of Self-Representation*. Bloomington: Indiana University Press, 1987.

Solomon, Martha. *Emma Goldman*. Boston: Twayne, 1987.

Spacks, Patricia. "Selves in Hiding." In Jelinek, ed., *Women's Autobiography*, 112–32.

Stanton, Domna C. "Autobiography: Is the Subject Different?" In *The Female Autograph: Theory and Practice of Autobiography from the Tenth to the Twentieth Century*. Ed. Domna C. Stanton. Chicago: University of Chicago Press, 1984, 3–20.

Watson, Julia. "Shadowed Presence: Modern Women Writers' Autobiographies and the Other." In *Studies in Autobiography*. Ed. James Olney. New York: Oxford University Press, 1988, 180–89.

CHAPTER 11

The Way We Work

JANE HALLOWELL COLES AND ROBERT COLES

We were married in July of 1960, and before that [we] knew one another three years. When one of us lived in Mississippi, in charge of a military neuropsychiatric service (part of Keesler Air Force Base hospital), the other one visited the South. The marriage preceded school desegregation in New Orleans by a few months, and took place a few months after the Greensboro sit-in, often regarded as the onset of the 1960s student civil rights struggle. One of us had lived for a month in Montgomery, Alabama, where Dr. Martin Luther King, Jr., began his political effort, before heading for Biloxi, Mississippi and Air Force medicine, under the old doctors' draft law that required two years of service from all young physicians. In a sense, as we look back at our lives, our marriage, our work, from the vantage point, now, of almost thirty years of marriage (our three sons are now grown and departed for college, graduate schools) we realize how powerfully our personal lives have been affected by the fateful circumstances in which, by sheer accident (an Air Force assignment), we found ourselves at the start of our marriage. Of course, we were who we were, and so something in us, individually and together, responded to the South of 1960 and the years thereafter. But in this century of exalted determinisms we want to emphazise the element of chance in our lives—even as all lives, and all marriages, hinge on luck, on the accidental: whom we meet, where we happen to be at one or another point, what is going on around us as we go about our day-to-day lives. With the foregoing as preparation, we begin our conversation in late January of 1989.

Jane Coles: We should probably start by describing the way we used to work together, and how we did the work for *Women of Crisis*.

Robert Coles: There sure has been an "evolution" to the work.

J. C.: In the beginning you were trying hard—painfully hard, I remember—to be a social scientist. We'd go to the homes of the children in New Orleans, to Ruby's home, to Tessie's, and later, to the Connors' [home, a white family that broke the boycott and sent two of their sons to the Frantz School, where Ruby had been alone as a first grade student] and you had all those questions written in advance, and you had all the psychiatric and psychoanalytic theory on the top of your mind, and you were trying to learn what the theory told you that you should learn. And that tape-recorder—it made its mark on our visits: a real presence!

R. C.: We should talk about that tape-recorder right away!

J. C.: Well, *you* should talk about it! I never liked it. I never liked what it meant about us, what it meant to the kids, the families we were meeting.

R. C.: Don't exaggerate! What do you mean?

J. C.: I mean the *investigators* we were. Every time we arrived, we went through our tape recorder ritual: all eyes on it, and your mind geared to it. Then the talking *to* it—the performance *for* it: I thought we were all losing our natural manner with one another, because of the self-consciousness that machine causes in people. No wonder I was glad to 'get away' with Ruby's mother, or Mrs. Connor. We would just sit and gab, while you had an eye and an ear focused on the machine, and then you were keeping tabs on all those [psychological] "defense mechanisms." It was as if you were half writing some paper while you were asking those questions.

R. C.: We had some fun times with those families, even early on!

J. C.: We sure did! I don't mean to be critical, I just want to remind us that we hung on for dear life to one kind of routine [in our inquiry], because we didn't quite know what else to do. We were learning not only what was happening to the kids, but something else: how to go about doing the work we were hoping to do.

R. C.: That's right. We weren't working out of an office or a clinic or a hospital or a school. You were a [high school English] teacher and I was a child psychiatrist, but we were going to homes, and asking parents and children to talk with us. They had plenty of trouble, without us! The black kids were going through mobs. Federal marshals took them to school. When the white kids finally went to school, the mobs turned on them. It was hell—and there we were, trying to find out how the kids were managing. After a while, when those families seemed so strong to us, and when the kids didn't develop symptoms—denied me what I was trained to see and then do something about, treat—we had to stand back and figure out what we were doing, and what we should do differently.

J. C.: Yes. You've described a lot of that [those shifts and turns in the work] in the *Children of Crisis* books. But we should be direct and blunt here: for months, for a year or two, we both floundered, thank God! You don't usually read about all the confusions that researchers experience, the shifts in thinking, the changes of tack. Maybe some research is different—a straight line from A to B. But we zig-zagged. I remember a picture I took with that old "Brownie" camera of you and Ruby sitting at the kitchen table. You're wearing a bow-tie, and a sport jacket, warm as it was then in New Orleans, and no air conditioning in the Bridges home. You've asked Ruby to draw a picture—of the school, I think—and she's obliging you. You're looking at her as she draws. Somehow, for me, that picture tells a story of us at the start. You're a doctor, and you're asking a patient to work with you, the way you did in the Children's Hospital in Boston. A year or two later you'd be without the jacket and tie. You'd be sipping a Coke and maybe drawing a picture yourself. You'd be laughing or talking, not looking so austere.

It took us time to get to know those children and their families. It took us time to feel our way, to relax a bit. We were white Yankees, and we'd gone to college—and you with all your training, and your ideas about what you should look for.

R. C.: I had to unlearn, I guess, as well as learn. I had to turn myself into an anthropologist, a journalist, a public health doctor. I became a documentary observer. More big-shot job titles! You were pushing me along—reminding me we were *guests*, we were strangers and visitors and eventually friends; reminding me of common sense and common courtesy, *their* "role" in "research."

J. C.: We began to enjoy ourselves with those folks. They fed us, and we brought soft drinks and food. We watched television. We played with the kids—their toys and games. We took them for drives. We visited their friends and relatives. Most important of all, I now realize, we went to church with them. Boy, did we learn from those long hours in church—the praying and singing, the shouting and crying, the intensity and passion of it all, the testifying and witnessing: people living tough lives and trying to figure out what mattered and what was silly or frivolous: a moral lesson for them, and for us. At last we began to see and hear firsthand what *inspired* Ruby and her family! No wonder she prayed for those people who wanted to kill her. No wonder she was willing to forgive them. Her parents taught her to remember the example of Jesus, and in church she and dozens of others spent a lot of time trying to "reach" Jesus. Their church-going wasn't the kind we had known up North!

R. C.: We were learning to notice all sorts of things about the *lives* of people. I was moving away from [an exclusive interest in] symptoms and the unconscious as it reveals itself in children's words or drawings. I was observing what pictures were on walls, what programs were watched, what music played, what food eaten, what was worn—the rhythms and styles of life, the cultural inheritance of the children I'd set out to study.

J. C.: You weren't making those observations casually, or to entertain yourself! I think we'd begun to realize that if we wanted to understand the strengths and weaknesses of those kids, we had to see the world through *their* eyes, not keep on imposing our psychological agenda on them. We didn't abandon your psychiatric and psychoanalytic curiosity; we tried to broaden it, so that it wasn't done in a social—and racial—vacuum.

R. C.: It was then, by 1962 or so, that Erik Erikson's work began to be so helpful to us. I remember buying *Childhood and Society* in that bookstore on Canal Street [New Orleans]. I was trying to figure out how to connect my medical life—its knowledge and assumptions—to the "street life" you and I were living: going from home to home, to schools, talking with white hecklers standing on the sidewalk and the federal marshals who escorted those children, and working with the civil rights student activists of SNCC and CORE in their "freedom houses." One day I was a pediatrician, helping a child who had bronchitis or a stomach upset. The next day, I was asking my psychiatric questions, though, Lord knows, I was getting better—the result of your prodding—at putting them in ordinary, plain words, and maybe some "common sense" was taking hold, so I rushed to fewer and fewer big-deal, ominous conclusions. Then there were days when I was one of those students, myself, working with them; or I was a journalist, doing a story for *New South*, a publication of the Soutern Regional Council, our sponsor in those first years. We were on our own, trying to learn how to do a kind of documentary work.

J. C.: That's what we both wanted, I now realize—to be "on our own"! You wanted to get away from a lot of rigid, uptight professional thinking (and living!). I loved living in the South, and loved meeting those children and their families. I'd taught in a fancy private school, and I'd learned that people can be white and well-to-do and well educated and not necessarily be solid, stable people able to live useful lives. I was glad to be with people facing real-life, honest-to-goodness struggles, and doing so with courage and even good humor. I'd had my fill of "the culture of narcissism"! (I suppose I'm saying it existed before the 1980's!) Anyway, we both had our reasons to be happy down in Dixie! Nothing like a little distance on your past in your younger years!

R. C.: We were doing "research"—you talking with parents and teachers, me with kids—but we were exploring, trying to figure out how we were going to live our lives, and what we believed to be important. Both of us during the 1950s had been apolitical—not really interested in social or racial questions. I was interested in literature, then medicine and pediatrics, and then psychoanalytic psychiatry. You were a history and English teacher, and a great reader of novels and stories. Slowly, even before we got married, you were pulling me away from the dogmatic, creedal, ideological psychoanalytic thinking of the 1950s and back to Dickens and George Eliot and Tolstoy and Chekhov. That "tension" in us—it *was* tense, sometimes!—was an important part of our lives then, and had a lot to do with the work we eventually did together. You were pushing me, I now realize, to be an observer, a witness, and to link arms with the people we met, with the struggle they were waging: a move from the "value-free" investigator to the "participant-observer," who is glad to learn from his "subjectivity," his personal involvements and commitments, rather than anxious to shun them to be rid of them. A big shift in my sense of the desirable, the ideal!

J. C.: We both loosened up a lot. I remember in the early days [of our work] I'd sit there, near you, as you tried to make conversation with those children. It was tough going for you; after all, they hadn't come to see you in a clinic. They were living their lives, and for some reason known only to you, they were seeing you a few times a week. They were as curious about you as you were about them; and meanwhile, you and I were our*selves* a bit "curious." We weren't this and we weren't that; we were wanderers, and we'd said goodbye to a conventional middle-class life, and to two professions, or at last [goodbye] to being the regular kind of doctor and teacher we'd once been. Add to all that the race question: for those families in the deep South of the early 1960s, we were the first whites who'd ever stepped foot in their homes. Maybe an insurance man had been outside, though there were black insurance agents, I remember, plenty of them; maybe some town official. They let us know, only after months, that they'd been quite afraid, never mind "curious," when we first showed up. Sure, we were taken to them by a person they knew and trusted [Mrs. Leontine Luke], and she explained to them who we were and that we were "friends," and yes, they nodded, but the looks on their faces told us something else, how nervous they were. You and I were nervous, too; maybe you and I were more scared then we realized. We didn't want to see how those folks felt about us being with them because we didn't want to stop and think about what we were going through. Those were tremendously challenging times for us, we *now* know, but I think we felt back then that we were on the brink of a big disaster. We seemed to be drifting, and we had no financial support, and no institutional support, and there were lots of people back home who thought we had gone off the deep end!

R. C.: It's strange, talking like that now; I mean, if feels strange to me. When I try to talk as you've just talked to others they think I've gone "off the deep end" for talking like that! To them—to me, sometimes, now—the work seems so "natural": an obviously sensible kind of study for someone to do. But it's almost thirty years ago that we began our work together, and *then* psychiatry was different, and psychoanalysis, and medicine, and not least, the South. Segregation was the law, and resisting integration was respectable in the universities and medical shools. Psychiatrists weren't involved in social and political issues in the way some of them are today.

J. C.: I think the verdict is [that] we were naive and maybe even a little simple-minded, and we were ready to take a few risks, and we were so glad *not* to be "locked into" fifty-minute hours (you) and an uptight school regimen (me) that we felt excited and happy, rather than frightened and anxious. You had plenty of reservations about the psychiatry you'd come to know in hospitals and clinics, and I was restless as a teacher: I'd been working in a private school—lots of well-to-do kids headed for the big-time—and I wanted to be challenged by other kids, that's for sure.

R. C.: Anyway, by 1963 we sure knew we were scared!

R. C.: Oh yes, when we got involved with SNCC.

J. C.: That was a big transition for us. The kids in Atlanta, the high-school kids we met when school desegregation began there, they were the ones who persuaded us to join the civil rights movements. You kept asking them what they did after school, and they told you! Then Lawrence [Jefferson, who at sixteen was one of two black youths to desegregate Henry Grady High School] asked you if you wanted to come to the SNCC headquarters, and you went just to see how he spent his time, and the next thing we knew, Jim Forman and Stokeley Carmichael were asking who *you* were, and why *you* were there, and you told them you wanted to be of help, and they put you to work sweeping the floor—one of your better moments in doing psychiatric research! They sure tested us both out—and why not? We hadn't been recruited on a campus. We were unknown whites who suddenly showed up, and they had plenty of reasons to worry about who we were and what we had in mind.

R. C.: We were tested for many weeks, and it was hard—harder on me than on you, because you accepted the desirability of that testing, and I got on my high horse from the very beginning and felt after a while that I should pull back. I guess I'd better say it outright: that testing came out fine, in the sense that we were accepted, eventually, but in the interim I sure learned a lot about myself. The gist of it: a snobbishness, a sense of self-importance, the high-and-mighty attitude of the professional man—how *dare* they question my credentials and treat me with such continuing skepticism! A day or two of sweeping the floors was fine, but weeks and weeks of the same! And of course I fought back with the weapon I knew best: psychiatric reductionism! Why were they so suspicious, so "defensive," so "paranoid?" What was their psychological purpose? What "problems" did they have?

J. C.: For a lot of us the civil rights movement helped in ways we didn't anticipate. We were struggling against the segregation of blacks and whites, but with a little looking inward we began to see other ways people have of keeping [themselves] apart—by neighborhood and occupation, for example. As I look back twenty-five years to those days, I realize how much we learned about the South, sure, but also about ourselves. It was too easy for plenty of us from the North to "dump" on the South—use it to keep being blind about the arrogance and insensitivity and smugness we didn't have to travel to Georgia or Louisina to find; in our own back yards there was plenty. Anyway, we were the lucky recipients of plenty of good teaching from those kids we were meeting, and their parents, and their teachers, the black folks and the white folks, too.

R. C.: The whites, as they struggled with social change, gave us powerful lessons in their own kind of courage, and also in the way fear or hate gave shape to lives. Our job, we began to realize after a year or two of important stumbling and floundering, was to connect what we were hearing to a written language. Some day someone should write an essay on the importance of floundering and stumbling in research; but then, I'm afraid, we'll all be told that there's the "floundering and stumbling stage" or phase, and that, too, will be part of our dreary secular psychological self-consciousness. Anyway, we were learning how to get along with poor Southern black people, with white people confronted by a major political change in their lives, with civil rights activists, and we were also abandoning the language of the clinic (I was, that is, prodded by you).

J. C.: You were doing so on your own as well. *Events, people, experiences* were prodding you, not only my preference for literature over psychology.

R. C.: Right. But you were always there, laughing at all the pretentiousness and banality that gets called *social science.* We were leaving the clinic and trying to learn how to tell stories—the stories of the people we were meeeting.

J. C.: Maggie Long was very helpful then, and Lillian Smith, those two Southern women we met, two Southern novelists.

R. C.: Yes, I don't know what we'd have done without them. They looked at some of my psychiatric reports and were aghast. They urged me to write in plain language, and as Lillian Smith put it: "Think of yourself as someone doing an *introduction* of someone else." A wonderful way of putting it. I'd sit in our home in Vinings [Georgia] and listen to our tapes, and read our notes, and remember scenes, comments, episodes, statements, accounts of this or that event, and I'd imagine someone in the room, standing and waiting to be told, to be informed—myself as an introducer of one person to another, a person in the middle—and then I'd write. Those two women and you, the three of you, bore down hard on a jargon-filled professional man looking for "data"!

J. C.: It was a big shift not only in the writing but in the way the work was done. I clearly remember that by 1962 we weren't talking so much about "psychological defenses" or "psychological adjustment." We were listening to people give us accounts of what happened today or yesterday, or what they hoped (or worried) would happen tomorrow; and then we tried to tell others what we'd heard, what we saw with our own eyes, or tried to see through the eyes of others.

R. C.: I became less interested in technology, too. We used the tape recorder less. I took more notes. I was back to my days with William Carlos Williams—all those notes he wrote to himself after he'd visited a patient, lines for future poems he'd heard from others, or lines they had stimulated his mind to come up with.

J. C.: I was glad, I have to admit. I typed up those tapes in the first years, and I used to think it was "overkill," too much taped, not enough "extracted" by us as we listened: the heart of things. That's what listening should be, close and careful attention paid on the spot. With the tape recorder present you tend to sit back and be a piggy eater, indiscriminate, the machine slurping everything in. Without the machine, it's your ears and your eyes and your brain, and then your fingers holding the pen: it's *you*, working and noticing and keeping what you think is important, what you've noticed in your head, and remembering it while at the same time thinking about what it means, and then writing it down so it makes some sense, and it fits into what you've learned before and are now learning and hope to learn: *context* is the word, providing a context (as a writer) for what you've heard as a person called *researcher*, who is . . . an eager, interested listener.

R. C.: I guess we've become long-term listeners! You started having conversations with the mothers and fathers while I was with the kids. We roamed through Appalachia and then came back North, and then went West, and then back to New England, American wanderers! Your notebooks and journals gave us *Women of Crisis*, and mine gave me the *Children of Crisis* series and *The Moral Life of Children* and *The Political Life of Children*, a lot of writing as a response, I now think of it, to thirty years of experience, of being taught by kids and by their families, and by what we've picked up in all those schools, from the classes of kids and the teachers.

J. C.: Yes, let's emphasize the school visits. They were always the high point for me, maybe because I'm a teacher. When I remember our work, I sometimes remember the moments with the children in their homes, but mostly I remember the times in all those schools, sitting on those low chairs, with the boys and girls in the first or second or third or fourth grades, hearing them ask questions or talk of what happened to them this time or that time, watching while they drew pictures, or drawing pictures ourselves, and then all showing them to each other. We were so lucky to be able to call all that *work*! It was a tremendous education for us, and the teachers were those children, and their families. I think it's great that professors write their textbooks, but I'd like to put in a word for some other "professors"—all the people who can sit down with you and "profess": tell you what's on their mind, and what they've gone through in their lives, and provide you with plenty of "knowledge" or "learning," whether colleges call it that or not.

R. C.: I've heard you talk like that for thirty years! You won me over to that way of seeing things, after a struggle. My head was full of psychiatric jargon and reductionist strivings when we started out. You kept smiling—and doubting; you listened to those folks we met, and eventually I began listening in the way you did.

J. C.: You were always attentive to the kids and their parents. It's not a matter of good or bad, or right or wrong. I think it's a matter of "attitude." For a while—and why not, given your training?—you saw them as patients, or soon-to-be patients.

R. C.: You saw them, many of the people we met in the civil rights struggle and afterwards, as heroes.

J. C.: Well, some were that. I guess in many of our lives—plain, ordinary folks—there will be trouble, sure, but also great personal dignity in the face of that trouble: the patient and the hero. There's also the teacher in many of us, and I think it took us a long time to address those children and their parents as teachers. I wish our college teachers had helped us think of the other teachers (the other kinds of education) we might find in the world.

R. C.: There are days when I think of you saying those words in Harvard Square, so some of us will come off our high horses.

J. C.: We left that place for the world of Ruby, to meet the people we were so damn lucky to meet, some of them right in Cambridge, but not in the Harvard Square you're talking about.

R.C.: True.

J. C.: True, and thank God.

CONTRIBUTORS

INDEX

Contributors

William L. Andrews is Joyce and Elizabeth Hall Distinguished Professor of American Literature at the University of Kansas. He is the author of *To Tell a Free Story: The First Century of Afro-American Autobiography, 1760–1865* (1986) and the editor of *Sisters of the Spirit: Three Black Women's Autobiographies of the Nineteenth Century* (1986), Frederick Douglass's *My Bondage and My Freedom* (1987), and *Six Women's Slave Narratives* (1988).

William Boelhower is Associate Professor in English and American Literature at the University of Trieste, Italy. He is the author of *Immigrant Autobiography in the United States* (1982) and *Through a Glass Darkly: Ethnic Semiosis in American Literature* (1984). He has published essays on Gramsci, Goldmann, cartographic semiotics in literary texts, literary anthropology, and ethnic and immigrant novels and autobiographies.

Lawrence Buell is Professor of English at Harvard University. His most recent book is *New England Literary Culture* (1986), and he is currently at work on a study of Thoreau and the American Literary Canon.

Jane Hallowell Coles is co-author, with Robert Coles, of *Women in Crisis*, published in two volumes in the Radcliffe Biography Series (1978, 1980). A graduate of Radcliffe College, she has taught in Georgia, Louisiana, and Massachusetts.

Robert Coles has written many books on a broad range of social and literary subjects, including his Pulitzer-Prize winning study of *Children of Crisis*, published in five volumes (1967–77). His most recent book is *The Call of Stories: Teaching and the Moral Imagination* (1989). Doctor Coles is Professor of Psychiatry and Medical Humanities at the Harvard University Medical School and Research Psychiatrist for the University Health Services.

Paul John Eakin is the author of *Fictions in Autobiography: Studies in the Art of Self-Invention* (1985). His edition of the essays of Philippe Lejeune, *On Autobiography*, was published by the University of Minnesota Press in 1989. His current project is a book on autobiography as a referential art. He is Professor of English at Indiana University.

Susanna Egan is Assistant Professor of English at the University of British Columbia in Canada. She is the author of *Patterns of Experience in Autobiography* (1984), as well as articles on contemporary autobiography in *The Literary Review*, *biography*, and *The Journal of Narrative Technique*.

Blanche H. Gelfant is Professor of English at Dartmouth College, where she holds the Robert E. Maxwell '23 Chair in the Arts and Sciences. She has published widely on literary figures and themes in twentieth-century American literature. Her recent book, *Women Writing in America: Voices in Collage* (1984), includes essays on noncanonical and popular writers, as well as on such established American figures as Willa Cather.

Carol Holly is Professor of English at St. Olaf College. Her recent publications include articles on Henry James's autobiographical writings, James family biography, and nineteenth-century American women writers. She is currently writing a book on Henry James.

Arnold Krupat is a member of the Literature Faculty at Sarah Lawrence College. Among his books are *For Those Who Come After* (1985), a study of Indian autobiography, and *The Voice in the Margin: Native American Literature and the Canon* (1989). He has just completed a study entitled *Ethnocriticism: Ethnography, History, and Literature.*

Daniel B. Shea recently edited the Quaker autobiography of Elizabeth Ashbridge, to be published in *Journeys in New Worlds: Early American Women's Narratives*, by the University of Wisconsin Press. He is writing an essay on the Adams-Jefferson correspondence. In 1988 his first book, *Spiritual Autobiography in Early America* (1968), was reissued with a new preface in the Wisconsin Studies in American Autobiography series. He is Professor of English at Washington University.

Albert E. Stone is Professor of American Studies and English at the University of Iowa. He is Series Editor of *Singular Lives: The Iowa Series in North American Autobiography*, published by the University of Iowa Press. He is also author of the forthcoming *The Return of Nat Turner: History, Literature, and Cultural Politics in Sixties America*.

Sau-ling Cynthia Wong is Assistant Professor in Asian American Studies at the University of California, Berkeley. She has published papers on Chinese-American autobiography and Chinese immigrant literature, and is completing a book-length thematic study on Asian-American literature for Princeton University Press.

Index

Abel, Elizabeth, 221, 222
Abramson, Edward A., 143
Adamic, Louis, 130, 134, 139, 153
Adams, Charles, 76–77
Adams, Henry, 3, 6, 9, 14, 15; Sayre
  on, 11; Stone on, 12; Cooley on, 13,
  71; and John Adams, 41; Buell on, 48;
  Egan on, 72–77, 80, 81, 83, 88–89; on
  Trollope, 75–76; Boelhower on, 125,
  126, 131, 132, 138; and the "quest for
  the new man," 125; and women's
  autobiography, 216, 226
Adams, John, 40–41, 58
Adams, Timothy D., 202
Addams, Jane, 81, 83
Addis, Patricia K., 97, 98
Affiliation, autobiographies of, 216–34
Afro-American autobiography, 6, 7, 8,
  15, 41–42, 133; Egan on, 83–88; Andrews
  on, 84, 195–215; and the black voice,
  as a political voice, 85; by women, 85,
  202–3, 208–10, 227; interest in, growth
  of, 97–98; Stone on, 97–99, 104, 111;
  definition of, 147; and Black Power, 196;
  "militant," 196–97, 201; publication of,
  198–99. See also Slave narratives; specific
  authors
Aiken, Conrad, 114
Alger, Horatio, 128, 137, 197
Alkon, Paul, 100
American Renaissance, 14, 47–69
American Revolution, 40, 51
Anarchism, 82–83, 238, 240–55
Anderson, Quentin, 19n18
Anderson, Sherwood, 71
Andrews, William L., 3, 8, 9, 15, 67n5,
  195–215; on Afro-American autobiog-
  raphy, quantity and characteristics of,
  84; on Foote, 85

Angelou, Maya, 99, 103, 199, 200, 202–3
Antin, Mary, 124, 129, 133–37, 153
Apes, William, 15, 180–85, 189n22,
  190nn23–26
Arno Press, 198
Arnold, Matthew, 74
Ashbridge, Elizabeth, 36, 38
"As told to" autobiographies, 41, 104,
  114, 115
Augustine, 11, 197
Auschwitz, 112
Autobiography. See specific forms

Baginski, Max, 248
Baker, Houston A., 3, 99, 205, 206–7, 211n9
Baldwin, James, 99, 199
Ball, Charles, 8
Bancroft, Hubert H., 86
Barnard, John, 38
Barnum, P. T., 4, 14; Buell on, 57–60, 61,
  62, 65; circus of, 77
Barthes, Roland, 207
Barton, Rebecca C., 195, 196
Beckett, Samuel, 176
Behavioral codes, 127
Belasco, David, 251
Bellah, Robert, 65
Bennett, Tony, 98
Bercovitch, Sacvan, 13, 52, 127, 134;
  concept of auto-American-biography,
  144; and the tradition of the American
  Jeremiah, 207
Bergland, Betty, 143
Berkeley, George, 38
Berkman, Alexander, 82–83, 241–53 passim,
  259n17, 260–61n22
Berthoff, Warner, 101, 197
Bibb, Henry, 198
Bible, 27, 31, 144

285